T0289872

ERASING THE INVISIBLE HAND

This book examines the use, principally in economics, of the concept of the invisible hand, centering on Adam Smith. It interprets the concept as ideology, knowledge, and a linguistic phenomenon. It shows how the principal Chicago School interpretation misperceives and distorts what Smith believed to be the economic role of government. The essays further show how Smith was silent as to his intended meaning, using the term to set minds at rest; how the claim that the invisible hand is the foundational concept of economics is repudiated by numerous leading economic theorists; that the several dozen identities given the invisible hand renders the term ambiguous and inconclusive; that no such thing as an invisible hand exists; and that calling something an invisible hand adds nothing to knowledge. Finally, the essays show that the leading doctrines purporting to claim an invisible hand for the case for capitalism cannot invoke the term, but that other nonnormative invisible hand processes are still useful tools.

Warren J. Samuels is professor emeritus of economics at Michigan State University, where he taught from 1968 to 1998. He previously served on the faculties of the University of Missouri, Georgia State University, and the University of Miami. One of the most prolific historians of economic thought, with cognate interests in the philosophy of economics, public finance, and law and economics, he has been president of the History of Economics Society and the Association for Social Economics. Professor Samuels was awarded the Kondratieff Medal by the Kondratieff Foundation of Moscow. He is the author of more than ten books and the editor of several dozen titles, as well as more than seventy volumes in the series *Research in the History of Economic Thought and Methodology* and *Recent Economic Thought*, as well as for the *Journal of Economic Issues*. He received his Ph.D. from the University of Wisconsin.

Marianne F. Johnson is professor of economics at the University of Wisconsin, Oshkosh. She is coeditor of the series *Research in the History of Economic Thought and Methodology* and has coedited two multivolume projects on early American economic thought.

William H. Perry is a professional lexicographer with more than thirty years of experience in constructing and searching large evidentiary and documentary research databases for special projects. For this work, he constructed a database containing, in machine-readable format, all significant philosophical, religious, scientific, political, and economic primary and secondary sources from the beginnings of Western and Middle Eastern civilizations until the end of the nineteenth century, searchable by concept.

Erasing the Invisible Hand

*Essays on an Elusive and Misused
Concept in Economics*

WARREN J. SAMUELS

Michigan State University

with the assistance of

MARIANNE F. JOHNSON

University of Wisconsin, Oshkosh

and

WILLIAM H. PERRY

CAMBRIDGE
UNIVERSITY PRESS

CAMBRIDGE UNIVERSITY PRESS
Cambridge, New York, Melbourne, Madrid, Cape Town,
Singapore, São Paulo, Delhi, Tokyo, Mexico City

Cambridge University Press
32 Avenue of the Americas, New York, NY 10013-2473, USA

www.cambridge.org
Information on this title: www.cambridge.org/9780521517256

© Warren J. Samuels 2011

First published 2011
Reprinted 2011

A catalog record for this publication is available from the British Library.

Library of Congress Cataloging in Publication Data

Samuels, Warren J., 1933–
Erasing the invisible hand : essays on an elusive and misused concept in
economics / Warren J. Samuels.
 p. cm.
Includes bibliographical references and index.
ISBN 978-0-521-51725-6 (hardback)
1. Free enterprise. 2. Economics. 3. Capitalism. 4. Smith, Adam,
1723–1790 – Criticism and interpretation. I. Title.
HB95.S27 2011
330.12′2–dc22 2011002436

ISBN 978-0-521-51725-6 Hardback

For Sylvia to whom
so much is owed

Science must begin with myths, and with the criticism of myths.

Karl Popper, 1957

Every religion is true one way or another. It is true when understood metaphorically. But when it gets stuck in its own metaphors, interpreting them as facts, then you are in trouble.

Joseph Campbell, 2008

Adam Smith's [invisible] hand was not in fact invisible: it wasn't there.

Joseph Stiglitz, 2010

When economists find that they are unable to analyze what is happening in the real world, they invent an imaginary world which they are capable of handling.

Ronald Coase, 1988

Contents

Acknowledgments

The author appreciates permissions to reprint from publishers, editors, and coauthors for the following: "The Invisible Hand," *The Elgar Companion to Adam Smith*, Jeffrey T. Young, ed. (Cheltenham: Edward Elgar Publishing, 2009), 195–210; "The Economic Role of Government" (coauthored with Steven G. Medema), *The Elgar Companion to Adam Smith*, Jeffrey T. Young, ed. (Cheltenham: Edward Elgar Publishing, 2009), 300–314; "Adam Smith's *History of Astronomy* Argument: How Broadly Does It Apply? And Where Do Propositions Which 'Sooth the Imagination' Come From?," *History of Economic Ideas*, Vol. 15, No. 2 (2007): 53–78; "Freeing Smith from the 'Free Market': On the Misrepresentation of Adam Smith on the Economic Role of Government" (coauthored with Steven G. Medema), *History of Political Economy*, Vol. 37, No. 2 (Summer 2005): 219–226; "An Essay on the Unmagic of Norms and Rules and of Markets," *Journal des Economistes et des Etudes Humaines*, Vol. 10 (Juin–Septembre 2000): 392–397, 405–407; "Hayek from the Perspective of an Institutionalist Historian of Economic Thought: An Interpretive Essay," *Journal des Economistes et des Etudes Humaines*, Vol. 9 (Juin–Septembre 2000) 392–397, 279–290; "The Political Economy of Adam Smith," *Ethics*, Vol. 87 (April 1977): 189–207; copyright 1977, The University of Chicago. Excerpts from the *Glasgow Edition of The Works of Adam Smith, The Theory of Moral Sentiments, An Inquiry into the Nature and Causes of the Wealth of Nations, Lectures on Jurisprudence*, and *Essays on Philosophical Subjects* are used by permission of Oxford University Press.

Every good-faith effort has been made in the preparation of this work to credit sources and comply with the fairness doctrine on quotation and use of research material. If any copyrighted material has been inadvertently used in this work without proper credit being given in one manner or another, please notify the author or publisher in writing so that future printings or editions of this work may be corrected accordingly.

Preface

1

Both the genesis and nature of these essays require explanation. I started working on the invisible-hand project in 1983. My initial examinations of material nourished my interest as an intellectual historian. As the examined materials continued to grow, so too did the facets, related topics, implications, and overall breadth of the topic and the magnitude of the relevant materials. Captivated, I gradually started to understand how human beings could become so enamored with invisibility in general and the invisible hand in particular, such that the invisible hand began to have a linguistic, ontological, and epistemological significance. Reference to the invisible hand is ubiquitous. The growth of the Internet, coupled with people's desire to have written materials they consider important made available to others (often in translation), has vastly increased the volume and ease of acquisition of relevant materials. The volume of relevant source material reasonably pertinent to a project such as the present one is daunting. This is especially true of a topic that has ramifications with so much else that goes on in society. Only a small percentage of such materials can be used in reaching understanding and conclusions, even if the researcher is avid. And the researcher has to be careful in amassing and interpreting information, for well-known reasons.

The physical problem of producing a detailed study under the conditions I allowed myself to develop cannot be overstated. It is not a project for a young person who, on the one hand, must publish, and on the other, lacks the time in which the range, complexity, and interconnections of ideas can be nurtured. It is a project for a team, not one person, however able and motivated. The enormity of the materials on which the account will ultimately be based is mind-boggling. I have the equivalent of at least forty file drawers (that is, ten four-drawer filing cabinets) of published and unpublished materials, to which must be added several sizeable boxes of note slips and one-quarter or more of a library running to at least twelve thousand books and journals.

It was my original intention to prepare a detailed, three-volume account of the result of my research and thinking. For several reasons, I have, however, with the cooperation of others, made different arrangements. The reasons are that I have given only about one-half of my research time to this project, which I caused to grow; that I have several debilitating illnesses that adversely affect my ability, though not my motivation, to work at the level I was capable of in the past; and because I will have turned seventy-seven before this book is published.

I should say something in defense of the project's enormous expansion. The results thus far, to my way of thinking, are deeper and more important and useful to others because of that expansion and should prove to be even more so in the future if and when the three-volume study is written and published, almost certainly by others, namely John B. Davis, Ross Emmett, Marianne Johnson, and Steven G. Medema. The expansion was not a transient or aberrational phenomenon. To make sense of the use of the term "invisible hand," an inquiry should correspond to that use and to encompass as much as possible of what that use signifies.

The following essays are intended to communicate an account of the parts of my findings that I consider to be important and of use to others. It is impossible for me working alone to present the fully documented account in all respects. Publishing this account of the conclusions I have reached so far implies no lack of faith on my part in what the group will eventually achieve. When they identify needed corrections, they should have the same freedom of thought and expression that I have had.

As I have consulted notes and memory in preparing this volume, I have yearned for the opportunity to complete the whole study myself. Writing would be even more fun than researching, and that has been a lark! As I wrote the text for this volume, I frequently wished that I had the whole completed study before me (with all the laborious preliminary work done!) so that I might, at an infinitude of points of controversy, present the deeper, subtler, more complex meaning of the story.

The key outline from which I have worked in preparing this book consists of thirty pages of small print. It is supplemented by several thousand 5- by 8-inch note cards or slips, plus other outlines. The reader can imagine the volume of underlying notes and annotated published materials by uncounted other scholars contributing to such topics as the market, the entrepreneur, and about four dozen other candidates for the identity of the invisible hand; order, coordination, equilibrium, harmony among self-interests and with the social interest – and the processes of working out the formation of each candidate for the function(s) believed to be achieved by the invisible hand; the Enlightenment in relation to the invisible hand; the kaleidoscopic topics of naturalism and supernaturalism, including Smith's position; the linguistic aspects of writing about the invisible hand; the nature and role of the belief, the mythic and symbolic processes of society; the meaning of "individual" and "social" in economics; the problems and variety of approaches to self-interest, rationality, the firm, spontaneous order, natural selection, government, and so on, each of which will likely require at least fifty pages of this book.

That situation accounts for what any reader is likely to judge curious: The text of this book, with its wide-ranging content, has only in certain parts the usual accompaniment of attributions and annotations with regard to the work of other authors. It is because of the situation described earlier that I have not been able to complete and use my schematic notes as a basis for this text and have not undertaken a completely detailed account. Furthermore, the nature of these essays is such that the text circles back on itself quite a bit. This is necessary (1) to show what is important to Smith, (2) to show the effects of these subjects on Smith, and (3) to show, in part, that every argument relates historically to all of the individuals discussed. Thus, I return to individuals and ideas in multiple contexts multiple times.

2

The project arose in part due to a long-standing appreciation that the concept of the invisible hand was widely considered to be foundational for economics; that, in part, the invisible hand was identified differently by different people and, indeed, that every aspect of its use has meant different things to different people; and that, in part, the notion of an invisible hand was downright strange, especially for an academic, scholarly discipline whose members reckon themselves serious scientists.

The invisible hand truly does not belong solely to technical economic theory, though that tie is important and, for many economists, commanding. The concept of the invisible hand is also a matter of ideology, theology, philosophy, sociology, linguistics, and intellectual history. In each of these respects, the invisible hand is given multiple specifications and meanings. As several scholars have pointed out, the subject of the invisible hand should not be approached solely from the history of the development of microeconomic theory. It belongs to the wider world of intellectual history and social theory.

In thinking about the invisible hand, it is inevitable that terms will be encountered that are so elastic that the terms themselves have multiple meanings and definitions. I have in mind such terms as the Enlightenment, capitalism, social control, psychic balm, history, order, natural, and so on. To say something important about the invisible hand would require that I use the "correct" meanings of those and other terms. I could neither do that nor need to do so in order to solve the numerous problems that enter into their putative meaning. For one thing, thousands of scholars were working on those problems and it would be presumptuous for me to try; I could not master and resolve these other problems. I did not have to provide *the* correct explanation of the Enlightenment or of social control in order to make sense of the concept of the invisible hand. I am confident, however, that my analysis, at least in its broad outline, is compatible with a wide range of particular theories in the case of each subject.

One of the more striking aspects of Adam Smith's uses of the invisible hand is that Smith himself anticipated the ambiguity and inconclusiveness of the notion of an invisible hand. He tells us in the *History of Astronomy* about doing so, but only in an oblique sort of way. Smith made mankind's coping with an invisible hand that is ambiguous and inconclusive a feature of a striking theme, one in which a belief is offered in the absence of a truth, a process that introduces absolutist formulation that sets minds at rest. If the truth of the economic role of government were a matter of truth rather than belief, very likely much of the invisible-hand discussion would be resolved; but it is not a matter of truth, so the opportunity exists for there to be a conflict of beliefs – much the same as a conflict over whether monkeys or alligators set the allocation of resources.

3

This book is an endeavor to make sense of the invisible hand. I never had a more elegant, prepossessing, or presumptuous statement of my objective. I was concerned with the concept of the invisible hand and of the uses made of that concept, as well as the fact that a considerable variety of functions were said to be performed by one or another identity of the invisible hand. Eventually I perceived the existence of a key difference, namely that the putative functions of the invisible hand were on one level of analysis and the putative functions of the use of the *concept* of the invisible hand were on another level of analysis. I had settled very early on a list of key questions around which to develop the study: What was the invisible hand? Where did it come from? What functions did it perform? What conceptual and what substantive problems faced anyone either using the term or conducting a comparable study?

Several connections that I made had an important role in working out the contents of Essays 4–7 and their relation to Essay 8, all based on the first three essays. I found that Smith's argument in his *History of Astronomy* applied to Smith's own use of the invisible hand, and that soothing the imagination was essentially the equivalent of psychic balm and social control. I further determined that many, perhaps arguably all, of the users of the term "invisible hand" – as to its identity and its function, see Essay 3 – were people seeking to set their minds at rest, doing exactly what Smith said they would do if they could not end up with truth.

4

Because the concept of the invisible hand has numerous aspects each of which has several formulations, it is very difficult to construct a consistent story about the invisible hand. Consider, as we will do in Essay 3, (1) the array of some four dozen identities given the invisible hand by different authors, (2) the dozen or so functions, each with numerous variations, performable in principle by each identity, (3) the huge number of possibilities and the unknown number of possible combinations that involve contradictions or inconsistencies that make no sense, (4) tautologies, (5) the large number of specific identities and function that have conceptual and/or substantive problems, and so on. Therefore, neither arguing the case that a consistent story exists nor setting out to construct such a story is one of my contentions or objectives.

Without either presuming or pretending any finality to the individual elements of the array or to the array as a whole, the following is a likely nonexhaustive array of types of invisible hand found in the literature: (1) specific combinations of identity and function, such as a competitive market generating efficiency; (2) Friedrich Hayek's principles of (a) unintended and unforeseen consequences and (b) spontaneous order; (3) invisible hand processes, (also) the result of interaction and aggregation; and (4) tautologies, such as the invisible hand being deemed to refer only to benevolent outcomes.

For numerous reasons, which accumulate in the successive essays, the concept of the invisible hand is ultimately ambiguous, inconclusive, not dispositive of the task of performing the function(s) generally attributed to it, and empty. The concept of the invisible hand is only that – a concept. For the most part, definitely not entirely, the use of one or another specification strongly tends to introduce, consciously or subconsciously, the idea that some transcendental force is at work in the universe of the economy; hence there is, for example, a harmonious self-regulating order. The use of the concept may introduce not only harmony, self-regulation, and order; its use is a mode of affirming conclusiveness. That it also serves as a trope with which to selectively influence policy is quite another matter.

It is important to recognize that Smith may have found it useful, necessary, or desirable to include a discussion of a policy that had a historic status yet may be considered to contradict either the nature of his "obvious and simple system of natural liberty" or his concept of how legislation should and should not be promulgated. Accordingly, when I write of "the moral rules," I intend to be read as referring to a category and not the moral rules themselves; and similarly with legal rules and other terms. As with the case of the moral rules, one of the principal themes of *The Theory of Moral Sentiments*, legal rules must be worked out.

Because of the enormous stature of Smith himself and of the image of the invisible hand, it is easy to forget that the subject of these essays is an interpretive field. It is laden with selective perception and the projection of feelings and sentiments; as Milton Myers might put it, it is a field full of "fancies and factions in place of facts and realities" (1983: 99).

5

I neither intended nor expected to reach the conclusions presented in this book. I have for a long time thought of the invisible hand as a rather silly and pretentious matter. It is not a joke, though some users of the term, by their claims, tend to make it appear to be one. It is a means of relating modern high theory to Adam Smith and, as such, an interesting example of the development of language. It does help set some minds at rest and it does engender hypotheses for serious work. It also opens wide doors to the human condition, the constitution of human nature, and what politics is all about.

The procedure through which I reached my conclusions involved the enormous amount of reading, annotation, and interpreting the meaning of lines of reasoning in relation to each other. I self-consciously endeav-ored to avoid antecedent premises that would drive the reasoning and, in various ways, project a personal point of view. A pluralist in methodology, theory, and otherwise, I concentrate my other research on the economic role of government, and do so as a self-professed institutionalist (in a blend of several other schools). Because of my interest in collective decision making, I believe that my work as a historian of economic thought and a methodologist has enabled me to take objective, arm's-length, but not necessarily the "correct," positions. My legal-economic analyses do not attempt to reach unique determinate equilibrium optimizing positions on issues of policy. My interest is in formulating models of what is actually going on in the process of working out more or less tentative solutions to problems of policy. Inasmuch as I have no particular policies and problem solutions to promote in my scholarly analytic and historical work, I do not need to engage in casuistic maneuvers to erect and defend an ostensibly impregnable intellectual fortress. I work with and on ideas and institutions that I disagree with, because I find them important, whatever my personal views. I learned later that when I included a long essay on nonlegal social control (morals, religion, custom, and education) as held by the English classical economists, some people thought that I was a social conservative, even fundamentalist in matters of religion, because, they reasoned, only such a person would devote their attention to those topics. Nothing could be farther from the truth. I have been told, by members of the Chicago School, that my deep interest in the theory of power put me "dangerously close" to Marx and rendered me "subversive." I invite the reader to suspend judgment on such issues and not to interpret my work and my ideas within narrowly defined conventional terminology.

I do not think that I am fooling myself. I also believe that it is impossible for a scholar to escape his worldview and to keep it from influencing his work. I also believe in criticism, not necessarily to reach Truth – more likely, to identify the matrix of positions taken by those in the process of working things out. I think that I am both more conservative and more liberal than many people find me to be. I accept that Smith's argument in his *History of Astronomy*, of which so much is made in this work, applies to me.

The opening essay documents the somewhat odd issue arising from the award of the Nobel Prize in Economic Sciences to economic theorists whose work is thought, by others if not by themselves, to further clarify the meaning of Smith's use of the term "invisible hand." Some people applaud it while others do not. I then enlarge the frame of reference to the conflict between those who affirm the invisible hand as the foundation of economics and those who consider that affirmation to be exaggerated. The essay also surveys the history of the use of the term – a history that extends back to the period of the ancient civilizations. The intent here is to put *finis* to the oft-stated belief that the term originated with Adam Smith. I also suggest that the term seemingly was given different uses depending on doctrinal matters as well as social circumstances. My purpose in doing so is to document the pre-Smith use of the term by various religious groups over a widespread area. Next I examine Smith's three known uses of the term. The two other uses are not unimportant, but the status of Smith and the *Wealth of Nations* is largely owing to his general argument in that book and to his use of the term.

Essay 2 presents Smith's synoptic and synthetic system that flows from his tripartite model of society, and its consequences. It combines (1) the moral sentiments and the moral rules that emanate from the principles of approbation and disapprobation as individuals seek respect and recognition; (2) the development of government and law as these become the object of capture and use of a widening range of interested parties; and (3) the case in favor of a market economy, or what Smith called the obvious and simple system of natural liberty, and simultaneously opposed to any system of extraordinary encouragements and extraordinary restraints, most notably mercantilism. Whether pursued through the extension of the rejection of mercantilism to the rejection of ostensibly most governmental activism, or through the denigration of both moral and legal social control, such rejection and denigration have misrepresented Smith's system of social science as presented by him.

Essay 3 takes up two of the questions addressed either directly or obliquely in the literature dealing with the invisible hand, namely what is the invisible hand? And what are the functions that the individual hand, so identified, is seen to perform and promote? One of the conclusions of this study – that of multiplicity resulting in ambiguity and inconclusiveness – is based in large part on this essay. One of the major implications of Essay 3 – centering on such questions as whether the invisible hand should be taken to be competition and its function to be efficiency – is that, aside from other considerations, no invisible hand can accommodate all the complications and explanatory and interpretive burden thereby placed on it. That implication, however, is mild when contrasted with the findings that come in Essays 4–8.

Consideration of the functions deemed to be performed by particular specifications of the invisible hand raises the very different question about the function of the use of the *concept* per se of the invisible hand, which is the subject of Essay 4. The analysis is based on Smith's argument in his *History of Astronomy* that people settle for propositions that soothe the imagination, or set minds at rest, when truth is unattainable. The propositions are extraordinarily wide-ranging. They are found in the system of social belief, including the mythic and symbolic systems of society, and are deployed in issues of social control as the social construction of reality and the struggles over both the structure of power in general and over the state in particular. Essay 4 therefore examines Smith's argument in his *History of Astronomy*, with its distinction between propositions that are believed to be true and others that serve to soothe the imagination. Also covered are the questions of the breadth of application of his argument, the sources of propositions that set minds at rest, and the systems of belief and of myth that are intertwined with the system of language. These propositions provide a logical sequence of cause and effect (or otherwise) allowing people to feel that they are not victims of unexplained forces.

The concept of the invisible hand, as distinct from candidates for its identity and function, has proven remarkably powerful in serving as social control and psychic balm in the western world. Use of the term "invisible hand" seemingly transfers to something else – the responsibility for business decisions that may flow from a quest for power, perhaps in the form of market share or market structure. Placing responsibility on the invisible hand – or "the bottom line," or the belief that every business decision either is efficient or contributes to efficiency, or some other euphemism – not only absolves business from responsibility but obfuscates the power that business has and the power that motivates business.

Essay 5 surveys a number of conceptual and substantive problems that, individually and together, further emphasize the ambiguity and inconclusiveness of the notion of the invisible hand. Among these problems are the multiple paradigms in which Smith operated; the character of the Enlightenment and related considerations; the various meanings of "nature" and "natural"; supernaturalism, including the question of Smith's theology; Smith's stages theory; the mythic and symbolic systems; the sociolinguistic system, including the problems of whether the invisible hand is a matter of a definition of reality or of language, which figure of speech is the invisible hand, and related issues; the problem of the invisible hand as self-interest, including the formation of self-interest, the meaning of rationality, institutions, and environment; an array of dualisms of interpretation; the problem of Hayekian deliberative versus nondeliberative decision making in the design and creation of institutions – that is, his principles of spontaneous order and of unforeseen and unintended consequences; and the relevance of power to the invisible hand and the invisible hand as a mode of working out the structure and use of power. Altogether, these conceptual and substantive problems so empty and emaciate the concept of an invisible hand, that the contents of this essay alone seems sufficient to render it useless, except for the purposes of ideology, namely to marshal and manipulate individual beliefs and behavior.

Essays 6 and 7 take up the question of the invisible hand as knowledge. The overriding conclusion is that the category of invisible hand is empty as language, on the ontological level, and with respect to the epistemological criteria of various kinds for the status of knowledge. On several grounds it is concluded that there is no invisible hand; that the invisible hand has no meaningful status as knowledge; and that no increase in knowledge is achieved by calling something an invisible hand.

Essay 6 considers the important topics of the political nature of language, Smith's contributions, metaphors in general and in economics, and language as social control and the social construction of reality amid the struggle for power and control of the state. Essay 7 examines the ontology and the epistemology of the invisible hand.

Much discussion of the invisible hand tracks or parallels substantive discussions of comparable topics in theoretical or empirical economics, notwithstanding that vacuity. Obscured by that parallel discussion is the putative fact that there is no more substance and hence no more justification of the claim to comprise knowledge than there is to the assertion that the allocation of resources is accomplished by a group of monkeys in Bay Front Park in Miami. Most claims about the invisible hand are pure assertion and are the result of cultural habit, wishful thinking, ingenuity, and gullibility. Furthermore, there is no increase in knowledge if two groups of economists argue which is correct, that resource allocation is governed by one or another group of believers and their supposed researches and/or logomachy. That some people do survive and others do not after being bitten by snakes in a box when their hand is placed therein may help give rise to the knowledge that the venom of some types of snake is poisonous and that of other types of snake is not poisonous. No such increase of knowledge is ascertainable in the case of the invisible hand in comparison with the more substantive, empirical parallel research on the same subject. To say, that is, that "the allocation of resources is the result of competition" is to produce nothing more and nothing less than the statement, "the allocation of resources is the result of competition operating as the invisible hand."

Essay 8 first discusses Smith's treatment of the economic role of government. Like the rest of this book, the essay is concerned first with what Smith actually seems to have understood on the topic, and second with what is historically and analytically wrong – or misperceived – and marketed as the laissez-faire, noninterventionist, libertarian, and similar interpretations of the economic role of government. The essay is concerned with neither how any type of economic system can be institutionalized nor the normative case for any economic system (except insofar as that normative case is affected by historical and analytical errors).

Here it is argued – contrary to the predominant Chicago School interpretation of Smith – that government is an important part of the economy, not least in that government defines, assigns, and revises the content of private property, and that something is lost when Smith is said simply to favor – or require – the institution of private property. Again contrary to conventional wisdom, Smith understood that the economy is what it is to no small degree because of the purposes to which it is put by those who have control of the government. The mainstream belief system of western civilization and of neoclassical and other schools of economics obscures the continuing – if muted – contest between classes of rich and poor, that is, between groups of individuals some of whom are rich and some are poor, largely – albeit not completely – because the one group and not the other group is able to, by means of its control of government, have its interests drive or constitute government policy. The key role of the use of the concept of the invisible hand is its selectivity.

Lecture notes taken in Milton Friedman's first year of teaching at Chicago suggest that he had a deeper and more complex model of the regulatory systems of a market economy. Much of this model is implicitly repudiated in his later, better-known work, enabling him to take as absolutist what in his lectures was relativist.

Essay 8 next takes up Friedrich Hayek's treatment of the economic role of government, the formulation of which comprises a relatively popular substitute for arguments often attributed to Smith. Although Hayek sometimes insinuates into his discussion his own possible agenda for government, such as revision of corporate law restricting the power of corporations to be predatory (possibly including expansion of the term "predatory" from its narrow confinement in contemporary antitrust theory), as well as his own version of the welfare state. The discussion focuses on Hayek's two "principles": that of "unintended and unexpected consequences" and that of "institutions of human origin but not of human design." These propositions are shown to be valuable as positive propositions but not with the twist Hayek gives them on the basis of his normative formulations. Indeed, in Hayek's hands, these propositions serve to introduce into the legal-economic decision-making process the agenda items the process desires and the exclusion of those agenda items it does not desire. To argue for laissez-faire is, once again, to fail to open to scrutiny the uses to which government will be put by those who claim to have no or very minimal uses of their own. Much the same applies to two other "principles" promoted by Hayek, namely "spontane-ous order" and "rule of law." For Hayek and his disciples, much as for those who claim allegiance to Smith's invisible hand, the invocation of an invisible hand constitutes a special kind of linguistic, ontological, and epistemolog-ical sleight of hand.

Government is important and inevitable as a mode of social control, social change, and social construction. Nominal positions of laissez-faire and nonintervention are shown to be the selective agendas they funda-mentally are. It is through pretense that the concept of the invisible hand selectively serves as social control and psychic balm, that it is selectively grounded in the mythic, symbolic, and belief systems of society, and that rhetoric about the invisible hand comes selectively to dominate debate over the economic role of government through which the details of government activism, *always* ubiquitous, are worked out. The alternative to one program of government activism is not the natural order of things to which human-kind should, if not must, submit. The alternative to that program of govern-ment activism is another program of government activism.

In some respects, what I found in Smith on the economic role of govern-ment, and the various glues used to tie ideas together, echoed my earlier findings on the Physiocrats. They, too, were doing what later people had been doing, namely masking (inadvertently or otherwise) the important economic roles of government by identifying their system as part of the natural order of things, and also opposing any system of economic policy deemed by them to be contradictory, all the while seeking to use and to manipulate government for their own purposes.

A persistent problem is the role of language. While studying the alterna-tives that arise in discussions of the invisible hand, I eventually focused on the linguistic term used by most people to classify the notion of an invisi-ble hand, namely metaphor (though comparable questions could be raised regarding simile, trope, and so on). One question I pondered was, if B is a metaphor for A, because A came first, then what about a situation in which B came first; was A a metaphor for B? I also posed to myself the following questions: Was the invisible hand a metaphor or something else? For what was the invisible hand a metaphor, what did it tell us, and did it matter? And for what purpose was the invisible hand a means of introducing into the legal-economic decision-making process the agenda items (and their supporting arguments) desired by the introducers, to the exclusion of those agenda items they do not desire? The purpose, I concluded, is to put one group and not another in a position to control government, thereby effec-tuating its interests and not the interests of some other group(s) – in other words, to promote certain consolidations of social interests and not others. To argue for laissez-faire or nonintervention is to fail to acknowledge (admit to) and open to scrutiny the uses to which government had already been put and will be put by those who claim to have no or very "minimal" uses of their own. I further concluded that the significance of discussions as to whether the term "invisible hand" was actually one thing or another, metaphor or simile, and of discussions of the specific identity and correlative function(s) of the invisible hand, was that those discussions already assumed and – by using the term – reinforced the belief that the invisible hand actually did exist.

Many people consider the invisible hand to be a metaphor. Does it matter? I then made two connections: I found that the argument of the *History of Astronomy* applied to Smith's use of the invisible hand, and that soothing the imagination was akin to psychic balm and social control. It eventually became clear that virtually all of the discussions of the invisible hand – for example, about its identity and its function – were by people seeking to set their own minds and the minds of others at rest by doing exactly what Smith said they would do if they could not end up with truth, including, I surmise, if they thought that they could generate truth but not of the type they were seeking.

Essay 9 raises a highly neglected topic, one unknown even to many economists: the survival requirement of Pareto optimality. Inasmuch as the invisible-hand reasoning has assumed the form of Pareto optimality, it seems important to consider that Pareto optimality applies only to marginal decisions, and that nonsurvival, or death, is not a marginal decision. I examine some important writings that introduce and support the survival requirement, some reactions to those writings, and a variety of materials, by economists and noneconomists, suggesting that the topic is alive and well. Essay 10 recapitulates and somewhat extends the argument and conclusions of the preceding eight essays. It focuses on the problem of the exercise of discretion about the conflict of continuity and change, the invisible hand as argument, Lionel Robbins's approach to the interpretation of Smith, the part of the invisible-hand literature known as invisible-hand processes of explanation (in their positive rather than the more common normative formulations), and the context in which invisible-hand analyses acquire their meaning.

I found very revealing and suggestive the variety of meanings attributed to each and every facet of the Enlightenment. The important matter was not that the Enlightenment in the eighteenth century putatively was about the independence of man, but what its subsequent interpreters have been trying to portray as the Enlightenment in order to influence the society and the economic role of government in the present. Hayek, like many others, was engaged in undertaking the very things he criticized others for doing. Then, too, even putting aside such intentions, individuals define reality as they see it, based on the array of intellectual movements in which their minds – and the minds of those who taught them or with whom they identify and/or interact – were enmeshed and their mentalities formed.

The invisible hand is also involved with something far different from the concept as it is usually defined and whatever function it is said to perform. The function of the invisible hand has to be dealt with as a concept on a different level from that of its particular identities and its particular functions. To appreciate my analysis, the reader must recognize that economics is the only discipline, science, or field of inquiry where practitioners pride themselves on having something invisible as the foundational concept of their discipline. I had been cognizant of the idea of economics both competing with and supplementing religion as social control. I had been aware of the ideological role performed by individual economists or by certain groups, or schools, of economists. I had concentrated, in part, in my work as an economist on developing an understanding of the economic role of government that satisfied neither conservative nor liberal view of it, but rather the one that would enable people to discuss their systems of thought over the centuries. I had concluded in that effort, for example, that government – or decision making, or governance – was important; that government was the object of competition to control the uses to which it would be put; that there was much sense in Lionel Robbins' market-plus-framework approach, especially when one incorporated in it the government as a means of change – that is, legal social control and nonlegal social control such as religion, morals, custom, and education – and went beyond that approach to the analysis of power and what I came to call the legal-economic nexus.

The critical time came when I tried to outline the essays and fit them together. Essay 1 is relatively traditional in its account of Smith's three uses. Two subjects had to fit in and somehow be tied together. One was the praise of the invisible hand as the foundation of economics, coupled with criticism – by economists at the highest levels of the discipline – of that praise as exaggeration. The other was Smith's argument in his *History of Astronomy*. I had found fascinating how economists and others wrote about the identifications and functions of the invisible hand often without labeling them as such, trying to make a case for one or another as *the* invisible hand.

6

My thanks go first to Marianne F. Johnson, one of my last two doctoral candidates and dissertation supervisees. Her calm and composed demeanor combines with ability, motivation, diligence, and work ethic to yield academic perfection. She has graciously helped me in a large number of ways, notably in preparing and polishing archival materials for publication in *Research in the History of Economic Thought and Methodology*. My greatest debt was incurred when she responded favorably to my request, on account of illness, to help in the completion of this book.

My second thanks go to numerous other former students and colleagues at Michigan State University and the History of Economics Society. They have shared with me information on items about (in one way or another) the invisible hand they have encountered, often giving or sending me a copy. They have critiqued my ideas and my work, both published and unpublished. I was fortunate to have department, college, and university funds for copying and for either undergraduate or graduate student help (mostly the latter) in searching for and copying materials already on hand at the Michigan State University Library and/or for securing copies through Interlibrary Loan (mostly the period when the computer and the Internet were not as research-friendly as they are now). Steven Medema has humorously remarked that working for me was like getting a doctorate in Xerox copying. At any rate, they fed my ego and self-image by letting me think that I knew more than I do and by assuaging my self-esteem when they thought I was enough wrong-headed to warrant criticism. I could not prepare with confidence a complete list of the individuals who have helped me in one way or another. Those who belong on the list know it and know how thankful I am for their support. I have retained the acknowledgment lines for several essays in which the individuals are mentioned by name.

My third thanks go to Holly Floyd of the Reference Department at the Michigan State University Library. Holly has given me invaluable help, especially after I retired and moved with my wife to Gainesville, Florida. Holly has helped on this project and on my work in editing the three annual volumes of *Research in the History of Economic Thought and Methodology*. I owe special thanks to Edward Elgar and Scott Parris. Edward has for more than twenty years provided moral support for my projected three-volume study of the invisible hand, and has agreed to publish a significant collection of invisible-hand materials, which I will edit with Marianne Johnson. Scott and I have discussed for some time the possibility of publishing my work with Cambridge University Press. He, too, has provided moral support.

I have been exceedingly fortunate to have been joined by William "Bill" H. Perry. He is an expert with the use of computers. He is highly knowledgeable about the history of religion. He knows how to use computer programs to find and download all manner of materials dating from well before 1776. Bill speaks of securing documents from the second century c.e. through the eighteenth century almost as if he were planning a visit to the nearest branch of the public library. He is, needless to say, highly motivated. I met Bill at George Mason University, not by accident; we were brought together by his wife, Jane Perry. Bill later introduced me to Ken Ewell, another computer whiz who lives in Gainesville, Florida. We are extremely fortunate that so many groups in possession of the kinds of documents we have needed have had them translated and put on the Internet in order to make them available to other scholars and/or to proselytize. Some of the pre-Smithian historical materials and most of the more recondite items – all examples of the use of the term "invisible hand" – presented in Essay 1 are due to Bill's efforts. The first volume(s) in the Elgar series mentioned earlier hopefully will likewise reflect his genius. To him and his wife I owe immeasurable gratitude.

One of my friends, Jim Qualizza, a computer specialist, after first commenting that the use of the invisible hand seemed to point to prediction, remarked that it was useful in giving a name to hide ignorance. Both comments seem to me to be propositions providing for the soothing of the imagination. If the propositions have the ring of truth, it is not because they are true but because people desire to have the music, as it were, of truth, and accept the propositions asserted as belief, notwithstanding their contrivance. This leaves them exposed, to serve as targets of those who seek for them to have the plausible assurance provided by belief in the invisible hand.

I also want to say that much of the picture or model that I have assembled in these essays resembles or is congruent with Vilfredo Pareto's *Treatise on General Sociology*, also published as *The Mind and Society*. In my 1974 volume, *Pareto on Policy*, I presented – using modern terminology – his ideas on both the deep and the broad processes of decision making centering on power, knowledge, and psychology, and the mutual manipulation through which policies are worked out. Pareto was perverse where Smith was proper. I would relish having both men in my home for an extended period.

Adam Smith's Invisible Hand and the Nobel Prize in Economic Sciences

1.1. The Research Protocols of Economics, the Ironies That Result from Them, and Other Preliminaries

By the end of the twentieth century, if not earlier, economics could be seen as science, as political and moral philosophy, as ideological self-projection by the people of the Euro-American nations and their way of earning a living, as both derived from and generally reinforcing the existing structure of power, privilege, and so on. The terms "science," "political and moral philosophy," and "ideological self-projection" each has a wide array of meanings. Language is a political phenomenon. Certainly such is the case with the term "the invisible hand." Each effort at definition is, in one way or another, an attempt to influence, for purposes of policy making, the definition of reality – the social belief system – by which we understand and, often unwittingly, socially reconstruct the economic world. The essays comprising this book are an attempt to make sense of a concept – the invisible hand – widely used in the corresponding plethora of assertion, argument, and controversy. A great deal is involved in this literature, much of which is rarely understood to constitute social control.

In light of this, it is fair to say that the nature, meaning, and significance of the concept of the invisible hand arise within the social construction, practice, and enforcement by strategically positioned economists. Certain research protocols are enforced that control (1) the scope of economics, (2) the way in which the economy is dealt with, and (3) how economic research is undertaken. Several ironies that have arisen in this situation must also be understood. As matters turned out, very little of all this derives from actual economies. Much more important is what strategically placed economists opine and enforce in regards to how economics is to be organized and controlled.

The protocols are adopted and enforced by a system of social control that is in the hands of the strategically best-positioned economists. These economists are the ones who make decisions as to the hiring, promoting, remunerating (notably merit raises), and distributing of professional or institutional awards. Other strategically situated economists include, among others, journal editors, the organizers of conferences (and of sessions at conferences), and the nominating committees charged with supervising the nomination of candidates for election to departmental and other organizational offices and committees, in each case depending on the organization's constitution and bylaws. So ubiquitous as to be readily overlooked are those faculty members that teach courses in economic theory and those that write course and, especially, comprehensive qualifying examinations. Variously called preliminary, general, qualifying, or comprehensive exams, only the doctoral candidates who pass them may continue in the program. A variety of rules govern these examinations.

In the late 1960s, in part as a result of student activism, graduate students acquired rights to membership on departmental and other committees, electing their own representatives. The rationale was the same as that advanced, since the late eighteenth century, in support of the extension of the franchise to all adult males and, later, all adult females – namely, that peoples should participate, through their elected representatives, in decision making with regard to matters that impact their lives.

Considerable freedom of action, or independence, is enjoyed by departments. This autonomy has several possible sources. One source is the establishment of academic freedom, which also operates at the level of the individual faculty member but is influenced by hiring, promotions, and other incentives. Another source is the establishment by faculty and higher administration of a charismatic leader, in the Weberian or some other sense, as department chair. Faculty can de facto quietly override, within more or less variable constraints, certain decisions by the state legislature in the case of a public university or the governing board of either a private or public institution. A common example is the legislative determination that the chair of a department is a head and not *primus inter pares*. The head is legally responsible, and has the legal authority, to make all curricular, personnel, and operating decisions. Election to the position of chair, or to a list of three submitted to the dean from which the dean chooses, may be restricted to only those faculty that agree to share decision-making power with the rest of the faculty or an advisory committee. Complete authority is never lodged in a department. Budgetary decisions can be imposed on a university, college, or department by legislative committee, governing board, president, or dean.

We come now to the first protocol and the first ironies. These economists, in their work, although they identified the economy as governing the allocation of resources, considered the economy to be self-contained and generating its own laws of allocation and distribution. After countless articles on the scope (and method) of economics had been mulled over and debated, discussion converged on a definition of the economy as independent of the rest of society, with its own laws of operation and development. All of that constitutes the first protocol. Considerations of the structures of decision making, power, and social control – that is, whose interests would count in the organization and operation of the economy – were excluded, minimized, or trivialized. The same is true of the working out of the structures themselves.

Yet all the while, economists took as their special domain the making of recommendations of policy, believed by them to be privileged because of their special expertise, which also was generally deemed to exempt them from the injunction in favor of laissez-faire. Numerous lines of reasoning, some of which shall be examined later, have been advanced in support of these positions; in most, if not all, cases, however, the arguments assume the very point that they assert. Such is the first irony.

The second irony derives from the protocol governing the way in which the economy is dealt with, and in such a way as to reinforce the narrowing effects of the first protocol and the first irony. It should go without saying that no model and no theory can encompass every relevant operating variable in the economy. The number of variables has to be made manageable, and it is sensible to commence the study of an economic question with those variables that appear to be the most important – sensible so long as one does not cease serious research involving the variable(s) in which one is most interested, inasmuch as those variables may have been chosen with a view to protect and promote certain interests and beliefs. The second protocol goes beyond manageability to the nature of the economy with which the theorist works. This protocol stipulates that economic theory be conducted with and within a generalized, *a-institutional*, purely conceptual economy – that is, an economy understood to possess the *institution* of "private property" but *largely approached only in generic and conceptual terms*. The pure a-institutional economy with private property lacks any specification and assignment of the particular bundles of rights enjoyed by the owners of particularly defined and assigned property (whose interests, and the uses to which that property is put, are thereby protected). The purely conceptual economy also lacks official cognition, recognition, specification, and, of course, protection of those whose interests are not protected as property. In actual economies, the other assets of these unprotected economic actors are left exposed to the choices and actions of those whose interests and ability to act are protected.

The second irony derives from the second protocol in three ways. First, inasmuch as the second protocol omits the specification and assignment of rights, those economists (and others) who apply the theory ensconced in the generalized, a-institutional, purely conceptual economy have no basis for their application(s). They have no reason to believe either that the purely conceptual economy and the actual economy have anything in common or that the purely conceptual economy can be meaningfully applied to the actual economy. Not all models of a generalized, a-institutional, purely conceptual economy necessarily apply either to a particular actual economy or to each and every actual economy. Secondly, even though the second protocol omits the specification and assignment of rights, the design of the generalized, a-institutional, purely conceptual economy may actually give effect to hypothetical institutions that are in conflict with actual institutions; or the design is applied to existing institutions that are specific to existing detailed arrangements of social control. Thirdly, the actual existing institutions, notably private property, may derive from one stage of society – of social control – whereas the network of forces presently active in society may relate to a later or to a current stage of social control and social change, with the conceptual model of the economy an object of control with which to advance one or the other stage of society or economy.

Undoubtedly, every stage of society/every stage of social control has conflicting elements inherited from multiple earlier stages. In the discussion of Friedrich Hayek's theory of nondeliberative and deliberative decision making, I adopt and invoke Carl Menger's version of that theory. As a result, except in the case of so-called spontaneously arising (i.e., nondeliberative) institutions in their first period, *all* institutions, *pace* Menger, are blends of deliberative and nondeliberative decision making. I mention that here because it appears to me to arise in the case of both Smith's stages theory and his legal-economic analysis as found recorded in the two sets of students' notes from his lectures on jurisprudence. As a result, still another irony arises, as will be seen in Essay 8, when the universal University of Chicago misperception of Smith is contrasted with what Smith actually wrote (on power, etc.) and is recorded as saying (on law, on the conditions of its genesis, and on its change) in his lectures. The foregoing holds even when one emphasizes, in his case, the allocation of resources through markets (but decidedly not markets that are, by their very nature as markets, competitive [*pace* Stigler]).

I now turn to the third protocol and the fifth irony. The third protocol governs how economic research is undertaken. The protocol requires that an exercise in economic theory produce a unique determinate equilibrium optimal result, or solution. This research protocol has an extraordinary narrowing effect. For example, choice must be made between different meanings of optimum. Further, if the choice be Pareto optimality, inasmuch as each possible structure of power or each possible set of assets will likely yield different Pareto optima, choice must be made between different power, or rights, structures. To produce a unique determinate equilibrium result (i.e., aside from optimality), assumptions must be made that rule out all determinate equilibrium results other than the unique determinate result thereby reached. In sum, the production of unique determinate results and so on assumes some specification and assignment of property rights, as well as that such rights are fully defined and unchangeable, and makes similar assumptions regarding all other relevant institutions.

The irony arises insofar as the processes in actual economies in which all variables are worked out by actual economic actors are replaced by sets of assumptions such that it is the economic analyst or theorist who produces the ostensible unique determinate equilibrium optimal result and not the economic actors.

Different theorists and economists will make different choices insofar as they interpret and apply social control to the problems constituting the work of economists; the same is true insofar as they construct different a-institutional, purely conceptual economies; and likewise insofar as they make different assumptions, thereby producing different ostensibly unique determinate equilibrium optimal results. The result is ubiquitous variety and ubiquitous controversy in actual economies but not so evident in purely conceptual economy configured to produce unique determinant equilibrium optimal results.

Considering the protocols made or followed by economists and the consequential ironies of those protocols, the introduction into economics of the concept of the invisible hand comprises a means of establishing absolutism into economics, doing so in several ways, one being the further narrowing of what economics is all about.

The foregoing can be exemplified by briefly considering the history of value and price theories. Value theory constitutes the various efforts to establish an absolute and invariable basis of price. The two historically important theories of value (each manifesting, however, in a variety of formulations) are the labor theory of value and the marginal utility theory of value. The labor theory of value holds that the value of any reproducible commodity is a function of its labor content, that is, the labor required in its production. A generalization and extension of the labor theory is the cost of production theory that holds that the value of any reproducible commodity is a function of its cost of production and of nothing else. The marginal utility theory of value holds that the value of any reproducible commodity is a function of the marginal utility of the equilibrium unit and of nothing else.

It appears that most economists, for whatever reason(s), have considered neither proposed absolute and invariable basis of price to be a satisfactory solution. The alternative solution is price theory that holds that the price of any reproducible commodity is a function of demand and supply (logically of demand, supply, and the irrelevant). It is vital to understand that the new solution does not contemplate an absolute and invariable basis of price but instead posits price as the result of market structures and forces. The structures have to do, in general, with kinds of competition and the nature of rationality. The forces are demand and supply. Price theory is not a theory of the absolute and invariable basis of price. Price theory is a relativist theory in which value = price is a function of demand and supply. Such a relativist theory is offensive to anyone who requires the absolute determinacy and closure of value theory. (To the labor and marginal utility theories of value now must be juxtaposed the actually older theory of the just price, a theory apparently usually expressed in terms of some formulation of cost of production or marginal utility but also in terms of some theory of individual merit).

Price theory may be more satisfying to those displeased with uni-valued value theory – that is, those who are comfortable with indeterminacy, open-endedness, and ambiguity of relativism. However, price theory, with its possible multivalued concept of price (as a function of demand, supply, and market structures) is less satisfying to those who require determinacy and closure.

Economics, for all the belief by some economists in the scientific quality of their discipline, has been sufficiently burdened by multiplicity and conflict that it appears to other economists as having an exaggerated confidence in that quality. The conflicted nature and usage of the concept of the invisible hand in economics is reflective of the differences to be found among economists in all aspects of the subject. I shall begin with the controversy over the status of the invisible hand in regard to the Nobel Prize.

1.2. Adam Smith and Some Nobel Prizes

The Nobel Prize in Economic Sciences was first awarded in 1969 to Ragnar Frisch of Norway and Jan Tinbergen of the Netherlands. Both men were honored for their work in the major fields of what then constituted economics. They were followed by several Americans, most notably Paul A. Samuelson. Substantially all of them and those awardees that came afterward made significant advances in both well-established fields and in areas of economics that they helped establish. Much, but not all, of their work utilized mathematics and econometrics, often using procedures that they themselves had developed. Another characteristic was their conception of the economy as a whole, perhaps divided into fields. This characteristic they shared with Smith, although, as Robert Dorfman pointed out, they shared neither the mathematics language nor the precise modeling form or structure (Dorfman 1983: F15). Smith was a professor of moral philosophy rather than of economics alone, who took substantially all of social science, including economics (as it then was to be found), history, and law, as his domain. As will be examined in Essay 2, Smith had a tripartite structure of those fields in his mind: moral rules, government and law, and markets. Another characteristic that Smith superficially shared with modern economists was the notion of the invisible hand.

In November 1983, shortly before Gerard Debreu was to receive the Nobel Prize in Economic Sciences, Harry Anderson reported in an article for *Newsweek* entitled "Explaining the 'Invisible Hand'" that "Debreu has created a model of a theoretical marketplace and has provided an analytical framework for some of the most fundamental tenets of classical economics." Anderson noted that economists since Smith had accepted as "an article of faith" that the conflicting interests of supply and demand could be reconciled through the price mechanism creating equilibrium between them: "The best explanation that Smith could offer was that individual economic agents were guided to the common good 'as if by an invisible hand.'" Here Anderson slipped into committing a common error, for Smith had written that individuals actually are "led by an invisible hand," not "as if by an invisible hand." However, it was Debreu, together with 1972 Nobel Laureate Kenneth Arrow, who developed a model in which "at least in his theoretical world ... equilibrium could, in fact, be attained." Debreu did this by confirming "'the internal logical consistency' of the classical view of markets" (Anderson 1983: 59; the internal quote is from the Royal Swedish Academy of Sciences award). Fourteen years later, shortly before Leonid Hurwicz, Eric S. Maskin, and Robert B. Myerson were to become Nobel Laureates in Economics, the *Economist* headlined the relevant column "Intelligent Design" and followed it, in the print edition, with "A theory of an intelligently guided invisible hand wins the Nobel Prize."

Some three weeks prior to Anderson's 1983 article, writing in the *New York Times*, Robert Dorfman quoted the invisible-hand passage in the *Wealth of Nations*, saying that Smith's "words carry immediate conviction, and they have served as the unifying principle of economics ever since they were written. But they do not bear close inspection." The key question concerns the coordination of all this activity: "Smith's explanation of the invisible hand – occupying barely a page – does little to answer such questions" (Dorfman 1983: F15). (Actually there is no explanation, only an assertion, and it runs to only a few lines. It is likely, possibly very likely, that at best he had only an incoherent vision or understanding when he used the term in his *Moral Sentiments* and *Wealth of Nations*.)

The next step was taken by Leon Walras a century after Smith. Walras's was a theory of general equilibrium utilizing a huge number of equations, but his demonstration was defective and could produce nonsensical negative prices and negative amounts purchased. Some sixty years later, Abraham Wald produced an equilibrium model with "some very restrictive assumptions about the nature of the economy. His demonstration, therefore, provided only modest comfort: The invisible hand might work as alleged in the Waldian economy, but whether it could do so in any real economy remained an open question."

The development of linear programming by Leonid V. Kantorovich and George B. Danzig led Tjalling C. Koopmans to look at Smith's problem in a new way, avoiding "the complexities of dealing with all of Walras's supply and demand equations." The next step was taken by Debreu and Kenneth Arrow, showing that "the equilibrium conditions could be satisfied under much less unrealistic conditions than Wald's." The significance for policy of that sequence of developments was, as Dorfman expressed it, that "it underlies all policies that rest on the belief that economic decisions are best left to the operation of free markets." Matters were not quite so simple, however. In a Debreu world, corporate size and no uncertainty (i.e., a complete array of futures markets) would eliminate economic instability. However, all that is "far different from our economy." Moreover, Debreu established only that "the invisible hand could work effectively, he did not show that it would." Dorfman provided a mixed evaluation:

Professor Debreu's achievement, though the most advanced yet, falls far short of showing that reliance on the invisible hand is the ideal economic policy in any feasible economy. But there is every reason to think that the invisible hand is more powerful and subtle than it has yet been proved to be ....(Dorfman 1983: F15)

Dorfman concluded with the question, "Is it likely that Adam Smith's brilliant conjecture will be confirmed in the end?" to which he responded:

I say no. In the first place, there is not going to be any end ... Besides, the progress made so far supports the common-sense view that no such simple dictum can be relied on in all circumstances. (Dorfman 1983: F15)

Two days later, in the October 25, 1983 edition of the *Detroit News*, Edwin M. Yoder. Jr. queried, "Was Economics Nobel a Mistake?" His answer was given in several parts: Economics "is too limited a field to sustain a suitable myth of distinction." Economics "produces few great originals." The only two who seem likely to be chosen would have been Alfred Marshall and John Maynard Keynes – "both of whom were, alas, long dead when the prize was established."

An alert reader of both articles might have asked him – or oneself: Are there two invisible hands, or are there two theories of the invisible hand? What is the "invisible hand"? What does it do? Where does it come from? If this reader had some knowledge of philosophy, he or she might have also asked, in what sense or in what way is the invisible hand "explained." Is there a difference between what people think they are doing when they say something like "the invisible hand is X and X performs Y function," and the social function performed by doing so? Is there a test, perhaps a new test, by which the explanation is reckoned? Is this explanation a matter of setting down some "first principles," or some premises or axioms, or a mathematical model, and working them out? Can these techniques permit more than one, perhaps numerous, answers, and if so, can they be reduced to one answer? How can such reduction be undertaken? Is the process of explanation, therefore, one of deductive logic? If so, what of empiricism, or resort not to some set of equations but to empirical data? Even then, on what basis is the empirical data reckoned to be empirical data? Along a different path, are the foregoing procedures to be understood as one or another mode of doing science? Experimental and other scientific practices are the result of some combination of deduction and induction. Deduction is a matter of logicality, of drawing conclusions from premises, conclusions that do not necessarily yield truth, descriptive accuracy or correct explanation. Induction involves drawing conclusions on the basis of evidence, conclusions that may or may not produce truth that requires repetition and falsification. In any case, what about one's social belief system, or ideology, or, for that matter, theology? How does one choose from among different explanations? And how do we know that there is an invisible hand to be explained? Are there conceptual problems or substantive problems with any or all of the answers? Does meaning flow to the invisible hand from the words used to discuss it, or does meaning flow from the invisible hand to the words? What about the invisible hand being "a suitable myth"? After all is said and done, if one intends for the invisible hand to be (a metaphor for) competition, what does the term "invisible hand" add to the term "competition"?

The experience of the reception of the Nobel Prize in Economic Sciences seems to have been mixed when the Prize came to the invisible hand. In part, inasmuch as the invisible hand has been lauded as a foundational concept in economics, that very claim has been criticized as being exaggerated.

1.3. The Foundational Concept of Economics

The foundational status of the concept of the invisible hand in one specification or another has been widely affirmed in the literature of economics. It has been called the "central principle of classical political economy" (Buchanan 1986: 267), the "core of traditional economics" (Meek 1977: 183), and one of the "the basic propositions of neo-classical economics ... its show-piece theorem, the invisible-hand theorem" (Mueller, in Wiles and Routh 1984: 160–1), as well as the "heart of economics" (Desai 1986: 4). Kregel (1984: 34) is but one of many who have echoed the widely known and influential assertion by Arrow and Hahn (1971: 1) that:

[T]he notion that a social system moved by independent actions in pursuit of different values is consistent with a final coherent state of balance, and one in which the outcomes may be quite different from those who intended by the agents, is surely the most important intellectual contribution that economic thought has made to the general understanding of social processes.

It has been called the "first principle of economics" and also the "only principle of economics" (O'Driscoll, in Spadaro 1978: 116). It has been called the "unifying principle of economics" (R. Dorfman 1983: F15), "a key unifying concept" (Hirschleifer 1976: 12), and "a great unifying scientific conception of economics" (Hirschleifer 1960: 140).

The concept of the invisible hand has been said to have "been the essence of economic theory since Adam Smith" (Reder 1982: 15) and "the common possession of economic thought in the large ... of the genus economist in general" (Davenport 1913: 513; quoted in Fetter 1914: 551), to "embrace the whole of pure and applied economics" (Walras, quoted in Hunt 1979: 266), and to constitute the nearest thing to "a universal principle of explanation able to cope with all economic phenomena" and the "one sole all-encompassing Principle of Nature, a theory which explains everything by a unified conception of what the cosmos is" (Shackle 1966: 31, 30) – that is, a single principle that "could explain the whole structure and metabolism of economic life" (idem: 64). In one specification or another, it is "literally a general organizing principle of economic society and of economic analysis" and thus "quite literally the sine qua non of economic analysis" (McNulty 1968: 646–7).

It also has been said to constitute "the basic analytical paradigm of orthodox economic theory" (H. S. Gordon 1980: 89–90; see also Coats 1969: 292; D. F. Gordon 1963: 123), "the heart of the economist's Weltanschauung" (Marris and Mueller 1980: 32), and "the proposition in economics that becomes a part of the working system (the so-called paradigm)" of economists (Stigler 1976: 1200).

The concept has been said to be the basis for defining "alternative paradigms in economic thought" (Garrison 1985: 309–10, 313n.10). The acceptance or rejection of the doctrine has been said to constitute the basis for the categorization as well as the evaluation of economic theories; and to constitute the paradigm that is the maintained hypothesis of economic theory (Wilber and Wisman, in Samuels 1976: 79–93, and Samuels, idem: 373–4), thus serving as the paramount filtering mechanism in the development of economics.

The concept has been called the "foundation stone for the entire superstructure of modern noncommunist economics" (Hirschleifer 1980: 14; cf. Giesbrecht 1972: 64) and "the rock on which economics is built" (Kristol 1980: 204). It is said to operate at the foundations of the science (R. Dorfman 1983: F15) and to constitute the basis for "almost the whole body of organized economic thinking and doctrine for the last hundred years" (Keynes in Clower in Howett 1998: 169), the "explicit foundation of the whole of economic theory" (Myrdal 1969: 121).

The belief is also widely held that the concept of the invisible hand is responsible for not only the central paradigm of economics but the very identity of economics. Smith's theorem, it has been written, "ultimately partitioned economics from moral philosophy and gave it legitimacy as a separate discipline" (Hébert 1984: 290), and provided "the entire conception of 'efficiency' which gives *raison d'etre* to the subject of economics" (Blaug, in Latsis 1976: 176); without the principle, "economics ceases to be a scientific endeavor" (Vaughn 1979: 677).

Smith's conception of the invisible hand has been called "the most important intellectual contribution that economic thought has made to the general understanding of social processes" (Hahn 1973: 33). Some facet or implication of the doctrine of the invisible hand has been called "the most important substantive proposition in all of economics" (Stigler 1976: 1201) and "perhaps the major intellectual discovery in the whole history of economics" (Buchanan 1986: 75). It has become "an article of faith to the general public" (R. Dorfman 1983: F15).

The concept of the invisible hand has been deemed the nucleus of both the interpretation and the evaluation of capitalism, that is, the basis of both positive and normative economics. It is "common to all political doctrines in economics," claiming "to tell us what, on certain assumptions, is objectively right" (Myrdal 1969: 147). It is "neo-classical economics' showpiece normative proposition" (Mueller, in Wiles and Routh 1984: 179), the key factor in "economics as a mechanistic intellectual defense of capitalism" (Gramm 1980: 127), the "basis for arguing the superiority of free markets over politically controlled economic processes" (Vaughn 1979: 677), and "the intellectual core of the support for the private-enterprise economic system today" (Bach 1966: 381; 1968: 321), where it is also said to be "For some ... a 'norm' of ideal behavior against which to measure actual conditions" (idem: 322).

The concept is central to the defense of capitalism, but it has also been held central to socialism because, in one sense or another, it involves a vision applicable to all economies as the essence of industrial reality. Thus one writer has written several times that "every economist feels in his bones that the Invisible Hand theorem is almost as relevant to socialism as to capitalism, coming close indeed to a universal justification for the role of the price mechanism as a rationing device in literally any economy" (paraphrasing Blaug, in Latsis 1976: 176; Blaug 1980: 131–133).

Inasmuch as economics' "theoretical structure crystallized in Adam Smith, it has not basically changed much since" (Boulding 1981: 791), for the reason that "Smith gave his message a resonance that has not been stilled for two hundred years" (Buchanan, in O'Driscoll 1979: 113). It is not surprising to read that "there is an Adam Smith in every economist," and that "[i]n the model of society and economy ... the importance of the invisible hand 'principle' would be hard to overestimate" (Schneider, in O'Driscoll 1979: 53).

If "the history of economics over the past two hundred years can be adequately characterized as a series of footnotes to Adam Smith" (Rosenberg, in O'Driscoll 1979: 19), it is also true that "[t]races of every conceivable sort of doctrine are to be found in that most catholic book, and an economist must have peculiar theories indeed who cannot quote from the *Wealth of Nations* to support his special purposes" (Viner 1927: 207).

It is perhaps the nature of fundamental doctrines to be permissively kaleidoscopic, whether due to the classic expositor of the doctrine or its users. There is no aspect in economics where this is more empirically correct than regarding the foundational concept of the invisible hand. The preceding paragraphs indicate the variety of ways in which the foundational theme has been advanced, its advocacy by leading economic theorists, and its acceptance as such by a wide range of other economists. Both the foundational status of the concept and its evident heterogeneity form one basis of this study.

1.4. Exaggeration Criticized

It is widely perceived and affirmed that the concept of the invisible hand embodies, or at least penetrates to, the fundamental assumptions of the mentality of western society; that the concept is woven into the fabric of society is perhaps ultimately constitutive of our perception of reality; it governs the ways in which people perceive themselves, their behavior, and that of others, and how they experience their own private and public lives, in part by expressing and shaping values, attitudes, political orientation, and personal perception of individual and collective experience. The thesis of the invisible hand, it has been said, represents the fundamental world view of the West (Canterbery and Burkhardt, in Eichner 1983: 23) and, as we have already seen, has become "an article of faith to the general public" (R. Dorfman 1983: F15). As a facet of traditional liberalism, it has become a potent and persistent presupposition in western thought, embodying a deep-seated mental attitude toward the nature of relationships in human society centering on the ideal of harmonious interplay free from coercion (De Ruggiero 1937: 435). "The problem of social order is undoubtedly the most fundamental issue in social science" (H.S. Gordon 1980: 139). The concept of the invisible hand is one expression of the problem of social order, such that "the doctrine of the harmony of interests [is] the starting point of sociological thought" (Mises 1951: 64). Moreover, the interpretation of the *Wealth of Nations* has become "a part of the social control system of the Western economies" (Gramm 1980: 135n.6, quoting Samuels 1976: 4).

There are abundant materials whose authors' point of view is to affirmatively reiterate the doctrine of the invisible hand. There are also abundant materials that support particular identities and functions of the invisible hand. Numerous historians of economic thought have devoted considerable attention to the evaluation and interpretation of the literature on the invisible hand, whether free-standing or as part of a larger analysis of Smith's writings. The subject of this section concerns the materials whose authors, often from among the foremost ranks of economists, find the approval to be overly strong, the advocacy to be overdone, and the panegyrics excessive, in all respects exaggerated.

Apropos of the status of the idea of the invisible hand itself, for example, Frank Knight (1956: 267) has written that "[t]he accusation that Adam Smith, for example, believed in a universal harmony of interests among men is merely one discouraging example of what passes widely in learned circles for history and discussion." William Grampp (1968: 544) has written of Smith's "famous and unfortunate phrase … [of] 'the invisible hand'"; Thomas Wilson (in Wilson and Skinner 1976: 78) wrote that "[t]he metaphor of the Invisible Hand – though used by Smith on only a very few occasions – was particularly unfortunate for it laid him open to easy attack and to ill-considered ridicule as the Dr. Pangloss of the early capitalist system." Samuelson (1977: 44) has referred to "the half-truth present in his [Smith's] INVISIBLE HAND doctrine." Scott Gordon, one of the most subtle and sophisticated interpreters of these matters, envisioned the concept of the invisible hand expressing the relevant belief system in terms of an ambiguous deterministic metaphysical harmonism, readily interpretable as a higher foolishness but by no means fully representative of economic though from Smith onward (H.S. Gordon 1991: 144–6, 169–217). Gordon has called it "the most widely known and least understood concept in the history of social theory" (idem: 144). Baumol (1952: 19) has written that "at times economists have expressed views on the subject which seem dubious in themselves, or which appear to be based on grounds whose sufficiency is questionable." (Apropos of the point of insufficiency, see also Brenner 1979: 272.) Dahl and Lindblom (1976 [1953]: 195, 196) have called it "an intellectual accomplishment of such magnitude" but also "a good idea … somehow … dissolved in a mixture of dubious metaphysics or psychology which had to be thrown out." William Letwin (1963: 224–5) has written that the argument of the *Wealth of Nations* has "gaps and errors." Frank Hahn (1973: 14–15) has written that "practical men and ill-trained theorists everywhere in the world do not understand what they are claiming to be the case when they claim a beneficent and coherent role for the invisible hand." Somewhere I have read that the predominant but not exclusive view among the Nobel Laureates in economics is that economies are not self-regulating mechanisms (one of the notions giving meaning to the concept of the invisible hand) and do not tend to optimal positions (another such notion), so that there is much room for active, discretionary intervention (on which there are differing views as to what the concept implies). Apropos of the notion of benevolent harmony, Mark Blaug (1978: 699–700) has classed the invisible hand with other "loosely stated" propositions and written of the "vulgar doctrine of the spontaneous harmony of interests" (idem: 63). Blaug (1985: 57–8) refers to "this kind of naive reasoning, the so-called doctrine of 'the spontaneous harmony of interests'." (Importantly, Blaug goes on to argue that the invisible hand "turns out upon examination to be identical with the concept of perfect competition; the 'invisible hand' is nothing more than the automatic equilibrating mechanism of the competitive market" (idem: 57–8). Frank Albert Fetter (1904: 427) wrote that harmony ideas "are partial truths, never to be ignored, but quite false if taken, without modification, as practical rules of conduct," and Fetter (1923: 582) commented that the doctrine of the "economic harmonies" was "an extremist expression" of "belief in the benefits of competition and the virtues of economic freedom." (For a similar view emphasizing exaggerated completeness, see Hadley 1896: 14–15). Paul Samuelson (1977: 610) wrote that Smith "had no right to assert that an Invisible Hand channels individuals selfishly seeking their own interests into promoting the 'public interest' – as these last two words might be defined by a variety of prominent ethical and religious notions of what constitutes the welfare of a nation. Smith has proved nothing of this kind, nor has any economist since 1776." (This an example of a rejection of one specification of what the invisible hand does. It also raises several other questions considered at various points later in this essay.)

With regard to further affirmative and negative evaluations, as a sample from a much larger collection of other pertinent comments, there is Ely's (1938: 229) critical statement about "... a series of extracts from the works of Adam Smith and John Stuart Mill which, considered by themselves, conclusively proved that both Smith and Mill must have been radical socialists! Of course, the extracts, in their proper context, had no such significance." There are Desai's (1986: 6) dictum that "[i]n economics as well, Marx did not challenge the empirical, factual validity of the Invisible Hand theorem ... while we are in the capitalist mode of production the market works just as well as for Marx as for Ricardo." There is also Macfie's (1967: 124) statement that "[t]his consumption based economic theory is of course basic as fact, and always will be. It requires no support from an invisible hand" (contrast, however, infra, discussions of the a priori versus empirical status of the theorem, whether the theorem works always or less than always, the assumptions required for and the meaning attached to "the market works," and the limits of the range of the theorem of the invisible hand). Finally, there is Schumpeter's (1950: 19) statement about "the old harmonistic view – full of nonsense thought that was too … but less of absolute nonsense than in Marxian analysis."

Jevons (1894: 13) wrote that man "cannot enjoy the society of other men without constantly coming into conflict with them"; Davenport (1916: 114) distinguished between the operation of harmony in production but not in distribution; and Carver (1915: 35, 41, 49–50) argued that conflict was inevitable and ultimately due to scarcity, that "a deep underlying harmony of human interests is the profound belief of some. But this belief, like that in a harmony between man and nature, is not susceptible of a positive support" (idem: 42), and therefore there is need for principles of justice "for the adjustment of conflicting interests among men" (idem: 35). Lionel Robbins (1953: 28) wrote that "[i]n general … it is really very hard to maintain that it gives any strong support to cosmic optimism, still less to a belief in a comprehensive pre-established inevitable harmony of interests. The most that can be said" is that it affirms the existence of mutually advantageous relationships in a world of free enterprise. It is no surprise, then, that Commons (1990 [1934]: 93ff. and passim) insisted that conflict, not harmony, of interests was the starting point of institutional economics; and that Knight (1947: 208, 275, 385) emphasized the practically ubiquitous combination of harmony and conflict in human affairs, also calling attention to the inevitable overlapping claims to freedom and to power, which created conflicts of interest (idem: 306; see also Spengler 1948, 1968).

Finally, it may be pointed out, first, that whereas some microeconomics texts do use or invoke the concept of the invisible hand, others do not, or at least do not list "invisible hand" in their indexes (at least some of the former doing so); and second, that whereas Cannan's index (in Smith 1937: 937) does have an entry for the "invisible hand," that of McCulloch (in Smith 1846) does not.

1.5. Some History of the Use of the Concept of the Invisible Hand

An author is quite frequently encountered who credits Adam Smith with coining the term "invisible hand." William Shakespeare, among others, has also had the term attributed to him. Shakespeare used the term in *Macbeth* but did not coin it. Nothing could be farther from the truth than to say its use began with Smith. Indeed, it is questionable that Smith even popularized the term in economics where it did not become widely used and interpreted until the 1980s.

The concept of the invisible hand has been around for more than two millennia, possibly in part because of the attraction of a presumed mysterious nature of the "invisible." It seems to derive from numerous sources, including powerful fascination with the idea of invisibility as such; the idea of seeing without being seen; from repeated invocation of invisibility by shamans; the limited ability of all people, shamans included, to refute the concept, should they attempt to do so; and the invocation of Deity in an acting but unseen role. Talk of the actions of unseen actors (or of a part of an actor, such as an invisible hand) and its effects on normal individuals brings to mind the social control role of Smith's Impartial Spectator. Eventually, in part because the gods of polytheistic systems were said to be invisible, in part because the God of Judaism and organized Christianity's monotheism was also said to be invisible, the "hand" seems to have been connotative of action or activity. So far as is evident, the term's widespread use originated in religion and spread to literature. In 1776, it began to take on another type of existence. Whereas religious users generally concentrated on the invisible hand of God, the use that seems to have commenced in 1776 (and not the economic use in Smith's 1759 *Theory of Moral Sentiments*) with the publication of Adam Smith's *Wealth of Nations* had to do with economic affairs. By the end of the twentieth century, the invisible hand had been identified in several dozen different ways. Not all of those uses pertained to God, though several did; indeed, God continued to be one of the uses and some others of them were given sacral connotation. Most uses of the term related to what Alfred Marshall called mankind in its ordinary business of life, earning a living. After a slow start in the nineteenth century, by the end of the twentieth century, the use of the term had been extended to virtually all phases of life, including politics. Some – perhaps most – uses, especially by economists, were apparently intended to convey positive sentiments; others, negative ones; and still others, no specific connotation or sentiment. The term has also spun off a vast number of imitators.

Some indication of the enormous magnitude of materials potentially involved in this study can be gleaned by examining some of the results of computer searches that I have or have had made for the term "invisible hand." Unfortunately, the lists tend to have both duplicate entries and erroneously included entries, as well as different specifications of search domain, including timeframe. Of unknown significance is the impact of statements like the following: "Usage is subject to the terms and conditions of the subscription and License Agreement and the applicable Copyright and intellectual property protection as dictated by the appropriate laws of your country and/or International Convention." Still, the volume of entries can be mind-boggling.

Distinctions can be made between religious and secular uses and between economic and political uses. The distinctions may break down, the former in a society in which much of life is ruled, at least in part, by religion, and the latter in society in which much government activity is economic in character while much of business is politically oriented. Still, many uses seem to amount to a cliché. In any event, classification is unnecessary for present purposes. Here is a sample:

ProQuest Smart Search: January 22, 2010: 11,126
Microsoft Search: December 16, 2009: 3,780
Microsoft Search: December 7, 2009: 3,760
Microsoft Search: December 7, 2009: 4,150
Wiley Interscience: November 13, 2009: 229
Wiley Interscience: October 28, 2009: 230
History of Political Economy, March 5, 2009: 253
Time: November 6, 2009: May 1924 – November 2009: 931
EH.Net, HES: November 17, 2005: 27
Web5.silverplattter.com: January 9. 2006: 128
HOES Archive: October 26. 2009: 152
Scirus: December 24. 2002: 14,909
Dell via Google: November 22, 2007: 250,000

The foregoing examples of search results were requested for Invisible Hand. The results of searches for laissez-faire, laissez-faire leadership, and visible hand include the following:

Bing: Laissez-faire Leadership Style: December 11. 2009: 247,000
Bing: Laissez faire: December 7, 2009: 9,260,000
Bing: Visible Hand: December 7, 2009: 24,500,000
Amazon.com: Invisible Hand: Books, December 5, 2009; 33,888
Amazon.com: Invisible Hand Law Books, October 8, 2009: 1,493

Incomplete data for materials published in the English language and acquired by me – principally, but not solely, economic writings – suggest that between 1816 and 1938, the average annual level of writings in which the term "invisible hand" appeared was very low. Thereafter, from roughly 1942 through 1974, the average annual level doubled; from 1975 through 1979, it roughly doubled again; and between 1980 and 1989, it was approximately 6.5 times higher than it had been during 1942 through 1974. Between 1990 and 1999, the average annual level was a little more than eight times that of the 1942–1974 level and slightly less than 20 percent higher than the 1980–1989 level. During the period 2000–2006, the average annual level seems to have receded to a level slightly more than 60 percent of the 1990–1999 level, the highest level reached thus far.

I hypothesize that the vast increase in the volume of economic literature on the invisible hand, which began in the 1960s, came at about the same time that the neoclassical mainstream of economics established – that is, stabilized – the protocols discussed in Section 1.1. Those protocols in turn led to the ironies also identified in that Section. No doubt the pressures of the Cold War contributed to the ascendance of interest in the absolutist formulation properties of the invisible hand and other concepts. The seeming availability of the concept of the invisible hand was conveniently at hand and, most importantly, accessible. The explanation itself can be stated in neoclassical supply-and-demand terms: The stabilizing of the foundations of neoclassical conceptualization and practice served to establish the *supply* of lines of reasoning with certain properties and the formation of the Cold War, provided one *demand* for those lines of reasoning (Weintraub 1991; see also Kadish and Tribe 1993).

My hypothesis regarding the explosion of research on the invisible hand during the Cold War brings up the interest of the military in invisibility. The possible military use of invisibility has been a particular interest of the United States Department of Defense for more than sixty years. In the 1950s and 1960s, research by many leading economic theorists was funded by the Office of Naval Research (ONR) of the United States Navy. (One fundamental component of U.S. strategy, Mutual Assured Destruction, was a product of game theory developed by economists and other decision theorists financed by ONR.) Stealth aircraft enables military operation as if the planes were invisible – which they are, insofar as the relevant construction material, coupled with the planes' configuration, enables their evasion from detection by radar. Major recent successes by American and Japanese scientists have reflected continued military interest and led to public acknowledgment that suspicions were correct that the so-called Philadelphia Experiment of June 1943 was in the field of invisibility. David R. Smith of Duke University and other researchers in this country and in Japan have been developing the technology with which to produce what they have already demonstrated to work. The developments seem to have been principally along two lines. One is the development and use of metamaterials that either absorb or guide and steer light and whose invisibility-inducing properties derive from their structure rather than their composition, through a negative index of refraction. The second is the use of electromagnetic energy to bend light waves around an object, thereby rendering the object invisible to sight. Some researchers in the field seem to expect the United States and some other nations' military forces to become largely invisible by 2030. Like most military innovations, the advantage is dissipated when both sides in a conflict have adopted the same or a countering innovation.

It is striking that if one considers the function of the term "invisible hand" to be that of obfuscating the fact and specifics of the structure of power in society, then the concept of the invisible hand has rendered *power* invisible.

The following are examples from more than two millennia of the use of the term "invisible hand." The evidence documents (1) that Smith did not theorize and write on a *tabula rasa*; (2) that the use of the term in religious matters was not confined to a narrow segment; and (3) something of the overall range and variety of its use. Classification is tricky: Was the use of the term by George Washington in an inaugural address religious or political? Does it make any difference for present purposes?

The volume of religious and other documents pertaining to the use of the concept of the invisible hand is vast. However, those archives are a thin slice of the total written record of religious relief and practice. The same comparison may be made with economics writings.

Left undocumented here is the enormous expansion of the fields and range of circumstances in which the term "invisible hand" has been used, both in and beyond economics. The invisible hand helps and hinders, rewards and punishes, and is often invoked or criticized. The great majority of pre-Smith citations seem to be to the hand of God, though some relate to the occult, the supernatural other than God, and the "witch craze" of the seventeenth century. Some pieces of evidence or their authors may surprise some readers. The conclusion seems accurate that the "invisible hand" – either alone or in the form of one or another adaptation or variation – is one of the most popular and adaptable tropes in the history of the western world and of humankind in general. The term "invisible hand" is amenable to all sorts of linguistic usage, including giving rise to comparable, alternative, or modified terms. Most of those who read or write about the invisible hand seem to believe that they have some sense of what is involved; but there is no way of testing for that. When confronted with a list of the approximately four dozen identities, each said by someone to actually be the invisible hand, they are not so sure, though many resist modification of the status of their favorite identity or function.

One problem is that much of its use may well have been in sermons, homilies, and the like, and thus largely unrecorded. So far as I can see, the site of most contemporary published uses is the newspaper and magazine column and op-ed piece, Internet home pages of businesses, and, of course, the writings of economists.

The following examples of the use of the concept of the invisible hand were selected by me from much longer lists compiled by myself and by Bill Perry, with assistance by Ken Ewell. They are presented roughly in order of date of appearance of the cited document (different dates of publication for several writings by one author are relatively frequent, and some dates are not known; also, birthdates of most contemporary writers are not given).

Aeschylus (525–456 B.C.), Greek poet and dramatist:

Agamemnon: Aegisthus: "But me avenging Justice nursed, and taught me, Safer by distance, with invisible hand ..."

Eusebius (263?–c. 340), Christian theologian and historian and Bishop of Caesarea for approximately four months:

The Oration of Eusebius Pamphilus: "In short, in every way they directed their attacks against the unseen God, and assailed him with a thousand shafts of impious words. But he who is invisible avenged himself with an invisible hand."

St. Basil (329?–379), Bishop of Caesarea:

Theological Works of Basil, Homily I: "You will finally discover that the world was not conceived by chance and without reason, but for an useful end and for the great advantage of all beings, since it is really the school where reasonable souls exercise themselves, the training ground where they learn to know God; since by the sight of visible and sensible things the mind is led, as by a hand, to the contemplation of invisible things."

St. Ambrose (340?–397), Bishop of Milan:

Exposition of the Christian Faith, Book 1: "With this Wine, also, Lord Jesus, purify our senses, that we may adore Thee, and worship Thee, the Creator of things visible and invisible. Truly, Thou canst not fail of being Thyself invisible and good, Who hast given invisibility and goodness to the works of Thy Hands."

St. Augustine (354–430), Bishop of Hippo:

The Harmony of the Gospels, Chap. XII: "... it is only by the hidden will of the true God, in whose hand resides the separate power in all things, that the kingdom was given them and has been made to increase ..."

To Consentius, Book II, Chap. 60: "Or else, if they shall be ashamed to confess what with long-continued simulation they have concealed, by the hidden hand of God healing them shall they be made whole."

St. John Damascene (c. 676–749):

Barlaam and Ioasaph: "And, by thine infinite compassions, I pray thee Lord Jesus Christ, Son and Word of the invisible Father ... do thou now also stretch forth thine invisible and almighty hand ..."

William Shakespeare, (1564–1616):
  Macbeth, III.II.48–50 (1606):

> Macbeth: "Be innocent of the knowledge, dearest chuck,
> Till thou applaud the deed. Come, seeling night,
> Scarf up the tender eye of pitiful day,
> And with thy bloody and invisible hand
> Cancel and tear to pieces that great bond
> Which keeps me pale. Light thickens ... "

Henry More (1614–1687), English philosopher:

An Attitude Against Atheisme (1653): "as he walked the streets, sensibly struck upon the thigh by an invisible hand ... returned home ... and grew forthwith so mortally sick, that he dyed within three days."

A Modest Enquiry into the Mystery of Iniquity (1664): "It were likewise a good roosing miracle, and bigger then belief, that a certain Holy House of the Virgin's should be carried out of *Palestine* into *Italy* by an invisible hand through the aire."

William Annand (1633–1689):

Pater noster (1670): "The soul here was bouy'd up by a miraculous and invisible hand ..."

Anonymous, *Miscellaneous and Collections*, Volume 1 (1683):

> Wou'd you this Riddle understand;
> Distinguish 'twixt the Butcher's clumsy Hand,
> And the invisible Command,
> Divines allow, the unseen Powers
> May wonders work; and why not our's,
> Whether on Scaffolds, or in Towers?

Increase Mather (1639–1723), American preacher and writer:

An Essay for the Recording of Illustrious Providences Wherein an Account is Given of Many Remarkable and Vermemorable (1684): "There was no great violence in the motion, though several persons of the Family, and others also were struck with the things that were thrown by an invisible hand, yet they were not hurt thereby ... The People of the House threw it on the Hearth, where it lay a considerable time: they went in to their Supper, and Whilst at their Supper, the piece of Clay was lifted up by an invisible hand, and fell upon the table ... and several things were thrown by an invisible hand, powerfully convincing, and thereby discovering the Hypocrisie and Theft of the Man ... She was to the amazement of all Spectators, pricked and miserably beaten by an invisible hand; so as that her body from head to foot was wounded ... These characters would remain for several Weeks after the invisible hand had violently impressed them on her body ..."

Thomas Flatman (1637–1688):

> *Poems and Songs* (1686):
> There, Thou dost understand
> The motions of the secret hand,
> That guides t h' invisible Wheel,
> Which here, we ne'r shall know, but ever feel

Thomas Burnet (1635–1715), theologian and writer:

The Theory of the Earth (1690): "Let us not therefore be too positive or presumptuous in our conjectures about these things, for if there be an invisible hand, Divine or Angelical, that touches the Springs and Wheels; it will not be easie for us to determine, with certainty, the order of their motions."

Richard Dirby (1649–?), English writer:

Dreadful news from Wapping New-Stairs (1693): "... received a Stroke on her Back by an invisible Hand, which struck her ..."

Madame Guyon (Jeanne Marie de la Motte-Guy on *nee* Bouvier (1648–1717), French mystic:

Autobiography of Madame Guyon (dictated in 1709): "After having been several months without any news of my papers, when some pressed me to write, and blamed my neglect, an invisible hand held me back; my peace and confidence were great."

Daniel Defoe (1661?–1731), English novelist:

A Journal of the Plague Year (1722): "... it was evidently from the secret invisible Hand of him, that had at first sent this Disease as a Judgment upon us ..."

Moll Flanders (1722): "... when a sudden Blow from an almost invisible Hand ..."

Colonel Jack (1723): "... if it has all been brought to pass by an invisible Hand in Mercy to me ..." and "... how an invisible overruling Power, a Hand influenced from above ..."

The Family Instructor (1795): "It is as testimony that nothing befalls us without an invisible hand ..."

James Ralph (1705–1762), American essayist:

The Astrologer. A Comedy (1744): "Ha! Death and the Devil! Disabled by an invisible Hand ..."

George Berkeley (1685–1753), Irish bishop and philosopher:

A Treatise Concerning the Principles of Human Knowledge (c. 1750): "... ideas are not anyhow and at random produced, there being a certain order and connection between them, like to that of cause and effect; there are also several combinations of them made in a very regular and artificial manner, which seem like so many instruments in the hand of nature that, being hid as it were behind the scenes, have a secret operation in producing those appearances which are seen on the theatre of the world, being themselves discernible only to the curious eye of the philosopher."

Tobias George Smollett (1721–1771), English novelist:

Peregrine Pickle (1751): "The painter, who did not think proper to own the truth, said, that he had been transported thither [in that corner] by some preternatural conveyance, and soused in water by an invisible hand."

Ferdinand Count Fathom (1753): "... his ear was suddenly invaded with the sound of some few solemn notes, issuing from the organ, which seemed to feel the impulse of an invisible hand."

Henry Brooke (1703–1783), Irish novelist and dramatist:

The Fool of Quality, Volume 4 (1765–1770): "On the third night, I dreamed that an invisible Hand came and, seizing me by a single Hair of my Head, hurried me aloft, through the Regions of the Air, till it held me right over a fiery Gulf, in the Pinnacles of whose Flames a Variety of Daemons appeared to hover ..."

François Marie Aruet Voltairé (1694–1778), French philosopher, historian, dramatist, and essayist:

Philosophical Dictionary entry on the Soul, section 1 (1764): "Does anyone know how his limbs obey his will? Has anyone discovered by what art his ideas are traced in his brain, and issue from it at his command? Feeble automata, moved by an invisible hand which directs us on the stage of this world, which of us has ever perceived the thread which guides us?"

Philosophical Dictionary entry on Passions: "Poor puppets of the Eternal Artificer, who know neither why nor how an invisible hand moves all the springs of our machine, and at length packs us away in our wooden box. We constantly see more and more reason for repeating, with Aristotle, 'All is occult, all is secret.'"

Philosophical Dictionary entry on Ignorance: "Who then produces them [thoughts] in me? Whence do they come? Whither do they go? Fugitive phantoms! What invisible hand produces and disperses you?"

Henry Home, Lord Kames (1696–1782), Scottish philosopher:

Sketches of the History of Man, Volume 3 (1774): "The dread, when immoderate, disorders the mind, and makes every unusual misfortune pass for a punishment inflicted by an invisible hand ... and when a single invisible being is understood to pour out blessings with a liberal hand, good men, inflamed with gratitude, put no bounds to the power and benevolence of that being."

William Hayward Roberts (1734–1791):

> *A Poetical Essay on the Existence of God* (1774):
> … See what rocks,
> What mountains rise, that cast their evening shade
> Far o'er the plain beneath: tho part the wind
> Sweep with its wings away; tho earthquakes tear
> Their yawning cliffs; tho Time from year to year
> Working with stealthy, and invisible hand,
> Moulder their crumbling sides, they bend not yet
> Their summits to the vale …
> Nor these alone the dangers that beset
> The mortal pilgrim, wandering thru the vale
> Of tears, and pain, and sorrow, yet upheld
> By that invisible hand, which still supports
> Man's feeble race, and from extinction saves
> His undiminish'd progeny …

Soame Jenyns (1704–1787), English writer:

View of the Internal Evidence of the Christian Religion (1776 edition): "This argument seems to me little short of demonstration, and is indeed founded on the very same reasoning, by which the material world is proved to be the work of his invisible hand."

Charles Louis de Secondat, Baron Montesquieu (1689–1755), French philosopher:

Familiar Letters, The Temple of Gnidus (1777): "An invisible hand drew me into this fatal abode, and in proportion as my heart was agitated, its agitation increased."

The Spirit of Laws (1777): "They with-held a part of the gift and yet concealed the hand that did it."

William Paley (1743–1805) English theologian, philosopher and clergyman:

Natural Theology (c.1780): "For my part I never see a bird in that situation, but I recognize an invisible hand, as the even proves, the most worthy of the sacrifice, the most important, the most beneficial."

Clara Reeve (1729–1807), English novelist:

The Old English Baron: A Gothic Story (1780): "he thought he was hurried away by an invisible hand, and led into a wild heath …"

George Keate (1729–1797):

The Monument in Arcadia (1781):
Nature! – Nature!

Who with thy pow'rful, and invisible Hand
Shak'st my whole Frame with Tumult

George Washington, April 30, 1789,

"First Inaugural Address," as printed in *Oracle Bell's New World* (London), June 11, 1789, Issue 10:

No people can be bound to acknowledge and adore the invisible hand which conducts the affairs of men, more than the people of the United States.

Ann Ward Radcliffe (1764–1823), English novelist:

The Italian (1797): "I was too much engaged to know how; I was led on, as by an invisible hand," and "... for at she apprehended that the strong and invisible hand which governed her course ..."

Oracle and Da3ily Advertiser, London, August 29, 1799, Issue 22:

"Potier – 'To retard the admission to the Legislative Body, of those who are elected by the People, is a violation of the social compact. Where is the invisible hand which prevents the Council of Elders pronouncing upon the operation of the Electoral Assembly of the *Bouches du Rhone*?" From a column entitled "Jacobin Society" and signed "21 Thermidor – August 8."

Charles Brockden Brown (1771–1810), American novelist:

Wieland (1827): "Was this the penalty of disobedience? This the stroke of a vindictive and invisible hand? Is it a fresh proof that the Divine Ruler interferes in human affairs, meditates an end, selects, and commissions his agents, and enforces, by unequivocal sanctions, submission to his will?"

Thomas Cole (1801–1848):

Hope and Trust Spring from the Contemplation of the Works of God (1835):
Is there cause for tears the spirit saidWhen all these ponderous words are thus sustained
By thin visible hand and gently led
Through the wide fields of heaven; ...

William Alexander Caruthers (1802–1846), American novelist:

The Knights of the Horse-shoe (1845): "The whole machinery of the world, both moral and physical, is managed by the same Almighty invisible hand, which strikes sparks from these electric chains."

Hunt Hawkins (1904–?):

The Invisible Hand Meets the Dead Hand High Above
Washington, D.C., from *The Domestic Life* (1944):
There! In the clouds can't you see
The Invisible Hand prancing, tumbling?
It soars over the Reflecting Pool,
Pirouettes atop the Washington Monument.
I think it must be Adam Smith's,
the Hand he said would harmonize
all selfish interests, miraculously making whole
a society of pure individuals....
And what is the Dead Hand doing here,
This skeletal yellow apparition? O, it just came
to Party. It chases the Invisible Hand

George Sand [pseudonym of Amandine Aurora Lucie, *nee* Dupin]: "Sketch of Talleyrand," *The United States Democratic Review* 17 (November 1945):

I can endure the inevitable existence of those nobler reprobates whom Providence, in its mysterious designs, leaves to accomplish their mission upon earth. Destiny exerts a direct influence upon remarkable men, whether for good or for evil. It need not concern itself about the vulgar; the crowd obeys passively the impulsion of those levers which are moved by an invisible hand.

Saul Bellow (1915–2005), Canadian-American writer:

More Die of Heartbreak (1987), p. 144:

... there's a funny piece about Milton Friedman. Somebody asks him, 'Are you sure that Economic Man *is* completely rational – can we depend on it? Many qualified thinkers have asserted that the behavior of *Homo sapiens* is distinctly paranoid and some even say that there is a widespread physiological condition described as *schizophysiology* and producing effects of *schizopsychology*. Koestler made such an argument. Now, how does this incontrovertible insanity square with your theory of Economic Man? Friedman answers that no matter how crazy people are, they still remain sane about money. What do you think, is this fact or faith? Well, he doesn't speak of Good and Evil. He doesn't even discuss psychology, which is greatly to his credit. All he seems to say is that between humankind and full chaos there stands only the free market. Belief in the invisible is narrowed down by him to the Invisible Hand.

Contemporary uses include such examples as the following:

Xtramsn, Travel newsletter distributed by Air New Zealand, June 16, 2004:
One of them [the Scots], Adam Smith, even came up with the wacky idea of the invisible hand of capitalism.

Azore Opio, "Review of Nfamewih Aseh, Political Philosophies & Nation Building in Cameroon," in AllAfrica.com, March 17, 2008:

Aseh skillfully weaves in globalization as a world of continuing slavery with the West constituting itself into a "ubiquitous invisible hand that manipulates the global economy and the relations of power both on the international scene and in almost all non-European societies, and particularly in African societies."

Robert H. Frank, "The Invisible Hand is Shaking," *The New York Times*, May 25, 2008:

... Smith understood that the invisible hand is often benign, but not always.

Ronald Bailey, "Does the Invisible Hand Need a Helping Hand?"
   Science, June 20, 2008:

policies designed for self – interested citizens may undermine "the moral sentiments." Case of day care centers imposed fines on parents who pick up their children late, the result being they came to pick up, now believing that lateness is just another commodity they could purchase, thus undermining the parents' sense of ethical obligation to avoid inconveniencing the teachers.

Steve Brady, *The Monterey* (California) *Herald*, June 23, 2008:

"Ancient law" letter a good laugh. Speaking of laughing out loud, I had a good one Friday while reading the letter from that kook in Carmel Valley, when he referred to the "ancient law" of supply and demand. This would be the one written in the Bible by the invisible hand? The credulity of these true believers defies analysis.

The Underwire from Wired.com, June 26, 2008:
   Invisible Hand Studios (to produce television and radio features).
   Chris Floyd, "Invisible Hand: Washington Role in Iraq Oil Deal Revealed,"
   Baltimore Chronicle & Sentinel, June 30, 2008:

"The Bush Administration has admitted that American government officials and selected corporate cronies 'helped' the Iraqis draw up the sweetheart contracts that will bring the original exploiters of Iraqi oil back to their old stomping grounds." George W. Bush said to be waging a "never-ending war on – not terror ... – but on anything and everything that might impinge in the slightest degree on the profits, power and privilege of the tiny clique of predatory elites that he represents."

Jerry Mazza, "Ahmadinejad calls oil price hikes 'manipulated,'" *Online Journal*, June 26, 2008:

He ironically attributed the oil price manipulation to "visible and invisible hands." (See my The "Invisible Hand" is picking your pocket for clarification on that last term.) Ahmadinejad reiterated that one of the world's largest problems is the continuing decline of the value of the dollar. One wonders what "Invisible Hand" is engineering that fiasco?

CondiNet iStockAnalyst, June/July 2008:

Presented is a chart of volatility suggestive of a "triple bottom" with possibility of an Invisible Hand rally, adding "triple bottoms usually don't end well ... In a socialized market helped by the invisible hand I don't know what would happen at a triple bottom, since we have little historical record. But in a free market, it usually ends badly."

Jason Lee Miller, "Analyst: VC Confidence at New Low," *WebProNews Search 101, A Guide to Online Advertising*, July 14, 2008:

Don't cha just love that market correction? The invisible hand readjusting the balance in your checking account?

Mazal Mualem and Zrahiya Zvi, "Despite no confidence vote, Olmert won't dismiss Labor ministers," *Ha'aretz*, July 15, 2008:

Barak harshly criticized the prime minister's conduct in regard to what he described as a reneging on previous agreements. According to Barak, "an invisible hand changed all the deals we agreed upon with the prime minister."

Kirk Johnson, "Preparing for Protests," The Caucus: *The New York Times* Politics Blog, August 24, 2008, 4:36 PM:

Security at the Democratic National Convention is mostly in the hands of the United States Secret Service, which prides itself on a kind of invisible-hand style.

Peter Morgan, "I Fell for Tricky Dick," *Newsweek* (December 8, 2008: 63):

Nor did I set out to write "Frost/Nixon" as a metaphor for the failed imperial presidency.

Mike Marquee, "Cashing in on Cricket," *The Hindu* (Online edition) 2008:

Regarding criticism of legal arrangements creating a labor market for cricketer labor enabling league club owners to auction players, thereby, it is said, of privatizing a public asset and commodifying a social activity that "In addition to guaranteed revenue streams and monopoly control of markets, the private owners enjoy the right to exploit a variety of public assets at little cost." Hence, "This vaunted triumph of the free market proves, on examination, to be less about what Adam Smith called 'the invisible hand' and more about a sleight-of-hand, a collusion between public authorities and private interests."

I conclude this subsection with an example of the use of the term "invisible hand" that is *unequivocally and unsurprisingly literally true* from *World* (London, July 17, 1790, Issue 1104): "The inferior ones [characters in a play] are to be played and directed in the usual puppet-shew manner on the stage, by an invisible hand behind the curtain."

1.6. Adam Smith's Three Known Uses

Adam Smith employed the term "invisible hand" three times in his published work. Given the antiquity and long history of use of the term, it is likely that Smith also used it on other occasions, both in speech and in writing. The three known uses have been sufficient to help ground enormous interest in the term.

In the *History of Astronomy*, Smith used the term "invisible hand" to describe how early thinkers ascribed to "the invisible hand of Jupiter" the governing of "the irregular events of nature." Regular events, or "the ordinary course of things," are driven, the thinkers felt, by "the necessity of their own nature" and needed no further explanation:

> ... it is the irregular events of nature only that are ascribed to the agency and power of their gods. Fire burns, and water refreshes ... by the necessity of their own nature; nor was the invisible hand of Jupiter ever apprehended to be employed in those matters. But ... irregular events were ascribed to his favour or his anger .... Those ... intelligent beings, whom they imagined, but knew not, were naturally supposed ... not to employ themselves in supporting the ordinary course of things, which went on of its own accord, but to stop, to thwart, and to disturb it. (Smith 1980: III.2: 49–50)

In what Smith called "the lowest and most pusillanimous superstition" (Smith, 1980: III.2: 50), Jupiter acted so as to change the course of events or interfere with the normal processes of nature. Irregular events are attributed to the action of the Gods or God; earthquakes and even eclipses remain examples to this day among naive and primitive peoples.

In the *History of Astronomy*, Smith writes of the "invisible hand of Jupiter" as part of a grander and more complex sociological discussion. This discussion is sociological, at least in part, because Smith analyzes what he thinks transpired over time while holding the theological element at arm's length, and with seeming ease simultaneously weaves together several strands of development.

Smith also identified a great and profound tension in the work of scholars and others, and, we can presume, in his own work. Indeed, Smith made it a centerpiece of his *History of Astronomy*. The tension is between achieving truth and the setting of minds at rest. People prefer to know the truth but will settle for propositions that will "allay this tumult of the imagination." Smith wrote that:

> Philosophy, by representing the invisible chains which bind together all these disjointed objects, endeavours to introduce order into this chaos of jarring and discordant appearances, to allay this tumult of the imagination, and to restore it, when it

surveys the great revolutions of the universe, to that tone of tranquility and composure, which is both most agreeable in itself, and most suitable to its nature. (Smith
1980: II.12: 45–46)

Such inquiries are undertaken "to sooth the imagination, and to render the
theatre of nature a more coherent, and therefore a more magnificent spectacle, than otherwise it would have appeared to be" (Smith 1980: II.12: 46).

At the end of *History of Astronomy*, Smith uses himself as an example of
how easy it is for the mind to go from a belief that soothes the imagination
to a truth that commands the intellect:

And even we, while we have been endeavouring to represent all philosophical
systems as mere inventions of the imagination, to connect together the otherwise
disjointed and discordant phaenomena of nature, have insensibly been drawn in,
to make use of language expressing the connecting principles of this one, as if
there were the real chains which Nature makes use of to bind together her several operations. Can we wonder, then, that it should have gained the general and
complete approbation of mankind, and that it should now be considered, not as
an attempt to connect in the imagination the phaenomena of the Heavens, but as
the greatest discovery that ever was made by man, the discovery of an immense
chain of the most important and sublime truths, all closely connected together,
by one capital fact, of the reality of which we have daily experience. (Smith 1980;
IV.76: 105)

A modern version of the "soothe the imagination" theme was written by
George Shackle:

All we can seek is consistency, coherence, order. The question for the scientist is
what thought – scheme will best provide him with a sense of that order and coherence, a sense of some permanence, repetitiveness and universality in the structure
or texture of the scheme of things, a sense even of that one-ness and simplicity
which, if can assure himself of its presence, will carry consistency and order to their
highest expression. Religion, science and art have all of them this aim in common.
The difference between them lies in the different emphases in their modes of search.
(Shackle 1967: 286)

Accordingly, Shackle wrote, two pages later, that "The chief service rendered by a theory is the setting of minds at rest" (Shackle 1967: 288).

Smith's use of the term in his *History of Astronomy* is typically treated
as a curiosum and, because it seemingly has no economic significance, is
quickly left behind inasmuch as the other two uses arise in economically
relevant contexts. When one considers his treatment of it in the *History of
Astronomy*, however, it should be clear that Smith's approach establishes
him to be a sensitive and deep-thinking analyst and, for his time, a sociologist of religion and of language, and at a premier level at that.

In *Astronomy*, Smith is reporting on the beliefs of others. In *Theory of Moral Sentiments* and *Wealth of Nations*, the "invisible hand" is given a different status of his own construction. Much of Smith's analysis of religion in the *Theory of Moral Sentiments* is sociological rather than theological in nature, especially his treatment of the formation of moral rules. God has given man the principles of approbation and disapprobation. Individuals desire to have others think well of them, in part so that they can justifiably think well of themselves. This behavior leads to the formation of moral rules as mankind works out what is approved and disapproved. This view of the formation of moral rules may be significant for the process of forming an opinion of Smith's position on key issues of religion. It would appear that most interpreters of Smith are themselves religious, so the sociological element may be discounted in favor of the theologically correct element, either consciously or unconsciously. The opposite effect may accrue either from the situation that economists may be the persons most interested in these matters or from the role of nonreligious sentiments, in either case discounting the religious element:

In *The Theory of Moral Sentiments*, Smith argues that spending by the rich gives employment to the poor, in effect making the distribution of consumption more equal than the distribution of wealth. The rich only select ... what is most precious and agreeable. They consume little more than the poor, and ... though they mean only ... the gratification of their own vain and insatiable desires, they divide with the poor the produce of all their improvements. They are led by an invisible hand to make nearly the same distribution of the necessaries of life ... had the earth been divided into equal portions ... and thus without intending it, without knowing it, advance the interest of the society ... (Smith 1976b: IV.I.10: 184–5)

Four characteristics may be remarked: Smith says "is led," not "as if led" – literal rather than metaphoric language. The individual behavior of the rich is said to promote the interest of society. The language of "without intending it, without knowing it" is that of the principle of unintended and unforeseen consequences, seen by some as the invisible-hand mechanism or process. The argument about spending by the rich and employment to the poor is interpretable as the trickle-down theory serving in defense of the existing upper levels of hierarchy. Smith's emphasis on setting minds at rest applies to our assessments of the evolution and impact of institutions.

In the *Wealth of Nations*, Smith discusses how the study by an individual seeking "the most advantageous employment" for his capital "necessarily leads him to prefer that employment ... most advantageous to the society." A businessman's added concern about the insecurity of investment abroad will lead to increased domestic investment and thus more domestic income and employment:

As every individual, therefore, endeavours as much as he can both to employ his capital in the support of domestic industry, and so to direct that industry that its produce may be of the greatest value; every individual necessarily labours to render the annual revenue of the society as great as he can. He generally, indeed, neither intends to promote the public interest, nor knows how much he is promoting it. By preferring the support of domestic to that of foreign industry, he intends only his own security; and by directing that industry in such a manner as its produce may be of the greatest value, he intends only his own gain, and he is in this, as in many other cases, led by an invisible hand to promote an end which was no part of his intention. Nor is it always the worse for the society that it was no part of it. By pursuing his own interest he frequently promotes that of the society more effectually than when he really intends to promote it. (Smith 1976A, IV.ii.9: 455–6)

Smith again writes "is led," not "as if led." The principle of unintended and unforeseen consequences is again present through the treatment of intentions and knowledge. Only two pages earlier, however, Smith argued that the individual employs his capital with his own advantage in view: "But the study of his own advantage naturally, or rather necessarily leads him to prefer that employment which is most advantageous to the society" (Smith 1976a: IV.II,4: 454). An internal conflict therefore exists between Smith's use of "necessarily" on the one hand and "generally," "in this, as in many other cases," and "frequently" on the other.

Notice, too, that Smith seems to anticipate the modern neoclassical view that postulates a unique determinate result. Smith postulates that there is an employment of capital "which is most advantageous to the society." And both he and the modern neoclassicists are wrong. There is no unique employment of capital that is most advantageous to society. Different distributions of wealth yield different employments of capital most advantageous to society; that is, different initial entitlements yield different allocations of resources. If there is an invisible-hand type of process at work, it produces the optimal allocation of resources for the correlative distribution of capital or entitlements. However, with a different distribution of capital or entitlements, different interests will be satisfied.

The use in *The Wealth of Nations* has been the principal one; it is seen to be wider ranging and the basis of the concept as foundational. The use in *The Theory of Moral Sentiments* is conventionally taken to be coordinate with it but its context narrower. But the invisible-hand language in both of his books takes up only a few pages. He does not go into elaborate detail, certainly not to the degree required, one would think, by the extravagant invocation of Smith's discussion made by those who seek to ground the case for capitalism.

All of which engenders questions, questions that elicit conflicting answers: What is the substance of social welfare and how is it known? Is society an independent entity? What are the directional flows of meaning: from individual to society or from society to individuals, or both? Is the social interest the sum of private interests, something given, or something to be worked out? The substance of economic performance has been defined differently: satisfaction, utility, production, value of output, welfare, happiness, wealth, and so on. The test of economic performance, whatever the substance, likewise has been variously identified: efficiency (by one definition or another), growth, most productive, Pareto optimality, stability, progress (by one definition or another), distribution, and so on. Efficiency, for example, can be defined in terms of exhausting gains from trade or maximum/optimum production.

The idea that modern theory has gotten to the bottom of and refined Smith's vague idea is both widespread and problematic, and has involved increasingly technical and narrow terms. "Refinement" has generally been defined in formal rather than substantive terms. It has also involved what is for some the curious role of the Walrasian auctioneer, which may or may not be a metaphor for the Hayekian spontaneous-order process.

The combined length of Smith's *Theory of Moral Sentiments* and *Wealth of Nations* is approximately 1,500 pages. Of these, only a handful are devoted to the invocation of an invisible hand, and nowhere is a discussion of the hand per se to be found. It may be that the term was used to set his own mind and the minds of his readers at rest. It may be that he used the term to achieve closure in his own mind, or to obfuscate the fact that he knew nothing very substantive of what he was writing about. Or perhaps he had something on his mind, some hint or intuition of an invisible-hand process. He neither informs us of the reason nor returns to the term time after time in either book, both of which one would expect of an author setting down and using a proposition or principle that he or she deemed fundamental. A handful of pages out of about 1,500 pages: Its elevation to canonical status by those who worship at its altar may well exemplify the use of a relatively few words on which to erect an addition to society's stockpile of kaleidoscopic mythic systems.

In a society becoming increasingly, if glacially, an individualist society, it is no surprise that self-interest would be given a linguistic rhetorical treatment. In a society in which theism was inherited, and in which absolutist formulations were rampant, it is no surprise that individuals would be thought to have the makings of order implanted in their minds or derived somehow from their actions. In a society inured to expect references to an invisible hand in the most authoritative context individuals are likely to encounter throughout their lives – their church – individuals are likely to respond well to its use in another important sphere of their lives.

There is much in Adam Smith that most of us would do well to learn. We should also have a sense of humility inasmuch as we have sometimes grasped at straws in order to set our minds at rest. We should be conservatively diffident in bringing to bear on policy ideas whose source seems to be their service in soothing our imagination (Samuels 2007b: chap. 17), which is not to say that Smith fully practiced diffidence. He was more interested in the process of working things out than in the substance of the legal and moral rules that were worked out. Our tendency has been to accept what seems plausible, even if unproven, in assessing the evolution and impact of institutions.

1.7. The Fecundity of Smith's Analysis as Shown by E. K. Hunt

I close this essay with an example of the use of the concept of the invisible hand that will be analytically helpful in several aspects that will arise later, even though it will irritate some readers. One aspect is that in almost all cases in economics, the use of the term is essentially an exercise in assertion. This applies also when the initial assertion is by someone other than the person quoted. The latter is presumably responding to that initial assertion in good faith or at face value; in the likely event of conflicting positions, the use of the term by either or both sides is also a matter of assertion. The chief argument, however, is that there clearly resides in Smith's work the operation of not one but two invisible-hand processes, one of which has eclipsed the other, and although Smith presents much evidence for it and comes close to formulating it, he does not do so.

E. K. Hunt first points out that the common theme throughout Adam Smith's work is that of interpreting individuals' pursuit of their selfish interests along the lines that "there was operative in the 'laws of' nature' or in 'divine providence' what Smith called an 'invisible hand' that guided these seemingly conflict-creating actions into a benevolent harmony. The invisible hand was not the intentional design of any individual but was simply created by the systematic working out of natural laws" (E. K. Hunt 1979: 37–38).

We will see in subsequent essays that if one begins with such a view and eliminates from it all notions of natural laws, divine providence, and a transcendent but invisible hand, whether or not unequivocally mythical, one is left with interaction and the aggregation of the results of human interaction, and the positive use of the principle of unintended and unexpected consequences to some or much of which the name "invisible-hand process" has been given. The ideological power of such a concept is, however, considerably limited; thus the attractiveness for ideological purposes of invisible-hand process explanations is much less than those questioned by Hunt, which are the mainstream of invisible-hand thinking.

Hunt next points to the deception argument of *The Theory of Moral Sentiments*, in which nature is said to have imposed on humankind the illusion that more goods is better than less, the result of which is the promotion of industry (idem: 40). Vanity and status emulation thus have the unintended effect of promoting economic growth. Such reasoning, Hunt argues, leads to the affirmation of a free-market economy, social harmony, and laissez-faire – for example, Smith's "obvious and simple system of natural liberty" (idem: 54). Hunt then identifies one of the flaws in Smith's reasoning:

Given Adam Smith's assertion that "civil government, so far as it is instituted for the security of property, is in reality instituted for the defense of the rich against the poor, or of those who have some property against those who have none at all," it behooved both Smith and Ricardo to show why government would not be used by capitalists in exactly this way. Without such a demonstration the invisible hand argument would inevitably be used simply to justify any observed outcome in a market, capitalist system. (idem: 109)

Which brings us to Hunt's identification of the alter ego of the invisible hand – the invisible foot. Capitalists are not, fundamentally, against government. They seek, rather, for government to do their bidding and to do so whenever there exists a need to identify which interests government will protect as property rights. This determination enables one party to impose negative externalities on other parties and to do so in a manner that obfuscates the role of governmental activism operating behind the power of some people and not others to create negative externalities. This obfuscation is accomplished by simply considering externalities, "for which they advance the establishment of property rights and markets, as somehow being metaphysically given and fixed" (idem: 369). Moreover, bargaining between economic agents is seen as evidence of the harmony-producing invisible hand. However,

[i]t follows from the orthodox assumption of maximizing economic exchanges that each person will create a maximum of repugnant and pernicious social costs that he

or she can impose on others. The general process can quite appropriately be called the "invisible foot" of the laissez – faire capitalist marketplace. The invisible foot ensures us that in a free market, capitalist economy, each person pursuing only his or her own maximum gain will automatically and most efficiently do his or her part to maximize the general public misery. (idem: 370)

We thus commence our interpretation of the concept of the invisible hand with the knowledge that leading economic theorists, among others, do not agree with the idea that the concept is the foundation of economics; that any issue can be treated as involving both (1) the beneficent and harmonious process and outcome and (2) the malevolent and conflict-ridden process and outcomes, and, moreover, that the conflict between the two views of economy and economics has been formulated in terms of an invisible hand in juxtaposition and conflict with an invisible foot.

2

The Political Economy of Adam Smith

2.1. The Interpretation of Adam Smith

Adam Smith and David Hume, as well as Thomas Hobbes and John Locke, are the premier philosophers of modern western civilization. Such stature is Smith's in part because he comprehended and analyzed the deepest levels of the newly developing industrial market economy.[1] I propose to interpret Smith's model of the market economy in terms of his total system of thought and analysis. This system, with all its oppositions and tensions, comprises Smith's solution to the problem of order, or of the organization and control of the economic system. Expressed somewhat differently, I shall inquire into the significance for economic policy and policy making of the central arguments presented in the *Wealth of Nations*, *The Theory of Moral Sentiments*, *History of Astronomy*, and the two sets of student notes from Smith's lectures on law and government. Smith speaks to the ages, or at least he is still being heard in our age. What does he have to say on the most fundamental level? What is really going on in our economic system, according to Adam Smith?

I first must acknowledge certain considerations involved in the retrospective interpretation of the history of thought in general and of specific classic literature in particular.[2] These considerations necessarily limit my analysis and argument.

---

[1] True, he has some interesting if not important things to say about practical issues and details of economic organization and policy, not all of which, by any means, we are obligated to accept. His views on interest rate regulation and the corporation are two examples. However, his opinions often are of interest because he is taking a position, more or less idiosyncratic, about some practical aspect of the fundamental structure and process of the market economy and/or its political correlatives.

[2] Several of these considerations are discussed in Samuels (1974b).

First, each generation has the task and the opportunity of reinterpreting Smith for itself. There is no escaping this, nor would we desire to.[3] Second, it should be clear that the understanding of Adam Smith is influenced by the problems, interests, and values that each interpreter, whether an individual or a generation, brings to his work. This is one facet of the inescapable tension between the data (or "facts") of history and the mind of the historian. Furthermore, the history of the interpretation of Smith influences our subsequent perceptions of problems, interests, and values. In both respects, the meaning of the man arises in and through our efforts to apprehend him. It is therefore both necessary and difficult to pierce several veils, not the least being one's own ideology, in order to approach Smith more closely.

Third, the interpretation of Smith has been influenced by a selective filtration process (Gramm 1973) that has permitted certain views to remain viable and others not – a process deeply channeled by ideology, power, and whatever governs professional or disciplinary concerns, including the felt needs of both orthodoxy and heterodoxy in economics, each of which has had its own dogmas and preconceptions about the past and present. No less perceptive an authority than Alex Macfie has remarked, with regard to the historical overemphasis on the economic side of Smith's work, that "the immense economic impact of the *Wealth of Nations* [arose] considerably out of the way it could be used to support the more dominant economic forces of his and later times" (1967: 13). Similarly, John Maurice Clark attributed the immediate success of the *Wealth of Nations* to a shift of "class interests" (1928: 73). Ideological and other filtration has permitted most economists and noneconomists to have only an aphoristic appreciation of Smith's view of the economic world. One wonders

---

[3] Interpretation, of course, serves several functions, among them social control. In the *Wealth of Nations* and in the *Theory of Moral Sentiments*, Smith examined the social control mechanisms of the existing society and economy. One indicator of the historic importance of Smith's work has been that the interpretation of the *Wealth of Nations* has become a facet of the social control system of the western economies. Yet this only illustrates the general view that the entire history of economic thought has meaning as knowledge, social control, and psychic balm, considering that economics may serve as both explanation and rationalization. The interpretation of the *Wealth of Nations* has become part of the quest for moral and legal rules, a quest that to Adam Smith, as we will see, was a very important part of the socioeconomic system; For example, see the disparate interpretations of the significance of the *Wealth of Nations* presented at the Political Economy Club centennial celebration; Political Economy Club, *Revised Report of the Proceedings at the Dinner of 31st May, 1876, Held in Celebration of the Hundredth Year of the Publication of the "Wealth of Nations"* (1876).

whether he would have thought the notoriety worthwhile if, in achieving it, his work and analysis were caricatured.

Fourth, I would recall the mixed reception that has been given to the *Wealth of Nations* as, in Frank Knight's phrase, "a propaganda for economic freedom" (1953: 279). Of course, the book and its reasoning have been frequently invoked and made increasingly sophisticated as an argument in favor of the market and commercial freedom. Yet many, like Knight, have perceived that Smith was too deep and subtle, and too admitting of unsafe thoughts, to permit his book to be readily effective propaganda once one looked beyond the ideas seemingly contained in certain obvious passages. The reception and status given to the *Wealth of Nations* have depended on many variables, including the interpreters' perceptions of Smith and of the necessary and desirable course of social and economic policy in their own times.[4]

Fifth, I would argue that the most significant aspect of Smith and the *Wealth of Nations* resides in the total matrix of interpretations and mutual critiques, not in any single one, however attractive, useful, ostensibly complete, or accurate it may be. No one interpretation can capture the complexity and fecundity of Smith's mind or the social meaning of his work.

Sixth, I should say that the history of the interpretation of Smith is as interesting and instructive, and as difficult to fathom, as the interpretation of Smith himself. Suffice it to say that the very nature and identity of vulgar Smithism is itself a matter of interpretation; that there is a tension between the confidence that one can determine "what Smith really meant" and the needs of reinterpretation; that it is difficult to transcend the filtration process, in part because its results inevitably help select our perceptions; and that I intend here not some "final" word, but one contribution to the continuing matrix of interpretations.[5]

Adam Smith was no ordinary economic writer; he was truly a premier philosopher of western civilization. He worked out many of the distinctive principles of a civilization newly coming into being (Mitchell 1967: 1, 167), and the complexity of such a task can hardly be overestimated. A philosophy of civilization deals with what Joseph Spengler has called the

---

[4]   The interpretation given later in the essay is largely in the tradition of Jacob Viner, Glenn Morrow, Alex Macfie, and Nathan Rosenberg, among others, all of whom deserve prior exculpation for the uses to which I have put their ideas. The influence of Joseph Spengler also will be evident.

[5]   Smith's element of cynicism here (Macfie 1967: 54) may be compared with Milton Friedman's criticism of what he considers intellectuals' "contempt for what they regard as material aspects of life" (Friedman 1962: 8).

problem of order, requiring continuous readjustments between freedom (or autonomy) and control, continuity and change, and hierarchy and equality (Spengler 1948; Spengler 1968). Each such philosophy encompasses not only freedom or continuity, but also the systematic handling of freedom and control as well as continuity and change, according to the authoritative principles of the civilization or of those who determine them. Vis-à-vis other civilizations and on its own terms, each civilization and its philosophy evolves a more or less distinctive resolution of the problem of order. This may be perceived and defined in terms of some view of freedom, or otherwise, but it includes within it all the elements that comprise the problem of order: freedom, control, continuity, change, hierarchy, and equality. Each civilization and its philosophy is thus a synthesis of often seemingly contradictory or antinomial elements, such as the controls necessary to permit a particular freedom to exist, and so on. Civilizations represent systems of social control, whatever the character and scope of elements, such as the controls necessary to permit a particular freedom to exist, and so on. Civilizations represent systems of social control, whatever the character and scope of perceived and actual freedom therein, whatever their resolution of hierarchy versus equality and of continuity versus change. At the level of a civilization, the problem of order is holistic, and one must speak of patterns of freedom and control, and so on. On a lower level, there exist particular conflicts regarding the details of the problem of order. Adam Smith must be interpreted in terms of such a context and on the level of abstraction required by the general problem of order.

Let there be no mistake about acknowledging the obvious: Adam Smith most distinctively stood for private enterprise, private property, self-interest, voluntary exchange, the limited state, and the market. He was the philosopher of a system of spontaneous economic activity, or resource allocation through market forces, and of efficiency (as it has come to be called) comprehended in terms of self-interest or maximization, or optimization, of personal well-being. The market, in the Smithian view, is a mechanism for resolving basic economic problems and for producing order without elaborate and overt central direction, the "mystery," as Mark Blaug (1968: 6) expressed it, of order achieved through exchange entered into by private individuals manifesting "the uniform, constant, and uninterrupted effort of every man to better his condition" (Smith 1937: 326; Smith 1976a: II.iii.28). All this does in fact characterize the distinctive argument presented in the *Wealth of Nations*, which heralds what we call the market system and its conceptions of freedom, welfare, and the nature, origin, and mode of their realization.

Yet, as I suggested more than three decades ago, there is a second model of order in the *Wealth of Nations*, a model of the economy as a system of power (Samuels 1973). Smith understood the deep forces of organization and control at work in the economic system. He realized how market forces operate only within, and give effect to, the structure of power, and especially how those with access to and (in some sense) control over government use it. Market order is achieved only within the structure of power. Both the market and power govern whose interests will count in the economy. Markets are structured by power, and market solutions are power-structure-specific. Power and market relations both constitute sets of variables in a general interdependent system.

It is possible to exaggerate the analysis of conflict and power in Smith, but it is also possible to exaggerate the analysis of voluntary market exchange, and it is the latter that has developed as a consequence of the filtration system governing the development of interpretation. Smith's realism and fecundity include both market exchange, narrowly considered, and power play over rights and other bases of access to and participation in the market, including the complex economic role of government. Smith includes both market and power models in his conception of how society works out resolutions to the problem of order. What is distinctive about the market economy is not the absence of fundamental power relations, but their particular form. It is necessary to examine the system on more than its own (ideological) terms and consciousness, and this is what Smith largely did.

2.2. Smith's Synoptic and Synthetic System

The juxtaposition and combination models of power and of market must be seen, however, as but one part of Smith's total conception of the economic system and its underlying processes. Smith, many of his contemporaries, such as David Hume, and many successors, such as Karl Marx, Carl Menger, Vilfredo Pareto, and Max Weber, each had a synoptic grasp on or approach to the world. Smith, and the Scottish school in general, "thought of economics only as one chapter (not the most important) in a general theory of society involving psychology and ethics, social and individual, law, politics, and social philosophy as well" (Macfie 1967: 16, 147 and passim). Smith had not only a synoptic view of the world but also, and most suitably, a synthetic way of thinking; results were a consequence of the integration or composition of complex and often seemingly contradictory elements.

Let me outline the important points that must be added to the juxtaposition and combination of market and power.

First, a fact that is quite well known but whose significance is not so well appreciated is that Smith's approach to moral philosophy encompassed four realms of thought and action: natural theology, ethics, justice (or jurisprudence), and expediency (by which he meant concern for wealth, power, and prosperity). The domain of ethics was explored in the *Theory of Moral Sentiments*; expediency, or wealth and associated power, in the *Wealth of Nations*; and justice was to be the object of another discourse, to consist of "an account of the general principles of law and government, and of the different revolutions they have undergone in the different ages and periods of society, not only in what concerns justice, but in what concerns police [policy], revenue, and arms, and whatever else is the object of the law" (Smith 1966: 503). In lieu of this latter volume, we have had two transcriptions of his lectures, including Smith (1964). The point is that the moral, market, and legal orders are distinguishable interacting subprocesses of a larger whole and that their interaction is an important part of their operation and explanation.

Second, it was Smith's view that what transpired in the life of the individual and society was a synthesis of a number of forces. These included self-love, self-interest, self-command, sympathy, benevolence, moral rules, and legal control. Individual thought and behavior represented a balance or synthesis of motives, each of which had complex origins. Social and individual phenomena were a product of both reason and feeling and of both rationalism and authority. There is both deliberative and nondeliberative choice in society (Macfie 1967; Samuels 1966; see also Essay 8 in this volume).

Third, society exhibits tendencies toward both harmony and conflict, with tension between them. There are great conflicts in society, and such harmony as exists does so within the existing system and structure and is very rough and limited; moreover, it is a created and not a fully spontaneous harmony (Robbins 1953: 25–9; Samuels 1966: 7–9).

Fourth, it is easy to lose sight of the foregoing because in both the *Theory of Moral Sentiments* and the *Wealth of Nations*, Smith himself presented a synthesis of naturalistic deductive lines of reasoning and factual inductive arguments. Needless to say, tensions exist between these two procedures (Macfie 1967: 108, 122 and passim; Morrow 1928: 168–71). As for society itself, there is a synthesis of "experience, induction from it, and the final faith."(Macfie 1967: 102–3, n4).

Adam Smith's mind encompassed the broad, dynamic, interactive, and open-ended processes of resolving the problem of order and the set of its ongoing solutions. The process was at any point constrained by the status quo and, for Smith himself, by certain normative pluralistic requirements, however ambiguous they may appear in retrospect (Samuels 1966: chapter 5; Robbins 1953: chapter 6; Coats 1971: 5ff). Smith's was an essentially modern, albeit undeveloped, theory of society. Inevitably, the tendency of interpreters is to see and emphasize portions of his analysis, but we must not lose sight of Smith's synoptic or synthetic whole, with its interdependence, ambiguity, and tensions, or of the fact that even at the present level of discussion, the terms with which we articulate the whole can vary between reasonably objective interpreters. The strength of partial analysis is necessarily associated with its limits, including the neglect both of interaction between subprocesses and of the general interdependent character of the whole. What happens to or within one subprocess profoundly affects and is affected by what transpires in the others. This is a system that Gunnar Myrdal called cumulative causation. Interpretation cannot properly reduce Smith's analysis to single-factor or unidirectional explanations or to narrowly normative systems without doing injury to his synoptic and synthetic views of the realities of economic life. Apparent closure, vis-à-vis the open-endedness of his analysis, is a result of ideological filtration that, however inevitable, necessary, and even salutary, nonetheless fails to present the entire Smithian analysis. His work serves to caution us that basic problems must be defined in such a way as not to foreclose analytical consideration of important variables and forces, but rather to stress certain critical antinomies ensconced within them. There are inevitable interactions, tensions, and problems characteristic of the working out of solutions to the problem of order.

The greatest difficulty in both positive and normative analysis is to project adequately the system of freedom under analysis while providing an important and explicit place for the system of control necessary for that system. The same is true with regard to continuity and change. It was Adam Smith's genius to have treated this as a critical part of his synthetic and synoptic analysis. As Macfie remarks, "Some of Smith's arguments seem to conflict with others, and the charge of inconsistency has been brought against him, with undoubted justice. But while consistency is certainly a virtue and an ideal, we live in a world shot through with inconsistencies. In this regard, I like to remember the saying of Emerson: "With consistency a great soul had simply nothing to do: an exaggeration, no doubt; but in due measure true, at least for geniuses" (Macfie 1967: 139; Anspach 1972: 203–5). The same point has been made by others: Reinhold Niebuhr wrote that "life is full of contradictions and ambiguities," and that "we live our lives in various realms of meaning which do not cohere rationally" (Nye 1975: 52). F. Scott Fitzgerald wrote that "the test of a first-rate intelligence is the ability to hold two opposed ideas in the mind at the same time, and still retain the ability to function" (Cerruti 1976: 59). Niels Bohr distinguished between "minor truths, whose opposites are plainly false, and great truths, whose opposites are also true" (Schlegel 1973: 480). However much ideological filtration may have distorted and emasculated Smith's analysis, his was a first-rate intelligence and his was a brilliant accomplishment – one that has been infrequently attempted and even more rarely achieved. He did comprehend great truths whose wisdom and accuracy resided in their synthesis with opposites that were also true in distinguishable respects. Nowhere is this insight more important than in regard to his analysis of market and power and of freedom and control, but it is also true, and important, in regard to his analysis of moral rules, law, and institutions generally.

2.3. Interdependence and Tensions

This section will sketch the interdependence and tensions contained within Smith's synoptic and synthetic analysis. Most of the discussion concerns the nature and role of the market, its relation to other institutions of social control, and the relation of self-interest to the market and to moral and legal rules, all involving the socialization of the individual. We will see that the usual formulation of his message "completely short-circuits much of the real substance of Smith's work" (Rosenberg 1960: 557).

Smith viewed the market as a regulatory system, itself an institution of social control. The invisible hand is supposed by many people to control individual conflicts and the excesses of competition, and to "safeguard the public good through healthy competition. Such is his faith" (Macfie 1967: 62). The market, above all, is an institutional mechanism to compel men to pursue self-interest in social rather than antisocial ways (Rosenberg 1960: 558). As Rosenberg has also said, "The price system, as Smith saw it, was an intensely coercive mechanism [which] tied the dynamic and powerful motive force of self-interest to the general welfare. Its free operation would, in most cases, leave the individual producer no alternative but to pursue his economic interests in a manner conducive to the national welfare" (1960: 560). Smith's emphasis is not solely, or not so much, on the self-regulatory character of the market as on the regulation of self-interest by the market. The regulatory function of the market is obfuscated by the modern emphasis on market solutions as being a priori optimal, or on an a priori free market, or the assumption that business decisions are not only beneficent but optimal. This often-blind invocation of the market neglects the fact that Smith's simple and obvious system of natural liberty was a shrewd method of harnessing and releasing the human propensities deemed favorable to the creation of opulence and good order and suppressing the unfavorable ones. Quite a few writers have noted and articulated this method of harness and release inherent in the market system. Alas, seemingly many more writers present a presumptuous and harmonistic explanation of what markets do; for example, writing as if the market economy is thoroughgoing freedom, thereby neglecting the correlative structure of social control, and also private controls, making the case for the market system in question-begging anticontrol terms. (My first exposure to the harness-and-release characteristic, as I recall, was in James S. Earley's lectures on the history of economic thought [see Samuels 2003: 246–7 and passim].)

Notice the merely tentative propriety attributed by Smith to market results. It is true that the individual's search for "the most advantageous employment for whatever capital he can command ... naturally, or rather automatically leads him to prefer that employment which is most advantageous to the society" (Smith 1937: 421; 1976a: IV.ii.4, 454). But his most elaborate statement of the general principle, as already shown in Section 1.5 of Essay 1, is considerably qualified:

As every individual, therefore, endeavors as much as he can both to employ his capital in the support of domestic industry and so to direct that industry that its produce may be of the greatest value; every individual necessarily labours to render the annual revenue of the society as great as he can. He generally, indeed, neither intends to promote the public interest, nor knows how much he is promoting it. By preferring the support of domestic to that of foreign industry, he intends only his own security; and by directing that industry in such a manner as its produce may be of the greatest value, he intends only his own gain, and he is in this, as in many other cases, led by an invisible hand to promote an end which was no part of his intention. Nor is it always the worse for the society that it was no part of it. By pursuing his own interest he frequently promotes that of the society more effectually than when he really intends to promote it. (Smith 1937: 423; 1976a: IV.ii.9, 456)

Notice that Smith here does not say that in all cases self-interest is led by an invisible hand to promote the public interest; only "in this, as in many other cases" does it occur. Again, pursuit of self-interest does not always promote the interest of society, only "frequently." The market, as a regulatory system, is seen by Smith as a more or less newly discovered institution of social control, but its operation is not a priori optimal. The market must be associated with the operation of other institutions of social control; there is no presumptive optimality of market solutions. The principle of the optimality of markets and market solutions, in all its forms, is a later principle with both explanatory and legitimizing roles, and does not adequately reflect Smith. The market must be seen to be qualified in its operation by the impact of moral and legal rules and other institutions that are themselves a matter of choice and evolution.

Two very different, even substantially conflicting, lines of reasoning coexist within no fewer than three pages in the great work – with no clear and direct treatment of the problem of which applies in particular cases. In one line of reasoning, the pursuit of one's own advantage "naturally, or rather necessarily leads him to prefer that employment" of his capital in the manner "most advantageous to the society." In the other line of reasoning, "[b]y pursuing his own interest he frequently promotes that of the society . . .: Necessary or problematic? In all cases, or only in some?" (Smith 1937: 421, 423; 1976a: IV.ii.4, 9: 454, 456).

Two consequences follow: One result is that no test has been designed, and none exists, to know what is going on. All parties come forth with what basically can be only assertions. The second result is that no test exists to be applied to any aspect of the previously mentioned topics – topics that are essentially welfare economic inferences.

The market, in Smith's total scheme, operated within and gave effect to the rest of the institutional system as well as to individual choice within the system. Voluntary exchange takes places only within legal and moral rules as well as the market. The market, according to Smith, must be comprehended within the larger system involved in the continuing resolution of the problem of order, however much it may contribute thereto. The order produced by markets can only arise if the legal and moral framework is operating well; as Rosenberg has written, the "decisive superiority" of the price system "as a way of organizing economic life lay in the fact that, when it was surrounded by appropriate institutions, it tied the dynamic and powerful motive force of self-interest to the general welfare" (Rosenberg 1960: 560). The market does not do so alone.

This signifies a dual flow in the creation of moral meaning. Individuals help produce moral rules through the operation of the principles of approbation and disapprobation, and the rules thus formed help in the socialization of the individual.

It is a fundamental argument of Adam Smith that institutions, including moral and legal rules and rule making, function as social control. Morrow (1928), Macfie (1967), and Rosenberg (1960, 1965) have elaborately spelled this out. As Macfie has argued, for example, "the central and fruitful proposition of the *Moral Sentiments* is not the natural theism, but the inductive argument based on the sympathetic feelings of the impartial spectator, with its historical setting of societies developing through the growth of social institutions, education, custom, moral rules and the institutions of justice" (1967: 107). For Rosenberg, "one of the major themes of the *Wealth of Nations*, of course, is its exhaustive examination of the manner in which institutional arrangements structure the decision-making of the individual, sometimes in a manner which harmonizes private interest and social interest, and sometimes in a manner which disrupts them" (1965: 129). "The question is, in each case, whether institutions do, or do not, harness man's selfish interests to the general welfare" (Rosenberg 1960: 560). The *Wealth of Nations*, then, is Smith's "attempt to define, in very specific terms, the details of the institutional structure which will best harmonize the individual's pursuit of his selfish interests with the broader interests of society" (Rosenberg 1960: 559).

Among other things, in Smith's analysis, institutions govern distribution. For example, he was concerned with the social gains and costs of the division of labor. One of his points, in modern terms, is that institutions govern their distribution among classes. In other words, there is a complex set of distributional, hierarchical, and aggregate-income-level trade-offs and related choices to be made through institutions (Rosenberg 1965: 136 – 138). As expressed by Rosenberg, "Smith is constantly searching out the impact of specific institutional forms upon the human actor. Given his basic conception of human motivations and propensities, the specific kinds of behavior which we may expect of any individual will depend on the way the institutions surrounding him are structured, for these determine the alternatives open to him and establish the system of rewards and penalties within which he is compelled to operate" (1960: 563).

For Smith, as for Hume, predictability of human behavior was brought about by the continuity generated by stabilized relationships embodied in institutions. "Once the institutional framework is specified," says Rosenberg, "human behavior becomes highly predictable" (1960: 563).

Institutions also govern the answer to the question of *whose* liberty is to be achieved, or liberty for what (Macfie 1967: 148). Smith was surely influenced by Stoic natural liberty and natural harmony doctrines, but he was also aware that social action of one form or another was necessary to discriminate among liberties and among actions. Selectivity is necessary unless all action be deemed harmonious and all exercise of liberty be sanctioned as natural. Belief in ultimate rationality and harmony does not avoid the problem of evaluating the status quo with regard to the actual elements of harmony and disharmony, and of rationality and irrationality, in accordance with the principles of approbation and disapprobation. It is precisely the role of moral and legal rules, and of their respective underlying processes, to govern such evaluation. It is the business of morality and law, as well as of the market, to regulate the detailed realities of freedom and of exposure to freedom. Speaking of banking regulations and firewalls, Smith said that "those exertions of the natural liberty of a few individuals, which might endanger the security of a few individuals, are, and ought to be, restrained by the laws of all governments; of the most free, as well as of the most despotical" (Smith 1937: 308). Moral and legal controls constitute part of the basis of the market, so that sympathy as well as division of labor may serve as social cement; whatever harmony and freedom exists is a function of other institutions besides the market (Rosenberg 1960: 559, 560, and passim; Macfie 1967).

The process involved in the foregoing may be examined by surveying Smith's conception of the socialization of the individual. Self-love is restrained by the growth of the moral rules and the social institutions that control it "appropriately" through informed sympathy (Macfie 1967: 81). Smith "concentrated on the social sanctions of morality rather than the individual one" of conscience (Macfie 1967: 97–8). The critical factor to Smith is not individual self-interest as such, but the moralization of the passions "through the gradual establishment of general rules, in the course of social progress, and through the reactions of individuals to such rules and conventions, in the course of their social living" (Macfie 1967: 117, 118). As Morrow explains, "It is because the individual is in his very nature socialized, a product of the social environment, that he can in general be left without external interference to act in accordance with the demands of his individual nature" (1928: 178, 166–7, 172, 177. See also Bryson 1968 and Schneider 1967.)

The Smithian model is one of controlled freedom; freedom of behavior and choice exists only within the socially established norms of conduct. Smith "certainly believed that it was only on ethical grounds that controlled liberty for individuals was justified and essential. This justified freedom (within limits) is the personal foundation of his individual and moral economic theory. The strategic factor, however, is not so much the freedom of the individual, which has received too unqualified attention since 1776, as the limitations on freedom which Smith always added were necessary, if freedom to pursue self-interest were to be moralized" (Macfie 1967: 117–8). Hence the paradox that "in his main argument, Smith was always fundamentally the sociologist, though in his equally basic argument for the (suitably controlled) freedom of the individual he was the eternal radical" (Macfie 1967: 91, n23). The individual is elevated to be the prime element in the economic system; however the individual not only operates within a moral and legal framework, but is also a socialized or moralized individual.

We might also say that the individual is a legalized individual. Self-love and self-interest go hand in hand with social control and socialization. It is true both that vanity has a social function in motivating self-interest and that "the great secret of education is to direct vanity to proper objects" (Macfie 1967: 72–3; Smith 1966: 380; 1976b: VI.iii.46, 259). In Smith we have both self-interested behavior and the control of self-interest by moral and legal rules. Self-interest exists only within social control (Morrow 1928: 16–7, 172, 177–8). Self-interest not only is operated upon by the market but also is defined, channeled, and restrained by moral and legal rules and by the operation of benevolence, sympathy, and the principle of the impartial spectator. Socialization operates through sympathy and the impartial spectator as internalized social control (Macfie 1967: 70–1, 75, 128, and passim; Anspach 1972; Coats 1975: 132–6).

Smith charts the operation of individual conscience (the impartial spectator plus the sense of propriety) and of social conscience (the general rules of conduct) that interact and together constitute the formation and internalization of social control. Individual choice and rationality exist within collective choice and rationality, which are in turn influenced by individual choice and rationality. The operation of the principles of approbation and disapprobation applied to the actions of oneself and others both govern and are influenced by the sense of propriety and the substance of moral rules. The impartial-spectator principle helps build up the moral rules and customs that serve as social cement, yet the principle depends for its content on already internalized social control. It is truly a process of cumulative causation or general interdependence and not one in which particular rules or particular patterns of socialized behavior may be taken as given once and for all time. Interdependence signifies endogenous change.

Several elaborations of topics warrant brief notice. Two concern the role of social conditioning in Smith's analysis. Of these, the first treats the social basis of man's general motivational system. I refer, in part, to Smith's argument that it is the deception of the "pleasures of wealth and greatness ... which rouses and keeps in continual motion the industry of mankind" (Macfie 1967: 47, 53–4, 60–76, 122–4; Smith 1976b: IV.I.9–10, 183; Rosenberg 1968: 371; Samuels 1966: 37). This has, of course, profound implications for Smith's individualism. He took for granted an organization of life that promoted material welfare, the propriety of which was channeled and reinforced by the dominant socioeconomic philosophy of life, that is, by socialization processes. In part this performed the social role of overcoming indolence (Rosenberg 1974: 1187 and passim). But it is important also to recognize that Smith was clearly interested in other, nonmaterial dimensions of welfare; that he recognized the moral corruption of over-emphasizing wealth and success (Macfie 1967: 78); that he distinguished between the role of the lure of wealth and the corrupting influences of wealth acquired by both oneself and others (Rosenberg 1960: 557 and passim); and that he seems to have felt that self-interest is not to be equated with selfishness, although he provided no conclusive principle for differentiating useful self-interest from selfishness, holding instead that such had to be worked out in society.

The second aspect of social conditioning involves Smith's view that preferences are endogenously determined within the economic system broadly considered. They are a partial function of moralizing and socializing processes that help define self-interest, including, of course, the proper objects of vanity (Rosenberg 1968: 367, 370, 372). Institutions, in Smith's analysis, help form the incentive-and-reward system of individuals (Rosenberg 1965: 129–30). And, of course, the market itself is a partial source of endogenously generated preferences; as Rosenberg says, "The growth of commerce is instrumental in shaping character, in altering tastes, and in providing new and more powerful incentives" (Rosenberg 1974: 1185).

Next, I would reiterate that the dualism of power and the market should not be forgotten. Both complement Smith's analysis of the origin, operation, and impact of moral and legal forms of social control. In this connection, three incidental points may be made. First, Smith appreciated the complexities of power. He appears, for example, to have been quite sophisticated in his understanding of how the union of Scotland and England served in the former to diffuse power (by limiting that of the local aristocracy), notwithstanding the somewhat more apparent centralization of power (Macfie 1967: 137). Second, it appears that institutionally produced inequality was more important to Smith than natural inequality (Macfie 1967: 120, n43). Third, I note the open question of the relation(s) between the division of labor and the power structure in Smith's work.

Another point worth noting is Smith's policy consciousness, a product of his relative empiricism, secularism, and down-to-earth realism. He treats institutions not as inevitable but as subject to redesign and change, as the product of past choice and subject to revised choices. He did not sacralize and revere the institutional status quo; rather, he represents the eighteenth-century version of concern to increase deliberative decision making in modern society (Macfie 1967: 49ff; Samuels 1966: chapters 2 and 5). Nonetheless, there is in Smith a sense of both the possibility of improving humans and their condition and the severe limits thereof (Macfie 1967: 117).

Smith, it should be apparent, blended methodological individualist and methodological collectivist levels of analysis, and he used both the individual and society as units of analysis. There are both voluntary exchange and a system, structure, and process of power. The individual is in one sense the prime element or unit in the economic system, but the individual exists and acts only within the evolving moral, legal, and institutional framework as a socialized individual. There are both individual choices and social forces. As Morrow has argued, Smith used two analytical procedures: the method of regarding society as a derivative of the individual, and that of regarding the individual as a product of society. Regarding his consideration of the concrete social environment "in explaining the nature of the individual man ... Smith is one of the very few thinkers of his time who had any realization of this complementary point of view" (Morrow 1928: 172). The filtration system has substantially worked to disregard this aspect of his thought.

The final point, treated only in passing, relates to Smith's complex attitude toward businessmen vis-à-vis (or, should I say, versus?) consumers. His views may be summarized as follows: (1) a functional emphasis on the critical role of the business class in regard to the organization and direction of production and thereby economic growth; (2) a normative and perhaps positive emphasis on consumption as the "sole end and purpose of production," and on the consumer as the primary beneficiary (Smith 1937: 625; 1976a: IV.viii, 49, 660); (3) a view of the market as a system of control to overcome indolence but also to constrain the rapacity of businessmen through their socialization; and (4) a celebration of the business system but not of the individual businessman. Indeed his views of the behavior of businessmen were often critical; as Heilbroner notes, Smith was "an admirer of their work but suspicious of their motives" (1972: 51). In sum, Smith provided no defense of the market on pro-business terms; there is no more presumptive optimality of market solutions than of business decisions in Smith – all that came much later, with ostensibly more sophisticated formulations of the central myth of capitalism.

This brings me to the central topic of the evolution of legal and moral rules and institutions. Smith acknowledges – indeed emphasizes – the inductive development of moral and legal rules, their changing character and content (Macfie 1967: 83–7 and passim). There is an evolutionary dimension to the evaluative process in society (Macfie 1967: 89–90). Moral and legal rules evolve through the principles of approbation and disapprobation operating through the impartial-spectator principle, expressing a refined sympathy and moral sensibility, as part of the larger evolving system (Macfie 1967: 83, 87, 89; Morrow 1928). "It is by our gradual evolution of moral rules and customs from innumerable cases that we develop those human institutions which are at once the safeguards and the growing points of human societies, In them the clashes of 'self-love' and benevolence, of sentiment and reason, are so far reconciled – reconciled in no absolute way, but pragmatically ambulando" (Macfie 1967: 57). Smith's argument in the *Theory of Moral Sentiments* is that moral and legal rules must be worked out and revised over time and cannot be set down once for all time and for all people (1966: 499; 1976b: VII.iv.33; 339). Not all unintended consequences of the market are, or are to be accepted as, beneficent. Such consequences may have adverse impact on desired legal and moral rules or on human welfare, and such rules may be changed to correct for adversity (Viner 1928). As I noted earlier, the historical interpretation of the *Wealth of Nations* had been part of the process through which moral and legal rules have been revised, sometimes in one direction and sometimes in another.

Smith's analysis thus provides for reevaluation: of institutions, including the market, in regard to the incidence of the reward-and-incentive system (Rosenberg 1960: 562); of legal rules in the light of changing norms and circumstances (Samuels 1966: chapters 4 and 5; Viner 1928); of the congruity of received values with new economic realities, including the terms of fellow feeling, for example, in regard to the distinction of ranks and respect for wealth and greatness (Macfie 1967: 124); of the reformulation (redefinition and reassignment) of property and other rights through law; of wealth vis-à-vis other considerations; of the definition of injury in regard to the doing of what one likes so long as it does not injure others (Smith 1937: 308; Viner 1928); of the meaning of "extraordinary" in what Smith referred to as "extraordinary restraints" and "extraordinary encouragements" (Smith 1937: 650); of the proper objects to which education is to direct vanity; and, inter alia, the substance and exercise of self-interest and egoism (Macfie 1967: 78 and passim; Morrow 1928).

It follows from this understanding of Smith that the interactions marking his synoptic and synthetic systems involve inevitable tensions. There is tension as to the content and direction of social control. There are tensions between the market, market forces, and institutions, and between market social control and legal and moral social control. There is tension between self-interest and the market as a regulatory system: individuals seek to escape from market control, there are conflicts of self-interest, and the market has an open-ended role as a conflict-resolving system that, perhaps paradoxically, is capable of being channeled by those who can control it (Samuels 1973). There is tension over the appropriateness of institutions, over the nature of injuries that should be avoided or prevented by rules and rights, and over when the liberty of one is endangering the liberty of another in such a way as to call for remedial action. There is tension over all the incidents of the socialization process: If the great secret of education is to direct vanity to proper objects, there is tension as to which (or whose) objects are proper and as to how vanity is to be so directed. There are inevitable tensions over the evaluation of aspects of the general motivational system, for example, over the morality and immorality of wealth and self-interest, including the structure of "institutional arrangements [within which] to cut off all avenues (and there are many) along which wealth may be pursued without contributing to the welfare of society," that is, over "the conditions under which [the] market mechanism would operate most effectively" (Rosenberg 1960: 560, 569). There is tension over the power structure as such (Clark 1928: 58, 62, 73–4); and, inter alia, over the conditions "wherein consist[s] the happiness and perfection of a man, considered not only as an individual, but as the member of a family, of a state, and of the great society of mankind" (Smith 1937: 726; Smith 1976a: V.i.f.30, 771). These tensions characterize the processes of socialization, collective action, and group existence. They were recognized as such by Smith, although they have been obscured by some interpreters who seem to have sought to sanction certain resolutions of the problem of order, and thereby of these tensions, and not others, all in the purported image of Smith. Such interpretations presumptively overstate the degree and overspecify the substance of the closure that Smith's system permits.

I urge, then, that change, reevaluation, and tension are necessarily critical aspects of Smith's synoptic and synthetic analysis. It is only by a static partial equilibrium-like approach to the problem of order – one that abstracts from the larger analysis – that one can reach conservative and laissez-faire doctrines and conclusions. I say this notwithstanding Smith's status as premier philosopher of the market system, the important conservative and free-market elements in his analysis, and without trying to make a case for any particular set of moral and/or legal controls or of changes therein. The deepest understanding of these aspects of Smith's analysis requires consideration of his larger system. Without doing so, we will not understand the conflict between those who see any act of government as an impediment of the market and those who see in government activity a change in the legal and moral foundations of the market. Above all, the previously presented account of Smith's total system and its tensions, its mode of working out continuous revision, and the great questions of changing legal rules and moral rules is correct whatever status is given to the notion of the invisible hand, even the denial of its existence or meaningfulness.

2.4. Present Significance

What, then, is the significance of Smith for contemporary analysis and policy? Smith can be and is, of course, interpreted, evaluated, and applied from any number of specific positive or normative perspectives. His analysis is broad enough to encompass quite a wide range of applications. His larger analysis – his total system, of which the invisible-hand argument in the *Wealth of Nations* is but one interacting part – permits and indeed has an important place for many diverse phenomena. There are two key points here: The scope of his system is broad, and its details – that is, the details that characterize a market economy and its moral and legal elements – are quite open and subject to revision. There is in Smith's total system what may be called a joint determination process: On the one hand is the determination of optimality through markets as individuals engage in voluntary exchange, and on the other is the ongoing socialization process that governs the reformulation of legal and moral rules, institutions, the power structure, and thereby the substantive conditions or content of optimality, always in combination with individual choice. Smith is quite obviously pro-market but not in a way that deems market solutions optimal per se. He does not propose, let alone establish, the exclusive or a priori presumptive optimality of market solutions. Rather, he articulates the role of the market as a regulatory system that performs either well or not, depending on the role of institutions and other forces of social control. Smith did not use his economic theory to justify conclusions that were beyond its scope, given the terms of his larger analysis, although he seems to have been easily enough interpreted as having done so. To Smith, reality is not a simple question of market optimality versus standards or norms of legal and moral social control; rather, the market gives effect to and operates upon such social control. His system is much larger than the dominant view of his work has admitted. Indeed, his larger analysis actually serves to explain the continued conflicts over proposed changes of moral and legal rules, institutions, power, values, and so on: Such conflicts are central to his conception of the evolution of the total economic system. And herein is to be found a major contemporary significance of Smith. Interpretive overkill, perhaps in an effort to make Smith's analysis safe for the system, has tended to obfuscate the larger process he deemed to be a crucial part of the social system, in part that arguments over freedom, change, and so on, whether or not conducted in the specific light of his work or considered more broadly.

Contrary, then, to the more typical usages of Smith and especially of the *Wealth of Nations*, I urge that he provides not a set of immediate policy

solutions or presumptions but a framework within which, given that it postulates and legitimizes what we consider to be a market economy, there can
be no unequivocal or conclusive a priori determination of practical policy
issues. It is Smith's message that these issues need to be worked out through
the principles of approbation, disapprobation, the impartial spectator,
and so on. Policy requires more than market-premised economic theory,
in part because there is more to the operation of the economy than such
theory incorporates. The theory of the market does not itself explain the
larger system of which the market is a part, nor does it conclusively assert
the superiority of market solutions within the existing systemic structure.
Smith's emphasis on the market tells us much about the general character of
his desired economic system and how it works in general, but it provides no
test of the congruence of any particular substance with his general model,
and tells us very little about the details of the continuing resolution of the
problem of order under its aegis. Smith was aware of the limited probative
value of his economic reasoning and therefore of the fact of the limits of what
science (itself subject to multiple definitions) can and cannot do (Macfie
1967: 13). The ultimate message of his synoptic and synthetic analyses is
the openness of the empty boxes that they present and therefore the choices
that they both permit and require. This conclusion stands in marked contrast to the more conventional view that Smith's message is to leave things
alone. His inclusion of tensions, which I have discussed, serves to indicate
the vacuity of the leave-alone view. To Smith, such tensions were not going
to be resolved once and for all, nor were market solutions the only ones
permitted or justified. It is a result of cumulative past filtration of Smith's
analysis that such a view as I have given may be perceived as statist.

Even those people who emphasize continuity do not want to retain every
detail of the status quo. They are selective and, above all, pragmatic, always
given the circumstances. The same is true of those who emphasize change.

The evolution of the interpretation of Smith, and of the doctrinal
defense of the ongoing system of which that interpretation has been a
part, has been a process of both filtration and conversion. Through filtration much of the substance and significance of Smith's larger system has
been excluded, including some fundamental social processes and many
continuing tensions. Through conversion, his analysis of the market – for
many, the invisible hand – has been transformed from an analysis and justification of relatively small-scale individual activity to that of large-scale
enterprise to which some economists refer as the corporate system. Both
filtration and conversion are inevitable processes. They function not only
to rationalize selected aspects of the changing status quo, but also, in that

respect and others, as important parts of the social valuational process. The point here is that in all these respects, Smith's total system and analysis have been transformed, in part to provide support for positions of the day on the issues of the day.

Much has changed since Smith's time; the modern world is vastly different in technology, institutions, political geography, historical experience, worldview, social stratification, and economic organization and control. One does find in the *Wealth of Nations* the germs of many of the conflicts of modern western civilization, but Smith largely antedated the conflicts between capital and labor and between property and nonproperty rights and positions in the economy. Yet these conflicts – for example, between masters and workers (Samuels 1973) – have a place in his system. He offers no genuine, unequivocal, and conclusive solution to any of those conflicts, but the probability that they will arise is predictable from his total analysis. Nevertheless, past uses of Smith have functioned either to deny the propriety of many of those conflicts or of certain positions on them, or to channel their resolution. There is no more conclusive ground for citing Smith in favor of a pro-business or property solution than there is for citing him in repudiation of the conflicts themselves. Given a market system, Smith's is a relatively open system. His analysis also recognizes, of course, that labor and capital are each jockeying for position to control the other, that government is an instrument of those who are in a position to use it, and that much asymmetry of position characterizes all such conflicts (Samuels 1973). Neither the conflict between laborer and capitalist nor that over property rights was considered essentially antimarket or antifreedom by Smith, despite the uses made of certain aspects of his ideas by subsequent partisans.

The fact of the matter, of course, is that the defense of the market, quite properly often in the name of Smith, has also served as a defense of existing power structures. Market theory has been used to obfuscate the importance of power, of moral and legal rules, and of the use of government, and to canonize existing power positions and their use of morality and law. One does not find in Smith the gains-from-trade and voluntarism arguments used in such a way as to rationalize and legitimize the existing power structure. Rather, Smith delineates the deep processes, no matter how laden with controversy, through which institutions, legal and moral rules, and power structures have been made subject to nonmarket revision. One cannot speak to Smith's reaction to a world of large-scale economic units, but it seems obvious to me that he very well might say that moral and legal controls – indeed the very institution of the corporation and the details of its existence and power – should be subject to revision (Clark 1928: 54n; Macfie 1967: 120). Surely Smith would have sympathized with Henry Simons's statement that "we may recognize, in the almost unlimited grants of powers to corporate bodies, one of the greatest sins of governments against the free-enterprise system" (Simons 1948: 52). In Smith's view, market solutions are not necessarily optimal; one must consider the power structure and other factors before one can reach that conclusion. It is a gross and misleading oversimplification of Smith to invoke his or any similar conception of the market without further examination of these other factors (Rosenberg 1960: 570). There always are at least several "optimal" results, each a function of the structure of rights and power actually or potentially in place. It is fallacious to identify the legal arrangements of a theoretical model with the extant legal arrangements. The conventional linguistic model that postulates private property as a foundation of the economic system is substantively empty. Friedrich Hayek proposed elimination of the right of corporations to hold equity securities in, and issued by, other corporations. He also proposed canceling the rights that allow corporate boards to determine the disposition of profits. Except for a possible contribution from current annual profits to maintain a reserve account, corporate managements, under his proposal, would have had to distribute all of their firm's other current annual profits to stockholders. The former proposal would restrict the opportunities of managers of some companies to engage in dubious schemes of personal self-enrichment at the expense of their stockholders (ostensibly their bosses). The latter proposal would allow the capital market to respond to the decisions of individual investors rather than interpose between individual and market the goals and calculations of managements. Hayek was hardly a radical in making these proposals. Most corporate boards and other managerial personnel would likely consider such changes to be incongruous with capitalism.

Adam Smith was a premier philosopher of the market economy, more so than our intellectual heritage has often allowed. The greatness of his analysis is that it is an open system in much the same sense that the market economy itself is an open system – notwithstanding the efforts of the already established and the powerful to the contrary. If we understood Smith better, it might be an even more open system, but that is quite another story.

3

On the Identities and Functions
of the Invisible Hand

3.1. Introduction

It should be clear from Essay 1 that with the obvious exception of Smith's noneconomic example, the invisible hand of Jupiter, Adam Smith does not indicate what he believes to be the "economic" invisible hand of the *Theory of Moral Sentiments* and the *Wealth of Nations*. It is notable, however, that in both economic uses he chose to say, in the first, that the rich "are led by an invisible hand," and in the second, that the individual intending "only his own gain ... is in this, as in many other cases, led by an invisible hand" (Smith 1976a: IV.i.10, 184; Smith 1976b: IV.ii.9.456). In a note at this point in the earlier work, the editors, Raphael and Macfie, note that "In both places Smith says that the end unintentionally promoted is the interest of society, but there is a difference: the TMS passage refers to the distribution of means to happiness, the WN passage to maximization" (Smith 1976a: IV.i.10.184n7).

Smith wrote "led" and not "as if led." He also wrote "an invisible hand" in both places. He may or may not have had one invisible hand in mind. I have shown that in his explanation of the etiology of the division of labor, Smith uses several causal factors (Samuels 2004: chapter 1). He may have been sloppy or forgetful but each tends to be presented in a manner that accords with the immediate argument of his essay on *The History of Astronomy*, that when a person is unable to establish the true explanation of something, then he or she is willing to accept whatever belief will "soothe the imagination," or set minds at rest. It is this linguistic strategy that Smith's writings emphasize by illustration.

When analysis comes to the invisible hand, an initial threefold interpretive problem arises. One can interpret Smith; one can interpret the vast literature of uses (identity candidates and functions), and one can interpret the "real world." There is not much to go on with which to ascertain what Smith "really meant." Nor are we here interested in interpreting the real world. Not that that is unimportant; it is just not the task of the historian and interpreter of economic thought.

The researcher is left with the vast literature of uses – of identities and of functions – of the invisible hand. And that is quite a story. In this essay we examine the identities that people have attributed to the invisible hand and the functions of the invisible hand, that is, what the invisible hand does or signifies. Many writers on these two topics are nearly as casual or blasé as Smith seems to have been. I suspect, but cannot prove, that the identity and function of the invisible hand was extremely important to Smith (and he also used it in accordance with his argument in *History of Astronomy* [Essay 4]); he has some things to say about its function but very little, almost nothing, about its identity. Most recent interpreters discuss what seems obvious to them, settling on their respective candidate or on the version they try to convince others to accept. The fact is that there is no test of either the identity or the function of the invisible hand.

One particular preliminary consideration is warranted. Neither space nor time permit taking up the problems encountered in elaborating each proposed candidate for identity. I take up for purposes of illustration the problems of a relative handful of candidates. The problems themselves could have been postponed to Essay 6. That essay, however, already deals with a large number of important conceptual, substantive, historical, and linguistic problems.

An important caution is also warranted: Nothing that I write in this Essay should be taken to be a clue to what I personally think is the invisible hand. I will, however, give the clue away on two fronts. I think that the idea of an invisible-hand process or mechanism is more important than any candidate for the identity of the invisible hand. And I suggest that the economy is comprised of numerous invisible hands. But what they do, or do not do, is another matter, which I will take up later.

3.2. The Identities of the Invisible Hand

Applicable to the questions of identity and of function are some widely found but not mandatory differentiating criteria. A designation of identity or of function can be classified as:

A. operative (1) always, (2) sometimes, (3) conditionally, (4) problematically, or (5) within limits;

B. (1) structural or (2) behavioral;

C. active in (1) production, (2) exchange, (3) distribution, or (4) institution;

C. pertaining to exchange and having (1) distributional or (2) allocative effects;

D. (1) empirical or (2) normative in nature.

Finally, the notion of an invisible hand seems to be used as a rhetorical device, as a means of capturing attention, by authors and others who believe they have something original and/or important to say. It is possible that as a discipline matures, less use is to be made of terms such as the invisible hand. That hypothesis, however, seems to have been negated by the enormous use of the term during the post–World War II period, which for the most part was the period of the Cold War, which implies a psychic balm role akin to that discussed in Essay 4.

The reader is encouraged to ask of each proposed candidate for the identity of the invisible hand, whether that candidate can have the qualifications that enable it to do what is expected of the invisible hand as, one supposes, given by the array of putative functions of the invisible hand. Although a candidate may have a more-or-less ubiquitous presence, that presence alone may be insufficient for the performance of one or more functions. The Appendix to this essay contains some examples of dissection, or deconstruction, in which I endeavor to show how a scholar, examining a manuscript at arm's length, can disentangle any confusion, in the process enabling the author of the manuscript to reword his or her text so as to make the desired point.

"The market" is one of several widely used identifications of the invisible hand. It is not surprising that several combinations of market, price system, and competition are also widely used. The price system is almost a synonym for the market; to that extent, the market price system is redundant. The competitive market system or competitive price system, or competitive market price system are also found in the literature. When, on the rare occasion, I have been asked what the invisible hand is, I will say it is the competitive market – unless I have the time to elaborate.

These widely used candidates for the title of the invisible hand may be obvious to most people but they are not without serious complications – a state characterizing the totality of the identifications, as each may be considered a substitute for one or more others. This is illustrated by the relatively longer discussion of several candidates.

The "market" as the invisible hand is such a rich concept that even without the introduction of the invisible hand, it could be considered the foundation of western modern social science. Yet even then it is rarely thought of in that manner.

The market as the invisible hand, however, encounters several very deep and important problems. We need only to identify them in outline form (as we do with other candidates for the identity of the invisible hand) in order to suggest the difficulties that confront the candidacy of the market to be the invisible hand.

There is no one market, and no one market necessarily produces the "best solutions." To elicit the importance of the point, one only has to query of someone who argues that "the market works" the balloon-puncturing question: "Which market?" This is similar to asking a devotee of the "rule of law": "Which law?"

The market under consideration can be a pure conceptual market or an actual market. Purely conceptual markets do not exist, and actual markets are due to the institutions that form and operate through them, that is, markets as the consequence, cause, and/or vehicle of power. This is true whether the analyses of Alfred Chandler, Ronald Coase, or Gardiner Means, for example, are followed. In each case, markets are in part a function of firms and their influence on or control of government; simultaneously, firms are a function of markets. Business strategy and induced change in relevant law are primary factors in how markets are "made." This situation could possibly stand for the identity problem as a whole: The invisible hand is caught up in a host of situations that challenge the proposed identity and render ambiguous and nondispositive the role claimed for the invisible hand. If business has a role in the making of markets and if markets "work," then markets *pro tanto* give effect to business strategy. The role attributed to markets then would seem to be taken over by competition; but, as will be seen immediately following,, this does not solve the problem.

Another problem is whether markets operate on their own or conditionally upon some structural or other feature.

Markets are sometimes interpreted in terms of natural selection. This means that markets are both selection processes and the result of selection.

In certain respects, markets exhibit characteristics of a mechanism, in others, of an institution, and in still others, of a process.

Those people who think the market is the invisible hand occasionally use language that seemingly modifies that formulation. Among the examples to be found in the literature are the following: The invisible hand is not the market but the hand of the market, the market as controlled by the invisible hand, and so on.

Much of the literature that examines the market (and other features) linguistically identifies the invisible hand as a metaphor. Some of those who identify the invisible hand as a metaphor also identify the market as a metaphor, leading to the awkward result in which one metaphor is employed to identify another metaphor. Serious linguistic problems will be taken up in Essay 6.

We must also note several things that are almost never said in public and even rarely in private: That the market of free trade may indeed look like it is behaving like an invisible hand, but it may be both giving effect to and obfuscating an invisible imperialism of trade, commerce, indirect control, and, as had been said of Great Britain in the nineteenth century and of the United States and its partner, United Fruit Company, in the twentieth century, even direct control. Ronald Reagan, I recall, invoked the market to explain away his inaction in the face of OPEC production controls. They were what led to the price in the market but it was not *the* market price. Similarly with capital flows: What governs is not the market alone but the structure of power making and operating through the market power process. Money flows to where money can be made, but it is not the market alone that controls this; it is national policy. Conversely, it is not the "free market" that punishes "evildoers"; equally likely it is their tool. Do markets know best or work best when they are tools of power and reflect power? This applies within nations and between nations – almost always worded in support of, and by, the winning side. Nationalism and its synonyms tend in actual situations to trump economic liberalism and political relativism, doing so by invoking *raison d'état* and *realpolitik*. This may all be blamed on the breakdown of the mentality of Naturalism (Natural Law, Natural Rights), but that too is a mode of trumping relativism. There is no single transcendent character of markets or of rights; there are multiples in each category.

We have already glimpsed the price system, which may or may not be equated in people's minds with the market, and the relation of price system and/or market to competition. Some people posit the invisible hand to be the price system; others posit competition to be the invisible hand. Thus some believe that markets by their very nature are competitive. The idea of competition, often if not typically left undefined, is otherwise given a number of different definitions such that two "competitive" situations may be contradictory. One group of definitions tends to be concerned with structural features and another with behavioral ones. In that situation, rivalry will tend to be competitive by the behaviorist approach but noncompetitive by the structuralist approach. The traditional approach attributed to Adam

Smith tends to be that in which competition is a large enough number of economic agents on each side of the market that neither one agent nor one side (demanders or suppliers) has an effect on price. Competition can be between all buyers and/or all sellers, or between all demanders on one side of the market and all suppliers on the other side of the market, but not all economists will agree with each of those connotations. Further surveying the history of economic thought, economists have differentiated pure competition, perfect competition, small-number and large-number competition, monopolistic competition, countervailing power, and so on, including some combinations thereof.

Again, ambiguity, inconclusiveness, and nondispositive with regard to the function the invisible hand is supposed to perform renders analysis so open-ended as to be lacking in substance. This situation is rendered even more ambiguous and inconclusive when courts take up the meaning of competition in cases brought under the antitrust laws. The notion of "relevant market" is one such complication.

So much for the market, the price mechanism, competition, and so on. The literature also includes such formulations as choice in a market, the profit motive, private enterprise, free enterprise, and private property. Choice in a market is somewhat like markets being necessarily competitive. The individual who faces an oligopolistic or monopolistic market is not unlike the individual who must buy under a regime of managerial or central planning. The significance of choice in a market varies with the potential consequence of that choice. In an economy in which output is produced by managerial or central plan, the individual consumer can choose from among what is made available, but that is different from the exercise of choice that has some effect on what is produced and is available for sale. A number of writers, most notably John Kenneth Galbraith, have argued that instead of markets translating demand into supply, present-day markets translate supply into demand. The profit motive may be no different to the user than the motive of gain or of self-interest.

Private property is probably used more by those authors who desire to use the luster of the invisible-hand idea to promote private property, or vice versa, than by people with a different objective. The idea of private property is itself a candidate for the invisible hand, depending on one's preferences as to what the invisible-hand story is all about. Private property is a means through which or with which to engage in trade or participate in a market. The institution of private property must be distinguished from particular rights of property. Property rights are a means of controlling or checking the power of government. However, the power of government is a means for determining what will and what will not be protected as private property and the range of protection given individual choice. In that respect, "private" property is every bit also "public" property. Issues of the continuity or change of existing rights seem nefarious to potential losers of rights but legitimate to those whose exposure under the existing law of property is nefarious. Change of rights constituting property must be understood in the light of several circumstances: recognition that externalities are reciprocal in nature; change in the values of people in society; business control of government and thus of private property; and the nuances of the institution of property in a world of inequality.

The ubiquity of standardized contracts or contracts of adhesion is largely ignored by most people, including most economists. These are contracts in which one side and one side only specifies its terms, without the possibility of bargaining to change those terms, in which the noncontract-writing party can only take it or leave it.

The term "self-interest" is one of the most widely cited identities given the invisible hand. Nonetheless, the identification of the invisible hand as self-interest contradicts the perhaps even more widely held idea that rather than self-interest constituting the invisible hand, it is the task of the invisible hand to control self-interest. In such case, the invisible hand might in principle be any candidate comprehensive and powerful enough to control self-interest. Further aspects will be considered in Essay 5.

The term "entrepreneurship" or its equivalent has been proposed as the invisible hand largely, but by no means entirely, in the late twentieth century. An early emphasis on the social role of whatever entrepreneurship was taken to mean is not the same thing as calling it the invisible hand, which became an arguably more common activity much more recently.

As might now be expected by the reader, a number of distinctions and other problems have arisen in discussions of the identity of the invisible hand. One intractable problem is whether the topic under discussion is a person or a function. Some people have insisted that the notion of entrepreneurship (used to avoid the issues of comparison) to be significant must apply to a group of people who perform the functions of entrepreneurship, ergo are the entrepreneurs. Other people insist that entrepreneurship is a function more or less performed by most, if not all, persons in their capacities as economic agents. The foregoing consideration also turns in part on the specific entrepreneurial function one has in mind, that is, what makes an entrepreneur an entrepreneur as opposed to something (or someone) else. Historically, a difference between entrepreneur(ship) and capitalist has been important to European thinkers, with the entrepreneur providing decisional skills and the capitalist the financing. Increasingly the growth of the large corporation in which high-level employees have their positions for reasons other than ownership or provision of capital has rendered more or less significant the distinction between ownership and control. Another aspect, now decreasing, is that of adventure, in which capitalism is comprehended as a civilized game of power in money form rather than violence. (I do not believe that there is a case in my records in which entrepreneurship along such lines has been identified as the invisible hand.) Whereas attention has been given to college and university presidents and others as educational entrepreneurs, to politicians and government officials as political entrepreneurs, and athletic team officials, including owners and managing partners, as sports entrepreneurs, I know of no case of one of them being called a manifestation of the invisible hand, though I would not be surprised to come across one or more who had.

A different line of demarcation has arisen between understanding entrepreneurship in terms of niche finding and niche creating, or between passive actor versus active agent of change. Along a different but not entirely isolated line is the use of the term entrepreneur(ship) to identify a system-specific honorific channel of achievement motivation or designation of achievement.

Thus far I have not specified the forms which entrepreneurship can take – for example, the specific meaning of the concept whether deemed to apply to a function or to persons, or to some persons or all. Humberto Barreto, in his book, *The Entrepreneur in Microeconomic Theory* (1989), has identified the specific activities or functions that have, for different economic theorists, defined the term. These include the entrepreneur as coordinator (within a particular theory of production and distribution); as arbitrageur (within a particular theory of human action); as innovator; as bearer of uncertainty; as speculator; and as owner, with a concluding emphasis on bearer of uncertainty. The individual theorists whose work was concentrated on by Barreto were Jean-Baptiste Say, Israel Kirzner, Joseph Schumpeter, Frank Knight, Richard Cantillon, and Frederick Barnard Hawley.

A symposium on entrepreneurship in a special issue of the *Journal of Interdisciplinary Economics* was received as this essay was initially being written. Hoo Sook Lee, the editor of that issue, treated entrepreneurship as a principal source of economic growth, concerned with commercializing new products and services. Lee (2007) emphasizes that entrepreneurship "is a major driver of technological advancement and a primary source of wealth creation not only to those who undertake it ... but also to the society at large." Lee also writes that "In a generic sense, all firms undertaking entrepreneurship follow a common set of processes: they all engage in identifying, evaluating and exploiting opportunities for wealth creation and growth" (Lee 2007: 113). Further, he examines how "variation in entrepreneurial characteristics exists across cultures … and … how sub-national institutional factors can impact variability of empirical studies." A quite different perspective is offered by Scott A. Shane (2008), who stresses "the illusions of entrepreneurship" and "the costly myths that entrepreneurs, investors and policy makers live by."

Another pair of candidates is the economic system per se and Smith's system of natural liberty. Most writers interested in the identity of the invisible hand seem to feel that a totalist specification is too much and thereby too little. The invisible hand may have a systemic emphasis; however, that emphasis may lack precision and determinateness. To speak of the invisible hand of capitalism is not unlike speaking of the invisible hand of the market: In both cases, is it the market (capitalism) that is or has an invisible hand; in both cases, the language of invisible hands serves to obfuscate power and its exercise. Smith's "system" has greater breadth and open-endedness than is acknowledged by conventional interpretations, especially the ideological ones.

One possibility of a systemic identity is that of an interactive adjustment process, which, for example, produces harmony, order, self-regulation, and so on. The same is true of a system that has a specifically informational nature. An informational system would presumably operate to provide knowledge with which to constrain ignorance and uncertainty, a point that can be made independent of the definition or model of those terms. Such identities seem closer to invisible-hand processes than others.

An identity seemingly relevant to several of the foregoing comprises the spontaneous-order principle and the principle of unintended and unforeseen consequences of Friedrich Hayek. Hayek argues that order can be achieved spontaneously if decision making is principally nondeliberative rather than deliberative. Accordingly, Hayek prefers institutions that originate and evolve nondeliberatively. A number of problems seem to render Hayek's analysis nugatory. One problem is that there is no such thing as an institution that is nondeliberative. As articulated by Carl Menger, a founder of the Hayekian Austrian-school analysis, it is the burden of every generation to deliberatively critique and reform received institutions. If an institution or proto-institution arises in period one, given Menger's principle, each institution will in each subsequent period both evolve nondeliberatively and be reformed deliberatively. It is therefore impossible to adopt Hayek's scheme without accepting deliberatively making choices, which are within the ambit of Menger's model and which contradicts Hayek's. Another problem is that the domain of putatively spontaneous activity is always within the system of moral and legal rules, rules that partly produce that activity, rules that are always subject to change. Hayek's final formulation relies on the concept of the rule of law, a concept itself manifesting the foregoing problems, suggested by once again posing the questions of (1) which laws form the rule of law and (2) which are to be changed – which content is precisely the point at issue and a process that is inevitably in part deliberative.

A candidate for the identity of the invisible hand that is perhaps implicit in the three preceding candidates is that of an interactive adjustment process. It is also at the core of what are called invisible-hand processes. Game theory in general and prisoners' dilemma relationships are common examples. Game theory, however, is not a perfect substitute for competition. It can seem to be like a complexity theory.

One characteristic of the literature on the invisible hand is the numerous authors who have attempted to adopt, and also to adapt to or transform, something from a new area or a new version of past work and convert it into a candidate for the invisible hand, or something like it. Natural selection has been a particularly attractive area in which economists and others have sought to derive lines of thinking, modes of change, and congenial results. That so many and so varied a group of natural-selection modes of reasoning have been developed suggests the protean nature and potential heuristic value of the Darwinian approach and reminds us of the protean nature of other candidates, yet may well be inconclusive because of the variety of natural-selection lines of reasoning. Nowhere is it established, however, that natural selection cannot properly yield such variety. A complementary point is the absence of any independent test with which to ascertain which is the correct candidate for the identity of the invisible hand; which of these variegated lines of reasoning is correct if in fact natural selection is recognized to be the invisible hand; and indeed, whether there is an invisible hand, either in fact or for experimental or hypothetical purposes.

Intersubjectivity is another candidate for the identity of the invisible hand. Conventional microeconomic theorists, often by explicit premise, have tended to explicitly postulate that individual economic agents are ignorant of each others' preferences and knowledge. In the event, some theorists now maintain that the basis of mutual knowledge does exist; such would, or at least might, constitute intersubjectivity. For economic agents to have mutual knowledge, intersubjectivity would be a productive premise. If all this were operative, it might be possible to contemplate that intersubjectivity is the invisible hand. Whether intersubjectivity is strong enough to carry the weight often attributed to the invisible hand is quite another matter. It may be neither strong enough nor ubiquitous enough to carry the burden that the devotees of the invisible hand would posit for their particular purposes.

It may be the case that intersubjectivity is at the bottom of several arguments emphasized by Adam Smith himself. These include condition bettering, status emulation, recognition and approval, the famous "deception," and also the key concept of sympathy of his *Theory of Moral Sentiments*. The desire of every individual to better their condition presupposes that every individual knows what will better their condition (a psychological relationship) in their own eyes and in the eyes of others; today we might say in the eyes of one's peers or reference group or significant others. This also applies to status emulation as such, perhaps broken down and motivated by a desire for recognition and approval. It will do to quote Adam Smith, who, in a sense, motivated all that is done within the covers of this book, and who tells us of

[t]he poor man's son, whom heaven in its anger has visited with ambition, when he begins to look around him, admires the condition of the rich .... He thinks [that] if he had attained all [the good things of life], he would sit still contentedly, and be quiet, enjoying himself in the thought of the happiness and tranquility of his situation. He is enchanted with the distant idea of this felicity .... With the most unrelenting industry he labours night and day to acquire talents superior to all his competitors.... For this purpose he makes his court to all mankind; he serves those whom he hates, and is obsequious to those whom he despises. Through the whole of his life he pursues the idea of a certain artificial and elegant repose which he may never arrive at, for which he sacrifices a real tranquility that is at all times in his power, and which, if in the extremity of old age he should at last attain to it, he will find to be in no respect preferable to that humble security and contentment which he had abandoned for it. It is then, in the last dregs of life, his body wasted with toil and diseases, his mind galled and ruffled by the memory of a thousand injuries and disappointments which he imagines he has met with from the injustice of his enemies, or from the perfidy and ingratitude of his friends, that he begins at last to find that wealth and greatness are mere trinkets of frivolous utility.... [The good things of life] do not require that their masters should point out to us wherein consists their utility. Of our own accord we readily enter into it, and by sympathy enjoy and thereby applaud the satisfaction which they are fitted to afford him.... They are therefore less reasonable subjects of vanity than the magnificence of wealth and greatness; and in this consists the sole advantage of these last. They more effectually gratify that love of distinction so natural to man.... But in the languor of disease and the weariness of old age, the pleasures of the vain and empty distinctions of greatness disappear. To one, in this situation, they are no longer capable of recommending those toilsome pursuits in which they had formerly engaged him. In his heart he curses ambition, and vainly

regrets the ease and the indolence of youth, pleasures which are fled for ever, and which he has foolishly sacrificed for what, when he has got it, can afford him no real satisfaction.... Power and riches appear then to be, what they are, enormous and operose machines contrived to produce a few trifling conveniences to the body.... But [i]f we consider the real satisfaction which all these things are capable of affording, by itself and separated from the beauty of that arrangement which is fitted to promote it, it will always appear in the highest degree contemptible and trifling. We naturally confound it in our imagination with the order, the regular and harmonious movement of the system, the machine or economy by which it is produced. The pleasures of wealth and greatness, when considered in this complex view, strike the imagination as something grand and beautiful and noble, of which the attainment is well worth all the toil and anxiety which we are so apt to bestow upon it.

And it is well that nature imposes upon us in this manner. It is this deception which rouses and keeps in continual motion the industry of mankind. (Smith 1976a: IV.i.8–10, 181–183)

The previous excerpt is from the lengthy prelude to Smith's use of the invisible-hand argument in the *Moral Sentiments*.

It may be submitted that bettering our condition, achieving social recognition and approval, successfully engaging in status emulation, and falling for the "deception which rouses and keeps in continual motion the industry of mankind" may well constitute the invisible hand. This suggestion – and it is no more than that – has the following in support: first, the proximity thereof to the use of the invisible-hand story in the *Moral Sentiments*; second, that one wants to be well thought of by one's peers; third, that people can appreciate the desirability of wealth being available for one's old age; and finally that all that is what the nature and origin of the *Wealth of Nations* is all about. All that is clearly Adam Smith, though one might well add that recognition of what in 1776 was the obvious and simple system of natural liberty is nothing less than, nothing more than, and nothing different from the values and definition of reality of a middle-class society.

Smith's emphasis on sympathy in the *Theory of Moral Sentiments*, identified by several authors as the invisible hand, points to a society with sufficient mutual trust, respect, and decency to have established a moral basis for the type of economy Smith seems to have applauded. Such a view would be consistent with Smith's tripartite model of society, namely moral rules, legal rules, and the market. Each would have been one of a larger number of possible economic systems inculcating their respective value systems through socialization into appropriate institutional individualist behavioral patterns. Moral rules will not only vary between nations with different power structures; reliance on an explanatory invisible hand may well obfuscate the role of power in governing which type of behavior receives recognition and social approval.

Natural selection has been chosen by numerous political and economic positions; it may well be the poster boy of the hermeneutic circle, insofar as the specific form of natural selection given effect is that of the Platonist policy claimants sitting around a fire in a cave. Speaking generally, however, "evolution" is typically defined in seemingly broad and inclusive terms but largely only as primitive terms, the more-or-less precise definition being supplied by each reader or auditor. The political and economic emphasis of natural selection is marginalism or incrementalism, one function of which is to torpedo radical, structural, or systemic change. Not all adherents to natural selection – what John R. Commons thought was, in human society, more artificial than natural selection – oppose incremental change; some decidedly favor serious structural change. As Thorstein Veblen insisted, natural selection was no more and no less than an application to institutions, ideas, habits, conventions, and custom.

Given the substance of the introductory chapters of Book I of the *Wealth of Nations*, it is not surprising that several key concepts developed therein have been proposed to be the invisible hand. These would include the division of labor, or specialization; the propensity to truck, barter, and exchange; the faculties of reason and speech; self-interest; noneconomic foundations; commercial society as a particular stage in economic development, opportunity, and advantage; the nature and source of human nature; rhetoric in the service of social recognition and moral approbation; and so on (Samuels 2004: chapter 1).

I next take up a diverse group of possible identities of the invisible hand, a group each one of which has been proposed to be the invisible hand. These are labor, consumer sovereignty, the credit system, and the Walrasian auctioneer.

Several of Smith's lines of reasoning lend themselves, singly or together, to support the proposed identification of labor as the invisible hand. These include labor as the (principal) source of income; the division of labor; labor as the real measure of exchange value; labor suitability to the demand for labor; the demand for labor favorable to population growth; labor's productivity enhanced by capital simultaneously with capital rendering labor unemployed; the wages of labor being a continued subject of contest between them and their masters; and so on (Smith 1976b: 1049–50).

The doctrine of consumer sovereignty has had a lengthy history but its having an explicit central place in the *Wealth of Nations* seems doubtful. Moreover, although Smith looked favorably upon the economic well-being of the mass of the people, he cannot be said to have adopted a line of reasoning that, in the guise of the sovereignty of consumers, served to exculpate the masters whose property hired labor and organized production. Around the onset of the second half of the twentieth century, the ideology that formed part of the belief system of the United States was bifurcated. The ideology originally promulgated by business stressed American individualism. To that ideology was added, after World War II, another, one that portrayed the businessman as playing the role of a sort of philosopher king arbitrating, as it were, between the various claimants of the (other) factors of production. Whereas the original ideology was deployed to deny or obfuscate the existence of business power, the later one attempted to openly defend that power (Sutton et al., 1956).

The credit system has been discussed and evaluated differently over the years, which obviously raises the question: If the invisible hand is the credit system, which credit system is it, or does it not matter? The credit system, both proposed and actual, has often been at the center of political and economic controversy in the United States. The elements of that system have engendered questions about and controversy over the relative roles of banks (and which type thereof), the several states of the Union, and the Federal government, the nature and basis of the supply of money, the conditions of issuance of money, who has access to new credit and the nature of that access, and so on. The elasticity (in the sense of variability) of the temporary solutions to those controversies renders highly unlikely, if not impossible, the identity of the invisible hand as the credit system. But if one accepts the importance of the credit system, given the monetary and banking standards in place, and if one accepts also that the performance of the system would include the foregoing issue, it seems reasonable for the credit system to be given the status of the invisible hand. It seems that very few persons have given it that status, and, more important, if one looks at credit as one form of money, then it would be the entire monetary system that properly was identified as the invisible hand. Perhaps more important, the divisiveness of the issues and unbending attitudes of people for or against various monetary and banking systems, and the nature, rules, and limits of their existence, would prevent serious consideration of them as the invisible hand. Of course, if the money supply (including credit) adequately funded economic growth, the case would be strengthened. But such further questions as the definition and roles of money supply, credit, and reserves would likely deny the attribution.

Perhaps the most remarkable, even startling, candidate proposed for invisible-hand status is the auctioneer in the general-equilibrium theory of

Leon Walras. Indeed, it is almost impossible to take the proposal seriously. The auctioneer was necessary to bring the Walrasian system to a close. Such a need is not congruent with most commonplace understandings of the invisible hand.

Still, insofar as the chair of the Federal Reserve Board in recent years has actively controlled the money supply and the conditions of its supply, as well as the fate, shall we say, of the banking industry, the housing industry, and the firms' remortgage market, and insofar as this has pointed to "saving" the financial system (or industry) and even the economic system, both this and the proposed identity immediately preceding take on credibility. Such an explicit position, would, however, be abrasive to the believers in automaticity and laissez-faire.

The next two candidates for the identity of the invisible hand are capital accumulation and technology. It is difficult to know several things: How much, if in fact at all, did Smith understand the industrial revolution, one aspect of which is the nature and rate of technological change, during, say, the last thirty or forty years of his life? Another aspect encompasses what he understood, and did not understand, about the processes of political revolution, its nature, direction, and rate of change. It is difficult for contemporary historians of economic and/or political thought to have a confident, meaningful sense of his views of revolution and of aspects of the cumulative interactions between them a quarter of a millennium ago.

Because we do not know and, with the possible exception of (some) economic historians, likely do not have even a sense of all that, it is hazardous to force the issue. Two things we can do: First, we can seek evidence, notably from what he wrote and did not write, to which we can add whatever insight we can discern from Smith's lectures on jurisprudence. Second, we can try to establish what we would need to know in order to have something more confident to say. All this would be in aid of reaching a judgment as to the probative value of capital accumulation and/or technology being designated the invisible hand.

Of course, Smith is not the only relevant thinker whose ideas can be considered. Karl Marx and Thorstein Veblen, the latter perhaps as revised by Clarence Ayres, have identified technology (or what may be reduced to technology) as a driving force. Ayres, at least during certain periods of the development and expression of his ideas, distinguished technology from institutions, holding that the former was progressive and the latter inhibitive or antagonistic to progress. Ayres did not, however, provide any system by which one could be differentiated from the other. And, of course, none of these men would expound their ideas in the language of the invisible hand;

that term was too ideological, too much associated with religion, and too orthodox in economics.

For analytical, or hypothetical, purposes, the *Wealth of Nations* can be converted from an argument concerning the nature of wealth (Smith's antimercantilism) and its origins to a simple but straightforward model of those categories. Wealth is reduced to consumable goods and the capital goods used in their production. The causes of improvement of those consumable goods are the division of labor, as limited by the extent of the market, the use of money, and the freedom of trade (which, for practical purposes, we can stipulate as the absence of the extraordinary encouragements of exports and the extraordinary discouragements of imports). Capital accumulation and technology would be both consequence and cause of economic growth. Whether that situation is sufficient to designate capital accumulation and technological improvement the invisible hand is difficult to say. Perhaps the two should be combined with entrepreneurship to identify the invisible hand.

Several scholars writing on what is required for economic growth have suggested that the critical variable is having a group of people with an interest in, and the ability and power to organize for, the production of the goods that constitute economic growth. The scholars may or may not have as boldly expressed the point as I do here. But if the argument is correct, that group might well constitute the invisible hand. I say *might* and not *would* because neither of Smith's economic uses clearly and unequivocally amounts to that. In the *Moral Sentiments*, the hiring of the poor by the rich is not said to staff factories. In the *Wealth of Nations*, the increase in risk to foreign investment redistributes economic activity from one sphere or nation to another, and *ceteris paribus*, any net change in either direction likely would be small.

The next candidate for the identity of the invisible hand is positive externalities. At first glance, one wonders why or how positive externalities can be the identity of the invisible hand. Presumably their candidacy would turn on the relation of positive externalities in one or more of the functions attributed to the individual hand. A second glance, therefore, at the list of identities both already covered and yet to be covered may suggest that numerous other candidates have characteristics (good results, beneficial outcomes) amounting to positive externalities. It is a rather ingenious finding. The problem is that it is tautological. It does not account for the "other side" of positive externalities, namely negative externalities or bad results – the same situation with the Ayres-Veblen dichotomy and with those Hayekians and others who credit the invisible hand for the beneficent result.

The historical process, final cause, nature, and God are the penultimate candidates proposed to be the invisible hand. If any one or more of these had satisfying supporting evidence, they presumably would make a strong candidate. Of the four, the historical process, if one exists, might derive from nature and/or God and constitute a final cause except for the other three. It is possible, however, to discern an historical process that is not derived from some combination of the other three. In the eighteenth century, naturalism did not replace supernaturalism; for the first time in western history, naturalism had an explanatory status that hitherto had been associated only with religion. Historically, all four were imperfect substitutes for each other. Moreover, the other three seem to have been eclipsed by the notion of a God who was the final cause of the historical process and nature. The two critical problems with the attribution of the invisible-hand status to God are, first, the matter of evidence vis-à-vis faith, and second, the connection of any of the four with the array of invisible-hand functions discussed in the next subsection (3.3). Even if one accepts a God who created the universe and everything in it and who also takes an active role in the life of society and of individuals, it is difficult, first, to explain variation in culture, institutions, and, perhaps, human nature, and second, that a Deity would be interested in the allocation of resources to the production of fish and country homes and the allocation of victories in athletic contests between, say, the University of Michigan and Michigan State University.

Overriding much of the preceding discussion is the Problem of Job. That Jacob Viner, considered one of the foremost historians of economic thought of the twentieth century, late in life changed his opinion from the invisible hand not being God to being God has entranced many believers and some nonbelievers but has left other believers feeling that it was about time he saw the light, and nonbelievers that the change was related to a gamble with God. Aspects of these candidacies will be taken up throughout this book.

We come, at last, to the candidacy of institutions as the invisible hand, either institutions in general or – more commonly, I think – governmental institutions. It is possible to contemplate that, for example, God or nature operates to produce the invisible hand in the form of institutions. If the invisible hand can be one or more of the previous candidates, then it seems odd that institutions would be excluded. However, the suggestion that institutions, especially governmental institutions, are the invisible hand has a delicious irony about it. The reason is that for many users, the role of the invisible hand as social control is that of trumping and rendering relatively immune to change all existing arrangements, especially institutions. Viner and Lionel Robbins held rather comparable views on economic policy, but

where Viner finally settled on God as the invisible hand, Robbins identified
the role of the statesman to be the invisible hand.

Consider the vast array of uses of the concept of the invisible hand. A
program examining the CIA was broadcast on the Discovery Channel on
American television during the evening of November 25, 1997. A speaker
addressed the invisible hand as the exercise of covert power at a distance,
saying, "The CIA has been the invisible hand of American power for half
a century." A somewhat similar point was made in the *New York Times* in
The Caucus Blog, August 24, 2008 (4:36 PM, The NYTimes.com). Under
the title, "Preparing for Protests," Kirk Johnson wrote, "Security at the
Democratic National Convention is mostly in the hands of the United
States Secret Service, which prides itself on a kind of invisible-hand style:
understated, dark-suited, always on alert."

In the late 1970s, I undertook an analysis of the operation and significance of the takings clause of the Fifth Amendment to the United States
Constitution. While studying court cases, I also interviewed officials of the
government of the State of Michigan. One view that emerged (on both sides
of the normative issue) was that many more "takings" existed from which
no litigation emerged than the relative handful of cases that were brought
and decided by courts. With the "non-case" in mind, it seems worthwhile to
note that some possible identifications or attributions have not been made,
or at least I have not found instances of them: the interest rate, the marginal
efficiency of capital, and the multiplier-accelerator interaction effect, for
example, have not, to my knowledge, been identified as candidates for
invisible-hand status. The only explanation I can find is that the invisible
hand strongly tends to be a concept of a certain type of orthodoxy, whereas
the examples just given were mostly from Keynesian economics (either not
orthodoxy or a different type). Even during the heyday of Keynesian economics, its status as orthodoxy was still sufficiently weak as to preclude
Keynesians from adopting such an orthodox concept.

It is apparently easy to be recruited into the ranks of the believers in
the existence of the invisible hand and become a searcher for it. It has
never been shown, however, that an economic invisible hand exists. Nor
has it been shown that calling something the invisible hand adds anything to knowledge. Undoubtedly each of the candidates for the identity
of the invisible hand is an important factor in the economy; but singly or
together, they do not have the causal significance, or function, conventionally attributed to the invisible hand. Moreover, the fact that more than four
dozen identifications of the invisible hand have been made both renders
the exercise highly dubious and suggests that what is involved is soothing

the imagination for people who require determinacy and closure and/or for ideological purposes. Also involved, of course, is the use of a chosen identity of the invisible hand to legitimize certain institutions and other factors, and not others.

3.3. The Functions of the Invisible Hand

This essay comprises a substantial array of purported identities of the invisible hand. It is here that no conclusive test exists of the identity of the invisible hand. Indeed, it is further argued that there is no independent test that demonstrates either the existence of an invisible hand or identifies the invisible hand. It is also argued that the several dozen purported identities of the invisible hand results in ambiguity. It is further suggested that apropos of the multiple purported functions said to be performed by specifically identified invisible hands, each function can be understood in a number of ways, and that one result of such multiplicity is ambiguity; further, no independent test connects the putative performance of any of the functions to their purported genesis, and the results in all respects are ambiguity and inconclusiveness. Of course, if there no invisible hand (see Essays 6 and 7), all these considerations pretty much dissolve and evaporate into the air.

Much invisible-hand reasoning assumes the invisible hand to be a definition of reality, as well as part of the social belief system operating as psychic balm and social control. The invisible hand projected by such reasoning is believed to be in part about the economy but is also of the economy, part of the process of working things out. The rhetoric or belief system of the invisible hand is a self-projection of western civilization and the modern economy – an aspect of culture that resonates with, reflects, and reinforces other aspects. Such raises questions of self-reflexivity and, with Knight, whether objective thinking about an economy is possible by a person within an economy. The multiplicity of identifications of the invisible hand raises problem of philosophical realism: When (arguably) everyone accepts the putative reality of an invisible hand but differs as to its identity, the result is not only ambiguity but inconclusiveness. Virtually all of it is pure assertion, especially if the invisible hand is a figure of the imagination to soothe the imagination (of others).

The story is in the details. It is an exceedingly wide-ranging and complex story, so the details are mountainous. It is, however, a mountain of ubiquity, a ubiquity of assertion and interpretation. The study of the invisible hand is a study of human beliefs, not necessarily the nature of man other than its need to believe. It is a study of society and economy, and of the universe ("nature") – though useful in social construction of reality in both senses (construction per se plus interpretation)

The story encompasses several important tensions and numerous minor ones, all contested terrain: tension between the "free market" as alternative to systems of government control and the necessity and inevitability of social control and of fundamental economic roles of government; tension between public and private governance; tension between the "free market" and social control, with the former a system of plutocratic, capitalist domination; tension between the need to work out market decisions and the need to work out governmental-legal decisions; tensions between systems of social control.

3.3.1. Order

One function attributed to the invisible hand is the creation of *order*. Every society projects a sense of order as part of its subjective system of belief and it is accepted by people who think that such an order is congruent with their own. This sense of order romanticizes and legitimizes, in each respect giving effect to the self-image, power structure, and belief system of the regnant social order. As the variety of conceptions of order is compared, its thoroughgoing subjectivity is manifest. The projection of order can focus on a state of affairs or on a particular process. The two – state and process – can be mixed. Those nominally on the state side must provide some place for change – say, change congruent with the system or change. Those on the process side must identify some necessary principles that persist even with change.

In Essay 2, I referred to Joseph Spengler's view of the problem of order, which is continually being resolved through reconciliations between freedom (or autonomy) and control, between continuity and change, and between equality and hierarchy. His presently relevant points are, first, that in the nature of things, as it were, the conflict within each pair (including their particular specifications) must be worked out, and will not be so once and for all time; and, second, that in every society, again by the natural order of things, both sides of each pair will be found.

3.3.2. Automaticity

Another function attributed to the invisible hand is its automatic realization of the order that it takes as a given and projects. Order without automaticity is self-negating. Automatic self-regulation and adjustment is a particular feature of economic order.

3.3.3. Coordination

The nuances of order and automaticity are particular features of coordination in an economic system. Nonetheless, the meaning of coordination, the identity of what is coordinated, and coordination in relation to equilibrium, self-regulation, and harmony are both important and varied, corresponding, I should think, with the interests and agendas of the individual author.

The concepts of order, automaticity, coordination, self-regulation, equilibrium, and harmony are mutually reinforcing. This reinforcement is especially dramatic in an economic context, all the more so when these concepts are associated with markets. The reinforcement may always be the case or only sometimes be so; the reinforcement may be conditional, problematic, and/or subject to limits.

The terms "order" and "coordination" imply social control; even the market is an institution of social control, all of which conflicts with the imagery of "freedom," with respect to which tropes like "freedom within order" are seemingly calculated to terminate conflict, preclude deeper study of what is going on, and provide the bait with which to catch people with different views. Socialization into society is one thing; for it to be so close to what many believe is the fundamental principle of an advanced discipline is quite another, especially when it is used to inculcate an extreme version of an already skewed ideology.

3.3.4. Equilibrium

The term most closely associated with economics is equilibrium. Yet over the generations it has been given multiple definitions, the most common of which is the equilibrium of demand and supply through price and quantity. More subtle formulations have embraced and given effect to intentions, plans, and consequential economic actions, further complicated by variations and asymmetries in knowledge and expectations, emergent equilibrium paths, tight priori equilibria, and so on. Equilibrium can be defined as reality (actual equilibrium or equilibrating process), general harmony, beneficence, stability, and the like.

As intriguing as the foregoing functions are, the remaining ones are even more fascinating in respect to economic theory.

3.3.5. General Harmony and Benevolence

This group may be the most esoteric and abstract of all the functions. It amounts to preaching that the system is not only orderly but harmonious and, further, benevolent to all. It is difficult to say what the test of this function might be. To the claim that the masses are not in revolt, the response would be that this is because they have accepted, consciously or unconsciously, the claim advanced by this and perhaps other function. The objective of this function is to convince people that the status quo is harmonious and benevolent. The distinctions must be made between actual and desired and between independently given (real as in philosophical realism) and created by mankind, with respect to the existing system.

3.3.6. Harmony of/among Self-Interests

This function goes beyond the preceding function to claim that not only are general harmony and benevolence characteristic of the existing system, but harmony exists among and between individuals. As between individuals, the claim is that well-being is maximized for all participants in the economy. The basis of that is typically that of the next function, Pareto optimality. This function is typically stated in terms of individuals, but some authors have stated the function in terms of classes, nations, sections, and groups. Along with the others of this group, its claims are particularly ambitious. At best it would apply to a system in which every aspect of life is a matter of trade. The problem here, as with most of the other functions, is that market activity, to Smith, the acclaimed father of all this, is supplemented by the other two domains, namely moral and legal rules.

3.3.7. Pareto Optimality

This function is a major claim. It asserts that when gains from trade have been exhausted, the maximum welfare for the group has been achieved. Otherwise trading would take place. Most authors write in terms of trade between goods and services, but some do so in terms of bargaining over votes. The application of general Pareto optimality is often expressed in terms of such criteria as unanimity, consent, voluntarism, consensus, and freedom. Some authors apply Pareto optimality to government and the bargaining therein. A principal problem is that no unique determinate Pareto optimality exists. There is a Pareto optimal result conceivable for each distribution of property and other rights, such that the claim is reduced to a defense of the existing system and its distribution of property and other rights, rights that regularly are subject to change.

3.3.8. Harmony of Self-Interest with Social Interest, or Welfare

Although some authors are not happy with the notion that there is a social interest or a social welfare, quite a few authors write in terms of the harmony of self-interests with the social interest. This, the harmony of self-interests with the social interest, and not the harmony of self-interests, is the case with Adam Smith who, in the invisible-hand passage of the *Wealth of Nations*, uses the term "*publick interest*" and writes of the individual being "led by an invisible hand to promote . . . that [welfare] of the society" (Smith 1976b: I.ii.9, 456). This is the general theme of the book, although Smith and later writers tend to be casual about the matter. For Smith and most later writers, the directional flow is from the individual and his interest to the social interest; for a relative few, however, the flow is from the social interest to the individual interest. Smith never says what he means to be the public interest, just as he does not say anything about the identity of the invisible hand. The conflicts since Smith have focused on what is the proper usage, the substance of social welfare, whether society can and should be considered an independent entity, directional flow, the social interest as the sum of all private interests, and what amounts to whether the social interest is something given or something to be worked out. The difference between a harmony of self-interests and a harmony of self-interests with the social interest is rarely recognized in the literature.

3.3.9. Economic Performance

One meaning of social interest could be some specification of economic performance. It is difficult to come away from the *Wealth of Nations* not thinking that the goal of the book is the growth of output. A good many authors adopt some formulation of economic performance as the one that the invisible hand, however identified, promotes. Among the formulations of economic performance are satisfaction, utility, production, value of output, welfare, exchange, happiness, wealth, social rationality, and others, including the growth of physical output. Among the other topics interwoven with those formulations of economic performance are growth, resource allocation, efficiency, best allocation of resources, optimality in general, Pareto optimality, stability, economic progress, and distribution. Rarely will one find an extended discussion of these matters in the invisible-hand literature.

In the decades following World War II, the advances associated with the several Nobel Prize awards identified in Essay 1 supported the idea that in fully eliciting the meaning of the invisible hand, economists would have a refined concept with which to conduct their analyses. Among the problems that arose were differences in articulation of the meaning of "refinement" and on the realism of such a refined corpus of theory; whether refining the analysis trivializes what goes on in an economy; whether it is formal rather than substantive; and whether the refined analysis could meaningfully be applied to a socialist economy. On all these and on all other points economists adopted diverse positions.

3.4. Conclusion

Several statements of conclusion are warranted.

1. The purported identifications of the invisible hand have by themselves nothing to warrant any one or more of them to conclusively succeed in arriving at the invisible hand.
2. Many, if not all, of the most widely held candidates have sufficient problems either to succeed at all or to constitute a case for any of them actually being the invisible hand.
3. It is not outside the realm of the imagination that one of the popularly held identifications – or some other candidate for that matter – might well be taken as being the invisible hand. However, the choice of candidates seems to lack an independent test by which not only to choose the candidate but to ascertain beyond reasonable doubt that there is the invisible hand.
4. None of the candidates surveyed in this essay seems to have the singular and uncomplicated power to assuredly produce the functions typically adduced to the invisible hand. The conclusion seems warranted that the identities attributed to the invisible hand are incapable of producing those results.
5. In light of the foregoing lines of reasoning, problems, evidence, and conclusions, the question must be considered as to whether the invisible hand does exist.
6. All of the candidates for function are, in actuality, dependent on the structure of power for their specific performance. They are not unique.
7. The explication of price theory, for example, is reminiscent of mastering a catechism, and the professorial role is rather like that of the high priest – namely teaching and protecting the doctrine.

4

Adam Smith's *History of Astronomy* Argument

How Broadly Does It Apply? And Where Do
Propositions That "Sooth the Imagination"
Come From?

4.1. Introduction: The Principles That Lead and Direct
Philosophical Inquiries

In his *History of Astronomy* (Smith 1980), Adam Smith argues that
our imagination is disturbed by sentiments of wonder, surprise, and
admiration, owing, respectively, to new phenomena, the unexpected,
and the great or beautiful. Such disturbances induce philosophical (read:
scientific) inquiry into "the invisible chains which bind together all these
disjointed objects" to

introduce order into this chaos of jarring and discordant appearances, to allay
this tumult of the imagination, and to restore it ... to that tone of tranquility and
composure, which is both most agreeable in itself, and most suitable to its nature.
(Smith 1980: II.12, 45–46)

Such inquiries are undertaken "to sooth the imagination, and to render the
theatre of nature a more coherent, and therefore a more magnificent spectacle, than otherwise it would have appeared to be" (idem: II.12; 46).

The function of inquiry is to allay the tumult of the imagination, to soothe
the imagination. Thus, in his *History of the Ancient Physics*, the second of
Smith's three essays on the principles that lead and direct philosophical
inquiries, the motivation is again "[t]o introduce order and coherence into
the mind's conception ..." (Smith 1980: 107).

In their General Introduction to *Essays on Philosophical Subjects*, Raphael
and Skinner call attention to several important matters. One is Smith's practice of conjectural history, which resembles theoretical history, hypothesiz-
ing in the absence of direct evidence (Raphael and Skinner 1980: 3, 12; see
also Wightman 1980: 15). Raphael and Skinner treat the difference between
the philosopher and the ordinary man as due less to nature than to habit,

custom, and education (Raphael and Skinner 1980: 4; Smith 1976a: I.ii.4), relevant here because the principles and motivations are not restricted to the philosopher or scientist. As they express the point, "man is impelled to seek an explanation for observed 'appearances' as a result of a *subjective* feeling of discomfort, and that the resulting explanation or theory is therefore designed to meet some psychological need" (Raphael and Skinner 1980: 5).

Raphael and Skinner next consider the quest for truth. They point out that

Smith did not claim an *exclusive* role for the central principles of surprise, wonder, and admiration, but rather asserted that the part played by these sentiments was "of far wider extent than we should be apt upon a careless view to imagine." (idem: 12)

A system of natural philosophy or of moral philosophy "may appear very plausible, and be for a long time generally received in the world, and yet have no foundation in nature, nor any sort of resemblance to the truth" (Raphael and Skinner 1980: 12–13, quoting Smith 1976b, VII.ii.4.14). They conclude that "[p]assages such as these suggest that 'truth' *is* attainable while at the same time reminding us of the importance of opinion" (Raphael and Skinner 1980: 13).

To Raphael and Skinner, Smith argued that while truth is the premier objective, we very often have to be content merely with propositions that quiet and soothe the imagination. In any event, "different types of philosopher may produce conflicting accounts of the same phenomena" (idem: 14). Smith's theory itself can be given more than one reading. One is that just given: Truth is the desired objective, but we very often must settle for propositions that set minds at rest. Another reading is that truth is impossible, and we are left with multiple interpretations. Raphael and Skinner conclude: "What Smith does is to leave the reader of these essays in some doubt as to wherein exactly 'glory' is to be found: in a contribution to knowledge, or to the composure of the imagination, or both" (idem: 15).

The tension is clearly intentionally evident in Smith's concluding paragraph of the *History of Astronomy*, wherein he says, in regard to his treatment of Newton, that:

even we, while we have been endeavouring to represent all philosophical systems as mere inventions of the imagination, to connect together the otherwise disjointed and discordant phaenomena of nature, have insensibly been drawn in, to make use of language expressing the connecting principles of this one, as if they were[1] the real chains which Nature makes use of to bind together her several operations. (Smith 1980: IV.76)

Smith points explicitly or implicitly to several things, among others: taking the hypothetical to be the actual; reification; the naturalistic fallacy; and mere belief taken to be Truth. Important here is the tension between two uses of principles, or systems, to allay the tumult of the imagination and to define reality. In his Introduction to the *History of Astronomy*, Wightman records his judgment that:

in respect of its "systems" his [Smith's] inquiry was less about their truth than about "how far each of them was fitted to sooth(e) the imagination, and to render the theatre of nature a more coherent, and therefore a more magnificent spectacle, than otherwise it would have appeared to be." (Wightman 1980: 14, using II.12, quoted above)

Whatever the respective proportions of propositions (or uses of a single proposition) considered to allay the tumult of the imagination and considered to state the truth, it is clear that for Smith, the former proportion is large enough to warrant his attention and discussion.

Smith himself exemplifies the quest for propositions that close an explanation, or may be seen as doing so, and thus quiet the imagination. In a study of Smith's treatment of the origins of the division of labor, a surprising number of somewhat interrelated explanatory propositions are found in the *Wealth of Nations* against a background of conflicts and paradoxes (Samuels and Henderson 2004). The explanations for the division of labor can be identified as follows:

1. due to a propensity in human nature to truck, barter, and exchange;
2. due to the faculties of reason and speech;
3. pursuing opportunities in quest of advantage;
4. stage-specific behavior;
5. human nature;
6. rhetoric in the service of social recognition and moral approbation;
7. the use of first principles as postulates with which to explain what may ensue from them.

---

[1] The author is indebted to Ross Emmett, Jerry Evensky, Steven G. Medema, Leonidas Montes, and A. Allan Schmid for helpful comments on an earlier version of this paper. Leonidas Montes suggests that I should italicize for emphasis the phrase "as if they were" (Montes to Samuels, March 6, 2006). The point is well taken, inasmuch as the phrase is critical to my argument. The difference between "we very often must settle for propositions that set minds at rest" and "truth is impossible" need not be great. During the last several

Smith seems driven by a need to terminate his analysis by asserting an ultimate cause of the division of labor. Each of the several explanations is context-driven, and some are a matter of interpretation of what he wrote pertinent to the question. As in many other cases, clarification of Smith's intentions would have benefited from an editor's querying his conflicting and ambiguous accounts. Not only did Smith have different explanations; he seems to have been driven by both the quest for true explanation and the desire to soothe the imagination. The fact of multiple explanations may reflect both a multifaceted truth and the use in different contexts of different propositions to soothe the imagination. The ambiguity derives from our inability to determine proportions between the quest for truth and the provision of psychic balm, as well as between each of the explanations.

I submit that in proposing logical explanations of the division of labor, Smith was attempting to satisfy his own and his readers' presumed need for closure, to provide a sense that they have the subject under control and not left hanging, the victims of unexplained forces. (Ambiguity also arises from the difficulty of distinguishing when Smith is indicating his own belief and when the beliefs of others, and when he takes a proposition to be true and when it is only a matter of belief.) Smith's point is that the imagination is soothed by providing a satisfying proposition that yields closure. When Smith concluded that it was insufficient to attribute the division of labor to a propensity in human nature to truck, barter, and exchange, he proposed that the propensity itself was due to the faculties of reason and speech, and when he felt that this did not satisfy, he resorted to the proposition that the final link in the chain of connections was rhetoric in the service of social recognition and moral approbation – itself an example of the use of first principles as postulates with which to explain what may ensue from them. As for his other explanations, the pursuit of opportunities in quest of advantage was implicit in gain-seeking behavior itself pursued in order to better one's condition; stage-specific behavior gives effect to the necessary conditions for such to occur; and the nature of human nature was an explanation extraordinarily congruent with the eighteenth-century mind.

Professor Jerry Evensky (2005) authored a recent book on Smith's moral philosophy. A central element of Smith's vision presented in Evensky's first chapter is the argument from the *History of Astronomy*. Responding to an

years, I have had several enlightening conversations with Montes and with Eric Schliesser. All agree that for Smith, it is not truth alone that counts; belief setting minds at rest also matters; that he would prefer truth but often must settle for belief; the only principal remaining issue being the question of the proportion to which truth can apply. See, for example, Montes (2003: 206) and Schliesser (2005).

earlier draft of this paper, Evensky's position on the question of truth versus setting minds at rest is close to mine, albeit with a twist. He suggests that for Smith, there is no tension "between two uses of principles, or systems, to allay the tumult of the imagination and to define reality." There are, broadly speaking, two levels of inquiry – popular and philosophical:

In the former, systems of belief are often taken as truth precisely to allay the tumult of the imagination. These systems of belief evolve from the synthesis of common but unreflective observation that becomes habitual and in time become the natural order understanding of how the world "works" – very Berger and Luckmann. These systems of belief can include simplistic observations about how bread becomes flesh, or accepted norms of custom and fashion that – as you aptly point out – serve to justify and protect the status quo social construct.

Philosophical inquiry is discretely different for Adam. It is exploratory, it observes carefully with an eye on the invisible connecting chain that gives rise to what we observe. At its best it is not wedded to the status quo (indeed, when it is, it has ceased to be good philosophical inquiry) but it respects existing explanations to the degree they offer an explanation of the observed that a well informed impartial spectator finds persuasive.

Since these chains are invisible, we can never know the real explanation ... all of our stories of truth are just that ... stories – as was Newton's. The ultimate serenity of life for Adam was "secure tranquility." As a philosopher that goal was unreachable, but it was approachable. He would never be so arrogant ... to suggest that he had discovered Truth ... and so there was never a moment of full calm in his imagination. But he could at times feel comfortable that he had offered what he believed was the best available representation of Truth, and that would be a close approximation of such serenity ... which would last until something disturbed his comfort with his own story ... as, indeed, I think happened to him and which motivated him to work on the TMS even as he was fading.

Evensky then considers Smith on the division of labor issue, saying:

I don't think Smith was deeply concerned about getting the origins of his first principles "just right." He took them as a given and told his story from there. If the story offered a compelling, persuasive analysis of human events to a well informed impartial spectator, that was the measure of its success. He very consciously leaves "value" muddled, but moves on because he defines it sufficiently for his purposes. (Evensky to Samuels, March 9, 2006)

I agree with Evensky's analysis, although both he and I know of interpreters who place in Smith's mind a greater regard for truth, or Truth. I would suggest two points: (1) There are two domains or levels of inquiry, and Smith's analysis applies to both but to each in different ways; (2) these are not two different groups of people; each group has a different combination of levels of inquiry; even the philosopher can reason simplistically.

Robin Neill's interpretation of the position of Frank H. Knight, Joseph J. Spengler, and Harold Innis neatly poses Smith's predicament in terms of modernism versus postmodernism. "In Modernity," Neill writes, "rationality, objectivity, a generally accepted moral order, and truth, though not achieved, were thought to be achievable and approaching achievement." In postmodernism, "objective truth and emotion-free rationality are thought to be not attainable" (Robin Neill, book review, EH.NET, March 15, 2006).

The two questions in my title thus arise: How broadly does Smith's argument apply? And where do propositions that can soothe the imagination come from?

4.2. How Broadly Does Smith's Argument Apply?

Richard J. McNally is a professor of psychology at Harvard University. His research interests include the application of cognitive psychology methods to elucidate information-processing abnormalities in anxiety disorders, especially panic disorder, post-traumatic stress disorder, and obsessive-compulsive disorder. He has intervened in the controversy within psychology between traditional psychology insofar as it stresses the patient coming to terms with his or her past in order to satisfactorily exist in the present, and cognitive behavioral therapy (CBT), which holds that reviewing the past is not only unnecessary but can be counterproductive, and favors the correction of current cognitive disorders that lead an individual to act dysfunctionally in the present. In McNally's judgment, reviewing the past could be therapeutically important in helping patients construct narratives of their lives in terms of cause and effect. Reviewing the present, or recent past, can help the patient find a rational explanation for their disturbing experience, and that may be all he or she needs. The rational explanation – the rationalization – can be effective even when the explanation is not correct. *Merely asserting a logical sequence of cause and effect lets people feel that they have some control, that they are not victims of unexplained forces* (the preceding is taken from Spiegel [2006], emphasis added).

Professor McNally's work is with reality monitoring among those with emotional problems. What of the normal person, whatever "normal" is taken to mean, at least those without dysfunctional emotional problems?

On February 19, 2006, I asked him about incorrect explanations that, by asserting a logical sequence of cause and effect, let people feel that they have some control. I told him that my interest relates to Adam Smith's argument in his *History of Astronomy* that propositions can "sooth the imagination" independent of their truth status. In his reply, McNally underscored that his experience was with panic disorder patients who are taught via CBT to identify certain bodily sensations, their cognitive appraisal of their meaning, and the consequences that follow. His point was that CBT can identify and correct these misinterpretations, and even though it is often impossible to determine whether the conjured cause-and-effect sequence is correct, the therapy does work. He cited studies showing through clinical trials and experimental demonstrations, how a sense – indeed an "illusion" – of control can attenuate panic.

In two further emails, I asked, first, what he thought of the argument that as a general rule – that is, not restricted to panic disorder and so on – the acceptability of putative knowledge is a function of its capacity (derived not from itself but from the need or receptivity of the person accepting it) to set minds at rest; and second, whether the panic attenuation argument corresponds to religion as a psychic balm quelling anxiety in an unpredictable world. His response to the first query was, "I suspect that you may be correct," and to the second, "Beats me about religion" (the foregoing is taken from emails between Warren J. Samuels and Richard J. McNally, February 19, 2006).

It is obviously my intention neither to intervene in the controversy within psychology nor to opine on the relation between the psychology of the normal and the abnormal (or whatever phrasing is preferred). Rather, I query: What of the normal person, at least those without dysfunctional emotional problems, to whom having their mind set at rest is consciously or unconsciously important? What should we make of the predicament of individuals confronted with wonder, surprise, and awe in their ordinary lives, and as a corollary to the predicament of individuals confronting the prospect of their own death, or the deaths of others, and similar catastrophic events? I deal with these questions in the context of Smith's *History of Astronomy* and therefore within the domain of science or philosophy (synonyms to Smith). The trope, induced by disaster in ordinary people, that there is a reason for everything, even if known only to God, is an extension of that domain. My specific question concerns neither the truth or falsity of Smith's argument, nor anything about the relation of modern medicine to his argument, nor, ultimately, the role of religion, notably the problem of Job. The foregoing, however, does more than frame the present discussion. It suggests the possibility that Smithian reasoning applies not only to scientists or philosophers but to all people (see Raphael and Skinner 1980: 4; Samuels and Henderson 2004: 38–41).

Among economists' writings published during the second half of the twentieth century, two statements having to do with theory arguably stand out. One is Hicks's "There is, there can be, no economic theory which will do for us everything we want all the time" (Hicks 1981: 232–233; 1983, 4–5). The other is Shackle's "The chief service rendered by a theory is the setting of minds at rest" (Shackle 1967: 288). It takes no leap of imagination to perceive the Smithian tension in their juxtaposition. If no theory can answer every question put to it, then a tumult of the imagination arises. If the function of the theory is to set minds at rest, and instead the result is tumult, the tumult is exacerbated. Moreover, two modern developments in epistemology – developments beyond controversy, one would think – not to mention others, further aggravate and worsen the situation. One development is the appreciation that deduction properly yields only conclusions that have the quality of validity and not necessarily descriptive or explanatory truth. The other development is the appreciation that induction – empirical testing – properly yields only conclusions that at best have the quality of being probabilistically true. Assuming that a general theory is reduced to a specific hypothesis and tested with regard to certain social space using a particular criterion of acceptance/rejection, and the test is affirmative, one still cannot say that the hypothesis/theory is true. This is because further tests of variations of the specific hypothesis may be conducted with regard to different social space using a different criterion, and the result may be negative. It is very difficult, as Smith appreciated for less technical reasons, to attain truth, especially with a capital "T." Finally, the situation is further immensely worsened when propositions are adopted for political and public-relations purposes because of the spin they can provide to unfavorable developments – not by providing serious information but for the obfuscation and ignorance they can create (Samuels et al., 2004) in the process of mobilizing and manipulating political psychology and belief (Pareto 1963 [1935], Samuels 1974).

Our problem is that presumably all people and all aspects of life are amenable to the role of propositions in soothing the imagination. The point has been made by Raphael and Skinner, as we have seen. They conclude that, "man is impelled to seek an explanation for observed 'appearances' as a result of a *subjective* feeling of discomfort, and that the resulting explanation or theory is therefore designed to meet some psychological need" (Raphael and Skinner 1980: 5). In considering the quest for truth, Raphael and Skinner point out that "Smith did not claim an *exclusive* role for the central principles of surprise, wonder, and admiration, but rather asserted that the part played by these sentiments was "of far wider extent than we should be apt upon a careless view to imagine." (Raphael and Skinner 1980: 12)

Smith's argument has been given its sharpest modern statement by George Shackle:

> All we can seek is consistency, coherence, order. The question for the scientist is what thought – scheme will best provide him with a sense of that order and coherence, a sense of some permanence, repetitiveness and universality in the structure or texture of the scheme of things, a sense of that one-ness and simplicity which, if he can assure himself of its presence, will carry consistency and order to their highest expression. Religion, science and art have all of them this aim in common. The difference between then lies in the different emphases in their modes of search .... The chief service rendered by a theory is the setting of minds at rest.... Theory serves deep needs of the human spirit; it subordinates nature to man, imposes a beautiful simplicity on the unbearable multiplicity of fact, gives comfort in face of the unknown and unexperienced, stops the teasing of mystery and doubt which, though salutary and life-preserving, is uncomfortable, so that we seek by theory to sort out the justified from the unjustified fear. Theories by their nature and purpose, their role of administering to a 'good state of mind,' are things to be held and cherished. Theories are altered or discarded only when they fail us. (Shackle 1967: 286, 288)

Smith made his argument a chief element of his theory of intellectual history, but, with relatively few recent exceptions, it has been largely forgotten in that field. In my view, his argument applies not only to intellectual history, to philosophy-equal-science, but to all domains of human activity. Except for more or less trivial conversation, to which the argument also applies, the scope of what is sometimes now called justified true belief is extremely narrow. If I understand McNally correctly, his view that "*Merely asserting a logical sequence of cause and effect lets people feel that they have some control, that they are not victims of unexplained forces*" has an extraordinarily wide range in human affairs.

Perhaps the following examples will help the reader perceive something of the range and importance of the argument and of how much we get enmeshed in it. Ross Emmett has written that:

> Keynes' *A Treatise on Probability* argued that the probability assigned to a statement is a function of the subjectivity of our knowledge, not of the statement's ultimate truth or falsehood. Knight's *Risk, Uncertainty, and Profit* argued that the voluntary nature of human conduct renders the outcome of human action unknowable. Hence, while Keynes understood uncertainty to refer to the problem of subjective knowledge, Knight understood it to refer to subjectivity of human action. (Emmett 2002: 374)

In such a fashion, he provides another angle on Smith's argument.

In David Brown's biography of the historian Richard Hofstadter, aspects of the present argument frequently arise, some pointing to its existence and some indicating his subject's active role in its practice. In the epigraph to his Introduction, Brown quotes Hofstadter thus: "In a liberal society the historian is free to try to dissociate myths from reality, but that same impulse to myth-making that moves his fellow man is also at work in him" (Brown 2006: xiii). Several times Brown points to his subject's attitude toward the practice of business leaders:

In need of an ideological umbrella to rebuff the growing demand for regulation, industrialists found Spencer's views philosophically functional and morally convenient. (idem: 30)

The great barons, in their quest to build economic empires, choke competition, and turn a socially mobile working class into a subdued proletariat, manipulated Lincoln's legacy. (idem: 59)

Brown shows that Hofstadter attributed the same practice to a historian friend. Hofstadter criticized Charles Beard's "use of the new history as a tool to push the Progressive agenda" (idem: 75). Brown also shows Hofstadter's use of language to construct a particular definition of reality: Hofstadter, we are told, used "more than a dozen categories to denounce" Whig racism: He used "Anglo-Saxon" followed by mystique, clique, school, thesis, liberties, movement, lineage, power, heights, superiority, cult, myth (idem: 34).

Brown quotes the historian Eric Foner's conclusion that "Hofstadter's central insight [was] that analogies with science helped to shape the way Americans perceived and interpreted issues from the differences between the races and classes to the implications of state intervention in the economy" (idem: 36). Science here served not as a means to truth but as a way of grounding propositions constituting definitions of reality that also settled the mind and served as psychic balm. And psychic balm is explicitly present: Brown quotes Christopher Lasch as to Hofstader having a "disdain for the hopelessly muddled thinking of ordinary Americans, their inability to think straight about politics, their tendency to confused images with actions, their insatiable appetite for symbolic actions that provide the illusion that something is being down when in fact nothing is happening … "(idem: 55, quoting Lasch in Blake and Phelps 1994: 1317). Brown himself argues that the "message" of Hofstadter's *The American Political Tradition* was that "national identity is frequently the offspring of historical mythology" (Brown 2006: 62).

4.3. The Sources of Propositions That Soothe the Imagination

Where do propositions that "sooth the imagination" come from? The propositions could come from anywhere, from religion to economics itself.

Not only must propositions be available to the individual, but they must serve to soothe the imagination – that is, the individual must be receptive to a particular proposition performing the function of allaying the tumult of the imagination, whatever their nature.

My suggested answer relates to modern western societies and likely varies in other societies and cultures – vary at least in detail; the basic themes likely would still apply *mutatis mutandis*. For present purposes, my answer to the question of the sources of propositions serving the psychic balm function is limited to the broadest domain of study that concerns economists and historians of economic thought. This is the domain of the organization and control of the economy, and corresponds to the theory of economic policy, or what I have also called the legal-economic nexus (Samuels 1989; 2007). Here some notion of truth may occasionally actually be the premier desired objective. But we very often have to be content merely with propositions that are acceptable, that quiet the imagination, that are deployed to mobilize and manipulate political psychology, and that embody wishful thinking. Most statements about the economic role of government are *ought* statements and have very little, if anything, to do with truth and much to do with voicing sentiments. These statements may give effect to ideology, partial analysis, wishful thinking, and so on; they serve to allay disquieted imagination. Acceptability in the domain of economic theory has little to do with truth (a positive and nonnormative proposition). The economics of a pure conceptual a-institutional economy has little, if anything, to do with truth and almost everything to do with logicality and validity. The principal criterion of acceptability is, rather, consonance with the dominant paradigm. Such is what allays the disquiet and tumult of the imagination.

Economics is a part of a larger system of thought and derives its larger meaning, its true propositions, and especially its imagination-soothing propositions from that system of thought. I suggest that imagination-soothing propositions are to be found in something like the following structure of the system of thought and power (adapted from Samuels 2006b).

4.4. The System of Belief and the Mythic System of Society

G. C. Peden has written that:

The central article of faith in orthodox Victorian political economy was a belief in market forces as the best method of allocating goods and services, and as the best means of matching labour and jobs. The idea that individuals, who were pursuing their own interests, would be guided by competition to act in the economic interests of society, "as though by an invisible hand," had first been given authoritative expression by Adam Smith ... [Smith] saw the market mechanism as the most impartial means of resolving [conflicts of interest between producers and consumers].... (Peden 1985: 2)

Was this a set of concrete truths about economic reality, or a set of beliefs, encompassing, even constituting, the mythic and symbolic systems of society, perhaps a set of metaphors or other figures of speech? Was there "a tendency to apply market economics to social relationships in a way which Smith had not done" (idem: 2)? Was this "article of faith" a matter of economic science or a mythic account of how "sturdy independence improved a man's character," per Samuel Smiles. Similarly, was Darwinian struggles and natural selection the means whereby society would benefit from the strong? Was collectivism to be equated with socialism and socialism with slavery (idem: 3)?

Or was all that merely reasoning or assertions in terms of unsubstantiated metaphors? "Victorian faith in the market economy was based on moral philosophy as well as on general abstract assumptions and on the particular conditions of the Victorian labour market." Did not Alfred Marshall claim "that decentralized free enterprise encouraged rational forethought, initiative, industry and thrift, besides producing an optimum allocation of resources," and would not socialism "not be conducive to 'firmness of character'" (*idem*: 5)?

Peden also wrote that "*Laissez-faire* is an example of how historians try to explain attitudes and policies by bringing them together under some general concept" (idem: 5). But was not laissez-faire as much a concept pointing to social control as to economic freedom?

... a policy of keeping 'respectable' workers away from the Poor Law was a conscious attempt to maintain these workers' attitudes toward public relief. This brings one to the concept of 'social control' .... For other social historians, the key to the success of the British ruling class in maintaining its position has been a series of policies and tactics which, although apparently unconnected, are best understood if seen as different forms of social control. Examples which have been given include education, the media and even organized sport, all of which have been means by which the ruling class could consciously impose values, attitudes and beliefs which would maintain the class structure of an industrial society. Indeed, the term 'social control' has been employed so variously that there is some doubt whether the concept has been sufficiently closely defined to be useful .... Taken to its logical extreme, the concept might be applied to all social policy, in so far as social policy has made the working class contented with their lot while capitalism has remained untouched, or even strengthened. (idem: 9)

Luigi Pasinetti has argued that the Classical economists conducted their whole analysis at a level of investigation which the Classical economists called 'natural', that is to say, at a level of investigation which is so fundamental as to be independent of the institutional set – up of society. This feature could be kept quite easily with reference to prices and physical quantities ... (Pasinetti 1981: xii)

... But [it] did not take long to realize that introducing behavioural (savings) relations did not fit consistently into a theoretical framework which was basically conceived independently of institutions. (idem: xiii)

The Classical economists ... had accepted the society in which they lived as part of the order of Nature; [and] had generally been arguing in terms of harmony of interests among the various sections of society ... (idem: 12)

Roy Pascal finds one tension between the doctrine of unintended consequences and the assumption of rationality (Pascal 1938: 166–7) and another between belief in Natural Order and belief that natural disparity of talents and tastes of men of different classes is not so large as is usually believed, but is mainly a result of social conditions, "of the division of labor, ... as from habit, custom and education" (idem: 71, quoting Smith 1976a: 17). It is noteworthy that Pascal finds that Smith,

[t]hough he occasionally slips into mechanistic or abstract deductions ... is on the whole true to his main theme of showing the birth of all change out of transformations in the nature and distribution of property.... The abolition of slavery, Smith emphasizes, was not due to acts of enlightenment or Christianity; it arose from self-interest. (idem: 172)

Even new forms of government and new moralities are produced: "[M]odern civilization owes its existence to 'the insensible operation of foreign commerce and manufactures'" (idem: 173, quoting Smith 1976a, I, 386). Michael Parenti cites Bronislaw Malinowski's on the Melanesian Islanders for whom "a myth is not an idle tale but a powerful cultural force ... [which] served to legitimate the existing distribution of wealth in the society. Far from being innocent stories, myths taught acceptance of the prevailing arrangements – to the benefit of the more prosperous property-holders" (Parenti 1981: 425). Parenti also quotes Sigmund Freud's *The Future of an Illusion*, "that every culture seeks to defend itself; 'Its organization, its institutions and its laws' – and, one might add, its myths – 'are all directed to this end: they aim not only at establishing a certain distribution of property, but also at maintaining it'" (idem: 425–6).[2]

---

2 Parenti also asks, "[W]hat are the myths of American society? What are the mystifying social images and tales that seek to legitimate existing political-economic relations? ... First, there is the myth of pluralism ... that power in American society is widely distributed.... No social group or class predominates over another.... The government acts as a mediator.... This ... begs the whole question of structured, institutionalized class power" ... a

Wendy O'Flaherty argues that numerous types of theories of myth exist. Some theories affirm that many myths exist. Other theories portray an overarching pattern linking all myths. The overarching pattern may be a single but composite version of a myth. Some theories identify the cultural diffusion of myths, others their re-emergence. Some theories emphasize thick description of a culture as explanation; others affirm a context of numerous other but related myths from the same culture; still others emphasize the influence of other cultures and the intellectual history of the culture in which the myth occurs (O'Flaherty 1983: 3). Two major problems prevent a hypothesis about myth from becoming a proof or a scientific undertaking: One is the scarcity of available data, the other is the absence of a reliable way to deduce myths from physical facts or facts from myths (idem: 24). Especially important for our purposes, for some interpreters, the study of myth is a study of the deepest level(s) of reality, whereas for others, it is only a study of beliefs. (idem: 24)

Also significant is O'Flaherty's point that myth paints a selective picture:

[W]hat is more arbitrarily lost in Mr. Campbell's selection is ugliness ... Everything is beautiful. The world is beautiful, God is beautiful, what is archaic is particularly beautiful, and man's myths and rituals, however barbaric or perverse they may at first seem, express the beauty of man's awe in the presence of the sacred. (idem: 25)

I propose that the system of belief, including the mythic system of society, is a principal source of the propositions that, true or not, soothe the imagination.

4.5. The System of Belief

Thinkers such as Adam Smith, John Stuart Mill, Karl Marx, George Herman Mead, Vilfredo Pareto, and Kenneth Boulding have emphasized that what is important is not what people should believe – because it is true – but what they do believe, because it is the belief, even if meaningless, on which they act. People have a need to believe – to have their minds set at rest. Even

whole body of literature ... challenges this mythical vision of American society ... [arguing] that government most often represents the privileged few, not the needy many, that power is highly structured and institutionalized, controlled by the same class interests in diverse institutions, and that the *diffusion* of power does not mean the *democratization* of power" (Parenti 1981 : 426).

The capitalist system has its own fundamental myths. They are mainly the myths of the Lockean ideology, such as the myth of individualism which reduces human community to a conglomeration of competing atomized persons.... And somehow the whole thing comes out for the better for everyone, thanks to Adam Smith's 'invisible hand' – an invisible hand that has us all by the throat (idem: 426).

those who claim to have no system of belief hold that view on the basis of a system of belief. It may be very different from that of most people, but it is nonetheless a system of belief – possibly, but not necessarily, deeper or more "correct" in some sense than others' belief systems (Harris 1971; Kselman 1991).

How such systems of belief are used to set minds at rest is a function in part of the issues before the public and in part the particular positions with which an individual identifies. It is useful to contemplate people's mental states as a combination of two positions, one of which is usually dominant. For many people, a system of belief is attractive and defines reality for them to the extent that it offers a sense of determinacy and closure. Other people have a dominant reality-defining system of belief that they treat as problematic and pragmatic. These people are content with open-endedness and ambiguity.

Particularly attractive to those who seek determinacy and closure is the possibility of having only one explanation or a unidirectional line of causation in which to believe. In such cases, however, there always tend to be significant multiple variations. Multiplicity renders nugatory (but not impossible) all claims to determinacy and closure, yet even this is finessed by those who are willing to accept some one variation. It is not surprising, therefore, that constitutional law, theological doctrine, and economic theory exhibit similar problems of interpretation (Samuels 2006a).

Systems of belief are not scientific matters, even within a putative scientific discipline, but nonetheless define reality for people, who thereby are provided with principles of order and/or of authority, functioning together as a filter through which an individual processes and frames, among other things, experience and statements of putative fact. Different systems of belief enable different people to interpret what they read or hear differently. The use of "code words" in political and other discourse, including economic discourse, enables interpretation at the unconscious level.

Economics is a system of belief providing such a definition of reality; economic theory is an institution broadly and deeply defining and structuring freedom, power, and opportunity. The meaning of "competition," "freedom," "property," "money," and so on varies between individuals because of their respective, different belief systems (Straub 2006). Pareto is not the only scholar who combined belief system and noncognitive and rational behavior and choice with the structure and struggle for power (Samuels 1974). See, for example, Parsons (1949) and Moessinger (2000), who trace the stability of social structures – their concept of order – to nondeliberative conduct, somewhat in the manner of Hayek (Samuels 1999), in effect combining psychology and sociology.

From the 1620s to the present, Americans have exhibited two cultural belief systems. One is theological fundamentalism, which would have all people pursue a life of piety; the other is economic fundamentalism, which legitimizes the world of business and trade, hence of wealth accumulation. Each has its own goals, rules, concept of order, and so on, as well as varied ideational formulations (sects, schools of thought, sacred or near-sacred documents, etc.). The two can coexist quietly or clash, reinforcing (and perhaps changing) the distinctiveness of each as well as their contradictions – about God versus Mammon, democracy, work, capitalism, corporate capitalism, wealth, freedom, and so on, including notions like the Money Power, robber barons, and the power elite (see Ellul 1984; Cottrell and Moggridge 1988; Means 2001).[3] In the late nineteenth century, the conflict was between Social Darwinism and the Social Gospel. In the half century after World War II, the conflict was between economic and social conservatism. The ascription of terms is less important than their opposition and both the genesis of conflict in society and the genesis of society in their conflict. Herein is the source of numerous propositions, often assumed to be true in some sense, that set minds at rest.

In general culture, an interactive process may exist in which folk etymology and beliefs help form the collective definition of reality (Rundblad and Kronenfeld 2003 envision an invisible-hand process) akin to Thomas Kuhn's notion of scientific revolution. The folk belief system can become an established, ingrained, and encrusted status-emulative mode of social control, and in turn the object of scorn by new aspirants. Here is another vast source of propositions serving to allay disquieted imaginations.

Typically each side in a controversy offers its own putative factual support, selectively framed, incomplete, and inconclusive. Selectively formed facts also tend to be tautological with the theory on which the facts are constructed; the facts are theory-laden, and the theory is a function of a particular reading of the facts. Putative facts lack the capacity to be conclusive in choosing between sides. The system of belief is pervasive. Its attractiveness accounts for the power of the story so told, but individual psychological attachments account for the adoption of some proposition(s) from that story as psychic balm.

---

[3]   See also, for examples, Gatell (1967) and Means (2001). For money power as economic nationalism, see Hont (2005).

4.6. Social Control as a Social Construction of Reality: The Struggle
for Power and Control of the State

People tend to believe strongly that words correspond with and derive from
reality: "[T]he whole point is that if we define the terms precisely and sort
out the various possible scenarios, we can learn more about market clearing
than if we remain vague" (Gani 2005; see also Kendall 1995 on the selective
use of discourse in presidential campaigns). Ludwig Wittgenstein, however,
found that this was not how language operates. Words do not derive their
meaning from reality; our definition of reality is derived from the words
used in our system of belief. To believe that words derive from and correspond with reality is to neglect both the social construction of language and
the multiplicity of words each of which defines reality for some people. This
situation leads to numerous linguistic problems of specification and interpretation in economics and other fields (Jones 1983, Chomsky 1988, Samuels
2001). More generally – in the sense of greater ubiquity – money, language,
and thought (perception and definition of monetary reality) critically interact (Shell 1992 [1982]; see also Binswanger 1994 and Zelizer 1994; on the
recomposition of practices and ideas interacting with the recomposition
of markets, see Kwon 2004). Belief systems are part of the system of social
control. Taking social control for granted is tantamount to accepting the felt
hegemonic belief system as given. Few people fail to express belief in the
omnipotence of words. The psychology of belief (religious, political, or economic) reveals the ubiquitous practice of using words nominally to define
reality but especially to control reality (Anthony Smith 1980), as different
individuals identify with different mind-settling phrases.

Accordingly, belief system is an object of control; society, as spelled out
by Pareto (Samuels 1974), is very much a process of mutual manipulation
of belief systems and thereby of power and psychology. Democracy, which
posits individual political judgment, becomes a process of mutual manipulation and the manufacture of consent or pseudo-consent.

People hold on to belief systems for purposes of having their minds
set at rest, induced to do so by institutions of social control (having their
political propensities promote some meaning of "order" or at least keeping
quiet). Secularists may debate using some linguistic formulation reduced
to "My belief system is truer than yours." Nonsecularists use language ultimately reduced to "My invisible friend can beat up your invisible friend."
During October 2005, the sports network ESPN[4] televised commercials

---

[4] "The Entertainment and Sports Programming Network" (1979–1985), ESPN thereafter.

on its own behalf, one line of which ran, "Without sports, what would we hold on to?"

People are induced to adhere to a particular belief system, even when it is undergoing change. Pareto insisted that social control consisted of force and fraud, the latter involving the manipulation of belief through the use of pseudo-knowledge and manipulative psychology. In the 1960s, the sports editor of the *Miami Herald* wrote that the principal argument for sports is that sports help prevent communism.[5] Some observers of high school, college, and professional sports think of them as aphrodisiacal; the *Herald* editor seems to widen Karl Marx's thesis of religion as the opiate of the masses. The Cold War provided ample opportunity for various interests to promote their cause by investing it with the function of combating communism (or attributing the opposite to their opponents). The stockbroker Charles Merrill "argued that nothing 'would provide a stronger defense against the threat of Communism, than the wide ownership of stocks in the country'" (Wallace 2005: 30). Wallace also quoted Franklin Roosevelt's statement of concern over the money power: "[W]e cannot allow our economic life to be controlled by that small group of men whose chief outlook upon the social welfare is tinctured by the fact that they can make huge profits from the lending of money and the marketing of securities" (idem: 30).

The conservative columnist, George Will, has condemned the business, financial, and accounting practices that led to the Enron collapse, insisting that

[i]t will remind everyone – some conservatives, painfully – that a mature capitalist economy is a government project. A properly functioning free market system does not spring spontaneously from society's soil as dandelions spring from suburban lawns. Rather, it is a complex creation of laws and mores ... (Will 2002: 3; quoted in Mercuro 2005: 16)

Social control encompasses more than controlling individual belief and behavior, so that actions seen as coercion by some Alphas are seen as freedom enhancing by some Betas (Samuels 1984, 1995, 1996b, 1997). Social control also establishes the legal and moral foundations of the actual economic regime. Social control – the sum of and interactions between power players, agencies, and institutions of social control – is thereby engaged in the social construction of reality (Berger and Luckmann 1966; Sederberg 1984; Searle 1995); both are aspects of the problem of order (Samuels 1996b), and the engagement is in two senses: the actual construction of institutions broadly defined and our perception of social reality. The adjustment of

---

[5]   Unable to determine date or exact words.

continuity and change can be posed in terms of property and/or covenants (Taylor 1966) but must encompass both continuity and change. The legal-economic nexus (Samuels 1989) is the domain in which public and private sectors interact but, more importantly, each is continually being reconstituted through that interaction.

A key role is performed by expectations and change of expectations. If manipulation of the system of belief can achieve passive consent, if not belief, on the part of those negatively affected that their predicament is due to the natural order of things, then their predicament will less likely be perceived as a problem for redress by government. What people expect and/or do not expect form a basis on which conflicting claims of right are worked out by courts, and can serve as a foundation of the basic jural postulates in the sense of Roscoe Pound (1937) and Hans Kelsen (1945). Much legal change ensues from changes in expectations per se or from the expectations that the courts are willing to recognize. Conservatives will find such changes wrong and liberals will find them good, so long as they agree with them, which means that no one is solely or purely conservative or liberal. The positivist, empirically oriented analyst will find such changes to be inevitable – for example, that the present (the status quo) is due to past changes.

Pervading the social belief system, language, and social control are propositions and terms that function to create, give effect to, and/or sentimentalize conceptions of socioeconomic reality by serving as the ostensible basis and/or conclusion of chains of reasoning. These latter are used in both identifying problems of policy and working out their solutions. The terms include, among others, laissez-faire, nonintervention, deregulation, and regulation; all are matters of selective perception, however much they derive from the dominant mindset of western civilization. They also are instrumental in working out who can get into a position to use government and for what purposes.

The question "Who decides?" inevitably arises. The state itself is an answer to that question. Thus arises the struggle over control of the institutions of social control, including those of the legal-economic nexus. As Pareto emphasized, much of this struggle takes place through asymmetrical mutual manipulation of the system of belief and of language itself in order to mobilize the political psychology which is at the basis of policy (Pareto 1963; Samuels 1974; this includes the languages of class such as Jones 1983, DeGré 1985, Burke and Porter 1987, Reddy 1987, and Corfield 1991). Much money is spent on lobbying and litigation to influence government policy – the interests the state will use to promote or inhibit – not because government is unimportant, as some writers would have everyone believe, but because government (collective action) is in fact important.

I increasingly prefer to speak of the entirety of the system of governance, meaning by "governance" the making of decisions that importantly affect other people. Normally there is a more or less ambiguous line of demarcation between public government and private government. The situation is illustrated by the Federal Reserve System that is "privately owned" and an "independent" government agency. It is also found in the Constitution's seemingly exclusive assignment of power to the Congress "To coin Money, regulate the Value thereof, and of foreign coin" (Article I, Section 8) but which has precluded neither paper money, nor state involvements in matters of money and banking, nor the issuance by private banks of perhaps 90 percent of the money supply through credit creation, nor government bonds constituting satisfaction of private banks' required reserves. It also resonates in the enforcement of private contracts by the courts.

A millennium ago, the deep interpretive questions were whether the Church was operating in the name of and/or on the behalf of God, or in the interests of churchmen, or as an institution of secular social control (to which a large measure of absolutist legitimization had been added). More recently, the deep interpretive questions were whether government and other institutions, many of the latter operating under color of law, were serving God's will, or the will of their leaders and/or a ruling elite, or the functions of social control. As economic institutions developed during the transition from feudal and postfeudal to capitalist market economies, comparable questions arose. Money, banking, and finance became key parts of the institutions by which a new and still changing ruling class stood astride both government and economy. In time it became increasingly difficult to distinguish whether the economic system was a socially functional set of institutions or a vehicle of the ruling economic elite; if one accepted the dominant system of belief, the vehicle of the ruling elite was socially functional. Whether in some sense the economy was performing in one way or the other, or a bit of both, what came to count was what it was believed to be; thus, as with government as a whole, enormous efforts were made to manipulate the belief system of the great mass of people. Certainly no independent test was available; it was a matter of what people were induced to believe by the powerful who competed among themselves to control and use government, and who manufactured consent to that end. One interpretation of the Constitution would dominate and exclude another not because it was the *law*; rather it was the law because of whose/which interpretation served the interest of those whose interest counted for more than that of others.[6] The deepest problem may well have become balancing the need for order on almost any terms with the public discussion of whose interest is to count for more than that of others. Public discussion might mean that the order was threatened; quietude would tend to safeguard the status quo power structure. All this is encompassed in the promotion and inhibition of various propositions and terms through which policy was worked out, propositions and terms that caused, reinforced, or countered Smith's soothing (or aggravating) of the imagination.

One point, fundamental to the present argument and worth reiterating, concerns laissez-faire. For several centuries, some people have believed in laissez-faire and governmental nonintervention. Other people have believed, equally sincerely, in government intervention and rejected laissez-faire. These two systems of belief are solely that – systems of belief – and do not accurately describe the economic role of government. Government, like it or not, is important and ubiquitous. Government helps create the fundamental economic institutions, and whereas some nominally private interests have great influence on – even control over – government, government has great influence on and control over them. Government protection of certain interests ipso facto means government nonprotection of other interests in the same field of action. Regulation of Alpha means protection of Beta; deregulation of Alpha means government no longer protecting the conflicting interest of Beta. That some people treat them differently is a function of selective perception of government, a selective perception intimately connected by manufactured and non-manufactured belief systems and the propositions that settle or upset the imagination.

One implication of the foregoing is that laissez-faire, which is not descriptively accurate with regard to the economy and economic policy, nonetheless serves the Paretian function of mobilizing political psychology and manipulating belief systems for many people.

---

[6] The U.S. Constitution is silent on the people's right of revolution. However, the Ninth Amendment reads: "The enumeration in the Constitution, of certain rights, shall not be construed to deny or disparage others retained by the people," and the Tenth Amendment, that "The powers not delegated to the United States by the Constitution, nor prohibited by it to the States, are reserved to the States respectively, or to the people." Of what these other rights consist is unclear; but arguably both amendments could be interpreted to support revolution or at least revolutionary attempts, and the Tenth Amendment to support secession. To my knowledge, no actual constitution of a nation explicitly provides for either secession or revolution. Of course, the Constitution means not what it literally says in the ordinary meaning of words, but rather how the given the words and clauses are interpreted by the Supreme Court.

Another way of making the point is to say that while the dominant ideology is noninterventionist, the accurate positivist description of actual legal-economic systems is the ubiquity and importance of government and governance (Samuels 1995) and thereby of politics – meaning having to do with decision making that affects others. It is ironic that arrangements that are political and socially constructed are reified so as to appear given, transcendent, and grandiose. Absolutist legitimization to the contrary notwithstanding, laissez-faire is both an insubstantial sentiment and a name for another political agenda. The political meaning of monetary and banking institutions, for example, is not unique in society. The reach of politics is ubiquitous (Feibleman 1969); meaning is political (Sederberg 1984; Straub 2006). Like it or not, identity (Aronowitz 1992), knowledge (Lagemann 1989; Meja and Stehr 1990), including framing paradigms and theories of social change (Janos 1986), information (Anthony Smith 1980), music (Buch 2003), landscape (Turner 1979), and religion (Tinder 1989) have selective political aspects. Religion has been deeply involved in the political status of lending, banking, and interest (Jones 1989). The idea of a theology of the corporation is highly suggestive of both the use of religion for economic purposes and the use of economics for religious purposes, and thereby the possibility of a similar nexus between religion and government (Novak 1981a, 1981b, suggestive of the absolutist legitimization of business, paralleling legitimization through absolutist ontological realism). Relevant here is not only what passes for science, but also belief without substance (Robinson 1921; Pareto 1963; Samuels 1974). Knowledge – or what people accept as knowledge and act on – is often a matter of imagery (Boulding 1956; Bloor 1976) and therefore of illusion (Skillen 1978; Geuss 2001) and myth (Barbour 1974; Bondi 1967; Campbell 1972; Mishan 1986; Samuel and Thompson 1990; Fitzpatrick 1992). Politics is a domain of symbols (Eaton 1925; Boorstin 1958; Edelman 1964) and figures of speech (Lakoff and Johnson 1980; Ortony 1993), a domain populated by entrepreneurs of myth (Nossiter 1964) engaged in the defense and invention of tradition (Hobsbawn 1962, 1983), including demystification (Rex 1974). Each of these topics has been the subject of diverse explanations. For present purposes, it is the general theme in each case that counts, not the differences of theoretical formulation. Further apropos of mystification (and demystification; see Chomsky 1988), giving something a name seems for some or many people tantamount to establishing ontological existence.

Silence (see Achino-Loeb 2005 on the influence of silence on power; on silence and the unseen in a general theory of ignorance, including the manufacture of ignorance, see Samuels et al. 2004) as part of a-institutional economic theory means either that existing institutions are rendered unimportant or that they comport with or exemplify pure abstract theory, neither of which is necessarily true; indeed, it is widely recognized (though not practiced) that the pure theory of economics does not apply directly to existing institutions. Instead, theory obfuscates the processes of power through which institutions evolve, thereby facilitating the continuity of those processes and the applicability of what an earlier age called "God-given institutions." The world is made safe for economists and the institutions on which they cast luster. Economists become members of the ruling elite, occasional criticisms of, for example, monetary and banking institutions being miniscule in importance compared with the legitimacy provided by economics and its theory(ies) of the optimality of (money) markets. Considerations such as the previously discussed are far more important than the velocity of money, the functions of money, endogenous versus exogenous money, and so on; but on those questions hegemonic monetary theory is relatively silent. Economists tend also to be silent on the question of whether law is policy. Ending this silence would strongly tend to demonstrate the emptiness of the laissez-faire and noninterventionist approach to government. If the legal foundations of the entire economy are important and ubiquitous, if legal and law-based institutions are inevitable, if nothing of the foregoing is given by nature but is a matter of the parallelogram of power that is both cause and consequence of the struggle to control and use government, then both conservative and liberal rationalizations of temporarily favored policies are shown to be merely means of mobilizing and manipulating political psychology. Politicians can get away with this because much of it is unseen, some has deniability, most nonpoliticians are emotionally inoculated against the machinations of all politicians and are, besides, more interested in what is closer (they feel, and are induced to feel) to their own lives, and, a sense that, like it or not, this is the nature of collective decision making – in other words, politics is the way we govern ourselves, all the alternatives being less fine and more dangerous than "democracy."

4.7. Conclusion

The preceding discussion testifies to the power of Adam Smith's argument in the *History of Astronomy*. People have a need for an acceptable system of belief. They have a need for something that will render aspects of their lives intelligible, even if the propositions serving to allay the tumult of the imagination are pseudo-knowledge. They seek a sense of closure and determinacy. They like to base and conclude arguments on propositions that, in part, at best will prevent and if necessary allay the tumult of the imagination and create a sense – albeit perhaps an illusion – that they are in control of their lives, or can have, even do have, the knowledge to set their minds at rest. The deployment of such propositions also, in part, is a means of controlling others. The necessary (but perhaps not sufficient) conditions of manipulative success are that such propositions are not seen for what they are, and, somewhat tautologically, that circumstances are permissive. The propositions that provide such setting of minds at rest and such disjunction from politics are available from the sources and in the contexts partly outlined earlier in this essay.

This is true of all people, in all walks of life, in all aspects of life. Only a relative handful of major writers reached such insights. The problem for such a writer is that it is very difficult for them to converse with other people if those folks have bought into the dominant belief or mythic system of society. This may well explain some of Smith's circumlocutions, especially the language, which has seemed so ambiguous and is really so evasive on his part.

The problems facing the person seeking to allay the tumult of their imagination, to overcome anxiety, open-endedness, and ambiguity, to have their minds come to rest include, first, the burden of having to choose from among the relevant alternatives – whose scope they may not know – and opt for a proposition, concept, or term that will work to soothe their imagination, uphold their hopes, and allay their fears. The second problem is that once they have chosen, unless they have a special mentality, they will avoid further serious inquiry into the area. To rethink an issue – assuming that one had actually thought seriously about it – is to expose oneself to alien propositions and to question one's status quo position, to threaten the equanimity engendered by the soothing position.

I referred to having a special mentality. How many Ludwig Wittgensteins have there been (Wittgenstein 1958)?

As for Adam Smith: I have for some time thought that his theory of the moral sentiments, applied to the problem of the formation of moral rules, can make him the first (great) sociologist of religion. His theory of allaying the tumult of the imagination may well make him the first (great) psychologist of belief.

Smith's argument concerns the tension between truth and belief. A function of both is to set minds at rest. Highly apposite is Shackle's admonition, already quoted, that religion, science, and art have a common aim in providing "a sense of that order and coherence, a sense of some permanence, repetitiveness and universality in the structure or texture of the scheme of things, a sense of that one-ness and simplicity which," if people are assured of its presence, "will carry consistency and order to their highest expression." That to me is the psychic balm function of belief and knowledge. The language, symbols, beliefs, and knowledge of economics contribute part of the inventory of propositions that perform this function of soothing the imagination and providing the first principles or starting points of analysis. But not only is psychic balm served; so too is social control. Systems of belief and language contribute to the social construction of reality through social control. The propositions, provided by economics and other human domains, are a result of both the struggle over the structure of power and the contest over the control of the state; and it is these propositions that are used in motivating and conducting those struggles.

Let us return to the main argument as pertains to most readers. The question arises, how it is that politicians and others (including lobbyists, public-relations agents, lawyers, and specialists in purveying ideology) are able to reiterate the same old stories, ideas, lines of reasoning, rhetoric, tropes, themes, economic laws, patriotic tales or myths, and so on, and say (or do) other, improper, immoral, and illegal things – and the mass of voters, seemingly, has learned nothing from those experiences? One would think that they eventually would no longer fail to question what they had been told, why the language that had been directed at them, they were led to believe, was a transcendent law or force for good of the economic universe and yet was not.

Why, when the masses of people, from every income class, every country, every ethnic group, every political party, every religion have been told or have sensed what is wrong, incomplete, mythological, superstitious, or biased with what they have been told, they nonetheless, strongly tend to continue to accept the same old lines and illusions that are told to them, often in the tone of sacerdotal language? Why, when it is perfectly obvious that individuals of every point of view commit or do unconscionable things, do we feel that one side is more dubious in what they urge than the other?

I suggest quite strongly that the arguments are often seemingly about the economic system as a whole, as to the relationships between the seemingly logical, connected, necessary, sufficient, and/or inevitable, and yet neither governments nor peoples choose at the level of the system very often, if ever. The arguments comprise propositions masquerading as truth, or presumptive metaphor or other figure(s) of speech, or primitive undefined terms. Its use, especially its repeated use by important, recognized, celebrated persons, serves to help establish the argument as the absolutist definition of reality intended by the users for embedding and use in others' belief systems. As with any of the autonomous nervous systems, it automatically enables the term or line of reasoning to elicit the desired ideological results with the reduction of conscious intervention to a minimum. It serves to instil or reinforce in the typical person's belief system a belief that comes into play, like the autonomous nervous system, when the occasion prompts (the heart of all campaigns) – say, for certain distributions of income and wealth, as well as opportunity and class positions.

Republican candidates and their supporters will pontificate about freedom; individuals being more important than governments; how income taxes should be lowered for investors, upper-income families and individuals, corporations, capital gains, and likewise with property taxes; how confining and disillusioning regulations have become, and how deregulation would embolden the entrepreneurial spirit and other motivations; how all saving, all investing, and all consumer buying will lead to increasing real incomes for all people; how the total levels of government taxation, spending, and deficits constitute the road to national bankruptcy, and so on. One argument they do not make is that deficits, perhaps especially growing deficits, arising from tax cuts for upper-bracket taxpayers do not necessarily strengthen a country during or on account of any war, whether undertaken in the name of or to advance a nationalist war party, economic or political or religious imperialism, or to promote, through easy victory, the presidential reputation of the incumbent president.

Democratic candidates seek to implant visions of a universally beneficent partial but nonetheless important change in the legal and institutional foundations of the system. They do so by neglecting the need for choice within the party itself and by other Americans as well. Other arguments are planted by selectively equating some opponent, some policy, and so on with something negative.

What is gained by some people using the term "invisible hand" and others the term "New Deal?" Three things, if successful:

1. Getting their issues and arguments into the discussion over the public agenda of the nation.
2. Serving the selective reinforcement or rejection of social control.
3. Serving the selective reinforcement or rejection of psychic balm.

5

The Invisible Hand, Decision Making, and Working Things Out

Conceptual and Substantive Problems

5.1. Introduction

As is so often the case, the story is in the details. The "invisible hand" encompasses more than an identity and functions. Almost every discussion of the invisible hand inevitably raises questions concerning the terms of the specification, its environment, and the process of its operation, including the different ways in which people interact and the different objectives and perceptions they have. The aggregation of the interactions yields the principle of unintended and unexpected consequences. The story of the invisible hand is wide-ranging and incredibly complex, and made more so by the ubiquity and multiplicity of interpretations. There is a vast difference between the invisible hand as a general or generic concept and particular usages. The story is about human beliefs and these are protean and heavily and selectively nuanced.

Returning to the football game example, there is a difference between the category or concept of "football" and the details of specific rules. Exemplified by the different sets of rules encountered in different neighborhoods and at different times in the same location, in order to accommodate extant local conditions, the point especially applies to pick-up games not only in football but in basketball, baseball, and soccer. There is also more to the process of interaction in football games than was initially given. Rules likely will vary depending on whether the players have pads and helmets. The game as a whole varies if the rules permit or, alternatively, prohibit certain types of blocks and certain types of tackles. The ability of offensive linemen to protect their quarterback can involve a moving rectangle within which certain blocks are permitted correlative to the prohibition of other blocks outside the rectangle. More obvious is whether or not the rules permit passing as a means of advancing the ball. Less obvious are the rules that have changed the game so that *foot*ball no longer is what it once was; for example, the dropkick is no longer a part of the game.

Professional baseball, for another example, varies as a game through rules defining the strike zone and the substantive content of the baseball itself. A larger strike zone and a "livelier" baseball will engender more hits, more multibase hits, and more homeruns. Those rules are adapted to have a more exciting game, greater attendance, and greater revenues and profits. Apparently more baseball fans prefer excitement so generated than those who appreciate a low-hitting pitchers' duel. Likewise, we will see that the term "invisible hand" has meaning depending on what is imported into the term and what is omitted, on the roles of the concept of the invisible hand in generating social control and psychic balm, and on what is recognized as the process of working things out. The situation of the amorphous strike zone has given rise to the joke with a philosophically deep punch line. Three umpires are presenting their views to each other. After the first two umpires give their opinions of when and where a pitch is a strike, the third umpire says, "The pitch is nothing until I call it a ball or a strike." Life is more or less lightly structured by customs and other rules that stipulate how the game in question is played and who has what range of discretion.

Essay 1 suggested that neither all economists nor all conventional economic theorists have accepted the script, as it were, in which the discipline of economics is privileged to have in the invisible hand a fundamental concept that both distinguishes economics from the other social sciences and provides economics with the basis of its revered status as the foremost social science. Economists have different views as to what economics is all about, notably as to its central problem and its scope and method, and also, as was seen in Essay 1, the content and status of the invisible hand, that is, the story that a particular devotee tells.

Essay 2 examined Adam Smith's system as a whole. Smith was seen to have had a tripartite model of society: law, morals, and market. From the standpoint of an individual, all three comprised the system of social control by which he or she is socialized and more or less lightly controlled. All three domains exist and interact and thereby form a system of mutual determination. The result is a system that is synoptic and synthetic. Individuals act on their objectives and perceptions. The result of the aggregation of these interactions is the principle of unintended and unexpected consequences.

Such a system is laden with tension due to the interdependence among the three domains. The three domains are not transcendent and given to mankind. Each domain is comprised of individuals participating in a comprehensive process of working things out. The sources of inevitable tension and outright conflict among those working in a market, in government, and on value-clarifying rules are ubiquitous. What transpires is not always transparent. Tension derives from the shared social-control roles of market actors, politicians, and religionists. Where there exists a division of authority, it is inevitable that absolutist legitimizing proclamations making impossible claims will be issued. The task of the ideal judge (meaning anyone who decides conflicts of interest) is to come up with mutually agreeable accommodations among the parties at interest (I do not intend for that description to be exclusive). Where the domain of the legal ends and that of the moral begins; where the dominant practices of business come to have attributed to them independent moral (and legal) status and thereby acquire moral as well as legal standing of their own; where the domain of business judging business by its own standards (and then applying that business-developed set of rules to consumers); and where judges, arbitrators, moralists, ethicists, lawyers, and so on look to each others' decisions for new or reinforcing or weakening insights – such are derivative of the division of governing authority to encompass insights from most, if not all, sources and from the interactive system as a whole.

I cannot emphasize too much the difference between ostensibly transcendent and given absolutist formulations *and* the fluid, flexible, and ongoing process in which solutions to needs and problems are worked out as the needs and problems, and numerous other factors, are themselves worked out.

Essay 3 explored the variety of identities attributed to the invisible hand and the array of functions they are thought to perform. The multiplicity of identities and functions permits anyone and everyone to believe that something transcendental is in control and that in the end everything is going to work out for the best. The adherence to such a view was satirized by Voltaire as illusory in *Candide; nonetheless the conflicts are very real to the protagonists.*

Essay 4 distinguished between the attributed economic functions of the invisible hand and the social functions of the use of the *concept* of the invisible hand. The chief services performed by belief in an invisible hand are social control and psychic balm. The same service could be provided by the belief that the allocation of resources is governed by a group of monkeys residing in some palm trees in Bayfront Park in Miami.

It is here that I employ Smith's argument in his *History of Astronomy* that for purposes of social control and/or psychic balm, propositions comprising truth, which are so difficult to achieve, can be replaced by propositions that set minds at rest. The critical point is that whatever individuals come to believe they will actually be submitting to one or another soothing of their imaginations.

One ironic aspect of the foregoing is that although some or many advocates of the invisible hand treat it as an absolute transcending human decision making, or policy, the operative significance of their advocacy is to do exactly what they say cannot and/or should not be done, namely to introduce and legitimize their preferences as to moral and legal rules into the process of working out those rules.

A further ironic aspect of the situation is that the concepts of the invisible hand – and, as we shall see below, of self-interest – are often utilized to counter – or, actually, to channel – social control, but both are within the system of legal and nonlegal social control of a particular type of culture and society.

The invocation of ostensible absolutes serves several functions: It enables the more or less surreptitious introduction of social preferences into the process of working things out. It satisfies a desire for transcendent security, satisfaction here supplied through belief in an invisible hand that presumably coordinates, harmonizes, and so on. Finally, it enables the marshalling and manipulation of social preferences, à la Pareto.

Notwithstanding the advocacy of Hayek's principles of spontaneous order, unintended and unexpected consequences, nondeliberative decision making as superior to deliberative decision making, and the rule of law, the differences of opinion among Hayek's disciples is a microcosm of the larger society. (A joke parallel to the umpire situation, but less humorous, involves the legal student who asks, what is the law? And is given the answer, whatever the judge says it is.) On the basis of following the Hayek List on the Web for many years, as well as reading the participants' publications, I have found among them numerous and fundamental differences of opinion, or interpretation, of Hayek and the application of his ideas. These include:

- what Hayek's system would permit government to do;
- what Hayek believed government should do;
- the evolution of Hayek's ideas and positions;
- Hayek as libertarian or not, and the meaning of libertarian;
- a soft versus a hard Hayek
- the interpretation (definition and evaluation) of the status quo;
- the meaning of democracy and of democracy in relation to libertarianism, totalitarianism, and authoritarianism;
- Hayek in relation to Mises and others;

- Hayekian structure versus Hayekian results; and
- how people interpret the principle of unintended and unexpected consequences.

In his *Theory of Moral Sentiments*, Smith describes the processes of working out conflicts generated by differences of substance, language, and the like. From such issues emerge moral rules that typically are treated and applied as absolutes, yet which in fact are tentative and subject to reexamination and revision based on experience, new ideas, and abrasive contact with other rules. The same is true of the continuing reproduction of legal rules. In such a system, it is illusory to seek unique determinate solutions.

The foregoing, I think, reflects the spirit of Smith's writings and lectures: his tripartite division of society; his synoptic view of the world and his synthetic way of thinking; and his seeming refusal to issue a lengthy list of unilinear explanations and of propositions leading unequivocally to policy.

The term "invisible hand" arguably has three simultaneous domains of meaning. One domain has to do with the term as a definition of reality. Its objective is truth or belief, perhaps especially the former. The second domain has to do with the term as a mode of discourse. Its objective is truth or belief, perhaps especially the latter. The third domain is that of argument. Its objective is to persuade. The combination of all three domains yields the meaning of the term. The combination arises in different ways by different individuals. The result is very personal but is nonetheless driven by various systems of belief. It is these systems of belief that help govern the propositions for which people settle in the absence of truth. It is these propositions, often masquerading as truth, that are deployed by various interests and groups participating in the Paretian process of mutual manipulation.

Understanding Adam Smith in general and the invisible hand in particular requires recognition of the fact that just as there are questions about the invisible hand that receive multiple answers, there are questions about the various terms used in discussions about the invisible hand that also receive multiple answers.

Adam Smith was not a simple-minded fellow, and his unfinished tripartite study was not a simple system. What Smith referred to as "the obvious and simple system of natural liberty" (Smith 1976a: IV. ix.51, 687) was neither obvious nor simple. It would have been enormously helpful if Smith had had an editor, instead of performing that service for himself; an editor who did not shirk from asking, "Professor Smith, what precisely do you mean by X, and can we substitute what you just said for X?"

At any rate, the objective of this essay is to illustrate the conceptual and substantive problems wherein the details of the story are to be found. These problems introduce complications that call into question the simplistic assertion of an invisible hand, its identity, and its function(s).

5.2. Smith's Multiple Paradigms

Adam Smith's ideas have each given rise to multiple interpretations for several reasons. First, we cannot place ourselves in his shoes; we cannot think as he thought even though many of the words are the same; we cannot have the same substantive experiences he did; and so on. These add up to the problem of presentism, interpreting the past in terms of the present, in effect pretending that in Smith's time and place, only one future could result – ours. Secondly, at least equally important is the situation that Smith worked within a number of paradigms. These paradigms include supernaturalism, naturalism, historicism, pragmatism (utilitarianism), empiricism, secularism, materialism, and individualism. This list helps account for both the richness of his writings and how they can be multiply interpreted. Smith's use of the term "invisible hand" may reflect the ubiquity of religious perspective in eighteenth-century Scotland, that is, the effects of hearing about invisible hands in religious and nonreligious materials. At any rate, each of the various terms pertinent to his work is capable of being variably interpreted.

5.3. The Enlightenment

The Enlightenment clearly meant and continues to mean different things to different people, and not only to people alive and thinking at the end of the eighteenth century, who understood and valued different aspects of the Enlightenment differently, but also to people alive recently and currently who understand and value different aspects of the Enlightenment differently. Not only do we find different aspects understood and valued differently, but we find different individuals endeavoring to have the Enlightenment itself reinterpreted and reconstructed along the lines that will promote their interests, material and otherwise, in the present. Specific conceptions of the Enlightenment were then (in the late eighteenth century) and are now intellectual instruments with which to make and remake history.

One does not study the Enlightenment directly; one studies the Enlightenment indirectly, by which I mean that the Enlightenment did not exist in the same sense as a loaf of bread. Granted, my point of distinction should not be overdone; bakers of bread have their history, too. But remaking and reorienting a civilization is not quite the same thing as changing recipes. The Enlightenment is what one's authors make it out to be. When one studies Alembert, Beaumarchais, Burke, Catherine II, Condorcet, Defoe, Descartes, Diderot, Ferguson, Fichte, Hegel, Herder, Hume, Jefferson, Kames, Kant, Lessing, Mirabeau, Montesquieu, Paine, Paley, Quesnay, Robertson, Rousseau, St-Simon, Schiller, Sismondi, and, of course, Adam Smith, one learns, perhaps, what the Enlightenment meant to them. Depending on one's conceptual and substantive criteria, understandings and the respective weights we put on documentary evidence, the Enlightenment will have different attributes.

Whether one is working with eighteenth-century or twentieth-century materials, the Enlightenment was, as it were, what people sought to make of it and putatively did succeed in making it. One could say that what the Enlightenment became was the result of muddling through (Charles Lindblom), the process of working things out (John Dewey, John R. Commons). My chief point is that the Enlightenment was made, not found, as various groups and individuals sought to put their own cachet on it, perhaps to make it theirs, to repel it, to adjust it, and so on. One implication of that point pertinent to the invisible hand is that one cannot look to one or another study of the Enlightenment (or of the invisible hand) to determine the truth of some aspect of the invisible hand. Similarly, one cannot look to one or another study of the invisible hand to determine the truth of some aspect of the Enlightenment.

The Enlightenment has stood for progress, for rational study, for choice uncontaminated by religion and absolutist politics. It has also stood for rational skepticism, factuality, scientific objectivity, empiricism, materialism, and disenchantment with and dissolution of a divinely concerned universe. Certain meanings of the Enlightenment have absorbed themes and attitudes associated with the French Counterrevolution, and vice versa. Some religious people felt, for whatever reason, that the Church was a leader and neither an opponent nor a follower in the Enlightenment movement. Some opposed only one or two Enlightenment themes while supporting other themes. Instead of emphasizing religion as social control, promoting certain beliefs, religion was lauded by some as a nurturing of the human spirit. Some people lauded a policy consciousness that underscored the view that human institutions were human artifacts while rejecting religious and political claims that certain, if not all, human institutions were of divine origin. Some religious people accepted the moral rules of their church while either rejecting or ignoring its theology. Some people rejected the idea that moral rules were of divine origin, whereas others insisted that they had to be of divine origin. Some persons insisted on an absolutist stature for moral rules; others accepted relativism predicated on differences of practice. Some people engaged in conflict – physical and/or doctrinal – over the clash of old and new value systems. Some people preached tolerance. Some people accepted policy consciousness, that institutions were man-made and not divine in origin, whereas others recognized policy consciousness but seemed to have opted for an apolitical society. Some feared that policy consciousness would lead to conflict, whereas others preferred or believed that recognition of policy consciousness would temper religious enthusiasm. Some religious people distinguished between a Catholic and a Christian mode of living. (I knew a person who, when a youngster, had told his priest that he was taking swimming lessons at the local YMCA [Young Men's Christian Association]. The priest responded that he could not take swimming lessons there. The reason given was that the "Y" was Christian and that the young man was Catholic.) On the basis of Smith's *Theory of Moral Sentiments* and other documents, some people believed that moral rules were given to humans by God, whereas others believed that God provided humans with a moral sense, comprised of the principles of approbation and disapprobation, which people themselves put to use in a process of working out moral issues. Some people have believed that the Old and/or New Testament were free of error (inerrant); other people have distinguished between error in matters of morality and/or in matters of science.

Accordingly, several tensions have existed – tensions that have impacted the candidacy of God as the invisible hand. (1) There is tension between the use of political power for religious purposes and the use of religious power for political purposes, including tension over how to distinguish one from the other. (2) There is tension between absolutism and relativism in the fields of philosophy and morality. (3) There is tension between the belief that God originally created the world and ever since has been a passive observer, *and* the belief that God, having created the world, remains an active agent in the world. (4) There is tension between the belief that God is not only active in the world but is a personal God, *and* the belief that God is not a personal God, however otherwise active in the world. (5) There is tension over religion as a link transforming supernaturalism into naturalism and transforming naturalism into secularism and empiricism. (6) There is tension over whether such issues as have been raised here should or should not be discussed in public. (7) There is tension between the belief that mankind should concentrate on living not merely a moral life, whatever that might mean, but a religious/theologically oriented life, with a more or less minimum possible level of economic/materialist gratification. (8) At no time from the eighteenth century through the twentieth century was there an ontologically given, transcendental phenomenon given the name, The Enlightenment. True, building on several centuries of various types of advance in Europe, by the middle of the eighteenth century, a number of movements for reform were well underway. These movements were either the result or the cause of tensions and conflicts, and are to be understood within two time frames, namely (1) a several-century-long secular movement of incremental change from absolute monarchies to the modern state and its sense of citizenship, and (2) shorter periods, with, for example, the intrusion of a Lockean middle-class-dominated legislature into the historic governance structure, such as the period of mercantilism and/or the even longer period in which the landed aristocracy competed with the monarchical institution on the one hand and with the "middle class" on the other.

Several further findings, however preliminary and tentative, can be suggested at this point. (1) There is some, but relatively little, demonstrated connection between most identities of the invisible hand and most functions of the invisible hand. (2) There is considerable uncertainty as to how much and what specifically is known by most people about the tension in New England from the 1620s well into the eighteenth century. The tension was between those who favored a fundamentalist, Puritan way of life and those who sought the way of life of trade, that is, business and economic growth and advancement. The individual colonies had different cultural, economic, and religious histories, but I suspect that by relatively early in the eighteenth century, the commercial life was beginning to be successful over religious life. (3) There is similar uncertainty as to how much and what specific major transformation away from a philosophy of more goods is better than fewer goods would contribute to solving population pressure on nonrenewable resources and on the environment. (4) There is still further uncertainty whether Islamic success over Judeo-Christianity would have made a major contribution to any of the problems raised here. (5) One of the most profound ironies in economics, to which the entire career of Frank H. Knight stands testimony, is that the ostensibly foundational concept of economics, the invisible hand, functions as social control.

5.4. Naturalism

The eighteenth century arguably was the first – or possibly the second – period in which Naturalism became a major philosophical movement, or in which Naturalism became a significant part of the belief system of society, particularly of educated people. The losing, as it were, but apparently still-dominant mode of thought was Supernaturalism. Insofar as naturalism is a prelude to scientific investigation, it assumes that the phenomena under investigation are of like kind, not subject to an invisible hand producing irregular effect, in part so that tests can be meaningfully repeated (Bothamley 2002: 364). Naturalism is description or explanation, without invoking supernatural agencies, of the natural order inclusive of human phenomena (Bynum et al. 1981: 283). Some authorities emphasize a deterministic conception, permitting repetition while excluding supernatural, teleological, or spiritual elements and forces as well as revelation (Webster Dictionary 1994: 953). Several scholars have identified Adam Smith's multiple uses of "naturalism" in his *Wealth of Nations*. One investigator identified the following uses by Smith: (1) to denote the innate characteristics of a thing or person; (2) to denote behavior that is in accord with the set of innate characteristics that individuals possess; (3) to denote behavior that is consistent with stated characteristics of the actors, regardless of whether those characteristics are themselves innate or natural; (4) natural denotes a characteristic or operation of the physical world, construed to exclude mankind; (5) identifying a certain form of liberty, namely natural liberty; (6) to denote an event that takes place of its own accord, which in this case means in the absence of human action except insofar as that action is in accordance with humankind's innate characteristics; (7) natural price, the price that results under the system of natural liberty; and (8) a synonym for "ordinary" (Puro 1992: 74, 76, 78, 79, 81, 84, 85). That no less than eight distinct uses can be identified suggests the difficulties encountered in making sense of a key term pertinent to the invisible hand and other terms.

Naturalism is a mode of discourse, a belief system, and a definition of reality. The use of naturalism renders many discussions of the invisible hand empty, indeed vacuous, and inconclusive. Whereas naturalism was newly important in the seventeenth and eighteenth centuries, its possible meanings were sufficiently diverse that almost any use left considerable ambiguity. The use of "nature" and "natural" left any discussion open-ended. "Nature" could be juxtaposed to "artificial." Nature could be compelling on humankind. Humans could be in control of nature. Nature could refer to a good, to be followed: however as a bad, it was something to be overcome. Attitudes toward nature could be one of alienation, of compliance, of aggression, or as a resource. Mutation could be seen as natural or as caused by humans.

Then there was "natural law." But what law? Law was something made, not found; it served as social control, often by a ruling class. In such cases, it was not just any natural law; it was that of a particular instituted system or someone's interpretation of it. It amounted to the projection and reification of a particular status quo, or one selective version of it, thereby given a seemingly ontological "natural" status. Naturalism was a name for a fallacy: treating as natural what is a matter of human social construction. The problem was that humankind is part of nature. Naturalism got one nowhere. In pretty much every respect, these terms are a matter of interpretation, of human social construction.

5.5. Supernaturalism

In no respect is interpretation and human social construction arguably more evident and more inconclusive than supernaturalism. What has been written earlier in this essay about naturalism is multiply true of theology. I write that not to be derogatory, only to point out that the diversity of religious belief demands more than does naturalism.

My principal interest is to see not what Smith meant but to identify what evidence seems to have supported what belief system he may have had over time. I am not saying that if evidence E can support belief B, then B is correct. I am saying that if evidence E can support belief B or belief C, then we do not know whether B or C is supported, given E. One can construct a situation that if E can support B or C but not D, then if E is present, then B or C – but not D – follows, but we have no basis on which to say that E supports B, or C. (This is a variation on the proposition, R or S imply T and T is present, then what? Since either R or S can yield T, having T does not tell us where this T in this instance is caused by this R or this S.)

The issues or questions of Smith's theology or religiosity are reasonably clear: Did he believe in God, and if so, what did that mean? What was the relation of God to nature? Was Smith a Deist or a Theist? Was he an Atheist; a Christian? If God was important to him, was it because God was the progenitor of the universe and/or active in this world or because the conception of God is useful for social control and whose denial would generate punishment? What, for Smith, is fact, what is belief, what is intuition, and what is inference?

I do not offer answers to those questions here, because I have not yet worked out the relations of evidence to belief for Smith. Still, the following "conclusions" seem at present reasonably clear to me.

1. Smith seems to have been or acted as a sociologist of religion. He could hold religious ideas at arm's length. He seems to have had an idea, a

theory, of the secular origins of moral rules, of the operation of the principles of approbation and disapprobation in the process of working out not only moral but also legal rules. Such does not rule out the possibility that he was both a sociologist of religion and a believer.

2. It is not necessarily the case, and there may be no evidence to support it, but his evident hostility toward "superstition" does not mean that he applied the term "superstition" only to Catholicism.

3. The term "Deism" meant different things to different people. Some supporters of Deism likely defined it differently than other supporters. Some opponents of Deism likely defined it differently from some, or many, or all supporters.

4. The evidence for serious religiosity may be no more than the evidence for weak religiosity, but it is more likely that the evidence may be less conclusive.

5. Theodicy undoubtedly was given various definitions by different people, but defining theodicy weakly may or may not be more likely to suffice.

6. Much of the written evidence in support of Smith being a believer requires an additional premise to reach that conclusion; but that conclusion is possible.

7. Some or much of the evidence supporting the conclusion that Smith was a believer is consistent with Smith being cautions knowing the treatment given Hutcheson and Hume in light of what others felt were their transgressions.

8. Given that religion is political in nature, it is possible that certain behavior, by Smith or by his actual or potential critics or opponents, was political in nature.

9. If natural religion is religion without revelation, based on some conception of nature, the implication, given what is said above about natural and nature, is uncertain.

10. One must be wary of the possibility of circularity: Reason generates a notion of natural religion that is then used to channel and confirm reason.

11. Aside from the possibility that Smith changed his mind over time, it is also possible that Smith concurrently held two positions: his private view of God, theology, ontology, and organized religion; and his objective analysis of God, religion, an Established Church, religious sects, and moral sentiments.

12. It is not clear that any conclusion with regard to Smith and supernaturalism would necessarily be informative as to the invisible hand. It

is possible, however, that some evidence might turn up that would be informative. Smith had numerous opportunities to take his readers in that direction but did not pursue them. It may well be that Smith had other reasons for using the term "invisible hand," such as his argument in the *History of Astronomy*, his use of a figure of speech, and what he might have thought of the invisible hand as knowledge.

13. Smith had a stages theory of history. The stages are identified in terms of government and law, and neither naturalism nor supernaturalism. It is not clear that even a weak economic determinism is involved; Smith seems to have been silent on the issue. What is clear is that the movement to commercial society, compared to other shifts from one stage to another, is situated in law and government and is revolutionary. However, as is the case with many other matters, Smith is silent on the relation of the change of stage to an invisible hand. Indeed, Smith is silent on pretty much every aspect of the invisible hand.

5.6. The Social Belief System

We have seen in Essay 4 that the belief system of society is the source of propositions that, as Smith put it, soothe the imagination. Not each and every individual requires certitude with respect to having a soothed imagination, but those who do so require may well be driven and in a position to drive others. We have also seen that those propositions can serve humankind by defining reality, providing a mode of discourse, and constituting the stuff of which arguments are made and ostensibly settled. The propositions likely are of two types. One type is seen by believers transcendental, deterministic, exclusivist, and apolitical. The other type is practical and empirical. The former seeks to set minds at rest by negating social decision making. The latter seeks to set minds at rest by restricting change to incremental adjustments. Arguments may also be distinguished as sophisticated or naïve. The belief system in general and propositions in particular are the subject of multiple practices, theories, and analyses of myth and symbols, and of social control and psychic balm. The belief system is amenable to utopian (or dystopian) formulation.

The social mythological system can be considered a human construct. Like the social belief system as a whole, it has been generated in part through the principle of unintended and unforeseen consequences. It is a result of nondeliberative and deliberative decision making.

The most conspicuous parts of the deliberative elements of the social mythological system are the judiciary, the executive branch (including institutions commonly labeled the administrative branch), and the legislative branch. Closely connected with these formal branches are the pursuit of strategic decision making by business.

Myth serves the functions of social control and psychic balm. The propositions and images constituting the mythic system of society are a widely used rhetorical device to persuade and cast luster on an argument. The principal targets of the mythological system serving as psychic balm are death (including life in the hereafter) and anything else important to humankind in the here and now. Only two things are important to the same degree as life and death and similarly warrant the setting of minds at rest: One is social recognition and approval; the other is the acquisition of the goods that enable us to better our material condition and results in social approval.

The "invisible hand" has the characteristics of myth. It is not quite true that the invisible hand is finessed in present-day sophisticated western society. It is the case, too, that the invisible hand is part of the social belief system. But it is also part of the linguistic system of society.

5.7. Self-Interest

Let us next take up the problem of self-interest and related considerations. The first problem is whether self-interest actually meaningfully defines reality.

Other than the invisible hand passage of the *Wealth of Nations*, it is likely that the best-known passage of that remarkable book is this:

[M]an has almost constant occasion for the help of his brethren, and it is in vain for him to expect it from their benevolence only. He will be more likely to prevail if he can interest their self-love in his favour, and shew them that it is for their own advantage to do for him what he requires of them. (Smith 1976a, I.ii.2, 26)

As if he had not already made his point, its importance to his argument brought forth the memorable language:

It is not from the benevolence of the butcher, the brewer, of the baker, that we expect our dinner, but from their regard to their own interest. We address ourselves, not to their humanity but to their self-love, and never talk to them of our own necessities but of their self-love, and never talk to them of our own necessities but of their advantages. (Smith 1976a, I.ii.2, 26–7)

The problems that Smith in effect proposes for our edification are whether self-interest is the key to the definition of reality, what is the substance of self-interest and how is it formed, whether people actually are driven to excess by their self-love, and whether self-interest is a methodological assumption. Considered as a definition of reality, several versions exist; for example the actual version versus the ideal version. The ideal version is laden with romance, is utopian, and is either the ideal or an ideal type. A sophisticated versus naïve version of the argument has as a parallel the-strong-versus-the-weak argument or forms of argument. As a tool of analysis, self-interest is fiction – perhaps a form of science fiction. The problem reduces in part to ideology versus science, and its substance is a function of the regnant economic system, or "stage." The further issue raised by the problem of self-interest is how much is ignored or neglected by the self-interest and rationality assumptions whether functioning as a definition of reality or a limiting assumption.

The first problem, again, is whether the pursuit of self-interest actually defines reality. The pursuit of self-interest is actual economic reality, but saying so does not indicate much.

The second problem derives from the fact that some authors consider self-interest to be the driving force in the economic system whereas other authors consider self-interest to be the object of control. For self-interest to be the driving force, the agents of the driving force must have a wide range of discretion, thereby unleashing the driving force of self-interest. Self-interest is the driving force because it combines motivation with wide discretion. But self-interest is the object of control. As to why self-interest is the object of control, the component that seems common to many if not all answers to that question, or to a sufficient proportion of answers to warrant serious attention, is *abuse of discretion.*

The nature, even the genius, of the institution of private property and of particular rights of property, is that it locates the making of choices in nominally private hands. To exercise choice is to use discretion. Some combination of experience, moral rules, and other considerations from time to time lead us to consider that the opportunity to make certain choices, or to exercise discretion, may result in socially dysfunctional results. The same reasoning applies to institutions of public office. In the making of economic, that is, business, decisions, it is in the self-interest of a business decision maker to maximize – or, more properly, to optimize – profit. One means of doing so is to shift costs to other people and attract gains to one's self or to one's firm. This is a very complicated subject, and seemingly meaningful statements cannot be made without introducing antecedent subjective and normative premises as to whose interests count. Among the reasonably objective statements that can be made are: (1) the reciprocal nature of externalities, as shown for example by Ronald Coase, that is, no one party generates costs independent of some other engaged party; (2) taxes and subsidies perform the same function, namely making certain activity or results too costly to continue; and (3) policy decisions usually, if not always, involve subjective judgments – for example, holding that moral behavior should not require bribery. All these and still other factors contribute to what different parties consider to be in their self-interest.

As indicated earlier in this essay, the irony of the situation is that the concepts of the invisible hand and of self-interest are often utilized to counter – actually, to channel – social control by others, but both are within the system of legal and nonlegal social control of a particular type of culture and society.

The status of self-interest is mixed: applause versus condemnation. Self-interest is often criticized and defended as greed or excessive greed – also called avarice, cupidity, venality, rapacity, egomania, and narcissism, all sometimes translated and transformed into self-interest versus enlightened self-interest.

The late Milton Friedman is known for his insistent opposition to pressuring business to act morally or environmentally responsibly. He is less well known for having said (it is reported) that the market is only one of several systems of social control, the others being the family, moral rules, law, and so on. For some reason, Friedman rationalized the conduct of extreme self-interest in a manner that legitimized such behavior by negating those other constraints on abusive behavior.

The definition of extreme self-interest, perhaps even self-interest per se ("the business of business is to make a profit, period"), is surprisingly close to: (1) megalomania: a form of mental illness or a mentality marked by delusions of greatness and wealth; obsession with doing great things or with acquiring great power and wealth; (2) psychopath: a type of personality characterized by amoral and antisocial behavior; extreme egocentricity; and (3) sociopath: a person who is hostile to society. All three convey the absence of regard for the impact of one's actions, policies, and decisions on others. "'Vanity of vanities' says the Preacher' 'Vanity of vanities, all is vanity'" (Ecclesiastes 1.2).

The meaning of self-interest as a driving force, subject to being an object of control, varies with a variety of lines of reasoning. (1) Multiple specifications of the end pursued: maximum or optimum output, value of production, income, wealth, status, honor, Pareto optimal results, marginal cost equal to marginal revenue, marginal utility of Alpha equal to marginal utility of Beta. The usual models ignore the initial and/or consequential structure of power. (2) Multiple theories of behavior: numerous psychological and social psychological theories; multiple theories of the mind and of consciousness; multiple descriptions and explanations of the subtleties of human nature; problems of nonrational and irrational behavior; multiple theories of intentionality; and so on. Over the years, economists have often chosen to ignore psychology and any other variables that they elected to exclude from economics. It is difficult to say which is better (or worse): omitting arguably important variables, or including them but retaining the numerous ways in which they can be modeled, or including them and consciously seeking to achieve a consensus model. It is also difficult to distinguish between a model believed to adequately represent the agreed-on major forces and a model elected on the basis of a particular modeling strategy.

Two procedures have operated within microeconomics for the better part of the twentieth century. The second is the gradually evolved neoclassical research protocol that requires determinate unique equilibrium solutions. The other is the use of elements of that protocol as a sieve or filtration mechanism allowing the acceptance of some work and the rejection of other work.

Perhaps the subjects of greatest importance have been (1) the attachment of individuals to particular objects, (2) the socialization of the individual, including formal and informal learning, and (3) the role of structural variables governing whose identities, attachments, and selective perception is to count.

For some economists, behavior is deemed to be a function of relative prices. For other economists, behavior is modeled as a function of institutions, either with or without relative prices. Still other economists have modeled behavior as a function of relative opportunities.

It is often difficult to distinguish the "self" in self-interest from the formation of self-interest. The formulation of the self is in part that of forming one's self-image and in part the process and substance (honor or wealth) of status emulation. Inasmuch as people desire and more or less actively seek social approval and respect, individuals are more or less other-directed in their formation of self, self-identity, and preference formation. The assumption of given and unchanging preferences and identities has largely ruled the socialization process out of analytical bounds.

Inasmuch as the corporation is treated legally as a person and, in any event, acts as if it were a person, it is not surprising that economists generally treat it as a person. The problem of objective function is faced by human individuals and by corporations – legal individuals and economic institutions. Human individuals, who typically are defined as the family, have to work out what kind of life, within various constraints, they will lead. So too does the corporation. The life of managerial personnel includes participation in the process of working out the objectives of the corporation. This can be a matter of individual rivalry for control, the rivals either already in the managerial ranks of the corporation or on the outside. It seems clear that the neoclassical-type solution to such problems, such as assuming a market for corporate control, while theory-enriching compared to the omission of such matters, nonetheless tends to trivialize the overall problem.

Another facet of the large problem of identity and decision making is the problem of who is recognized to have an interest impacted by corporate decision making. The problem is obviously dual, one of joint determination. The determination of who is a member of the community is *pro tanto* the determination of whose interests are to be pursued as part of the objective function of the corporation, and the determination of whose interests are to be pursued is *pro tanto* the determination of who constitutes, as a member, the community. The resolution of who is a member of the community is thus a cause and a consequence. In the contemporary industrialized nations, correlative with other issues to be worked out, are the question of economic and social class, race, ethnic identity, and gender. For various reasons, decision making takes place very deep on the corporate ladder. From a Hayekian point of view, such participation in decision making is a way in which local and personal knowledge is made useful to others. This may be reckoned as the combination in various ways of informal and formal components. No simple or simplistic invisible hand can capture under the heading of one identity of the invisible hand the range and depth of decision making.

An individual's interests are neither "natural" nor unchangeable, but are in part a function of such factors as the structure of rules (of whatever type), the structure of power between groups or classes of actors/agents, and the process of individual identification that helps form personhood, if not also personality, as well as the technological and institutional context. A change in any of these factors will elicit a change of interests.

5.8. Self-Interest Further Considered

Earlier in this essay, we noted that some economists identify self-interest as the invisible hand; one candidate among many others but still a candidate for the identity of the invisible hand. We also noted that some economists considered self-interest very differently – as the object of control by the invisible hand. A driving force as the invisible hand versus a driving force requiring control by the invisible hand constitutes quite a contrast. The psychodynamics of that situation seem to have been comprised of beliefs somewhat like the following: (1) Something as important and honorific as self-interest could hardly be understood to be anything but an, or the, invisible hand; (2) self-interest as a check on self-interest is something of a definition of competition producing automatic self-regulation; and (3) the *ideas* of self-interest serving as control and of self-interest requiring control by the invisible hand, insofar as the ideas resuscitate affirmative roles for social control, including social control by government, are anathema to the discipline of economics, whose practitioners desire the status of scientist, to be safe, and to have something presumably solid and useful to offer as policy. That every other social science – political science, sociology, psychology – had a prominent place for social control was beside the point. Economists who presented the market, or the market system, as a control system seem to have been wary of overdoing the point. If it is dangerous for self-interest to be associated with social control, then making it the invisible hand rendered it safe.

If the formation of self-interests is within the purview of economists, then a host of factors would newly enter into the formation process. Ironically, those factors would interfere with the effective working of the invisible hand. Among those overlapping factors are the socialization of the individual, including his or her sense of identity and self-worth; the individual as a passive responder to market forces and signals vis-à-vis the individual as an active agent of choice and change; the formation of personal preferences and social preferences; the relative roles of Hayek's and Knight's deliberative and nondeliberative decision making; the formation of expectations; principal–agent activities and problems; the formation and role of incentive systems in colleges and universities, firms, law, and in the entire economy; the expansiveness of wants; the conditions and consequences of learning; path dependency; the formation of habits and routines; and so on.

One of the topics central to notions of self-interest and general economic theory is *rationality*. The significance of rationality for present purposes is the ambiguity and inconclusiveness it introduces into general economic theory and the invisible hand. Rationality has variable specifications within economics. Rationality also has variable specifications across disciplines, such as procedural versus substantive, legal, social, pragmatic, and so on. Rationality has several further aspects: as a fact, as a methodological limiting assumption, and as performing an ideological function. Further elaboration is not required to see that rationality introduces further sources of multiplicity and elasticity of meaning – a characteristic of every aspect of the invisible hand.

The impact on the meaningfulness and utility of the invisible hand of these difficulties can be identified through certain dualisms that emphasize the necessity of choice as to the source of causation and the route it takes. Among the dualisms are individual versus environment; individuation versus socialization; scarcity and its consequences, such as tragedy and the problem of Job, versus the imagery and partial reality of harmonism; determinism leading to reductionism versus an ambiguous projection of universalist laws of invisible hands; nature versus nurture; individual decisions and choice versus culture; institutions versus genetics; and so on.

Consider the topics of scarcity and the problem of Job. If any concept is seen to constitute a deeper foundational level than that of the invisible hand, it is *scarcity*. Scarcity in the Robbinsian sense leads to the notion of cost and, perhaps especially, opportunity cost. Robbinsian scarcity engenders the necessity of choice. Radical indeterminacy amounts to scarcity of knowledge of the future, in part because the future does not yet exist, because we have not yet (fully) acted so as to produce the future. Changing levels and density of population, changing technology, changing preferences, and numerous other phenomena are both produced by and contribute to changes in self-interests.

It is not my intention to support one or another theory of the eviction of human beings from the Garden of Eden or one or another theory of God. Notice, however, the initial apparent irrelevance of scarcity. The principal characteristic of Eden is abundance. Thomas Robert Malthus's population theory is ultimately grounded in eviction-induced scarcity because of original violation of a rule of divine control. One of the perennial questions raised by Malthus's population theory concerns why God did not create Adam and Eve so as to perfectly obey God's rule. An earlier form of the question had the background not of population pressure but of the eviction itself. Indeed, one interpretation of Christianity is that it is a story of theodicy – in short, why bad things happen to good people. To discuss theodicy at all meaningfully, one must have conceptions of goodness, badness, of divine intentions, and, ultimately, an explanation of why God designed an imperfect humanity. A God who was serious, omniscient, and omnipotent would presumably not have created an imperfect humanity, a humanity that would have to learn to be perfect, but would have fabricated a perfect humanity. All of the foregoing raises the generic or overriding question: If God was humanity's creator, at least apropos the argument from design, why did God use a faulty design?

Now introduce the concept of an invisible hand, one candidate for the identity of which is God, or the invisible hand of God. If God created humanity and did not use a faulty design, why is an invisible hand required to perform certain functions? If God designed everything, why do problems exist? This question arises whether the identity of the invisible hand is God or some other candidate.

It is also not my intention to deal with the theory of evolution, whether or not it is stipulated that (some form of) evolution theory – for example, random variation and natural selection – is an instrument through which God acts. Suffice it to say that economists and noneconomists have come up with a variety of theories of evolution, each theory congenial to the overall view of its author. (Often the proffered identity of the invisible hand tells more about the author of the proposal than the invisible hand itself.) Accordingly, the domain of evolution theory is very broad and laden with conflict. Furthermore, if the invisible hand is natural selection, it is not likely that it can solve all the tensions and conflicts for which function other candidates for the identity of the invisible hand have been nominated. On the other hand, the evolution theory of God as the invisible hand may actually be a theory of co-evolution. Interpreting natural selection as a theory of the survival of the fittest begs a host of questions, such as the specifications of "fittest" and of time horizon.

It is also not my contention that matters within economics relating to scarcity and the invisible hand, especially the latter, would be better if such tensions and conflicts did not exist. No, the significance of these tensions and conflicts and of the conceptual and substantive problems raised in this essay is that, if indeed there is an invisible hand, it cannot handle them. The world is too complicated for all these and still other differences to be resolved by an invisible hand. An active mind can picture an economy with invisible hands at every turn, each one projected to solve a problem, akin to how certain problems are finessed, solved, or what have you by simply assuming that a market exists – as, for example the market for corporate control. All problems would be eliminated by virtue of the action of the invisible hand – especially if God is the invisible hand and is given some reason to use an imperfect design. We have here, therefore, a concept, the invisible hand, that is essentially a metaphysical construction or projection; an invisible hand said to be a metaphor, but without a meaningful answer to the question: For what is the invisible hand a metaphor?

One characteristic feature that many of the discussions in this collection of essays have in common is the considerable range of discretion that exists in the economy and polity, and therefore in what I have called the legal-economic nexus. One hears that this country has due process of law and strongly recommends it to other countries. That trope vastly understates the extent of discretion exercised throughout government. I find that situation is inevitable (I do not feel any compulsion to normatively evaluate that situation). I find (as positive matters) that statements like those usually made about the invisible hand, are, first, to no small extent exercises in symbolism and mythology, that is, the exercise of social control; and second, they beg the question of what has to be worked out and thereby is finessed, obfuscated, and omitted from economic models and legal models. The finessing, the obfuscation, and the omitting are inevitable in the same way that passes to wide receivers are sometimes dropped by even the best of them, and in the same way that outstanding hitters in baseball – say, who have a batting average of 350 – still fail to hit 65 percent of the time. Adam Smith, in his *Theory of Moral Sentiments*, speaks of moral rules as a category, but not all specific moral rules will be accepted by everyone. The substantive content of the category has to be worked out, and Smith is more concerned with the process than with the content. The same is true in law with respect to which one can favor the protection supposedly accorded by the due-process-of-law clause in helping promote the rule of law but ignores the significance of at least two questions: "Yes, the rule of law, but which law is it to be?" and "When is abuse of discretion permitted and when is it prosecuted?"

It is one thing to assume and assert the existence of an invisible hand; it is quite something else to presume that this imaginary invisible hand obviates the process of working things out. I think that the content of this essay, coordinated with that of the preceding and following essays, raises serious questions: Does the invisible hand exist? What, if any, knowledge is given by the invisible hand? What are the actual functions performed by the concept of the invisible hand? What meaning is to be assigned to terms like "laissez-faire" and "noninterventionism"? Is economics less or more important than law in such matters? What is the significance for a discipline that, for many of its practitioners, accepts the mythological concept of an invisible hand as its foundation, when in fact the concept of an invisible hand has become a vehicle for importing into economics a particular approach to economic policy not all that different from other approaches to economic policy, all the while arguably misstating the legal foundations of our economic system and, indeed, of all economic systems?

Visualize, if you will, a model in which each and every term stands for all the subsidiary variables that comprise it. If the term is used without specification, then it has no substantive content. If the term is used with such specification, the resulting content more or less also lacks meaningful substance because the substantive content of each of its component variables is influenced and shaped by the content and their relative weights of the other variables, with each element of the model likely to help steer, as it were, the variable and one or more of its specifications. Development of the model will also be affected by the interpretations given it by the developers. The interpretations themselves will be more or less numerous, but whichever is chosen will be, in part, the result of personal ideological subjective belief system, hence of social control, and so on.

The invisible hand – I should write, instead: the imagery of the invisible hand – has helped provide the economics profession with eminence and celebrity and also with irritation and disparagement, all amid contentment and condescension. Noneconomists have taken the term to heart almost as avidly as professional economists. Economics is simultaneously an intellectual discipline and religion. Two of its roles are those of an institution of social control and psychic balm. Enveloping these two roles is the desire in people – more so in some and less so for others – for a sense – selectively, of course – or pretext of closure and determinacy. These folks absorb the social controls and psychic balm and, insofar as the imagery of an invisible hand is concerned, lead happy lives. Other folks rest and act content with the understanding that the world of humankind is open-ended and ambiguous.

The invisible-hand term is at the heart of one view of the world. This first view is that names and meaning come to us from the objects of our inquiry. This is akin to the beliefs that judges find, and not make, the law; and that the laws of economic life, if followed, would lead to an Edenic future. (Is that an amendment to the Book of Genesis?) The other view affirms that, like it or not, legal and moral rules have not been given to humankind but emerge, through various decision-making structures and processes – these structures and processes themselves emerge in the same manner – comprising the process of working things out. However one looks at the matter, the operative social process is that of working things out. Joseph Spengler, as I have pointed out, identified as the problem of order the process of working out the reconciliation of autonomy and control, continuity and change, and hierarchy and egalitarianism. In such a world, we must not forget that the group of people who require determinacy and closure, however selectively, are fated to suffer the disappointments arising, they think, from the success of those who are more or less content with open-endedness and ambiguity. In neither case is change due to the groups involved (any more than in the case of Hayek's principles). Yes, they act as if social motion or fate was their or their leaders' doing, whereas the problem of order is resolved in a continuing manner through the process of working things out. In all this, we can agree with Frank Knight who amended one of Marx's slogans and came up with the proposition that religion is not only the opiate of the masses, but also the sedative of the (upper) classes. I would add that economists may or may not sense or understand this but they play their role, while pretending not to. *What more could a discipline like economics reasonably expect?*

The invisible hand is a trope that is highly significant in the lives of people in seemingly all walks of life and possibly in all societies by religions, before and after the Reformation, with variations between religious movements. The term is also used in fiction, in business, in religion, and in politics. There is no question that people are both sensitive to and attracted to the very notion of an invisible hand. That sensitivity is a basis of its use. That different persons identify both the invisible hand and its functions differently transfers – and, in the process, transforms – the term from a metaphor (and other figures of speech) to that of a primitive term.

5.9. Infinite Expansion

One of the chief purposes of this essay is to explore the matter of self-interest, largely because it enters the discussion of the invisible hand in so many important ways, for example, driving force or object of control, the notion and formation of the "self," the relation of the individual to society, problems of modeling self-interest, and so on. Another purpose is to suggest that at every turn in the discourses on the invisible hand, one encounters subject matter that is not only capable of but is in fact treated in different ways.

Economists are, I think, as typically confused as everyone else on what is going on when they treat a term like self-interest in whatever way they do. The assumptions are that people have self-interest(s), or that they know their preferences, or that tastes are given, and so on. Such assumptions are of two types: methodological and substantive. As a methodological assumption, it is adopted to make the analysis manageable and/or to make explicit that the person making the assumption feels either that we are largely ignorant of the material ("we" meaning all economists or those who are a member of a particular school of economic thought), or that the excluded material is largely irrelevant to the author's purpose, or that given some assumed definition of the scope of economics, it is excluded, however relevant it may be. As a substantive assumption, it is adopted because the person making the assumption is either ignorant that he or she is doing so, or believes that people have settled tastes or preferences, or because, knowing or fearing, for example, that increased knowledge about the formation of self-interest will lead to the adoption of government policies to steer the formation of some direction and not others. It is difficult to give credence to ignorance of making the assumption. It is somewhat less difficult to believe that people assume actual constancy of tastes. I have known people who think it subversive to assume that the formation of tastes should be exposed to the winds of politics.

I raise this matter, first, because it is part and parcel of the problem of self-interest; secondly, because some people either are or seem to be ignorant of it and/or assume belief in given preferences; thirdly, ignore the possibility that in making the assumption, they are also buying into the antistate position; and fourthly, because there are people who either think it does not and/or should not matter.

I think the following is a credible position: A person should be able to assume given tastes as either a methodological or a substantive assumption. A person should know what they are doing and the consequences of their doing so. A person should be specifically aware that government is *already* in the business of forming tastes as part of its service as social control. Education is either provided by or influenced by the government. Wherever an institution other than government provides education, it, too, is an institution of social control, in effect governmental in nature. Education is merely an example of the general proposition that all of life is governed by law/social control, and that changing the law does not, or does not necessarily, constitute an increase or a decrease in government/social control. It is neither absurd nor inconsistent for an individual to be both antistate/anti–social control and an advocate of some restraint on people's behavior, though it may appear that they are one or the other, *if* they (1) recognize that the latter is an exception to the former; (2) do not attempt to evade the issue by asserting that *their* list of "exceptions" is part of the natural order of things or what the deity demands; and (3) recognize the ubiquity and importance of social control and of the process of working out the details of social control.

What is attractive about Robbins's market-and-framework approach, as either a *general* model or one expanded to include legal change and nonlegal social control, and what is attractive about his identification of the invisible hand as the law giver or statesman, is that the approach should (I do not say, will) help prevent the seemingly boundless absurd rhetoric of politics that serves the function of constituting a platform on which to run for public office. The "consistency" of a candidate's positions cannot and does not require that if the candidate favors one law (say, L1) on one subject, they need not favor another law (say, L2) on another subject. The law is a matter of freedom and control (as well as of change and continuity) in such a way that law involves a structure of freedom and a simultaneous correlative structure of control. In the language of rights, no right can be fully defined, and all rights are attenuated: Neither judge nor legislator (even when said to be the invisible hand) can know all of the possible or likely conditions under which reciprocal externalities will place conflicting rights holders in some position of conflict of claimed rights.

Adam Smith wrote that "The great secret of education is to direct vanity to proper objects" (Smith 1976b, VI.iii.46; 259). What constitutes vanity in relation to control and what constitutes a "proper object" is a matter to be worked out. Every topic to which discussion of the invisible hand turns and every position on which some position thereon rests is capable of what I call "infinite expansion." I use that term to emphasize the importance, multiplicity, and complexity of the topics raised by the invisible-hand discourse.

This encompasses all aspects of self-interest. It also applies to every use of the term "freedom" and other comparable phrases. For a professional economist to argue that one's own position on the issues is or should be exempt from public discussion, even to suggest that there should be no public discussion of the fact that the topic discussed *is* a matter of social control, is to adopt the high-priest role and to open widely the door to every sort of villainy. If, further, one feels that politics is corrupt, because, for example, politicians speak words that they either know or should know are misleading, the viable position is not to do away with politics. Politics is not so easily done away with. *Some* group is going to make decisions, whether we like it or not.

Politics does not only derive from corrupt people; it derives from the nature and structure of collective decision making, whether in some branch of government, in schools, in business, or in religious organizations.

A further and overriding purpose is to suggest that the presence of this multiplicity necessarily results in the omission of important topics or in their enormously incomplete treatment. Neither judge nor legislator (even when said to be the invisible hand) can know of or prepare for all of the possible or likely conditions under which reciprocal externalities will place conflicting rights holders in some position of conflict of claimed rights. No candidate for invisible-hand status will fail to encounter different difficulties.

6

The Invisible Hand in an Uncertain World
with an Uncertain Language

6.1. Introduction

Essay 3 presented the approximately four dozen answers, many of them given several formulations, that are found in the literature of economics (and related fields) to the question: What is the invisible hand? Also presented there are the approximately one dozen major responses that have been elicited by another question: What are the functions of the invisible hand? Here too most, if not all, of the individual answers have numerous formulations. The resulting multiplicity is a principal feature of the use of the term "invisible hand." The important consequence of this multiplicity, in regard to at least these two of the most fundamental aspects of the meaning of the term, is that the term is essentially ambiguous.[1] When the invisible hand is given some four dozen identities, the term is, for most, if not all, practical and theoretical purposes, empty – indeed, it should be seen as not having an invisible hand.

Terms that are given no specific definition are called "primitive" terms. Propositions that contain one or more primitive terms have little, if any, meaning. When such a term is used aurally and even if all auditors nod in agreement, more than likely they individually identify and understand the primitive term differently. The same is true of terms that are encountered in reading. Such terms are essentially assertions. Their purpose is in part to obfuscate the fact that there is now and likely never will be a meaningful answer to the question posed.[2] But, both more broadly and in the context

---

[1] These are two of the questions I determined as needing, in effect, to be put to all uses of the term "invisible hand." I suspect that if authors posed these questions to themselves, there might be an increase in the coherence of what they write and therefore a decrease in ambiguity.

[2] The identification of primitive terms should not be confused with the difference between a category and its possible specific content. For example, in *The Theory of Moral Sentiments*,

of this group of essays, such terms help define the world for us by serving to reinforce some larger category (such as one identity of the invisible hand also functioning to both take advantage of and promote the general category of identities of "invisible hand").

I sense that economists consider the term "invisible hand" to be a figure of speech, especially a metaphor or a simile, either because doing so lends an aura of substantiality and solidity to a concept otherwise suspected of being insubstantial, or because of an inchoate suspicion that there is in fact no invisible hand.

This essay examines two general topics. One is the relevant linguistic analysis pertaining to language in general, especially the political nature of language and the domains or respects in which it is operative. The other is the linguistic nature of the term "invisible hand," particularly how linguists interpret metaphor and other figures of speech.

6.2. Language in General: The Political Nature of Language

The field of linguistics resembles all other fields in the wide range of approaches taken or proposed by its practitioners. Nonetheless, a substantial degree of agreement exists on some basic issues. One of the latter is the study of the political nature of language. From at least the 1930s, it seems to this outsider, increasing agreement on the technical details in that area has outweighed increasing disagreement. Moreover, as the twentieth century evolved, the proliferation of topics was driven by opportunities for revision and dissent, while tensions over the use of propaganda during World War II and Viet Nam were contained. Linguistics itself grew and benefited from scholars from other fields (philosophy, political science, political sociology). The nature of both language and politics (political philosophy) was substantially enriched. The development of the field centered on the articulation of the importance of language (Sturtevant 1947; Black 1962), the vocabulary of politics (Weldon 1953) and the words of politics (Rodgers 1987; Luntz 2007), the politics of language (Degré 1985; Hoeflich 1986), various intersections of language and politics (Chomsky 1988) and of both of those topics and knowledge (Lagemann 1989), the linguistics of liberty (Sampson 1970), language and the definition of reality (Whorf 1956), political symbolism, myth, and ruling illusions (Edelman 1967; Skillen 1978;

Smith addresses the central category of "moral rules" but does not specify their content, leaving them to be worked out within the process identified in terms of the Impartial Spectator and the principles of approbation and disapprobation.

Calabresi 1985; Samuel and Thompson 1990), and the sermonic (Weaver 1970), cognitive, and political criticism (Shapiro 1990) aspects of the political nature of language. It is not too much to say that, from my general pluralist approach to epistemology, theory, and most everything else, the discipline of economics pales in comparison when one looks at its failure to welcome fundamental dissent, thereby losing opportunities for analytical enrichment. One reason for this failure is the mindset that lauds absolutist formulations such as the invisible hand when there is no scholarly justification for doing so.

When Alpha is constrained by law (statute, court decision) in order to protect the interests of Beta, the situation is generally called regulation. When the law is reversed, the new law no longer protects the interests of Beta; it protects the interests of Alpha and leaves Beta exposed to the actions of Alpha now allowed by the new law. This situation is generally called deregulation. Yet the two situations are analytically equivalent: The interests of one party are protected and those of the other party are left exposed; only the identity of the two parties has changed. If Beta had been constrained in order to protect Alpha, that would have been called regulation, and the reversal, now protecting Beta's interests and leaving Alpha exposed, would have been called deregulation. In each case, the initial protection of one party and the constraint of the other party are called regulation, and the reversal of protection is called deregulation, although in each case, one party's freedom to act is enhanced and the other's freedom is restricted.

People define the world with respect to issues of policy using the words, their definitions (insofar as they know them or however they use them), and any underlying concepts. If the field of economic policy is understood in terms of regulation and deregulation, given the topics that each individual selectively perceives and assigns to "regulation" and "deregulation," respectively, then people will treat differently situations that are analytically indistinguishable (but, to repeat, identified on the basis of selective perception).

Regulation/deregulation is but one of the artificial, misperceived, or illusory sets of terms that enter the stream formed by the convergence and interaction of linguistic, symbolic, and mythic systems. Such is but one example of simplistic phrase making that can have serious consequences. One can verbally oppose a war or any other purpose for which government spends money. But if one acts so as to be open to the charge of inciting a riot, encouraging others to evade the draft, or refusing to pay part or all of one's taxes, one can be convicted of a felony and end up in a federal penitentiary.

People tend to believe strongly that words correspond with and derive from reality: "[T]he whole point is that if we define the terms precisely and sort out the various possible scenarios, we can learn more about market clearing than if we remain vague" (Gani 2005; see also Kendall 1995 on the selective use of discourse in presidential campaigns).

Words convey meaning derived from their definition and connotations as well as the situation in which they arise. The term "invisible hand" is a pair of words, an adjective modifying a noun. There is, however, no necessary reality to which the term relates or from which the term is derived. That a word (or term) exists does not guarantee the existence of anything (for example, the Walrasian auctioneer). Words do not have "intrinsic or essential meanings which it is the aim of political philosophers to discover and explain" (Weldon 1953: 11–12). It is futile to search for the "essential meaning of words" inasmuch as many such discussions "are purely verbal, that is, they concern linguistic habits and conventions but tell us nothing about matter of fact" (idem: 13). Political terms "do not support the superstructure which they are supposed to support and could not conceivably do so .... All of them ...... involve the error of supposing that actual political institutions are imperfect copies of something else ..." (idem: 14). The key point is that inquiry into the meanings of words is doomed to sterility because words do not have meanings in the required sense at all; "they simply have uses ... they are not the names of anything. To know their meaning is to know how to use them correctly, that is, in such a way as to be generally intelligible, in ordinary and technical discourse" (idem: 19).

By "correctly" is, of course, meant that the rules of grammar are followed and that the definitions are consonant with general (say, current dictionary) usage. The belief that real essences exist has in the past led to the assumption that truths about facts could be discovered by enquiry into the meanings of words .... Thus it comes to be held not merely that nouns are always the names of identifiable things, but also that the things of which they are the names are unchanging and eternal (idem: 20). Such procedure suggests the way in which primitive beliefs can be reinforced and made intellectually respectable by a mistaken theory of meaning coupled with a convenient ontology (idem: 21). To engage in that procedure is, therefore, an endeavor to ascertain the true or real meanings of words, or alternatively become acquainted with the immutable essences or Ideas for which political words stand. (idem: 21)

Following this procedure creates an illusion of real meanings and essences. One can examine how the words can be used correctly, but that is inquiry into use, not reality or essence. Words are used to define reality, but one does not learn about reality by studying the meaning of words as if the meanings corresponded with, and therefore represented, reality. The view taken here is widely agreed on, but when, for example, a term comports with our belief system, the tendency is seemingly to attribute it to "reality." In any event, words are not necessarily a matter of truth. Following Smith, they also function to soothe the imagination; following Pareto, they function as means with which to manipulate or mobilize personal political psychology.

A corollary is the rule that believing or wishing that something is the case does not make it so. Doing so is to commit the fallacy of wishful thinking (which Wesley C. Mitchell argued was the most common mistake made in economics).

6.3. Adam Smith and the Tradition He Started

Adam Smith has a great deal to say about language, much of which is not directly relevant to our concern. The use of language is one of the sources of the division of labor. Language is serviceable in the human quest for social recognition and moral approbation. Language enters into his argument that people seek truth but in the absence of truth will accept and adopt a proposition that soothes their imagination.

The use of the term in economics likely was imported from religion and literature. The term can – not inaccurately – be said to have substituted for, rather than constituted, knowledge; or, in view of Vilfredo Pareto's system of general sociology, to have been constituted as quasi-knowledge rather than knowledge. What may well be more important than such a substitution is the evolution or use of economics as ideology and an elevated status as social control. If that is the case, *both* substitution and constitution may have taken place. In what seems to be – say, vis-à-vis medieval Church doctrine – an increasingly secular worldwide mindset, economic doctrines have both replaced (substituted for) and constituted theology as social control. One need "only" contrast pre-Smithian economic thought, namely mercantilism and the rich and diverse mosaic of sixteenth- and seventeenth-century economic thought, with the mainstream of economics, as outlined in Essay 1, Section 1.5 to encounter the rise, during the period, say, of 1776 to the present day, of the use of the concept of the invisible hand.

Adam Smith used the term, consistent with his *History of Astronomy* argument, to soothe his own mind and the minds of his readers. He had nothing either more precise or more persuasive to offer by way of explanation. His use of such ambiguous language suggests, first, that Smith recognized that he knew nothing more precise (and/or more persuasive) and, second, that he desired to hide his ignorance. Smith seems actually to have endeavored to render invisible both his ignorance and the fact that he was doing so. He achieved both by coming up with a name with which to fill the void, namely the invisible hand. It seems that neither Smith nor, for many years, anyone else appreciated what use and achievement would be made of his artifice.

Later writers have unwittingly followed Smith's precedent and made assertions as to what Smith's invisible hand was and did. In doing so, they produced the vast literature that uses or analyzes the term and/or someone else's writing. If Smith had not used the term in explicating economic subjects, then possibly someone else would have. If the term had not – so far from soothing the imagination – caught and inspired the imagination of people contemplating the economic system that was coming into existence among the western nations centered on Atlantic trade, economics would have been denied a remarkable, interesting, entertaining, and suggestive topic. All that with a topic that has been a piece of fiction – a piece of fiction that has motivated minds to seek knowledge – but has not itself constituted or uncovered knowledge (the latter except for students) – a piece of fiction that has served social control, psychic balm, and the entry and reinforcement of a political and economic ideology, as well as various material interests, and, let us not forget, has also done service as a teaching device.

In the *Wealth of Nations*, though he does not do the counting for us (and may, or may not, have appreciated being told how many he had), Smith had as many as five or six accounts of the origin of the division of labor (Samuels 2004), and does not say that any of them is the invisible hand. He identified neither identity nor origin of the invisible hand in either book. Consider his two economics uses of the term. In both cases, an individual's behavior is "led by" an invisible hand. His recent editors pointed out that in both cases "the end unintentionally promoted is the interest of society." (Some people who claim to follow – or to correct – Smith reject the idea of "society" having an interest.) The end in *The Theory of Moral Sentiments*, the editors write, is "the distribution of means to happiness," and that in the *Wealth of Nations* is "maximization" (1976b: IV.i.10, n.7, 184). Both are more statements of subject than of ends.

Smith is more precise as to the end, even though the specific purpose – if there is one – of saying "nearly" is unclear and the identity of the invisible hand remains unstated. What Smith does say is: "[T]o make nearly the same distribution of the necessaries of life, which would have been made, had the earth been divided into equal portions among all its inhabitants" (idem: 184–5). The overall point seems to have as the "interest of the society" that the distribution of consumption be more equal than the distribution of either income and/or of wealth.

The ubiquitous problem remains that of discerning some meaning to people in the use of the term. The role of the use of the term centers on its contribution to the fashioning and legitimizing of an economy in which the invisible hand, as defined, would dominate all other doctrines comprising the regnant belief system. Each use of the term is a contribution to and/or a mode of working out our understanding of the economic, or, shall I say, the legal-economic system; the use of the invisible-hand concept enables the introduction of certain ideas in the process of systemic reproduction and transformation. Its use is ironic for two reasons. One irony arises because the broadest *bête noire* of the concept in general is the identification of the invisible hand as transcendental to human choice. The eighteenth century was characterized – and not only in regard to the Enlightenment – by a recognition of *policy consciousness*, by which is meant the belief that institutions are the result the actions and beliefs of individual people and not the creation of God. This mindset also tended to repudiate the use of arguments such as the divine right of kings, which had been used to legitimize the power of monarchs. The earlier intermediary position of the doctrine of two swords, which legitimized the simultaneous and correlative power of King and Pope, was gradually replaced by a wider range of answers to the question: Who decides? Much of eighteenth-, nineteenth-, and twentieth-century economics (and what later became the other social sciences) was influenced by clashes between adherents of government by the few and government by the many. Sometimes the clash was between landed aristocracy, monarchy, and working class; other times, the clash was between labor and capital, and so on.

The second irony stems from Lionel Robbins's conclusion that the invisible hand was the law giver or statesman. The principal target of much normative invisible-hand usage in economics has long been government and law. The opposition to government is, of course, selective (see Essay 8). Government is important no matter which group of contenders controls and uses the state. Neither of Smith's two known *economic* uses, in the *Moral Sentiments* and the *Wealth of Nations*, involve government (the former case involves the exercise of choice by the rich among their spending alternatives and the latter the exercise of choice by investors based on differences in risk or changes therein, with the changes not necessarily being due to government action; see Essay 1, Section 1.6),

The invisible-hand term, as we have seen with nouns in general, cannot itself tell us its significance and etiology, especially whether it is a contribution to knowledge, or to social control and psychic balm, or to something else. The tension is clearly intentionally evident in Smith's concluding paragraph of the *History of Astronomy*, wherein he says, in regard to his treatment of Newton, that even Smith himself, while considering all philosophical systems as due to the imagination, has sometimes tended to treat them as if they really existed (Smith 1980: IV.76, 105). The problem, in part, is whether the enormous literature on the invisible hand is to be seen as dealing with something that is adopted as a matter of truth or as a matter of setting minds at rest (say, by inculcating or making use of a political doctrine).[3] The tendency to portray the economy as having laws of its own and to adopt absolutist formulations of ideas both derives in part and contributes in part to the working out of the aforementioned tensions and conflicts. The ground that sustained the concept of the invisible hand was nurtured by such tendencies and conflicts.

6.4. Language in General: Of Metaphors and Other Figures of Speech, Part 1

Some uses of the invisible hand can engender hypotheses for further study. Beyond that, no use of the invisible hand as a metaphor or any other figure of speech conveys any substantive meaning or any meaning without further substantive analysis. Precious few authors have suggested something actually new; not very many more have undertaken a comparison with the aim of convincing readers that one identification or function is more useful or more correct than another. Many of the terms used in conjunction with the invisible hand, such as nature, God, competition, and so on, are given so many different meanings or other characteristics, that the attribution of invisible-hand status adds nothing. The term introduces a poetic or mythopoeic aura into a discussion. What place does a poetic or mythopoeic element have in a putative science largely secular and material in practice?

---

[3] Waterman writes that he does not "see why it need be either of these. Whether a metaphor is a 'matter of truth' depends solely on how it is used. In some hands the IH can illustrate some things which actually seem to be happening. In other hands it can be merely an escape from careful thought" (Waterman to Samuels). I have no hesitation in concurring with "escape from careful thought." However, I seriously doubt if the invisible hand as a metaphor (or any other figure of speech) can *itself* communicate knowledge not otherwise available or, for that matter, at all. What advantage in these regards does "invisible hand" have over "group of monkeys" except the luster derived from the history of religious use? As for "matter of truth," the invisible hand would have to have true content to communicate, which seems to be missing. I also do not see that illustration or dramatization counts.

What if the use of the term is to serve as an eye-catching literary device and nothing deeper or more substantive?[4]

So many identifications of the invisible hand have been made that, notwithstanding the popularity of the "market,"[5] "competition," "price

---

[4] When asked to express a position on what Smith "really" meant by the "invisible hand," or on Smith's position on several theological issues, or on whether the term is a metaphor or something else, my responses have been as follows: My response to questions on Smith's religious position is that I have been collecting material putatively pertinent to the viability of different answers. My response to the question of his intended meaning of "invisible hand" is that I have no way of knowing what he meant, if anything, and as for the term's status as a metaphor or simile or something else, my response is that the question is obviated by the argument presented in this book.

[5] Terms like "institution" and "mechanism" are sometimes said to be metaphorical inasmuch as "[t]hey point to particular abstractions from our total perception of the phenomena we are observing: abstractions we find helpful for some analytical purposes. Hence any phenomenon can wear any number of 'metaphorical' hats. We assign the one that best enables us to explain to others what we see that may interest them." (A.M.C. Waterman to Warren J. Samuels, undated comment [see note 3, *supra*]). I do not think that metaphor per se necessarily has anything to do with the abstraction of one from a number of possible abstractions. To confuse the result of abstraction with the actual phenomenon itself is an error, as may be the application of a conclusion from one of the possible abstractions. If the analyst applies the result of abstraction, the existential significance of the excluded elements of the phenomenon is lost. Thus, for example, the application to policy of a conclusion from one possible abstraction amounts to holding that the elements excluded from the conceptual model are irrelevant on substantive and/or normative grounds. To designate one element (the invisible hand) (A) as a metaphor due to abstraction is to presume that that for which the term "invisible hand" (A) is a metaphor (B) in the sense that the invisible hand is, in an implied comparison, is a common feature of both A and B. It takes a considerable exercise of the critical faculty to see that the invisible hand is a common feature, abstracting from other potential and/or actual features. For example, if the invisible hand is the market, and if both are deemed metaphors, to identify the market as the invisible hand, as McCloskey (1983) wrote, is to define one metaphor by another. If, however, the invisible hand is the market and if "market" is given a nonmetaphorical definition, what is gained from equating market and the invisible hand? If B is a metaphor for A, what does B tell us about A except that all other elements or features of A are put in Marshall's pound of *ceteris paribus*, that is, any other common feature? When it is said that John is a poster boy (= metaphor) for hard work, laziness, poor educational design and policy, and so on, what is being said is not that John is a poster or a metaphor but that John is an advertisement asserting something about how and why he turned out. In what respect, then, is calling something an invisible hand making a comparison? If, somehow or for some reason, the claim that the market is the invisible hand is believed to be *literally* the case, then one is claiming something like this: Whether or not the object of discussion, the invisible hand, has material substance, upon a towel being draped over it, the towel thereby would take on some part(s) of the shape of a hand. If the claim is not literally that the market is the invisible hand, then what is learned by saying that the market is a metaphor for the invisible hand or that the invisible hand is a metaphor for the market? If, in contrast to simile, in which the likening of an A to B is made explicit, with metaphor the likening of A to B is not made explicit, what is learned by calling it a metaphor? Where does abstraction enter?

  Furthermore, both metaphor and simile are commonly designated to be "figures of speech." *Webster's New Universal Unabridged Dictionary* (1994) defines "figure of speech" mechanism," or a combination thereof, the use of the term is laden with ambiguity to the point of incoherence. Nothing substantive with regard to knowledge is added by the use of the term, whatever identity is chosen. Most usages seem nonspecific and inconclusive with regard to their intended use and purpose. So many possible meanings of the identity of the invisible hand exist that using it leads to confusion such that the use of the term not only adds nothing but detracts from the argument being made.

Each candidate proposed for the identity of the invisible hand identifies something important. One could, in principle, combine some or many of them and construct a general model of the economy. Calling any or all of them an invisible hand, however, adds nothing but saccharine attitude to what is otherwise likely already known. Most scholars seem to appreciate the argument being made here, but the weight of conventional usage and the latent sense that, after all is said and done, there *is* and *must be* an invisible hand strongly inhibiting or channeling arm's length analysis and the same credulity.

The domain formed by the totality of identities of the invisible hand found in the relevant literature is not a neat and tidy subject. It is possibly unsurpassed in messiness, due to the large number of alternative identities and hosts of complexities and ambiguities. Many invisible hand arguments overreach and tell us more about the arguers and their motives than about the economy.

A combined linguistic and epistemological characteristic is rarely labeled for what it is: aprioristic reasoning, argument by appeal to first principles, pure assertion, wishful thinking, and, often, a primitive undefined term; although assertion can be treated as combined conjecture and hypothesis. The etiology and character of political terms in which the struggle over the structure of social power and the control of government is conducted have the same character.[6]

as a matter of rhetoric, "any expressive use of language, as a metaphor, simile, personification, antithesis, etc., in which words are used in other than their literal sense, or in other than their ordinary locutions, in order to suggest a picture or image or for other special effect." The suggestion is made to see Definition 1 for "trope," where one reads, "any literary or rhetorical device, as metaphor, metonymy, synecdoche, and irony, which consist in words in other than their literal sense." Put aside the phrase "any expressive use of language." We are left with "words are used in other than their literal sense," "in order to suggest a picture or image or for other special effect," and "which consist in words in other than their literal sense." None of these constitute a contribution to knowledge, surely no more than if one claimed the invisible hand was our group of monkeys.

6   Waterman asks, "Which 'struggle'? In some times and places there is no perceptible 'struggle'. In others, where this [there] is one, it is usually many-sided and messy" (Waterman to Samuels). At the risk of reminding the reader of the Cold War cartoon in which the

The invisible-hand term is itself a linguistic vehicle of received wisdom. Its use selectively reinforces the version of the status quo with which it is associated. Inasmuch as most of the candidates for the identity of the invisible hand are attributes of the capitalist market economy, when some or all of them are deployed, the status quo system is further reinforced and legitimized. In western society, the widely perceived issue of the status quo is whether change is to be generated by the market (which may be the power structure operating through the market) or by law (ditto). Laissez-faire is the view of those seeking change through the market, or, more accurately, using the market-versus-law model to preclude change by law. But both market and law generate and require change, due to a variety of reasons (Samuels 2007a: chapters 1–8, 10–14). Some mechanism(s) of market adjustment and legal adjustment must be in place. Legal change (change of law) is, willy-nilly, a part of the invisible-hand model. By seeming to protect against legal change (by virtue of control of government) and against undesirable market change (by virtue of the invisible hand's contribution to harmony, etc.), the concept of the invisible hand ironically provides legitimization of both market and legal change (this is elaborately illustrated by regard to the Fifth Amendment's takings clause [Samuels and Mercuro 1980]). Ironically, Lionel Robbins identified the invisible hand as that of the statesman within a market plus legal and moral framework (Robbins 1953) Robbins examined neither the moral component of the framework nor the legal change part of the legal factor; see Samuels 1966). Even the identities of the invisible hand that one might think were antagonistic to the general character of the others serve a reinforcing and legitimizing role. The belief, mythic, and symbolic systems of society perform their role though the significations of language.

To those impressed by the term "invisible hand," the concept contributes a sense of attaining the transcendent. The term catches hold of the imagination and channels it in a certain direction(s). The term is thus a tool of social control and of psychic balm; its contribution is the transmittal of pseudo-knowledge. It is a term of art, a code word of a group, and as such, because of its multiple identities, has flexible meanings enabling its acquisition in one way or another by different people, depending on the psychic propensity to which it adheres. It is also a mode of forming and/

communist hunter says to the doubter, "You can't find them? That is because they are so well hidden," the absence of even perceptible struggle can indicate the effectiveness of social control (including invocation of the invisible hand). As for his last point, all of life, especially all decision making, as well as revolution, counterrevolution, and a state of contentment, is many-sided and messy.

or "confirming" one's own identity as one absorbs the image fostered by the kind of economy the invisible-hand identity and function project.

Precisely because the term "invisible hand" likely corresponds to nothing in reality,[7] it contributes nothing to knowledge; and even if the term corresponded to something in reality, it would add nothing to our knowledge from other sources. The linguistics of the term contributes nothing to knowledge.[8] Calling the invisible hand (or anything) a metaphor, simile, or any figure of speech adds nothing to knowledge of the economy. Doing so is a distraction and a diversion.

Social symbolic systems are an important aspect of society. A key question is, symbolic of what? These systems selectively project what is selectively attributed to them; hence, there is circularity. These systems are a major means of social control, personal definition of reality, personal equilibrium and stability in a chaotic world. Selective legitimization is an inexorable aspect of the social control process.

Ideology in modern society gives effect to the business view of the world and subtly presents a defense of the capitalist market system, including selective legitimization of institutional details.

6.5. On Metaphors in Economics

Several questions are often ignored. When is a proposition or term a figure of speech – say, a metaphor – and when it is literal? When is a proposition or term a statement about reality, when is it a mode of expression about reality, when is it a figure of speech, a rhetorical device? If a proposition is a metaphor, for what is it a metaphor? What about similes? Fictions are used in economics and in law. Discourse can be conducted with terms that make sense and provide putative description yet are metaphysical, if not entirely imaginary. Providing something with a name does not guarantee its literal existence. Language is a set of signs but not necessarily of something "real."

Markets are often perceived to be metaphors. But a metaphor for what? To the extent that an invisible hand is designated a metaphor, can the same

---

[7] Waterman queries, "How can you say that? Once again: whether or not a metaphor tells us anything about 'reality' depends on who uses it, and how." My response is this: Take any identity or function said by someone to pertain to the "invisible hand." What is there about the invisible hand that can tell us anything about reality that cannot be discerned from serious study or more than invoking the group of monkeys? The circumstance that a result is a function of interaction and aggregation could be deemed an exception to my claim about having nothing to tell us, as I do in this book. But it does not need to be, inasmuch as much of economics is recognizes and/or is the result of interaction and aggregation.

[8] Waterman: "*Agreed.*"

questions raised about individual identities also be raised about all identities for the invisible hand?

It is not clear that all invisible hands are metaphors. Is an invisible hand a metaphor in some circumstances but a different figure of speech in other circumstances?

Is knowledge produced by declaring a term or proposition one or another figure of speech?

A substantial percentage of people use the term without saying anything else about it other than its identity, function, and significance. Of the remainder, a substantial percentage identifies the term as a figure of speech. Of those who identify it as a figure of speech, the largest percentage say that it is a metaphor; next comes simile. Finally, there come several others. Most people do not give it a label. Some authors commit themselves only to a class of figures of speech. Does any such a designation constitute linguistic knowledge? Some relevant terms and their respective definitions are as follows:

Metaphor: an implicit comparison – for example, you are my sunshine.

Simile: an implicit comparison with a specific attribute and specification of the object compared with.

Analogy: a partial similarity between like features of two things, on which a comparison may be based.

Euphemism: an attempt to see things not as they are but as we wish them to be or masked or obscured.

Synecdoche: use of part of referent to stand for the whole – for example, all hands on deck.

Trope: stylistic and/or substantive effects created by choices of words; sign, signification; relation to allegory (akin to myth, symbol).

Metonymy: the use of the name of on object or concept for that of another to which it is related, or of which it is a part.

The class of figures of speech as a whole can be defined in a comparable manner:

Figure of speech: any expressive use of language, such as metaphor, simile, personification, antithesis, and so on, in which words are used in other than their literal sense, or in other than their ordinary locutions, in order to suggest a picture or image, or for other special effect.

The ambiguity latent in the foregoing illustrates, first, the inconclusiveness due to multiplicity and second, usages due to employing primitive terms (including the invisible hand itself), enabling selective identification as each reader supplies his or her own meaning.

Subject to selective perception, reification and the fallacy of misplaced concreteness are: "human nature," "self-interest," "rationality," "competition," "nature," "order," and so on – primitive terms – general conceptual categories with variable and selective content and nested meaning. For example, the content of natural theology and natural philosophy is a function of the meaning attributed to nature and to status quo society: elastic, a priori, a function of selective perception. For example, consider parallels in the utopist literature: different utopias and dystopias written with respect to the same society, due to different perspectives; "natural order" as selective perception, interpretation, reification, and projection of status quo, that is, Platonic idealization.

Perhaps a term or proposition is not a figure of speech, but something literal. A mode of abstraction can transcend a figure of speech. Can some uses comprise metaphors and others similes? Of what importance, if any, are these matters?

One problem is that of structure governing whose preferences are to count – say, in going from private interest to social interest. Loaded within that problem is another: using/finding euphemisms for an obfuscated power structure. A simple but suggestive model starts with the formation of individual identities and continues with the formation of individual preferences. Individual preferences then are weighted by their respective power (e.g., purchasing power). The process is to determine whose preferences count, and this is a function of their respective participation in the economy, which itself is a function of the distributions of income and wealth. No unique determinate allocation of resources exists because different structures of power yield, *ceteris paribus*, different allocations of resources and different results as to whose interests count. Insofar as the use of the term "invisible hand" signifies a process in which power is absent (that only one Pareto optimal result is possible), the term serves as a euphemism for the obfuscation of power structure.

Such is only one of a number of factors that result in a matrix or array of alternative equilibrium results in the event that one or another factor varies. Other problems include (1) importing analogies from the histories of physics and mathematics; (2) fitness; (3) comprehensiveness; and (4) conclusiveness. The same point applies to other comparable terms, such as *deus ex machina*; social contract; divinely ordained monarchy; and Hegel's "cunning of history."

A multiplicity of copycat usages has developed. These include: a palsied hand, a grabbing hand, a vanishing hand, an invisible fist, a visible hand (government, corporate management), an invisible hand with a green thumb (profitable environmentalism), and tracking the invisible hand (convergence of double auctions to competitive equilibrium).

The figures of speech that arise with the invisible hand and other terms are of dubious assistance in eliciting knowledge. This is the case for several reasons. (1) One analyst will work with an assumption whereas another will find a way to yield the same result as a conclusion. (2) Acceptance versus rejection on the basis of consonance with the reigning (or some other) paradigm. (3) In the absence of an independent test, (1) and (2) tend to be tautological. (4) Selective perception can yield any desired conclusion. Such is the raison d'être of the manipulation of language.

The problem of the *social* is especially intransigent. Society can be seen to be an entity or a process. It can also signify the sum of the individuals comprising it. "Society" carries a considerable amount of baggage. There is a widespread tendency to use the term to mean more rather than less. Society can be seen to be the division of labor plus institutions plus social structure. It can also be seen as the sum total of the work of social control. Whether one starts with individuals or with society, the problem of the structure of power is certain to arise, though often obfuscated.

6.6. Conclusions Up to This Point

Some conclusions can be reached based on the first parts of this essay. The invisible hand tends to project the ethos of an age. As society becomes more complex, not only is it likely that multiple utopias and dystopias will be formulated, but multiple candidates for the identity of the invisible hand will be forthcoming. The array of such candidates likely will reflect and help further formulate the economic civil religion – coordinating, bonding, "ordering." The age- or epoch-specific desire is for certitude, for the transcendent and the absolute, for absolutist legitimization, for the image of an apolitical world, for the search for the absolute principle with which to ontologically ground and legitimize self-interest. Altogether the issues and problems raised so far in this essay render ambiguous and greatly weaken the invisible hand.

The further conclusion is drawn that, with certain exceptions, there is no such thing as the invisible hand. The claim that there is no invisible hand is made in the sense that nothing is added to knowledge by calling something the invisible hand. The linguistic, ontological, and epistemological grounds and other considerations on which that conclusion is based will be identified as we go along in this essay and in Essay 7.

Designating something – for example, the market, the price mechanism, the entrepreneur – an "invisible hand" adds nothing to our knowledge of the market, the price mechanism, the entrepreneur, or anything else. Singling out one candidate for the identity or the function ostensibly performed by something called "the invisible hand" literally adds nothing: Neither a category of "invisible hand(s)" nor an actual example of an invisible hand has been established. Existing evidence of market, price mechanism, entrepreneur, and so on exists; the existence of evidence of something specifically called an invisible hand in the present, the past, or the future has not been established. Calling something an invisible hand does not suffice to establish either a category or an example of an "actual" invisible hand. To do so is only to assert. Assertion is not in itself evidence. Also neither lines of reasoning, nor suggestiveness, nor wishful thinking, nor fiction constitute in themselves evidence. There is evidence of increased or decreased unemployment, balance of payments debits or credits, and so on, but nothing of an invisible hand as such.

No existence – no accretion to knowledge. No category – no content for such a category. There was never, so far as is evident to me, a discovery of the category of "invisible hand" and thereafter a subsequent organized procedure or effort for either seeking or testing for the existence of an invisible hand. That a multitude of writers have chased after "the" invisible hand and its specific meaning, and have done so in a manner described, both deliberatively and nondeliberatively, as an "invisible college" is only a metaphor, a shorthand means of communication (for example, in teaching). There is no contribution to knowledge from anything that warrants being called an invisible hand. Those negative findings are overwhelming.

The term "invisible hand," so far as the great bulk of candidates is concerned, is only words. "Purple cow" would convey no less and no more, except for the history of use and its attendant aura antecedent to Smith.

The exceptions comprise the separate category of *invisible-hand processes*. These include interaction and aggregation, such as are operative in the principle of unintended and unexpected consequences.

The test of the existence of an invisible hand is whether knowledge of either the identity, function, operation, or any other aspect or topic deemed pertinent to the invisible hand is acquired through study making an independent contribution to knowledge other than or beyond that which is otherwise attainable. I know of no knowledge of economics made by the discussion of the invisible hand that has not been made by discussion without asserting an invisible hand. There is no substantive basis on which to take an informed dependent position as to their existence.

6.7. Language in General: Of Metaphors and Other Figures of Speech, Part 2

The initial question arising from the consideration of the invisible-hand term is whether the term is intended to be a definition of reality, a mode of discourse, a stratagem in a game, or simply the more or less random juxtaposition of two words, such as one would encounter in a game of Scrabble. If it is a definition of reality, presumably considerations of its truth (descriptive accuracy or correct explanation) arise. If, or to the extent that, it is a mode of discourse, technical questions of linguistic status arise. A third alternative is that the term is used as an argument without any necessary content or substantive basis.

The origin and meaning of a term may derive from one or more of several alternatives in a number of contexts. A term's origin may be a priori reasoning or an argument from first principles and may be related to the belief, mythic, and symbolic systems of society. On the ontological level, a term may be used in the context of supernaturalism, naturalism and/or secularism-materialism.

One of the difficulties in comprehending (attributing meaning to) Smith arises from the situation that elements of his work can be located in one or more of the following (and perhaps other) paradigms: naturalism, supernaturalism, pragmatism (utilitarianism), empiricism, historicism, secularism, materialism, and individualism.[9] A related set of interpretive difficulties derives from the Enlightenment context in which he wrote, in the highest echelon of the Scottish version of which he is often located and considered a leader. The attribution of meaning is influenced by how an interpreter treats several issues pertaining to the meaning of the Enlightenment, including multiple specifications of the meaning of the Enlightenment, such as progress, rational study, and choice uncontaminated by religion and absolutist politics, influenced by rational skepticism, factuality, scientific objectivity, empiricism, materialism, disenchantment with a divinely concerned universe, policy consciousness, each of those having its own issues, including wishful thinking. Also generating possible meaning are the relations of the Enlightenment to the past and the variety of its perceived meanings in the present and the future, especially its use as argument.

---

[9] It is important to remember that Smith did not use some of these terms, that his use of any term likely differs in material respects from its meaning today, and that both then and now each term has meant different things to different people.

How one approaches one's subject also has an effect. The phenomena of legal change, for example, permits several different foci of analysis: on the implicit or explicit vote trading among judges and among legislators and between party leaders and rank-and-file, on the rules governing voting, on the relations between successive bills or between successive statutes. Add other paradigmatic elements to the mix, and the possibilities can expand significantly. Asked by me how he came to vote as he did, a legislator replied that he first considered party doctrine to determine the consonance of the bill and his party's doctrinal tenets; immersing himself and/or his aides in the materials pertinent to the issue addressed by the bill, hoping to reach through immersion a judgment on the bill; trading votes on two bills with another legislator, each person agreeing to vote how the other stipulates on a bill of no consequence to the legislator but of interest to the other legislator; and the requests made by party leaders to rank-and-file legislators. Not mentioned were bribery and the purchase and sale of political favors.

Two important sources of the meaning of the invisible hand are nature (naturalism) and supernaturalism. Nature-naturalism is itself a definition of reality, a belief system, and/or a mode of discourse. The eighteenth century was perhaps the first in which nature and naturalism became an open, though not necessarily a dominant, position. Perhaps two dozen or more meanings have been attributed to "nature" including natural versus artificial, nature as compelling upon mankind, man in control of nature, nature as a resource, nature as good and to be followed, and nature as bad and to be overcome. Nature can be seen as the source of natural law – not just any natural law, but that of a particular instituted system. The concept and specific laws of nature likely are a projection and reification of a particular status quo, thereby given an ontological natural status. As already noted, just as a particular society can be the basis of several different utopias, so too can a particular concept be given different specifications.

The second source of the meaning of the invisible hand is religion (supernaturalism). Indeed, the historical origins of the term are believed by many to have been the theology and theological language of the medieval period and in the literature of the late medieval period. Essay 1, Section 1.5 provides evidence suggesting – more than that: demonstrating empirically – that neither Adam Smith nor Christianity created the term, although both vastly added to its historical significance. The issues pertaining to the language from which some or many uses of the term "invisible hand" derive are belief in God, deism versus atheism versus theism, with variants of each; God as the designer-creator of the world but subsequently inactive in the world versus God as active in the world, possibly a personal God; organized religion versus natural religion; God as the source of moral rules versus moral rules created by humankind with the ability to do so given by God; God made unhappy by man's quest for knowledge with which to become God-like, and vice versa; the intended scope of the term "superstition,"[10] and so on.

Understanding Smith's position on issues and tensions regarding religion and theology is of particular interest for understanding the term "invisible hand" and for understanding Smith himself. Evidence exists in support of a number of rival positions, one of which may have been held by Smith. It is also possible that his view was a composite of more than one view or that he held two views simultaneously or successively. As stated previously, it is also possible that he had two views: one a private view of God, theology, ontology, organized religion, and superstition; the other an objective, arm's length analysis of God, religion, the Established Church, sects, and the moral sentiments. Basic interpretive problems, however, are the illusive and circumstantial nature of the evidence, and evidence that can support more than one hypothesis, his circumspection, and the reasons for it.

The meaning attributed to the invisible hand may be caught up in, derived from, and give effect to the foregoing complexities and the open-endedness of interpretation.[11] With regard to the array of opportunities open to the legislator, for example, one can imagine the opportunities for use of figures of speech in political cartoons to both promote and oppose particular bills.

The term "invisible hand," for different people, can be a cliché or either nothing or something. In some areas of life, the use of the term "invisible hand" has been part of a broader linguistic or allegorical tradition. The notion of *invisibility* itself seems to have intrigued mankind for ages. People seem to have been taken emotionally with the idea of invisibility, resulting in something like an invisibility tradition. Exposure to the problem of the

[10] Waterman suggests that "superstition" referred to Roman Catholicism in eighteenth-century Anglican Britain. Smith's use of the term in the *Wealth of Nations* introduces no distinction, perhaps because he rejected the distinction or because he accepted it and for some reason (fear of reprisals, sense of irrelevance to his principal argument, and so on) felt it ought not or need not become part of his description.

[11] Waterman (2002) argues that Smith was associated with the eighteenth-century enterprise called theodicy: "It also seems to be the case that Smith's conception of a self-regulating market economy grew out of a tradition of 17th Century Jansenist theodicy that Boisguilbert transformed into 'economics,'" citing (Gilbert) Faccarello. (A.M.C. Waterman to Warren J. Samuels, undated comments inserted in email of first version of this essay). That Smith's version of Christianity was that of theodicy remains to be demonstrated. This is a splendid example of how Smith's *History of Astronomy* argument can be applied to work of the type done by Waterman, myself, and other historians of economic thought.

"unseen" can elicit a sense of the transcendental and mystical so far removed from normal, ordinary experience, it is beyond the capacity of most people to comprehend, for example, even a sense of fairness, or a mind set at rest given someone believed to be in control. The realm of the invisible seems, oddly or ironically enough, to point to some ultimate transcendental force or being, perhaps even to some perfectly working adjustment mechanism. The term "invisible hand" is attractive in part precisely because it cannot be seen. The term is also a vehicle of marketing and delivery of what are deemed to be conservative ideas on policy (see Samuels 2007a). The forms of the invisible are numerous and include an ultimate transcendental force or being, an operative adjustment mechanism, the exercise of power at a distance, and the working of the rules of morals, law, card, athletic, and other games.

Smith's argument in his *History of Astronomy* can readily be applied to the topic of invisibility. In order to deal with phenomena under the rubric of truth, it would appear that the phenomena must be visible, or transparent. When that condition is not satisfied, as is the case with invisible hands and other unseen phenomena, the quest for truth fails, and people must content themselves with propositions that soothe the imagination, or set minds at rest. Of course, today subatomic particles, germs, DNA, and the like are not "seen" in the same sense as one sees print or pictures in a book. In some cases, their presence is indicated by streaks of light on film.

Economics, like law, uses fictions to facilitate the reaching of conclusions. When is a proposition a fiction? Assuming that choice can be made as to which fiction to use (in some particular circumstance), which, how, and by whom is that choice to be made? By fiction is meant something imaginary, made up, used for the sake of convenience although not, or not necessarily, true or untrue. And if truth is the issue, how (within what paradigm or belief system) is it to be defined? Is construction and analysis within the terms of pure conceptual models of the economy, rather than actual economies, by definition, a matter of science fiction? What if the construction is a matter of setting minds at rest or communicating a political or religious message or feeling?

A term may be a mythological, symbolic, or linguistic construct and, in the view of many people, be a source of hypotheses for empirical, secular, material study. But language, considered as signs, is not necessarily indicative of something "real." Providing a name does not necessarily guarantee the literal existence of that which is named.

So many identifications of the invisible hand have been made that, notwithstanding the popularity of the market, competition, the price mechanism, or a combination thereof, the use of the term is laden with ambiguity to the point of incoherence; nothing substantive with regard to knowledge is added by the use of the term, whatever identity is chosen. Moreover, most usages seem nonspecific and inconclusive with regard to their intended use and purpose.

6.8. Language in General: Of Metaphors and Other Figures of Speech, Part 3

Very early in my studies, I sensed that the discussion of the invisible hand as a figure of speech did not contribute much, if anything, to our understanding of the term "invisible hand" and its use. This realization came as a considerable surprise to me, and I remain to this day concerned about my finding. Questions about the several terms listed and defined earlier, about whether the invisible hand was a metaphor or a simile, or something else, were taken up in the literature of linguistics and of economics. People who I knew and respected seemed to think differently. Surely, my native skepticism was taking me too far afield into the realm of error. During the better part of three decades, I read and thought and then paused, and then resumed.

For some time while I was writing these essays, I took my planned discussion of metaphors and related topics to be sufficient. What I needed to show was that whether or not a proposition was a metaphor added nothing to our knowledge and understanding. To say that the invisible hand was a metaphor for the market (or some other candidate) had at least three problems. One was that inasmuch as the market was but one of several dozen candidates for the identity of the invisible hand, could not much confidence could be placed in any identity when there were so many of them. Secondly, inasmuch as the case could be made that the market was a metaphor, saying that the invisible hand was a metaphor for the market was defining or identifying one metaphor by another. Thirdly, if the adding invisible-hand status to the market (or to anything else) added nothing to our knowledge and understanding of markets, no reason existed for getting involved.

I then saw that if I correctly understood the three problems, further questions existed, namely: What functions were served by discussion of the invisible hand as a figure of speech? Why was identifying the invisible hand as a metaphor or a simile important? And what function did doing so serve?

I decided, first, that I very much could use an analysis centering on the invisible hand as metaphor to supplement or modify my previous analysis, and second, that I had considerable notes on metaphor and related topics that I had taken and, in some cases, organized over the years. After reviewing many of the notes, I determined that considerable materials existed along a number of important lines of analysis, and that I could accomplish my purposes by concentrating my attention on one rich source. I had several such books and selected Andrew Ortony's edited collection, *Metaphor and Thought* (1979; all numbers refer to pages in Ortony 1979, unless otherwise indicated, and all names refer to authors whose work is included therein, unless otherwise indicated). I had borrowed a copy that was owned, and heavily annotated, by Nancy Brenner. I had read the book and had prepared a set of notes for my own use, simultaneously getting Nancy's permission to retain it until I was done preparing the linguistic materials for this book. Among the collection of books that could readily be treated both together and in the same fashion, are: Dicey 1981 [1905], Eaton 1964 [1925], Kellner 1989, Pagden 1987, Starr 1992, and White 1984.

These decisions were made only after I had determined that the three essays with sections on linguistics were undesirably repetitious. Putting the several sections side by side also convinced me that the discussion could use what follows.

The following model will be useful here and later in the essay. There are two phenomena named A and B, respectively. Each of the two phenomena has five features which may be related, feature to feature, with each other. Thus A has A1, A2, A3, A4 and A5, and B has B1, B2, B3, B4 and B5. Feature A1 relates to B1, A2 to B2, and the like. If A is a metaphor for B, or if B is a metaphor for A, it will be because one or more pairs of features constitute the common basis of comparison, say, A2 and B2 or A5 and B5. If A and B have an unequal number of features, comparison, along the line of A being a metaphor for B, or B being a metaphor for A, can occur only with regard to paired features: A3 and B3 but not A5 and B2, because these two do not form a pair. The first problem is when someone tries to establish metaphoric relations between A5 and B2, having A5 be the metaphor of B2 or B2 the metaphor of A5. It will not work. If A and B have no features in common, any effort to affirm metaphoric relations will not work. The problem has to do with knowing or not knowing that the two have no paired features. Someone trying to establish an argument may falsely affirm that A5 and B2 can yield a metaphoric relation, that is, lead to the problem of truth versus falsity, or of truth versus manufactured truth, or truth versus propositions that, although not true, do set minds at rest. It has also been established, by assumption/assertion, that opportunity for metaphoric relations requires the relevant pair, but such opportunity can be falsely claimed or actual relations need not exist but can be pretended to exist. In the absence of any effective test of a claimed pair being able to sustain a metaphoric relation, and distinguish between A as a metaphor for B, and B as a metaphor for A, much opportunity exists for false claims.

The general conclusion that my reading compels, and as illustrated by the material from Ortony's collection, plus some other sources, is this: The problems that I have encountered and the negative conclusions I had reached with regard to the "invisible hand" are worsened by any serious reliance on the analysis of metaphor in particular and figures of speech in general. The world of metaphor has multiplicities and conflicts to a degree comparable to the world of the invisible hand. Explication of metaphor as a means of enlightenment with regard to the invisible hand seems not likely to be of much help. The literature on metaphor is not a solution; it is an aggravation. I suspect that the reason why economists do not go further in pursuing the metaphoric character of the invisible hand is that there is nothing there. Economists seem to go into figures of speech only as far as is necessary to establish and reinforce to their satisfaction that the invisible hand has substance as a figure of speech – for example, that the invisible hand is a metaphor or simile. Linguists seem to have a similar motive. I again feel constrained to pause, but hope to learn from criticism. I have concentrated on metaphor rather than on another term, such as simile, for two reasons: Economists seem to emphasize the invisible hand as metaphor rather than as simile (though the latter is not without important support), and, it seems to me, possibly in error, that the theory of metaphor is more developed than that of simile. The reader will recall that I have concluded that more prominence should be given to understanding the invisible hand as a primitive term over any figure of speech.

The remainder of this subsection, with one exception, consists of further conclusions regarding metaphor and a sample of various passages constituting evidence for the conclusions reached, including two entries from Samuel Johnson's *A Dictionary of the English Language* (1755).

Under the heading of what I would call "the character of metaphor," one finds some interesting and revealing topics and themes articulated by the authors in Ortony's collection. The result is diverse recognitions of the lack of solidity in the analysis of metaphor. One wonders if the center of attention in the study of metaphor should move in the direction of identifying and analyzing different types of metaphor.

Amplifications of the model given previously:

We say a statement is literally true when we find an existing schema that accounts fully for the data in question. We say that a statement is metaphorically true when we find that although certain primary aspects of the schema hold, others equally primary do not hold. (Rumelhart in Ortony 1979: 90)

[M]etaphors are both restricted and systematic; restricted in the sense that not every way that one thing can remind us of something else will provide a basis for metaphor, and systematic in the sense that metaphors must be communicable from speaker to hearer in virtue of a shared system of principles. (Searle in Ortony 1979: 113)

[Problems are not given to man, they are made and understood by man. Even if problems are assumed to be given, they do not always have the same form.] New descriptions of problems tend not to spring from the solutions of the problem earlier set, but to evolve independently as new features of situations come into prominence. (Schön in Ortony 1979: 261)

[F]rame conflicts are not problems. They do not lend themselves to problem-solving inquiry ... because frame conflicts are often unresolvable by appeal to facts. In the case of two ... stories ... the adversaries do not disagree about the facts; they simply turn their attention to *different* facts. (Schön in Ortony 1979: 269)

Metaphors involve a juxtaposition of two phenomena or sites, probably one feature of each. The phenomena and feature chosen do not exhaust the possibilities of comparison. The truth status of the comparison is not necessarily a matter of fact; it is subjective and limited. When it is said that A is a metaphor of B, the speaker is telling a story about A and B in terms of a posited common feature. Several questions can be posed: What is "the point of using metaphors?" and What are "the distinctive powers of metaphorical discourse?"

The foregoing account ... treats a metaphor, roughly speaking, as an instrument for drawing implications grounded in perceived analogies of structure between two subjects belonging to different domains, has paid no attention to the state of mind of somebody who affirms a metaphorical statement. A good metaphor sometimes impresses strikes, or seizes its producer: We want to say we had a "flash of insight" ... (Black in Ortony 1979: 32)

Wide agreement on a fundamental understanding:

Among the mysteries of human speech, metaphor has remained one of the most baffling. [There is an] odd predilection for asserting a thing to be what it is not ... so perhaps the "mystery" is simply that, taken as literal, a metaphorical statement appears to be perversely asserting something to be what it is plainly known not to be. So a metaphor/user, unless he is merely babbling, would seem ... to say one thing and mean another. But why? (Black in Ortony 1979: 21–2; quoting Boyle 1954: 257)

Why stretch and twist, press and expand, concepts this way – why try to see A as metaphorically B, when it is not *B*? (Black in Ortony 1979: 34)

[T]he recognizable mark of a metaphorical statement is that *taken literally* it would have to count as a logical contradiction or an absurdity, in either case something patently *false*. (Black in Ortony 1979: 35)

An obvious objection is that this test, so far as it fits, will apply equally to such other tropes as oxymoron or hyperbole, so that it would at best certify the presence of some figurative statement, but not necessarily a metaphor. A more serious objection is that authentic metaphors need not manifest the invoked controversion .... The negation of any metaphorical statement can itself be a metaphorical statement and hence possibly true if taken literally. (Black in Ortony 1979: 35)

The problem of explaining how metaphors work is ... a special case ... of the problem of how it is possible to say one thing and mean something else, where one succeeds in communicating what one means even though both the speaker and the hearer know that the meanings of the words uttered by the speaker do not exactly and literally express what the speaker meant.... what the speaker means is not identical with what the sentence means, and yet what he means is in various ways dependent on what the sentence means. (Searle in Ortony 1979: 92–3)

Metaphors have two pairs of interpretive positions: the features being concentrated upon, and the interpretations forming the metaphor (the literal vis-à-vis and the (opposing) figurative, an affirmation vis-à-vis a negation, the position voiced vis-à-vis the position intended).

Are the following statements, originally given as examples of metaphor, homogeneous as to being metaphors? The final two statements are given as similes.

"The Lord is my Shepherd."

"John eats like a pig."

"My love is like a red, red rose."

Do metaphors and similes convey the same messages? If they do convey the same message/tell the same story, is there a point to the distinction? Does "The Lord is my Shepherd" convey less or more or the same amount of information? What about "The Lord is like my Shepherd" or "The Lord is to me like a Shepherd"?

Why have figures of speech been identified and labeled? To help us understand relevant discourse, or to prescribe/proscribe that language?

Further as to the Character of Metaphor:

Metaphors characterize rhetoric, not scientific discourse. They are fuzzy and vague, inessential frills, appropriate for the purposes of the politician and of the poet, but not for those of the scientist, who is attempting to furnish an objective description of physical reality. (Ortony 1979: 2)

Our recognition of a metaphorical statement depends essentially upon two things: Our general knowledge of what it is *to be* a metaphorical statement, and our specific judgment that a metaphorical reading of a given statement is here preferable to a literal one (Black in Ortony 1979: 35–6). And just as there is no infallible test for resolving ambiguity, so there is none to be expected in discriminating the metaphorical from the literal. (Black in Ortony 1979: 36)

... assumes that the determination of literal meaning is a necessary step on the way toward finding the conveyed meaning ... (Rumelhart in Ortony 1979: 83)

The subjective and psychological aspect of metaphor and other figures of speech:

A metaphorical statement is available for repeated use, adaptation, and modification by a variety of speakers or thinkers on any number of specific occasions.... The *very same* metaphorical statement, as I wish to use that expression, may appropriately receive a number of different and even partially conflicted readings. (Black in Ortony 1979: 25)

> [T]he underlying principles governing metaphor are of a general psychological sort and are thus not specifically linguistic. (Black in Ortony 1979: 46)

> Languages are the way they are in part because of historical accident, because of common psychology and experience, but also in part because of constraints peculiar to language. (Black in Ortony 1979: 49)

> As a psychologist, I find myself primarily interested in the mechanisms whereby meanings are conveyed.... In the comprehension of language ... psychological theory must concern itself with conveyed meanings. (Rumelhart in Ortony 1979: 78)

> [M]etaphors often serve to plug such semantic gaps as this. (Searle in Ortony 1979: 97)

> The comprehension of metaphor is basically a cognitive problem which centers around the following question: How does a novel conceptual entity arise from apparently disparate parts? ... for the creator of the metaphor must first grasp the significance of a metaphorical relation before it is uttered. (Paivio in Ortony 1979: 152)

> All psychological studies of metaphor involve meditational approaches ... concerned with processes that mediate the similarity, relational, and integrative reactions in the comprehension of metaphor. Contemporary cognitive psychologists would interpret such processes primarily in terms of structural and functional characteristics of long-term or *semantic memory*. (Paivio in Ortony 1979: 154)

> Contemporary memory theorists would analyze comprehension of metaphor primarily as a problem of long-term, or semantic, memory.... Comprehension ... involves the retrieval of such information from long-term memory.... Different theories assume different mediating structures. Traditional verbal associative theory assumes that the relation is mediated by the structure of verbal associations. Imagery-based theories might stress the structural similarities in perceptual memories. Other theories stress overlap in abstract semantic representations, which may be organized into networks or hierarchies. (Paivio in Ortony 1979: 155)

> [T]he metaphorical expression and the situation provide the retrieval context that guides the "search" through long-term memory.... the linguistic aspects of the retrieval process ... [have an] influence [that] will depend on their memorability, which in turn depends on such long-term memory characteristics as their concreteness or meaningfulness. (Paivio in Ortony 1979: 155)

> [Susanne] Langer finds the origin of metaphorical thinking, not in language but in the nature of perception itself, in abstractive seeing. (Paivio in Ortony 1979: 156)

A number of other psychologists have also emphasized the perceptual basis of the metaphor without necessarily referring explicitly to imagery. (Paivio in Ortony 1979: 157)

Such interpretations do not in themselves explain how the perceptual processes and images achieve their abstract functions, nor how they become linked to language, but they do emphasize the primacy of such processes in the origin of metaphor. (Paivio in Ortony 1979: 157)

[I]ndividuals within a culture largely agree in their metaphorical interpretations of the specific concepts ... (Paivio in Ortony 1979: 160)

[T]here is considerable evidence that imagery contributes to the comprehensibility of sentences.... It is reasonable to suppose that imagery contributes similarly to the comprehension of metaphorical expressions. (Paivio in Ortony 1979: 165)

Concrete nouns and pictures are effective pegs for storage and retrieval of associated information. (Paivio in Ortony 1979: 168)

The hypothesis that the vehicle functions as a conceptual peg suggests that it should have been processed before the topic, and as an image. (Paivio in Ortony 1979: 169)

[T]he ambience, tone, and attitudes that are ... projected. (Black in Ortony 1979: 31)

[T]he underlying principles governing metaphor are of a general psychological sort and are thus not specifically linguistic. (Sadock in Ortony 1979: 46)

The production of figurative speech is ... reflexively governed by the speaker's awareness of the hearer's expectation of cooperative behavior on his (the speaker's) part. (Sadock in Ortony 1979: 47)

[T]he telling of several different stories about the same situation, when each story is internally coherent and compelling in its own terms but different from, and perhaps incompatible with, all the others. Such a multiplicity of conflicting stories about t he situation makes it dramatically apparent that we are not dealing with "reality" but with various ways of making sense of a reality. (Schön in Ortony 1979: 267)

... problem-setting matters. The ways in which we set social problems determine both the kinds of purposes and values we seek to realize, and the direction in which we seek solutions. Contrary to the problem-solving perspective, problems are not given, nor are they reducible to arbitrary choices which lie beyond inquiry. We set social problems through the stories we tell – stories whose problem-setting potency derives at least in some cases from their generative metaphors. (Schön in Ortony 1979: 268–9)

... frame conflicts are not problems. They do not lend themselves to problem-solving inquiry ... because frame conflicts are often unresolvable by appeal to facts. In the case of two ... stories ... the adversaries do not disagree about the facts; they simply turn their attention to *different* facts. (Schön in Ortony 1979: 269)

The world of metaphorical statements is not that of truth, although truth may enter as a coincidence. Rather, it is a world in which the intellect is employed to generate statements that are produced by and satisfy the mind of the speaker, that is, soothe the imagination/set minds at rest – statements that are derived not from a given reality but from the state of mind, or attitude, of the speaker and, for that matter, the hearer.

The important implication may be drawn that inasmuch as policy depends on the definition of reality, what is true of the making of economic policy, indeed all policy, is true of the language with which policy is expressed and made: People will manipulate language in order to manipulate the thinking of others and to influence the policy adopted. Government is an instrument subject to its capture and use by interested parties; so, too, is language.

I conclude that the same fundamental framing assumption is made in working with metaphors. The assumption is that the statements in question relate to truth or falsity only by coincidence. The use of absolutist formulation is but one means of manipulation.

The theory of metaphor in late-twentieth-century English was anything but settled and homogeneous. For the purposes of comparison and to get a sense of the definitional situation in the middle of the eighteenth century in England, two entries from Samuel Johnson's celebrated *Dictionary* are reproduced just below. Adam Smith reviewed Johnson's *Dictionary* in the first of the two numbers of the *Edinburgh Review*, published in 1755. Smith was a founder of and major contributor to the journal whose editor was Alexander Wedderburn (Campbell and Skinner 1982: 37). The three men – Johnson, Smith, and Wedderburn – were among the leaders of British intellectual society in the eighteenth century. Johnson and Smith had mixed feelings for each other, neither of them, apparently, hiding their respective views of each other (idem: 152ff.)

The two entries are those for metaphor and simile (Johnson 2006: 376, 526):

> **Me'taphor.** n.s. [*metaphore*, Fr. ΜετάΦοοα.] The application of a word to an use to which, in its original import, it cannot be put: as, he *bridles* his anger; he *deadens* the sound; the spring *awakes* the flowers. A metaphor is a simile comprised in a word; the spring putting in action the powers of vegetation, which were torpid in the winter, as the powers of a sleeping animal are excited by awaking him.
> *The work of tragedy is on the passions, and in a dialogue; both of them abhor strong metaphors, in which the epopœa delights.*
> DRYDEN'S DEDICATION TO VIRGIL'S ÆNEIS.

Si'mile. n.s. [*simile*, Latin.] A comparison by which any thing is illustrated or
aggrandized.
> *Their rhimes,*
> *Full of protest, of oath, and big compare,*
> *Want* similes.
> SHAKESPEARE'S TROILUS AND CRESSIDA
> *Lucentio slip'd me, like his Greyhound,*
> *Which runs himself, and catches for his master:*
> *A good swift* simile, *but something currish.*
> SHAKESPEARE
> *   In argument,*
> Similes *are like songs in love,*
> *They much describe; they nothing prove.*
> PRIOR.
> *Poets, to give a loose to a warm fancy, not*
> *only expatiate in their* similes *but intro –*
> *duce them too frequently.* GARTH

Wedderburn was opposed on the larger stage of national politics and political philosophy by Jeremy Bentham. The central issue was then, as it remains
to this day, the principle of democracy, on which rested government responsive to the interest of the entire population, versus the principle of hierarchy, on which rested the equation of property and virtue, and

the sacrifice of the interest of the many to the interest, joint or several, of the one or
of the few.... Opposite to the interest of the greatest number – opposite through the
whole field of Government – is that same ruling interest.... which ... requires that
the quantity of power, wealth, and factitious dignity, in the possession and at the disposal of the ruling few, should be at all times great as possible. (Bentham in Bowring
1962: 245; Samuels 1966: chapter IV)

This conflict of interests is the backdrop, or context, for the efforts of the
upper economic and social classes to develop an ideology (or, as Frank
Knight envisioned classical economics, a "propaganda for economic freedom" [Knight 1953: 279]). Adam Smith's text seems to have Bentham's positivist description – civil government as functioning for the defense of the
propertied rich against the poor[12] (Smith 1976a: V.i.b.12; 715) – but normatively identified with Wedderburn and with Bentham in his procontinuity,
prosecurity passages.

[12] An echo of Smith's statement cited in the text is the analysis of synergetic relations between
public and private financial markets "which can serve to solidify an alliance between
wealth holders and the state, potentially at the expense of 'society' at large" though principally at the expense of the nonwealthy. *Inter alia*, "these insights undercut the classical
story of the neutral role of money, as well as the notion of a clear distinction between public and private, politics and markets" (Davis 2008: 1101).

The Invisible Hand as Knowledge

7.1. Introduction

The meaningfulness of the concept of the invisible hand depends on the status of the invisible hand as knowledge. Essay 6 examined the linguistic status of the concept. This essay is concerned with the concept's ontological and epistemological status. Considerably more attention has been given in the literature to linguistic issues than to ontological and epistemological issues. The results of this discussion were essentially negative. The ontological and epistemological issues, rarely directly discussed in the literature, are actually fairly straightforward. Once again, however, the results of the discussion are negative.

7.2. Ontology and the Status of the Invisible Hand

Metaphysics has to do with absolutes and ultimates. One branch of metaphysics, *cosmology*, deals with the origin and structure of the world, or universe, broadly defined. Closely related is *ontology*, which has to do with the ultimate nature of being, existence (both per se and nature), and/or reality, including first principles. *Theology* is the study of the nature of God and the relations of God to the universe and to humankind, as well as the study of religious doctrine. *Ethics* is the study of standards of conduct and of moral judgment, and comprises the domain of normative propositions (dealing with goodness, propriety, and ought). *Epistemology* is the theory of knowledge, which some scholars place within metaphysics. Cosmology, ontology, epistemology, theology, and ethics have in common the subject matter of existence whose ultimate content, nature, or first principles generally cannot be directly dealt with and/or experienced, and whose study is substantially conjectural. Accordingly, propositions that arguably form the content of these fields are matters of assertion. They provide no basis for study that permits either conclusive confirmation or disconfirmation of their existence or characteristics, nor do they have conclusive metaprinciples enabling comparisons and/or choice of competing principles.

The literature of metaphysics and ontology is by no means homogeneous in the definition and structuring by various authors in the fields previously outlined. However, the treatment given here of metaphysics and ontology does not bias their application to the concept of the invisible hand. Needless to say, not everyone will agree with any one treatment.

The absolutes and ultimates of metaphysical statements have to do with their truth, meaning their accurate description and/or correct explanation in dealing with the existence and nature of their content. It is very difficult, if not impossible, to determine the truth of metaphysical statements in the same sense or to the same degree that empirical statements can be determined. Truth value is a matter of epistemology, the study of the criteria by which propositions may be evaluated with regard to their truth value; this is taken up further in this essay.

Notwithstanding the assertion of absolutes and ultimates that form propositions about the invisible hand and evidently characterize their nature, many – possibly most, if not all – writers treat the concept of the invisible hand as either literally true or a matter to which criteria of truth apply. Many authors place the term within quotation marks, probably for varying reasons, one of which is likely to indicate reservation as to the truth or other status of the term. Many writers treat the concept as a figure of speech, typically a metaphor (which is why it is given so much attention in Essay 6). Terms with multiple alternative identifications or definitions, such as the invisible hand, exhibit wide variations of specification and application but, as previously mentioned, lack metaprinciples enabling conclusive comparisons and/ or choice of competing principles, identifications, or definitions. They are, however, amenable to question-begging assertions.

Users of the concept of the invisible hand have a strong tendency to confidently treat their candidates for identity and function as absolutes and ultimates – for example, as having singularity and universality – and to affirm their candidates with aplomb. Concepts of the invisible hand, however, are and remain ontologically empty and are but an exercise in assertion. Many such users are, indeed, eminently confident in the ultimate existence of their candidates for identity and function, so much so that they give them – and neither find nor prove – ontological status, giving effect to a belief that their existence somehow transcends human action. (The principle of unintended and unexpected consequences and invisible-hand processes can be exceptions to that statement, and in Essay 10 they are accordingly placed in a different category and treated differently than the candidates examined in Essay 3.)

Notwithstanding this readily projected confidence in asserting that the invisible hand has ontological status – that is, the existence of invisible hand as a category and usually with a particular identity and function, all at the ontological level – the invisible hand is not amenable to proof. Compared to my hypothetical assertion that all resource allocation is governed by a group of monkeys in Bay Front Park in Miami, Florida, or that the allocation of resources, the level of income, and the distribution of income are predetermined by the nature of the universe, no theory of the existence, identity and function, and others of the invisible hand has greater possibility than do these.

Smith compared propositions that are true, that is, capable of having their truth values determined and whose truth has been determined, with other propositions whose truth values are not, and perhaps cannot be, determined. These other propositions are either untrue, or have no truth value, or are incapable of having their truth value determined. Nonetheless, they soothe the imagination, or set minds at rest. (Propositions that are true may not [be able to] set minds at rest.) Many writers refer to the concept of the invisible hand as true, others consider it untrue, and still others seem to think the term is not capable of existence. Many writers define or identify the invisible hand as, for example, the market; some consider it to be literally so whereas others consider it to be a metaphor, a simile, or some other figure of speech. A metaphor can have truth value. It can also be devoid of possible truth value. It may also be only a primitive term.

If there is no invisible hand at the ontological or any other level, statements that purport to identify what it is and/or its function are empty or fictional; there is nothing to identify. If there is an invisible hand, statements that identify it or its function may be metaphysical. Various epistemological criteria may be applied to those statements. A statement may be true by one criterion and not true by another. In both cases, the multiplicity discussed earlier imposes a need to choose between candidates of identity or of function, which may have different truth values. The market and God may be considered to be same or different ontologically. Their respective truth value may be judged differently for comparative purposes by different criteria.

The invisible hand either exists or does not exist ontologically. If it exists ontologically, its existence and nature may be metaphysical and not amenable to analysis permitting, even in principle, a conclusive result. Like God (yes, I know this is controversial; also, God is, of course, one of the identities given the invisible hand in economics), assuming its existence as a matter of faith, the nature of the invisible hand is a matter of assertion. Many people consider that the existence of God is also essentially a matter of assertion. If the invisible hand does not exist, it is a matter of the imagination (including myth), and although its nonexistence does not prevent analysis of when and how individuals imagine it, the fact that people can imagine it does not guarantee its existence (we do not assume that people can imagine only what exists; imagining would thereby be its own proof). The reader can substitute the Bay Front Park monkeys, intra- or intergalactic vehicles, or anything else.

A proposition about the invisible hand may be ontologically empty (except for the proposition itself) but may comport with noninvisible hand – nonontological propositions that the proposition in question attributes to the invisible hand. We know a great deal about the working of the price mechanism, the propensity to truck, barter, and exchange, about technology, and so on, without having to rely on assertions of the invisible-hand status. A hypothetical model of adjustment mechanisms and processes could comprise a number of candidates for the invisible-hand status found in the literature, but omit any designation of the invisible-hand status. The loss through omission is asymptotic to zero.

Another principally relevant concern is normative status, having to do with statements of goodness, propriety, and ought. Most propositions about the invisible hand seem to be "ought" statements, even though they may have an "is" form. Such are statements that purport to be true but whose message is primarily that they ought to be, or ought to be considered, the case. The objective analyst, and not only the skeptic, will treat them as "ought" propositions masquerading as "is" propositions. One reason for saying that the invisible hand ought to be the case is that such will be deemed consonant with the ultimate nature of things – an untestable metaphysical proposition, an assertion. Another would predicate ought status on its presumed or desirable performance as social control, psychic balm, or ability to convey certain policy preferences into the process of working things out. This basis may be true, false, or conditional. Propositions about the use of the concept may be true or false, but they also may be rejected or accepted on the basis of different criteria of performance. The concept may be either empty or full of truth value. Even if empty, its use may have great normative value as social control and psychic balm. If it is full of truth value, its deployment may have little normative value of the kind just mentioned. As argued in Essay 4, in Smith's argument in the *History of Astronomy*, both propositions that have and propositions that do not have truth value may serve as instruments of social control and/or psychic balm.

The doctrine and use of the concept of the invisible hand can itself function as social control even if most people believe along conventional lines. Its serviceability for social-control and psychic-balm functions need not – and typically, if not always, does not – signify any correspondence of the invisible hand with ontological reality. It does, however, suggest the effectiveness of other, past social control.

If the invisible hand is to be deemed, say, a metaphor for the market, or some other candidate for its identity, then the market *et alia* functions as social control. Whether or not the invisible hand exists, or is (only) thought to exist, the meaning and utility (social function) of the *concept* of the invisible hand can be judged by its efficacy as social control and psychic balm. Propositions pertaining to that matter can be treated as empirical or metaphysical, and can have a low, high, or no truth value.

The concept of the invisible hand is a foundational concept in economics in the sense of being a key element in the social belief system. This is effectuated through the use of language. Foundational status as belief guarantees neither the existence of the invisible hand nor that this knowledge (in the sense of truth) can be acquired about it. To pull off such a gambit, however, is a common enough phenomenon.

The invisible hand as a mode of discourse is a residue of mythopoeic reasoning, with supernaturalism serving to legitimize it along the lines of absolutist formulation, notwithstanding the fact that the term "invisible hand" is purely metaphysical and "… merely illustrates the way in which primitive beliefs can be reinforced and made intellectually respectable by a mistaken theory of meaning coupled with a convenient ontology" (Weldon 1953: 21).

The combination of the quest for determinateness and ideological legitimization of the status quo, however selective, results in affirmation of determinacy and the propriety of a particular status quo, typically without any showing that, or how, the status quo, somehow defined, comports with the ideological formulation.

The antipathy of economists to subjects at the heart of this essay may reflect a desire to escape and obfuscate any realization that economics serves mythic-symbolic-religious functions of social control and psychic balm. Whatever the explanation – it could be training, self-selection, and so on – the antipathy does exist.

The belief, mythic, and symbolic systems of society order "reality" for us; they are not there to be found in any ontological sense. That reality may be imaginary and illusory, represent wishful thinking, imagination, and projection, and serve to legitimize through absolutist formulation.

Much – in fact, nearly all – of the invisible-hand literature seems to assume that the objective of the use of the invisible hand is the definition of ultimate reality, whereas in fact the objective is to influence the social belief system operating as social control and psychic balm, the former relating to the control of government and including service as a conduit for ideas into the policy process, and the latter relating, in part, to the (assumed or concluded) mythopoeic needs of the population, with both reflecting the human tendency to assign ontological meaning to the important things in life.

Selective perception and selective specification of the nature of ultimate reality is one way desired policies are elevated in ontological status and rejected ones are treated as artificial. I have heard one person argue that apartheid is a social reality and not due to government policy – this in a regime controlled by the white minority. The same person might not apply the same reasoning to abortion. In the former case, the role of government is seemingly diminished (if apartheid is part of natural reality, then, like hurricanes, it cannot be altered by humans), whereas in the latter case, the role of government is elevated (because abortion is not commonly thought to be a feature of natural reality, government can be used to limit it). *The reality, however, is that in both cases, government is being used for the purposes of those who control it.* The rhetoric of ontology being used to legitimize apartheid policy in an absolutist manner is an echo of its use in portraying slavery as natural, approved by the Bible, and not artificial. To the extent that socioeconomic reality is socially constructed through politics, truth is a partial function of politics. For example, the creation of time zones was initially intended to facilitate railroad schedules, and thus bore no relationship to the nature of reality. When Daylight Savings Time was introduced, some people opposed the policy as interfering with God's time.

To assert, for example, that markets are essentially competitive, regardless of their structure, is to make an ontological argument or claim, hopefully to remove the topic from the domain of government action, and to pretend that markets are found and/or are homogeneous rather than the result of a conflict between institutions, agents, and their respective policies. *Economics, as a science that purports to deal with the objective and the confirmable, ironically has as its foundational concept something metaphysical – the invisible hand.* Whether seen as a continuation of medieval mysticism or as ideological glorification – and laden with faith presuppositions in either case – the linguistic device selectively converts an *is* to an *ought* and a moral problem to a natural-theological one. The same applies to the concept of the invisible hand. The invisible hand is a quaint and fuzzy concept that, depending on a point of view, either has meaning or is meaningless (inexplicable and incomprehensible) on the level of ontology. In either case, it may only be a metaphor or another figure of speech, a primitive term, a projection of wishful thinking, and/or a recognized instrument of social control, and not – or not necessarily – a description of ultimate reality.

At work, also, are tendencies toward reductionism, exclusivity, and reification. The rival of truth (which may or may not be an empty set, depending on the chosen epistemological criteria) is, as with Smith, soothing the imagination (which is perhaps even more problematic than truth). Nonetheless, the substantive content adduced to the natural order of things vis-à-vis the social construction of reality is itself, to some significant degree, a social construction.

7.3. The Epistemology of the Invisible Hand

The invisible-hand term, examined with regard to linguistic and ontological considerations, cannot contribute to true propositions (though it can be *seen* as doing so). For linguistic propositions dealing with the invisible hand to have something to say about truth, words would have to have "intrinsic or essential meanings" (Weldon 1953: 12). Words, however, do not correspond to reality; they are verbal, linguistic, discursive; "they concern linguistic habits and conventions, but tell us nothing about matter of fact" (idem: 13). They "do not have meanings in the required sense at all; they simply have uses … they are not the names of anything" (idem: 19). For ontological propositions dealing with the invisible hand to have something to say about truth, not only would they have to be able to do what linguistic propositions cannot do; they would have to go beyond non–invisible hand propositions and deal in terms of existence, absolutes, and ultimates as to the absolute nature of things. The epistemological considerations remain.

Epistemology has to do with the credentials by which propositions are accepted or rejected as knowledge. Like linguistics and ontology, epistemology is a vast and diverse subject. The epistemological significance of the invisible-hand term can be approached as follows.

The two procedural approaches to epistemology are prescriptivism and credentialism. *Prescriptive epistemology* accepts only certain criteria of truth. *Credentialist epistemology* identifies the alternative criteria by which any statement can be said to be true, and individuals and groups can choose whichever they prefer.

The two methodological or scientific approaches to epistemology are deduction and induction, or rationalism and empiricism. Deduction or rationalism deals with the process of assembling premises, axioms, and the like and, given the rules of the system of logic employed, produce logically derived conclusions. This procedure says nothing necessarily about the world; its conclusions are solely matters of logicality and are either valid or invalid. Validity is not necessarily truth.

To my knowledge, no proposition as to the existence, identity, or function of the invisible hand has ever been derived through deduction. (I expect that some arguments could be converted to deduction.) The Walrasian auctioneer, for example, is what is necessary to close the Walrasian system; it is conceptually a matter of neither validity nor empiricism.

Induction or empiricism has to do with propositions that are aimed at accurate description or correct explanation. The propositions are hypotheses derived from a theory to enable the hypothesis to be tested (or, following Smith, to be adopted in order to set minds at rest). The elements of the testing process are the particular specification of the general hypothesis to be tested, the social space to which it will be applied, the data used in the test, the strengths and limitations of the tools used throughout the test, and the decision rule by which the hypothesis is accepted or rejected. If the test satisfies the decision rule and the hypothesis is accepted, the result is deemed true. However, the result of truth thus reached applies only to the hypothesis, social space, data, and other elements that form the test. It does not necessarily apply to every repetition of the test, with the same or different substantive elements, because the next iteration of the test, or the one after that, may prove false. Truth is thus limited and probabilistic.

No empirical test of a hypothesis of the existence of the identity, status, or functions of the invisible hand has ever been undertaken that provided knowledge that went beyond the empirical study of specific existence, identities, and functions without invisible-hand designations. If one's response is that one does not expect such demonstration in the case of the invisible hand, then (1) the exercise reverts to metaphysics and ontology, which may well be the domain of one's chosen epistemological criteria; and (2) one has to explain the efforts to simulate the process summarized in the paragraph immediately preceding this one.

Consider the following, from an email from Y. S. Brenner:

When we talked about your, actually Smith's, *invisible hand*, it reminded me of Newton's idea of gravitation. Today, tak[ing] into account his exceptions (namely the services that pay for themselves and those he believed to remain the responsibility of the state) his metaphor would have been better illustrated by the *immune system*. The immune system, like any other ruling system, reacts automatically to "attacks." But when it fails to restore the "equilibrium" by itself, we call in the doctor who will try to restore it by giving us pills etc. This in a way changes the corrective agent God, into a human corrective agent like the doctor. Naturally Smith believed in God and therefore Newton's vision was closer to him, but non-believers in God's direct intervention in the running of the universe may find the metaphor of the immune system better than gravitation for illustrating the idea of the invisible hand. (Y. S. Brenner to Warren J. Samuels, July 26, 2007)

I responded: "Interesting idea! I guess that different illustrations work for different people" (Samuels to Brenner, July 26, 2007). What status does this have as knowledge? What are its epistemological credentials?

The example is akin to the thought process that generated the idea of the Walrasian auctioneer. With the immune system example, we have God as a "corrective agent" being juxtaposed with the immune system in the same role. There are two identities plus the function, equilibrium, which bring closure. The thinking process that reached this conclusion is not deduction from premises yielding a valid conclusion. It is not the process of testing an empirical proposition. It is a thinking process that seeks an alternative to God that will better illustrate the invisible-hand metaphor, and it came up with the idea of the immune process. Others have come up with the auctioneer.

This example does not illustrate a better solution. It illustrates that nothing is added to our knowledge by the proposal of the immune system as a better illustration of the invisible hand. This process is akin to seeking the truth of what is going on by searching for the meaning of words. There is no "intrinsic or essential" meaning of anything to be discovered by using one's imagination to find an alternative to God as the closing "mechanism." The proposal of the immune system is not, or not necessarily, a priori, responsive to an invisible hand that exists and has an essential meaning. The task is to discover the invisible hand that generates closure – to discover what might generate closure and call it the invisible hand. If I say that the monkeys in the palm tree are a better illustration than God, the obvious silliness of my suggestion is enough to dismiss the proposal. But the immune system example, while better (more sensible) than the monkeys, adds nothing to knowledge. It is purely and simply the assertion of a hypothesis. The suggestion of either the immune system, the monkeys, the auctioneer, or, for that matter, Newton's God adds nothing to knowledge by their being possible instruments of closure – and based on an assumption about closure rather than causation. The examples merely reflect beliefs, that is, linguistic habits and conventions that, it is important to note, also may govern our choice of epistemological criteria. The examples tell us nothing about the invisible hand, including whether or not an invisible hand exists. Indeed, the invisible-hand investigation is not helped at all by assuming a particular closing mechanism. Once we come up with the immune system as the closing mechanism, we not only know no more than before about the identity of the invisible hand; we know no more than before whether there is in fact an invisible hand. The key point is that a search for the better illustration of the invisible hand is not a means of getting to reality. The candidates for the invisible hand (i.e., the closing mechanism) are simply words that have uses; they are not necessarily the names of anything. One uses those words to be intelligible in ordinary and technical discourse. If there are facts that can be discovered by inquiry into possible closing mechanisms, they all are at the stage of hypothesis formation. Were the monkeys' existence in the tree taken as fact, there obviously would be much more work to do. The fact of the monkeys may surprise someone, but their control of resource allocation is quite another matter and surely more surprising. The immune system as a noun provides no knowledge of anything pertaining to an invisible hand, not even to the existence of an invisible hand. (Weldon [1953: 20] writes that "it comes to be held not merely that nouns are always the names of identifiable things, but also that the things of which they are the names are unchanging and eternal." The two points – names of identifiable things and the things are unchanging and eternal – are separable.) The introduction of falsification into the analysis makes the analysis more interesting, more *au courant*, and more complex but does not alter the relevant result.

We have now seen that induction, or the use of empirical reasoning, used with regard to linguistic considerations cannot properly be held to contribute anything to true propositions. Used with regard to epistemological considerations, it cannot be seen as contributing conclusiveness to propositions.

The search for an invisible hand, or for its identity or function, leads to an epistemological conundrum: Once a putative invisible hand is identified, its invisibility is over and of no consequence. That the term continues to be used testifies to the political and social nature of language.

More importantly, the search for the invisible hand cannot lead to knowledge about the invisible hand. This is true of deduction, in which the drawing of a valid conclusion yields no necessary, substantive, true knowledge. It is also true of induction, in which no conclusion surviving the testing process can be said to be conclusive. Neither deduction nor induction alone adds to our knowledge of matters of fact.

The words of the invisible-hand idea have no meaning corresponding to anything known conclusively to exist and add nothing to our quest into whether there is an invisible hand beyond either wishful thinking or our imagination. And those words offer no proof of the existence of any absolute or ultimate.

Whether we consider the invisible hand to be a matter of language, or ontology, or epistemology, two conclusions emerge. One conclusion is that the claim of the existence, identity, and/or the functions of an invisible hand is a matter of pure assertion. The second conclusion is that analysis of any aspect of an invisible hand adds nothing to knowledge that goes beyond what is known without any invisible-hand language. Consider the most frequently attributed identities: the market, the price system, competition, some combination of these, self-interest, the entrepreneur, the division of labor, consumer sovereignty, and several others, including God. The literature on the invisible hand as such has arguably contributed nothing to our knowledge thereof, with respect to either the identity or the function of the invisible hand.

Consider, too, the so-called invisible-hand processes. The idea here is that, like much of Hayek's reasoning, there is a process of the unintended and unforeseen consequences of human action, a process that is for most, if not all, practical and theoretical purposes invisible. I do not doubt that some insight has been facilitated by contemplation of such a process. But businessmen and politicians, among others, in seeking to comprehend what will happen in the markets in which they operate, know this instinctively and operate accordingly. What is involved is a process of interaction and aggregation as well as the evolution and structure of complexity.

Take, once again, American football. In American football, the offense and the defense meet on the field. The respective coaches adopt, and adapt, their offensive and defensive formations respectively. The result may reflect what one or the other of the coaches had intended, or it may reflect neither; and if the two teams later in the game adopt the same offensive and defensive formations for a second time, the second result likely will differ from the first result. What went for a long gain, possibly a touchdown, now goes for a loss, no gain, or a short gain.

The situation is actually almost infinitely more complicated. The individual players at each position have their strengths and weaknesses; how they match up, or how it is thought they will match up, is basically known (by virtue of their expertise and experience) to coaches on both sides. This affects play-calling decisions by the offense and defensive strategy by the defense. Later in the game, the various players (as well as their substitutes) will be fatigued, perhaps to different degrees, and their performance – both absolute and relative to the player on the other side – will be differentially affected. Coaches devote much time to recruiting, which is also an invisible-hand process. They also devote much time to analyzing formation and play calling. They seek to understand the likely pattern of what their opponent does in certain situations as the game progresses. They make judgments as to when certain maneuvers by defensive linemen against certain offensive formations and play executions will and will not likely pay off. Just as likely, each coach analyzes his own team and the other team in the manner just described: Knowing what the other side, A, likely sees in their side, B, and how the other coach, A, will, given his manpower, react thereto enables the coach of B to react differently. (Some coaches will do this with the aid of their computer. At least one college coach decided to use offensive and defensive formations drawn randomly, preventing the opposition, especially when on defense, from selecting their formations in the manner described earlier. The coach apparently gave up on this system after one season.) Undoubtedly, coaches think of their situation as similar to a chess game (as do generals and admirals). They are all invisible-hand processes. Informing them, if they happened to be ignorant of invisible-hand processes (which I doubt), likely would have helped strengthen their choice, preparation, and execution of game plans. Later, the same information will be of little or no help. The point is that, Hayekian diffusion of information aside, society will have had no increase in knowledge, only a change in its distribution – plus, through the tactics outlined earlier, the intended creation of effective ignorance on the side of their opponents. It is somewhat ironic that certain maneuvers are called misdirection.

In an essay on Thorstein Veblen as an economic theorist, I endeavored to defend him against the dual charges that he was anti-theory and had no theory of his own. I suggested that neoclassical economists engaged in several forms of theorizing, and that Veblen also engaged in several forms of theory construction. I also included a two-page list of Veblen's theories arranged by general subject matter, with some overlap, each of which in varying degrees attempted to describe and explain.

Essay 3 of this volume presents lengthy lists of the identities and the functions that have been attributed to the invisible hand, each with enormous variations. In my list of Veblen's theories, one group was comprised of theories of capitalism and its development; other groups were of theories of methodology, belief system, behavior, the state, the firm, and economic instability. All but the group on methodology have a substance whose description and/or explanation has not only been Veblen's program but that of hundreds, if not thousands, of others. There is no question that there are elements of assertion in the list, but overwhelmingly Veblen and the others, including neoclassicists, have dealt with substantive topics and materials about the existence of which – *ceteris paribus* the limiting roles of the definition of the scope of economics, the substantive content of the conceptualized economy, and the protocol requiring the production of all unique determinant competitive equilibrium optimal results – there has been no or very little question.

This is not the case with assertions of the existence, identity, and function of the invisible hand. Virtually all the candidates for the identity of the invisible hand are found in the literature of economics as substantive topics; the same is true of the list of functions attributed to the invisible hand by various authors. The difference is that the lists pertinent to the invisible hand, aside from work on the individual topics in their own right, are assertions without substance pertaining to invisible-hand status. Certainly, one can compare all the lists and feel that some of the topics in the non-individual-hand literature will appear, at one time or another, to be assertions without much simultaneous corresponding substance. But this situation will overwhelmingly apply to an early period in the development of the topic and its corresponding substance. No such development of substance associated with invisible-hand status has taken place. The very existence of the invisible hand remains a matter of assertion. Whether seen as a metaphor or some other figure of speech, it often carries with it the aura of metaphysics, myth, and mystification.

One cannot look to definitions in order to determine the existence, identity, or function of the invisible hand. Nor can one look to philosophy, either ontology or epistemology, to determine if there is, in fact, a category called "invisible hand," what it is, or what it does.

The question of the existence of the invisible hand as such is not a question that has been seriously asked or answered; basically we have only assumption and assertion. Some authors "feel there ought to be answers; yet we do not know how to find the answers, and if answers which look feasible are propounded we do not know how to test them in order to decide whether they are correct or not" (Weldon 1953: 56–57). These are "questions of a type to which no empirically testable answers could be given, and such questions are nonsensical" (idem: 74). The assertion is of "a metaphysical view and, as such, ... [is] beyond the range of empirical confirmation" (idem: 94). What happens "is that an appeal is being made to the basic assumption" that the invisible hand exists and is somehow a reflection or expression of something that "stands behind and justifies them" (idem: 58). What is mistaken is to suppose that there is something natural or fundamental behind the assumed invisible hand (idem: 60). The ostensible functions of the invisible hand "are just what happens.... It is a mistake to give either a positive or a negative answer" about the existence of the invisible hand, "since the question is empty" (idem: 65–66). From the very beginning, the term has been "turned into a kind of slogan or propaganda phrase.... [The term] is a slippery term because it covertly implies approval of a particular type of ... [economic] system" or at least tends to do so (idem: 68–69). Like other terms dealing with economic policy and in other fields, the term tends to have "propaganda rather than informative value" (idem: 72).

Once one understands that what is going on is a matter of the formation and execution of social control, and not the conduct of linguistic science, the activities and beliefs denigrated by Weldon take on a meaning very different from that of political and economic activists. Weldon writes that

> it was once supposed that the Laws of England were not made up by legislators or judges but discovered in the same kind of way as that in which laws of nature were mistakenly supposed to be discovered. All this however is now of historical rather than philosophical interest. (idem: 68)

Here, however, Weldon was wrong. It remains commonplace for courts – in another form of absolutist legitimization – to assert that they find and not make the law. In regard to the concept of "rule of law" and the trope of "find, not make," see Samuels (2007a), chapters 3 (the nature and sources of rights), 10 (problems of language in law), and 13 (choice versus rule of law).

Fascinatingly, Weldon's book on the vocabulary of politics, or political linguistics, makes some of the same points as did Vilfredo Pareto in his *Treatise on General Sociology*, first published in 1916 and subsequently republished as *The Mind and Society* (1935). For the present purposes, we need to consider two of Pareto's major terms. *Non-logico-experimental* knowledge consists of things lying in whole or in part outside the world of experience and, therefore, experiment. Its conclusions concern and are offered as *a priori*, certain, absolute, necessary, and immutable, although they vary from writer to writer. Non-logico-experimental statements tend to blend nonverifiable statements of fact and of value; to invoke higher principles; to be dogmatic, exclusivist, and absolutist; to use indeterminate words and defective reasonings; to deal with metaphysical entities and essences; to ascribe objective existence to both arguments and the pseudo-objects of emotions; and, therefore, to be generally beyond the world of experience and proof. In general, the non-logico-experimental is the world of the metaphysical, theological, and ideological; it is the world of theories transcending experience, the world of mere assertion, and requires the direct support of faith and conviction (paraphrased from Samuels 1974: 28–29 and passim).

Derivations are the rationalizations (James Harvey Robinson) or myths (Georges Sorel) of a non-logico-experimental nature, which are essentially metaphysical and a prioristic assertions, allegations, and speculations with no foundation (or possibility of foundation) in fact. They are the substance, according to Pareto, of superstition, prayer, theology, morality, law, natural law, ideology, political formulas, and the like. They are, or use, indeterminate words or expressions that correspond to northing actual, which define unknowns by unknowns, and which combine definitions with unproven theses. They are the imaginary principles and theories to which prescriptive and objective existence is ascribed. Derivations function to make the relative, normative, and contingent appear as absolute, given, and required. Derivations are the myths, fictions, and arguments, with all their attendant casuistry, that are universally accepted as part of the national, cultural, economic, and religious heritage, as well as the rationalizing "truths" of reformers. Insofar as they are accepted as knowledge, consciously or unconsciously, they serve to mobilize and manipulate individual psychology using different propositions to manipulate definitions and psychic states as a framework for policy decisions, and thereby help structure social policy (paraphrased from Samuels 1974: 34–35 and passim).

In short, they are the terms that describe the "invisible hand." The term "invisible hand" itself can be a name with which to either hide our ignorance or pretend to know what it is, or even pretend it exists.

The Invisible Hand and the Economic Role
of Government

8.1. Introduction

This essay concentrates on the theory of economic policy, especially the economic role of government, to be found in Adam Smith's works, both his own publications and the notes taken down by students from his lectures on law and government. Considered first is the leading interpretation or ostensible application of his purported ideas that, in my view, is nothing less than the economic ideology or economic belief system of western civilization. It is sometimes called laissez-faire or noninterventionism, notably the ideology largely embraced by the discipline of economics and, within it, especially the Chicago School, notably Milton Friedman, and the companion ideas of Friedrich Hayek.

8.2. Laissez-faire

Laissez-faire is generally used in three contexts: minimization of legal change; a particular vision of an economy; and legal change to bring about that particular vision. Discussion here focuses on the first.

The concept of laissez-faire is simultaneously unambiguous and ambiguous. The difference turns, in part, on the issue of sentiment versus coherent substance. Both sentimentally and substantively, it stands for an economic system based on institutions of private property, private enterprise, competition, markets, meaningful private choice, and a presumption against government activism; that is, in which markets govern resource allocation. Sentimentally, it is an idealization and a projection of certain individualist sentiments. It is also simultaneously the propositions used to defend the upper classes against changes in the rights or privileges accorded them and their business activities. It also has substantive meaning in comparison to mercantilism and Soviet-type planning. Even though laissez-faire seems an attractive solution to social problems and to escape the burden of choice, and because movement toward an idealized image is perceived as neither government nor change, at the very least serious problems arise in its application within a market economy.

Running through these essays is the argument countering the belief that the invisible hand enables, even requires, laissez-faire. It is a mythical, false argument. There is no invisible hand. Anything even resembling laissez-faire is impossible. The role of the invisible hand considered here is to introduce into the decision-making process the agenda items to be imposed on government to advance the interests of users of the term, either wittingly or unwittingly.

Market economies are usefully modeled as market plus framework systems. Markets operate within frameworks of moral and legal rules structuring and operating through the markets they help form. This model gives effect to both private choice and necessary social control. Problems arise over the substance of rules, mode of determining rules, relative reliance on moral and legal rules, and changing the legal rules. The model postulates a joint process: optimizing market resource allocation, and reforming the framework. "Private choice" usually includes corporate choice, incongruous inasmuch as corporate decisions can be more important to people than government decisions.

Because the presumption against legal activism is easily rebutted, the substantive interpretation becomes ambiguous. Legal social control is necessary. The basic economic institutions are legal in character. People who believe they have problems in pragmatic, democratic regimes seek government help, and the government responds. Working all this out is messy. Politicians seeking reelection must attend, or be seen as attending, to citizen attitudes and perceptions of problems, problems often very real. For this and numerous other reasons, changing the legal rules governing property rights and other institutions happens frequently – to the dismay of sentimentalist believers in strict laissez-faire.

Modern western economies exhibit several practical models of laissez-faire. First, government is projected as an evil, to be removed from the backs of the citizens. Second, already existing important governmental activities are more or less taken for granted, treated as natural, not governmental. In the first two models, officials' principal function is to enforce the law, and neither expand its scope nor introduce change (the usually silent corollary is approval of changes in the law of which they, or some group of interested parties, approve – deregulation, for example. Third, typically inexplicit in ordinary discourse, government is the object of reform, making government do the correct things for the "right" people. The first model seemingly minimizes government; the second seemingly minimizes change of law and of the interests protected by government; and the third seemingly minimizes control of the agenda by the "wrong" people.

This practical orientation faces fundamental problems. First, conflicts exist between the three models considered as agendas for government. Second, all three are applied pragmatically and selectively, therefore inconsistently, with ambiguity and inconclusiveness the result. Third, economic policy is a function of contests among elites and between elites and nonelites to determine who are the "right" people to control and benefit from government. Fourth, a tension may exist between economic and social conservatives; the former want to enhance and the latter, to constrain the range of private discretion allowed by law, generally but not necessarily in different spheres of life.

Another problem is *governance*, defined as decision making importantly affecting other people. Official government is one institution of governance; others include other governments, international organizations, domestic and foreign corporations, nonprofit organizations, the social belief system, organized religion, education, and custom. Government has formal responsibility for the division of power within the nominally private sector and between the private and public sectors. But government is an object of a ubiquitous contest over its control. Limiting government, however, does not limit governance.

Common to much of the aforementioned is the view that government "interferes" in order to control the "interference" by others. Freedom to manufacture and to trade is a function of the total system of freedom and control. Legal rules both limit and enhance an individual's range of operative discretion, typically differently for different people. A historic example is the contest between labor and capital over the legal status of unions. Sometimes such "interference" is seen as necessary; other times, it is defended as only minimally necessary. Much depends on whose ox is being gored.

Private property is both what it is because of government *and* a check on the power of government – given suitable legislators and judges and the issues at stake. During the period of transformation from the old to the modern state and economy, new forms and new meanings of property arose and old ones fell. Property was not protected because it was property; it was property because it was protected. However, such did not prevent claims invoking the sacred character of property and the need to protect property against the claims of those who wanted government to protect their interests just as it had protected others, as property.

Laissez-faire has been fiction, an exercise in wishful thinking and the language of those who opposed changes – except the changes they favor. The concept has mixed sentimental and existential or substantive meaning, suffused with selectivity in application and ambiguity of meaning. Certain sentiments are effectively expressed, mobilized, and manipulated, yet they are fundamentally inconclusive with respect to the issues to which they are addressed, generally represented by the question: What should government do? The question is more complicated than the phrase and its underlying sentiment might lead one to expect. *Government will be protecting and promoting certain interests, and not others, no matter which answer to the question is given.* Laissez-faire is a simplistic and disengaging view of complex real-world problems, the dynamics of change, and the need for collective decision making. Accordingly, no country could or has practiced laissez-faire, though much has been done in its name and through its ostensible domestic program.

Domestic legislation and practice has inevitably had to take sides in issues involving conflicts between interests and therefore between claims of rights. Both professional and lay people have not appreciated the depth of importance of law in economic affairs. Moreover, domestic legislation and practice has been combined with neo-mercantilism and imperialism by Great Britain and the other European colonial powers in the nineteenth and twentieth centuries. Countries such as the European colonial powers and especially the United States have self-images of being and having been benevolent to others. The stronger powers, however, have used their advantages, their economic and military superiority, to structure markets and exchange in their favor. Those parts of the belief system that selectively serve domestic interests often also serve international interests. The nations with superior power apply to international economic affairs variations of the domestic belief system – for example, that trade benefits everyone. The advantages in trade enjoyed by the more powerful are obfuscated by the luster cast on "free trade" by the dominant ideology. Subsequent generations of citizens of the superior powers then are aghast at the antagonism displayed toward them by citizens of the dominated nations.

Contrary to the picture of harmony provided by the doctrines of laissez-faire and other psychic-balm functioning ideas, even if one grants the proposition that markets allocate resources, different allocative results will derive from different structures of power, both within and between nations. Market structures are made, not found, and trade often takes place within them under terms imposed by the superior powers.

The world is not as simple as either the laissez-faire or power-oriented explications seem to allege, but the relevance of power to the organization of markets is also illustrated by another domestic phenomenon. I refer to the effort of individual states of the United States to adopt mercantilist legislation in order to promote or protect the interests of certain industries. When, for example, oleomargarine became a threat to the dairy industry of Wisconsin, the state government of Wisconsin attempted to protect the home interest from the threat of competition from Iowa farmers whose corn was the basis of the oleomargarine. The Wisconsin state government simultaneously sought to overturn other states' legislation that attempted to do to Wisconsin dairy farmers what Wisconsin's legislature was trying to do to Iowa farmers. In the early 1970s, I heard a speech by a member of the governing board of the California university system, a gentleman who had been appointed by Governor Ronald Reagan. The first half of the speech was a brilliant discourse on free trade, lambasting Mexico for endeavoring to prevent the import of tomatoes from the United States. The second half of the speech was an equally brilliant discourse against free trade in defense of the United States' efforts to prevent the importation of plywood from Japan.

The foregoing is not the exception to laissez-faire; it is what takes place all the time and in all industries, that is, the practice of neo-mercantilism. It is what the ideology of laissez-faire selectively obscures. It is a picture of government as a responder to the inevitable conflict of interests among industries and to the efforts of parties to resort to government when they feel that they have problems. Inasmuch as it is impossible to distinguish between law that erects the framework of the economy from that which selectively benefits so-called special interests, such activity will continue. And laissez-faire will continue to be a means of selectively influencing public opinion.

8.3. The Misperception of Adam Smith on the Economic Role of Government: Freeing Smith from the "Free Market" – Prelude

Adam Smith was like the rest of us, only more intelligent and more knowledgeable, more of a scholar. Smith seems to have known that there are two levels of analysis and discussion of the economic role of government. One level was that of ordinary belief and discourse. What we have and own is believed to be a matter of right, ultimately a matter of the natural order of things. It matters little that the legal content of what we have and own has evolved over past centuries. It matters much if in the present, government interferes with our ownership and enjoyment of what we have. Such is the social belief system with regard to the economic role of government – the attitude, at best, of possessive individualism.

Such is also the adult result of juvenile or adolescent rebellion. The tormented teenager is torn between two forces: the desire to be independent from parents, to do one's own thing; and the desire for the security of knowing that you are or can be under the parents' protective wing. It is the clash of these two desires, further nurtured by hormones related to sexual maturation, that generates the abrasive, rebellious, and obnoxious behavior of the teenager, who has relatively negligible control over his or her feelings. A more or less satisfactory resolution of these conflicts of adolescence cannot be precisely specified, but one can generalize and say that it involves an adult who is relatively secure in his or her self-command and ability to act, while also able to accept the authority initially of parents and eventually of supervisors, coworkers, and government. One does not like social control, especially with regard to those activities with which our identity (financial future) is bound up, but for the most part, our having been socialized in the ways of our society both enables and compels us to follow the rules, including those that assign decision-making authority to others and that enable them to introduce damage.

Another level has to do with what characterizes most people some of the time and some people much but not all of the time, the combination of the serious conceptual and historical nature of government and the larger scheme of social control of which it is, in some form and in some way, an interacting part. On this level, one does not feel competent to specify the details of what government in particular and the aggregate of social control in general consists.

For the most part, it seems, serious thought about the economic role of government centers on the market-plus-framework model of social control and a correlative approach to the nature of property. In the market-plus-framework model, the framework consists of law and morals, elaborated as government and law, moral rules, custom, education, and religion. Neither legal nor moral rules are given once and for all time and all societies; rather, the content of legal and moral rules must be worked out. For Smith, moral rules are in part a product of individuals' drives for recognition and approval. One element is the great deception, as he puts it in the *Moral Sentiments*, which leads us to overvalue our possessions but nonetheless leads to their greater production. Throughout we are subject to the principles of approbation and disapprobation, as we pay attention to what others respect and disrespect, above all to what we think of ourselves along those same lines. Much the same is the case with the working out of legal rules and rights. Among the key dimensions of the process of working out the rules by which we live are the respective domains of law and of morals; the specific content of rules and rights; the conditions of the interaction between legal rules, between moral rules, and between legal and moral rules; and the determination of when old rules are to be retained or new rules adopted in their place.

The rules and the rights of law and morals do not have a transcendent, given existence. Nor are they uniform across societies; diversity, empirically, is overwhelmingly the case, although the set of rules of each society tends to have as part of its social belief system some absolutist formulations that provide legitimization on an ontological level.

The rules in each domain govern not only their respective domains and the content of rights, but also how the rules may be changed. A change of the rules governing who can vote and on what will likely lead to further change of rules, the rules governing who can vote and on what, and the content of those and all other rules. A change in the nature, form, and content of property rights will likely increase some people's decision-making capacity and decrease others' – actually, such a change will both increase and decrease any one person's decision-making capacity.

To conclude the market-plus-framework approach to the economic role of government, several points need to be made. Markets do not exist independently of mankind. Markets are a function of the strategic actions of business people and firms, law, and moral rules. Markets are like property, law, and morals: Each is simultaneously both a dependent and an independent variable. Each, that is to say, is a function of the forces acting on and through it, and each influences those same forces. Each contending force seeks to control government. This is because government is an institution open to the direction given it by those in a position to control government. Accordingly, one of the most fundamental social processes is that in which contenders seek to capture and control government in order to effectuate each contender's agenda. Laissez-faire, nonintervention, and similar phrases are in this model not a definition of actual reality or a meaningful description on the second level. They are, instead, linguistic devices utilized on the first level for the mobilization and manipulation of perceptions, preferences, and decision-making behavior. They seem to make sense only because they resonate with our adolescent and adult sensitivities, given each person's identifications that both help form and are the result of their identity, and so on.

The "interesting times" in which Adam Smith lived – eighteenth-century Scotland – was comprised of a civil war between Scotland and England; a political structure comprised of a landed aristocracy; a landed gentry; a more or less traditional European monarchy; an ascendant middle class of tradespeople; and rural and urban workers and their families. Insofar as elective power is important, the franchise was held by 5 percent or so of the population, and continued at that level until the Reform Act of 1832. The franchise was then and thereafter gradually extended to most adult males and, eventually, females. The contest for the control of government both influenced and was influenced by the distribution of the franchise and the particular issues, real and contrived, of each election.

That Adam Smith stands for laissez-faire, noninterventionism, and minimal government is a dominant theme in economics and elsewhere – including among those critical of the laissez-faire position. Innumerable examples of this view – which we *may* call the "minimalist" view of Smith – appear in the economics literature past and present. Against the background of government clearly comprised of a narrow group, it is hardly surprising that getting the government and those who control and use it for their own purposes off the backs of the mass of the people, as some express the point, would be an attractive position. In some respects, it was meaningful (see the United States' Declaration of Independence); in other respects, it was meaningless and/or deceptive. Especially, was it a misperception to attribute it to Adam Smith? Smith provided a spirited attack on mercantilism for its extraordinary restraints, but he did not extend the attack to government and law in general. Indeed, many of those who do extend the attack, wittingly or otherwise, are silent about Smith's candor:

Wherever there is great property, there is great inequality ... Civil government supposed a certain subordination. But as the necessity of civil government gradually grows up with the acquisition of valuable property, so the principal causes which naturally introduce property ... Civil government, so far as it is instituted for the security of property, is in reality instituted for the defence of the rich against the poor, or of those who have some property against those who have none at all. (Smith 1976a: V.i.b.2.3.12; 709–10, 715)

Moving on to the twentieth century, the minimalist view of Smith has long pervaded the Chicago and Virginia traditions in economics. George Stigler, Smith's best friend in the estimation of some, noted in his American Economic Association Presidential Address that "The main burden of Smith's advice ... was that the conduct of economic affairs is best left to private citizens – that the state will be doing remarkably well if it succeeds in its unavoidable tasks of winning wars, preserving justice, and maintaining the various highways of commerce" (1965: 1); elsewhere, Stigler (1976: 1201) argues that "The crucial argument [of Smith's] for unfettered individual choice in public policy was the efficiency property of competition ..."

Milton Friedman (1978: 7) speaks of "those elementary functions" of government "that Smith regarded as alone compatible with the 'obvious and simple system of natural liberty.'" He also says that "[t]he market, with each individual going his own way, with no central authority setting social priorities, avoiding duplication, and coordinating activities, looks like chaos to untutored eyes." Yet, "through Smith's eyes we see that it is a finely ordered and effectively tuned system, one which arises out of men's individually motivated actions, yet is not deliberately created by men" (idem: 17). And even though Smith "fully develops the self-regulating market mechanisms only in *The Wealth of Nations*, in *The Theory of Moral Sentiments* he was already fully aware of the difference between an imposed order and what he would have called a natural order" (idem: 18).

Within the Public Choice camp is to be found, for example, William C. Mitchell's contention that members of the Virginia school (among which he numbers himself) "seek not weak or impotent governments but ones having sufficient authority to carry out Adam Smith's limited government agenda" (Mitchell 2001: 6). This same sentiment is reflected in Edwin G. West's (1990: 14) claim that a "necessary Smithian condition for overall prosperity ... was *limited* government."

Economists who are typically classified as advocating a more interventionist approach to the economic role of government see Smith in a way virtually identical to this Chicago-Virginia view. Paul Samuelson (1962: 7), for example, speaks of Smith's "attacks on ... state interference and ... his spirited championing of *laissez faire*." Richard Musgrave (1985: 7) contends that "The traditions of British authors, from Adam Smith on, viewed the market as the rule and the public sector as the exception, needed to step in if and where a specific market failure occurs." And John Kenneth Galbraith (1987: 72) says that Smith "rigorously confines the activities of the state to provision for the common defense, the administration of justice and the provision of necessary public works."

It should come as no surprise that this view continues to pervade contemporary economics, including economics textbooks. In his public finance text, Joseph Stiglitz writes that Smith "advocated a limited role for government" and that "Adam Smith's ideas had a powerful influence on both governments and economists," including nineteenth-century classical thinkers "who promulgated the doctrine known as laissez faire, which argued that government should leave the private sector alone [and] it should not attempt to regulate or control private enterprise," because "[u]nfettered competition would serve the best interests of society"(Stiglitz 1988: 7). Stiglitz also asserts that "Smith argued that one did not need to rely on government or on any moral sentiments to do good. The public interest, he maintained, is served when each individual simply does what is in his own self-interest" (idem: 62).

A perhaps even more extreme example of this view of Smith is found in Harvey Rosen's public finance text, where Rosen equates Smith with "Libertarians, who believe in a very limited government" and "argue against any further economic role for government" beyond the provision of defense, justice, and public goods such as "roads, bridges, and sewers – the infrastructure required for society to function" (Rosen 2002: 5–6).

In spite of the prevalent attribution of this minimalist view of Smith in the literature and the illustriousness of many of its expositors, this interpretation cannot be sustained when one examines the entire corpus of Smith's writings. Even if individuals make claims like those of Stiglitz or Rosen, and believe that those claims can or do describe legal-economic reality, it is all substantially false.

A hint of this has been given in Essay 1: Smith does not discuss the invisible hand in connection with the economic functions of government. His use of the term comes in a discussion of differences or changes in the security of a businessman's assets as between some foreign market and his home market, not in a direct discussion of the economic role of government.

Reading Smith in such a manner as to minimize the intrusion of ideological lines of reasoning is not an easy task. His world and ours are very different, and language likely has, between the two, very different meanings and nuances. And always, notwithstanding absolutist statements, one has to recall that seemingly unequivocal and important statements may be composed of primitive terms, and further decision making is not only warranted but ineluctable. Examples of these and related points are readily available in all of Smith's economic discourse, but I select the following from the *Wealth of Nations*. First, we have Smith's proposition that "what improves the circumstances of the greater part can never be regarded as an inconveniency to the whole. No society can surely be flourishing and happy, of which the far greater part of the members are poor and miserable" (Smith 1976a: I.viii.36, 96). This statement departs from the extreme individualism of so many professed disciples of Smith. It seems to suggest that intersubjectivity and the interpersonal comparability of preferences is possible, even desirable – an argument unpalatable to many (perhaps most) conservative people, yet many arguments both for and against some economic policy will assume both comparability and implicitly either equal or unequal weighting of preferences and/or of individuals. In Essay 9, such considerations will be seen to pervade the problem of the survival requirement.

Secondly, we read that some regulations may, no doubt, be considered as in some respect a violation of natural liberty. But those exertions of the natural liberty of a few individuals, which might endanger the security of the whole society, are, and ought to be, restrained by the laws of all governments; of the most free, as well as of the most despotical (Smith 1976a: II.ii.94, 324).

Smith seems to contemplate the term "regulation" more narrowly than I do. I consider regulation (1) not to be an intrusion of government/law upon given, transcendental rights but one historic means of establishing or changing relative rights, and (2) to point to a two-way or dual or reciprocal relationship, such that a law/regulation may give effect to and protect Alpha's interests and thereby simultaneously increase Beta's exposure to Alpha's resultant capacity/freedom to act, and a repeal of that law may give effect to and protect Beta's interests and increase the exposure of Alpha to Beta's resultant capacity/freedom to act – in other words, freedom has, in both directions, its opposite in freedom from ("security" may be substituted for "freedom"). If so, Smith's is the more common usage, but, I modestly claim, mine is the more accurate. Even with a narrower usage, however, Smith's point is the opposite of believers in something called laissez-faire. Indeed, Smith's wording is quite strong, for he writes "might endanger" rather than "does endanger."

Still, the use of "might" may introduce more-than-expected ambiguity and competition between claims. Thus, elsewhere in his opus, Smith also writes, in one of his clearly negative remarks about businessmen, that "the interest of the producer ought to be attended to, only so far as it may be necessary for promoting that of the consumer" (Smith 1976a: IV.viii.49; 660). It is apparent that the term "necessary" may engender competing claims of reasoning as to what is "necessary." For example, public utility ratepayers may argue that lower rates promote their interests, whereas it can also be argued that lower rates injure their interest, by limiting the rate of return on equity capital (common stock) and thereby restricting the utility's ability to produce more of their product. Both propositions "make sense," but which applies when is a matter of the subjective specification of risk assumption and avoidance, as well as other factors.

Along a different line, we note Smith's claims that "[t]he establishment of perfect justice, of perfect liberty, and of perfect equality, is the very simple secret which most effectually secures the highest degree of prosperity to all the three classes" (Smith 1976a: IV.ix.17; 669). Also, "If a nation could not prosper without the enjoyment of perfect liberty and perfect justice, there is not in the world a nation which could ever have prospered" (Smith 1976a: IV.ix.28; 674). The two propositions, made some five pages apart, are rich in expressive and interpretive force, but also difficulties. First, it is obvious that the key words in the two statements – perfect, liberty, justice, and prosperity – are primitive terms lacking specificity. Secondly, in most – possibly all – propositions using these and comparable words, an assumption is made that has the actual arrangements of a society equate with the arrangements required by the definitions of those words. Thirdly, the twenty-first-century mind is likely more sensitive to the phrase "highest degree of prosperity to all the three classes" than is the mind of most of Smith's contemporaries, albeit with a caveat. The "highest degree of prosperity to all *the three classes*"?! Does not the affirmation of three *classes* raise questions about the respective incomes, opportunities, and influence on government policy of individuals in the three classes?

8.4. Smith's Legal-Economic Nexus

Smith's view of the economic role of government is not unambiguous. The minimalist interpretation of Smith has *multiple* competitors – some of which portray a more activist economic role of government; some of which suggest not a strict laissez-faire approach by Smith but a laissez-faire-with-exceptions approach, in which the exceptions are very important and sometimes rather broad-based (see, e.g., Viner 1926); and some of which interpret Smith, and the Classical School as a whole, not at all in laissez-faire terms but through a market-plus-framework model in which social control and social change through law figure prominently (see, e.g., Pack 1991 and Rothschild 2001). Smith clearly opposed mercantilism. The issue is whether or not this opposition to mercantilism is extended by him to oppose other forms of government "activism." The answer is, quite clearly, "no."

As was suggested in Essay 2, the interpretive problem arises in part because Smith has a tripartite mode of society comprised of three modes of social control: moral rules, law, and the market. Each works in its own way to channel individual behavior into socially apprehended directions. His *Theory of Moral Sentiments* covers moral rules; his *Wealth of Nations* addressed the market; and, although he never published his planned third volume, we have insights into his thinking from two sets of lecture notes, *Lectures on Jurisprudence*. Viewing any of these works in isolation is almost certain to lead to error, and this is the root of the problem with the "Smith as noninterventionist" approach.

An Inquiry into the Nature and Causes of the Wealth of Nations is the reference of choice for most commentary on Smith's view of the economic role of government. One must recognize, however, that Smith discusses the economic role of government here only insofar as he deems necessary for his particular purpose: the elaboration of a program to promote the increase of national wealth against the backdrop of the extant mercantilist system. Smith portrays a market economy, his "obvious and simple system of natural liberty," in which the market both provides economic freedom and serves as a mechanism of social control – the latter particularly by harmonizing the actions of self-interested agents.

In his discussion of the expenses of the sovereign or Commonwealth, Smith identifies three duties of the sovereign (Smith 1976b: IV.ix.51, 687–8):

1. that of protecting the society from the violence and invasion of other independent societies (Smith 1976b: V.i.a.1, 689);
2. that of protecting, as far as possible, every member of the society from the injustice or oppression of every other member of it, or the duty of establishing an exact administration of justice (V.i.b.1, 708–9);
3. that of erecting and maintaining those publick institutions and those publick works, which, though they may be in the highest degree advantageous to a great society, are, however, of such a nature that the profit could never repay the expense to any individual or small number of individuals, and which it therefore cannot be expected that any individual or small number of individuals should erect or maintain. The performance of this duty requires, too, very different degrees of expense in the different periods of society (V.i.c.1, 723).

The immediate discussion is continued in his next paragraph:

After the publick institutions and publick works necessary for the defence of the society, and for the administration of justice, both of which have already been mentioned, the other works and institutions of this kind are chiefly those for facilitating the commerce of the society, and those for promoting the instruction of the people. The institutions for instruction are of two kinds: those for the education of youth, and those for the instruction of people of all ages. (V.i.c.2, 723)

The defense of a society against the aggression of other societies is clear enough. Not so clear is what is and is not covered under the protection, "as far as possible," of "every member of the society from the injustice or oppression of every other member of it," or how the preceding language

equates with or is amplified by "the duty of establishing an exact administration of justice." Such protection in practice will depend in part on the
definitions of injustice and of oppression and of the evidence thereof – in
sum, on the specification of rights and the content given to them. Smith's
model provides for such a function, or duty, of government but seemingly
leaves it to society to work out the details. That is what political decision
making, or governance, is all about.

Similarly elastic is the notion of public works and institutions that comprises the third duty; someone paging through Book V of the *Wealth of
Nations* cannot help but be struck by the expansive set of tasks elaborated
by someone who is considered the godfather of laissez-faire. See Viner
(1927) for an elaboration. Moreover, government is portrayed by Smith
as, among other things, a *facilitator* of commerce. His position is not that
government needs to stay out of the way and let individual enterprise reign;
rather, he lays out a specific (and lengthy) set of activities for government to
undertake if it wishes to promote the national wealth. It is, however, a very
different set of tasks from those undertaken by a mercantilist government.
Providing the legal foundations of a market economy and promoting it in
order to produce greater wealth is still promotion.

Evidently missing from the minimalist view of Smith is that the
three stated duties, read narrowly, do not exhaust the economic role of
government – although a strong case can be made that the content given to
them by Smith itself negates any attributions of minimalism. Smith's criticism of the existing system points to the dynamic process in which existing law is made subject to critique and reform. Smith clearly intended his
work to be a contribution to that process of legal change. He understood
full well the ubiquity and importance of law, and his argument for "the
obvious and simple system of natural liberty" actually constituted a revolutionary doctrine in terms of introducing legal change. Indeed, the system
of natural liberty was, for Smith, a legal-governmental construct through
and through, and its establishment and maintenance a clear-cut instance of
governmental "activism."

Smith's broad-based conception of the economic role of government is
made clear when one pays attention, first, to what Smith has to say about
government and property, and the machinations of special interests; and
second, to the treatment of law and government, as well as property, in the
Lectures on Jurisprudence (Smith 1978). Of particular import is Smith's recognition that government itself is not exogenous to the system; as we saw a
few pages back, it is due to and to a large extent the instrument of the propertied, of those, that is, who use government to cement and institutionalize

their systemic social power. Smith is reported to have said to his students: "Till there be property there can be no government, the very end of which is to secure wealth and to defend the rich from the poor" (Smith 1978, 404). Also central here, as in the *Wealth of Nations*, is Smith's reliance on his stages theory of history. These stages are defined largely in terms of their respective systems of law and government, and point to the ubiquity and importance of legal social control and the effects of changes therein. From a practical perspective, also, in *The Wealth of Nations* the particulars of all of three duties are said by Smith to vary with the stage of history.

Smith's relative silence in the *Wealth of Nations* on topics of the structure and content of law, perhaps especially concerning property, should not be surprising. Like most people writing on the economic role of government, Smith typically took the regnant legal system and body of law as background. Also like most people, he did not hesitate to criticize either the legal system or the law. In other words, he was selective in what he implicitly accepted. He was lecturing on law and government, and planning, at least early, to write a volume on law and government. With this volume left unwritten, Smith's most elaborate treatment of government and law was his critique of mercantilist restraints on particular imports in Book IV. Smith the realist appears, not surprisingly, in his lectures on jurisprudence. The modern editors of the lectures quote the account of them given by John Millar, to the effect that Smith lectured on justice as a branch of morality, its gradual progress between stages or ages, the effect of changes in technology ("those arts which contribute to subsistence") and the accumulation of property in generating legal change ("in producing correspondent improvements or alterations in law and government"), and lastly "those political regulations which are founded, not upon the principle of *justice*, but that of *expediency*, and which are calculated to increase the riches, the power, and the prosperity of a State" (Meek, Raphael, and Stein 1978: 3). Moreover, in his discussion apropos of retaliation, Smith says:

To judge whether such retaliations are likely to produce [benefits], does not, perhaps, belong so much to the science of a legislator, whose deliberations ought to be governed by general principles which are always the same, as to the skill of that insidious and crafty animal, vulgarly called a statesman or politician, whose councils are directed by the momentary fluctuations of affairs. (Smith 1976a: IV.ii.39, 468)

Accordingly, it is clear from the editors' list of topics discussed in the lectures (Meek, Raphael, and Stein 1978: 24–7) that Smith covered under Public Jurisprudence the organization of government and the rights of subjects; under Domestic Law, the relative rights of family members and of slaves and others; under Private Law, property and its transfer, and injury to person, reputation, and property; and under Police, a short discussion of cleanliness and security and a lengthy discussion of cheapness or plenty – in other words, of the kinds of policies and theoretical topics also discussed in the *Wealth of Nations*.

The *Lectures* suggest that in working out, through changing the law, pragmatic resolutions to conflicts over property, a society – that is, government and law – is involved in more than a simplistic administration of justice: Government is involved in the continuing revision of the legal foundations of the economic system. The lectures have an empirical facet indicating that Smith appreciates both the ideal juridical and material economic facets of legal change. Systems of law are constantly working toward what they "ought to be," and it is only through experience/observation that policy makers can make decisions. Once a law is tried and fails to fulfill (or no longer fulfills) the social need for which it was intended, new laws are tried. This process is discussed repeatedly in Smith's works, appearing in discussions of property origins, secondary forms, transference, tax systems, voting systems, citizenship definitions, and so on. The government, here, is a player, a part of the economic system, and a necessary one.

Smith's empirical depth and perspicacity of understanding of economic and legal history were enormous. The potential negative impacts of those understandings on the empirical significance of two of the principal non-interventionist arguments are vast. Those who contend that legal social control should be slight, minimized, and neither increase nor change very much or very regularly in legal and economic history and the actually expectable course of affairs are contradicted by Smith, as is reported in lecture notes taken by his students. Smith develops his stages theory in terms of changes in government and law, as society moves from one stage to its successor and within each stage, with both types of situations manifesting both increasing change and growth of the law.

Smith *may* have meant the empty wording of the tropes calling for minimal change and only that growth of government that is necessary, that is tautological and without guidance as to degrees and specific content of change and growth of law, but the notes do not indicate that he did. Like the rest of us, he does not know where to draw the line. It is easier, as in the *Wealth of Nations*, to write grandly about the simple and obvious system of natural liberty and the invisible hand. It is also easier, as in the *History of Astronomy*, to use a term that seems to explain and thereby sets minds at rest. In his lectures on law, Smith dealt with legal rules much as he had done with moral rules in the *Theory of Moral Sentiments*, namely leave the construction of the specific content of moral rules to be worked out by people, not prescribe them himself. Here one can see, in detail, the changes wrought in individuals' economic autonomy, the operative meaning of property and other terms, and the change from feudalism to a market economy, and so on – that is, the gradual change from one stage to the next and change within each stage.

In his lectures, Smith took up the bases of rights to property and of injury. His interpretation centers on the reasonableness of expectations. He did not rely on some absolutist genesis of property rights. The right to own, including the right to exclude all other person from it, is the basic principle, but the details and assignment of property depend on the "concurrence betwixt the [impartial] spectator and the possessor" through the judgments of relative reasonableness of expectations (idem: 1.35–8, 16–17). Thus, in addition to the tropes "invisible hand," "simple and obvious system of natural liberty," and similar phrases, Smith uses "impartial spectator" to refer to public opinion, that is, the processes through which social preferences are formed and their inculcation into the mindset of the individual undergoing socialization (societization) and "reasonable[ness] of expectations." Inasmuch as Smith knew that he could not specify in advance – or even afterward – the particular rights that helped form a particular property, he followed and employed the argument expressed in his *History of Astronomy* that gave warrant to the substitution of propositions that soothe the imagination for the demonstrably true propositions that he, like the rest of mankind, lacked. At the level of generalization on which he theorized, the use of such primitive terms is acceptable so long as one did not presume to supply concrete substantive content. What Joseph Campbell wrote about religion, metaphor, and fact also applies to Smith on moral and legal rules as well as, it would seem, religion: "Every religion is true one way or another. It is true when understood metaphorically. But when it gets stuck in its own metaphors, interpreting them as facts, then you are in trouble" (Thinkexist: http://thinkexist.com/quotation/every_ religion_ is_true_one_way_or_another-it_ is/152697... December 15, 2008). This certainly been the case in economics, notably the use of the concept of the invisible hand.

Smith argues that in the various stages of society, "the laws and regulations with regard to property must be very different." In the earliest stages, inasmuch as there is little property and consequently not much to steal, "[f]ew laws or regulations will (be) requisite in such an age of society, and these will not extend to any great length, or be very rigorous in the punishments

196 The Invisible Hand and the Economic Role of Government

annexed to any infringement of property" (Smith 1978: 1.33, 16). The economic role of government, however, changes:

... when flocks and herds come to be reared property then becomes of a very considerable extent; there are many opportunities of injuring one another and such injuries are extremely pernicious to the sufferer. In this state many more laws and regulations must take place; theft and robbery being easily committed, will of consequence be punished with the utmost rigour. In the age of agriculture, they are not perhaps so much exposed to theft and open robbery, but then there are "many" ways in which property may be interrupted as the subjects of it are considerably extended. The laws therefore tho perhaps not so rigorous will be of a far greater number than amongst a nation of shepherds. In the age of commerce, as the subjects of property are greatly increased the laws must be proportionally multiplied. The more improved any society is and the greater length the several [sic] means of supporting the inhabitants are carried, the greater will be the number of their laws and regulations necessary to maintain justice, and prevent infringements of the right of property. (idem: 1.33–4, 16)

This paragraph must be considered the most sophisticated and accurate of any that Smith wrote bearing on the subject of this essay. It, and the support given it in numerous places in his lectures, directly contradicts the so-called noninterventionism of those people who are selectively marketing a so-called minimalist government.

The themes expressed by Smith in the preceding paragraphs recur from time to time throughout the *Lectures*. For example, economic and technological progress leads people to have less time to devote to resolving others' conflicts, yet "the causes of dispute also multiply." The result is pure Smith: Taking advantage of the division of labor, "A certain number of men are chosen by the body of the people, whose business it is to attend on the causes and settle all disputes." Moreover, the authority of these chosen people, or of some of them, "will grow very fast; much faster than in proportion to the advances made by the society" (idem: iv.15–16, 205).

He next discusses some sources of differences in organizing the structure of judicial and other governmental decision making. Although he does not say so explicitly, it is in the conflicts over that structure that global-like statements are made that later lead people, especially partisans, to take those statements out of their original context and apply them in impossible, question-begging ways.

Government is never an undifferentiated whole. Then, as now, the institutions of governance can vary as issues and economic and political environments change. Individual legislator's voting records can reflect a continuing singular great issue, such as mercantilism, imperialism, the budget, the scope of the franchise, poor relief, subsidies, and so on. The absence of such an issue, however, does not prevent a legislator from having a private fixation or a strategy for building coalitions.

If government and law seem anathema in the *Wealth of Nations*, it is because of Smith's opposition to the direction of certain *activities of government* at the time. The point of the *Wealth of Nations* is not that government is bad, but that government was doing bad things in promulgating mercantilist policy. This negates neither the subjective normative nature of policy nor the centrality of government and law in Smith's obvious and simple system of natural liberty, that is, the natural order of things. Combining both the *Lectures* and the *Wealth of Nations*, not only are law and government part of Smith's system and not only is legal change also part of Smith's system, but, relative to the mercantilist agenda he opposes, his system includes what established interests could and in fact did oppose as *revolutionary*. In sum, to favor the market process, with Smith, does not require the belief in a minimalist view of the economic role of government, and such a view certainly finds no support in Smith's writings. The ironical coda is Lionel Robbins's conclusion that to Smith, the invisible hand was that of the *statesman* (Robbins 1953: 56).

Lionel Robbins surely was among the dozen or so most influential English economists of the twentieth century. He was an economic theorist, policy analyst, historian of economic thought, public intellectual, administrator, and more. He was appointed or elected to numerous boards, committees, and similar institutions; he taught at the London School of Economics for more than fifty years. He was an Establishment man, fundamentally laden with conservative sentiments, while possessed of a large, capacious, and sensitive mind. He helped train a significant number and percentage of his country's next generation of historians of economic thought. Like other professors, Robbins was both held in awe by many of his students and colleagues and dismissed as pompous and arrogant by others (see Medema and Samuels 1998: xxii–xxiv). His conservative sentiments were strong, but unlike many others, he held his conservative propensities in check. His writings and lectures on the history of economic thought demonstrated his mastery of the subject and his self-restraint combined with the tone of authority. Nonetheless, his interpretations were not without controversy. Whereas numerous other conservative historians of economic thought not only misperceived but seem to have deliberately distorted the theory of economic policy of the English Classical economists (including Smith), Robbins's books on the subject (notably Robbins 1953) were judicious in their judgments and amply supported by evidence. In my own book on the subject (Samuels

1966), I extended the interpretive range to also include morals, custom, religion, and education, together comprising nonlegal social control, and the role of government as an instrument of change. The reader should appreciate that in our respective works on the subject, neither of us was seeking to promote a particular ideology. We sought only to establish the *correct interpretation* of the Classical theory of economic policy. Whether or not we individually agreed with it in some respects was an entirely different matter. The approach continues in this book. I have found it necessary and desirable, however, to state in what ways and how, especially with regard to invisible-hand thinking, economists have, wittingly or unwittingly, been in various ways advancing an ideology. Insofar as the invisible hand has been involved in this, economics has been made into a fundamentally normative and justificatory exercise, one with little, if any, serious ontological, epistemological, or linguistic support.

8.5. Milton Friedman

Milton Friedman has been seen differently by different people: as an economic scientist, an economic ideologue, an economic ideologue whose technical career as an economic scientist was driven by his economic ideology (with his ideology evident while a graduate student at Chicago in the mid-1930s [Samuels 2000]), or someone who found that his professional work and his normative views happened to happily largely to coincide. My late colleague, the agricultural economist Glenn Johnson, took Friedman's Economics 300A, given during the Winter term of 1947 (Johnson and Samuels 2008) and Friedman's 300B, given during the Spring term of 1947 (Johnson and Johnson 2009). Johnson's notes from 300A are complete and those from 300B are incomplete. The notes enable us to observe Friedman teaching economic theory during the first year of his long career at the University of Chicago. Summarizing, Friedman takes positions much deeper than and somewhat – perhaps quite – different from those that adorn his later reputation. The notes taken by Glenn Johnson suggest than Friedman had achieved in 1947 a depth and range of analysis achieved by very few economists. Judging by later student notes and some of his own writing, eventually Friedman excluded these ideas from his purview and, apparently, his teaching, either because it ran afoul of his price theory or because he changed his mind, for whatever reason(s), or he narrowed and tightened his approach to economic theory. Whatever the explanation, the account is fascinating and arguably an example on the micro level of professionalism driven by the desires, first, for economics to be, or appear to be, more technical and scientific; second, to render economics impervious to the pressures emanating from the Cold War; and third, to develop and strengthen his ideological position.

Friedman gave permission to publish his notes so long as the editors of the annual do not imply that he has checked the notes for accuracy. In using the notes here, I imply no such thing. It is poignant that he wrote that he "was not prepared [him]self to spend any more effort or energy on those notes," because Friedman died the following week (Milton Friedman to Marianne Johnson, November 20, 2006).

Friedman is recorded as making a number of interesting, even striking, points. Several are in the first lecture. One reads that the "Ultimate purpose of study is to improve social welfare" (Friedman 2008: 73). This sounds both innocuous and laudatory, possibly even saccharine. To a disciple of Friedrich Hayek, however, it would not only constitute scientism (the view that the methods of physical science can properly be applied to social science, which Hayek strongly rejected) but ignorance of the principle of unintended and unforeseen consequences generated by deliberative collective (that is, government) action (and by both liberal and conservative policies, though Hayek, it seems, played down its applicability to conservative policies). Friedman emphasizes that his is positive economics, albeit with a purpose: "The normative problem of how the system ought to work must await the study of the positive. This course," he is recorded as saying, "will be concerned with the positive" (idem: 73). He is seeking to develop or strengthen his ideological position – as a prelude to normative economics (idem: 73). For Friedman, welfare – as in "to improve social welfare" – involves implicit normative elements, such as, for example, those that deal with whose interests will count, through the choice of the standard of value, and the group whose interests will dominate.

Friedman is not as explicit as I am making him out to be, but he can be granted the point. In comparison, for example, James Buchanan juxtaposes his inclusion and promotion of a particular moral view to my Friedman-like "if you want to achieve a certain moral state of the world ... it seems to me you're better off knowing what really is going on so that you can take the right kind of action" (Buchanan and Samuels 2008, in Peart and Levy 2008: 34; Samuels 2007a: 156). Many, perhaps most, writers, of all schools of economic thought, seem preoccupied with their normative message, leaving their positive analysis narrow and underdeveloped.

8.6. Friedrich Hayek and the Marketing of Capitalism as the Free Market

Hayek was manifestly motivated by the desire to promote a free society. This meant not only that he favored freedom and loathed coercion but actively sought to construct the ideas and institutions that would permit and preserve a free society. There are, however, several initial problems with such an agenda. The first problem is that both "freedom" and "coercion" are not simple concepts. Each is multidimensional, and each dimension of freedom and of coercion may affect different individuals differently (Samuels 1995). The second problem is that individual freedom always exists within a system of social control. Some system of social control is necessary; without social control, individual freedom is nugatory and property is scarce, insecure, and unsafe. Social control both expands and limits individual freedom, differently for different individuals. The third problem is the ineluctability of choice: choice, for example, among the dimensions of freedom and of coercion, choice between forms of social control, choice among individuals, choice among the interests to be given putative effect by social control, choice between already existing law and proposed new law, and choice as to the mode of choice itself. It was both his genius and his predicament that Hayek came to understand, or at least give effect to, these problems.

The previous analysis is given poignancy by the following. Some decades ago, I attended a small conference organized by an economist who was, like Hayek, a member of the Mont Pelerin Society. The conference reviewed in some detail the principal literature of late-eighteenth–nineteenth-century liberalism. The organizer reluctantly found them all, from Smith on, to be interventionist. The question arises but has been neither then nor since answered: What precisely would constitute noninterventionism? Just how confusing the ideological position can be – for both analytical and ideological purposes – is suggested by a tale recounted by Milton Friedman. Discussion at the first Mont Pelerin Society meeting, on necessary social control, led Ludwig von Mises to announce, "You're all a bunch of socialists," and stomp "out of the room." Friedman remarks that it was "an assembly that contained not a single person who, by even the loosest standards, could be called a socialist" (Friedman and Friedman 1998: 161).

In his review of Lionel Robbins's *Theory of Economic Policy in English Classical Political Economy* (Robbins 1953), Frank Knight wrote of Robbins's search for a "propaganda for economic freedom" (Knight 1953: 279). In the second essay of this book, we examined Joseph Spengler's analyses of the "problem of order" as involving the inexorable continuing effort to reconcile autonomy (freedom) and control, continuity and change, and hierarchy and equality (Spengler 1948, 1968). Any propaganda for economic freedom necessarily encompasses the constituent *elements* of the problem of order, and is therefore a matter of both normative economics and selective perception of freedom, coercion, governance, and so on. And whereas most western discussions of such matters are conducted in terms of "individualism," the object of discussion is the "system" that will satisfy the normative and selectively perceived object of the propaganda. In part, this is because every system of freedom has its correlative system of control. The propaganda version of the problem of order in capitalism must emphasize freedom, or at least certain forms of freedom, while obfuscating the correlative system of control and other forms of freedom.

The second half of the twentieth century exhibited enormous attention to the "selling" of capitalism through the search for a suitable and effective "propaganda for economic freedom." Many, probably most, of the scholars who have that objective are the naïve epigones of far more sophisticated analysts. The most sophisticated of all may well have been Frank Knight. Knight understood the complexities and subtleties of the problem of order and felt compelled to write about them for the benefit of other scholars. Knight himself, I think, would have been delighted to have worked out the propaganda for economic freedom that met at least minimal requirements for coherence, consistency, and, *inter alia*, the fullness of the problem of order. (He may have but he seems to have thought not.)

Knight started out working on the theory of capital but eventually became preoccupied with issues of the problem of order. Because he wrote principally for the benefit of fellow scholars, he was not well known among the general public.

Friedrich Hayek became well known to the general public through his little book, *Road to Serfdom* (Hayek 1944), which made his name almost a household term. He, too, began his work as a capital theorist. Through several series of publications, Hayek pursued the holy grail of propaganda for economic freedom that would capture the loyalty he thought capitalism warranted. Hayek's efforts became increasingly concentrated on three so-called principles: the principle of unintended and unforeseen consequences, the principle of spontaneous order, and the principle of the rule of law. Several of the lines of reasoning pertaining to them can be traced to Adam Smith and other Scotsmen of his period, notably Adam Ferguson, and of antiquity, for example, Aristotle. The intended gravamen of the three principles is continuity, and whether one is an able and open-minded enthusiast for continuity or a comparable positivist analyst of continuity versus change, the principles lack the conclusiveness that the overall subject would require in order to become useful.

This lengthy part of Essay 8 focuses on Hayek's ideas because of the comparatively high degree of attention they have received. I would rate Frank Knight higher than Hayek for the depth and subtlety of their respective analyses. I would also rank Vilfredo Pareto and Smith himself higher than Hayek. Nonetheless, Hayek's is a mind to be reckoned with. He also had more to reckon with than Smith: the establishment of capitalism in the North Atlantic western community and elsewhere, the challenge of socialism and communism, and, *inter alia*, the development of new, more complex, more highly nuanced, and more anxious economic and philosophical discourse.

The lack of conclusiveness of the three principles derives from the fact that they come with a high degree of pragmatism or, as Smith might have put it, expediency, in which the three principles are held, further worked out, and applied. Each principle is selectively stated by him so as to bolster his case. All such principles and related policy analyses are more or less inevitably strongly pragmatist in their attention to consequences. Hayek's disciples seem to stress their ostensible "principled," that is, transcendent stature when, as a matter of fact, they allow and even require selectivity. Moreover, devotees and disciples of Hayek do not agree on the implications. Their exchanges partly constitute their contribution to the process of working things out.

Many years ago, I heard Hayek argue that the principal reason for opposing inflation (and, as I recall, similar topics) and supporting the gold standard and balanced budgets was to have these ideas serve as a check on the power of government. Hayek was engaged in the task of working out what Knight called "propaganda" and a set of institutions for what he considered economic freedom. This normative motivation drove much, perhaps all, of his work. He desperately – in view of fascism and communism – sought to identify and establish the nature of and case for a free society. This is an important venture and is not to be gainsaid. This weighty, high-priestly, and normative task motivated and infused perhaps all of his work and that of others, such as Friedman, Stigler, and Buchanan.

Hayek was also engaged in positive work, notably descriptive and explanatory analyses and general social theory. These endeavors were conducted at reasonably high levels of sophistication. They also were typically and selectively deployed in the service of his normative projects. Like most, if not all, other members of the Austrian School of Economics over the years, Hayek held two different, deeply conflicting positions: His positive analysis described and explained a world of power and power play, efforts to control government in order to attain the successful marketing of agendas, and so on. On the other hand, his normative analyses typically emphasized a more or less similar economic system, but one which he thought could properly be called a "free" society. I have no confident sense, however, of the degree to which Hayek recognized the Platonic idealist element in his work.

Hayek makes arguments that can appear antinomian and absolute but which, when due account is taken of his superimposed normative agenda, point to an inexorable necessity of choice. Hayek's case for a free society is therefore much more subtle and open-ended than it sometimes seems, and is taken by epigones, to be. One might, therefore, distinguish between the soft and hard Hayek, or the thin and thick Hayek, or the naive and sophisticated Hayek, meaning by "Hayek" that for which he is taken to stand. For all its sophistication, the Hayekian analysis leaves much to be desired, including provision for the working out of innumerable details.

Hayek is of interest here because his analyses of spontaneous order and the principle of unintended and unexpected consequences constitute and drive important parts of recent discussions of both the invisible hand and the theory of economic policy in general. This is true notwithstanding the power of the criticisms directed against his arguments.

Hayek and other leading marketers of propaganda for a middle-class, capitalist market economy – also including Friedman, Knight, Stigler, and Buchanan, among others – disagreed among themselves on the meaning, relevance, and effectiveness of various versions of the general case held and marketed by all of them. The defenders of the western economic system have suffered from their lack of unanimity in defining and explaining that economy, as well as their tendencies to emphasize and differentiate their own respective theories, as in Chamberlin's theory of monopolistic competition (Chamberlin 1950). The broad outline of the defense has major common themes, such as political freedom being predicated on economic freedom, the minimization of actual business power, rules over discretion in government, the importance of the price mechanism, security of property rights, anti-inflation, the superiority of monetary policy over fiscal policy, and so on. The defense case also has frequent tensions, such as regarding the explanation of economic instability, the problem of externalities, the price individual decision makers are willing for the government, society, and individuals to pay for the so-called welfare state, and so on.

The relationship, conceptually and practically, between a market economy and a capitalist economy is one of, if not the most important questions facing economists. What may or may not constitute the same issue is the relevance of an economy whose *raison d'être* is to enable social, political, and economic hegemony by the possessors of substantial personal or family wealth and that of the managers of substantial firms. Such hegemony is the middle-class equivalent of the hegemony enjoyed by the owners of substantial tracts of land in one or another type of landholding, latifundia, or feudal system. Another way of comprehending a capitalist economy is as a system of rule by effective capital in one, two, and/or three forms, namely money capital, finance capital, and landed capital.

In contrast, a market economy would not have a ruling class. It would have, that is to say, no group with either overt or covert power not enjoyed by every other group, which is also to say that every person has as rights what the historic hegemonic class had as privileges, that access to government officials was not dominated by private or corporate wealth (lobbying and litigation); in short, there would be no class with de facto and/or de jure privileges. Inasmuch as such a society does not exist, the conceptual version is either utopian (some would say dystopian) or normative.

The socialist view of the world, commencing in the second and third decades of the nineteenth century in England, became one in which the representatives of labor and the lower classes in general had a dual interpretation of the bourgeois revolutions of the early nineteenth century. They felt that the leaders of these predominantly middle-class revolutions (as cause or effect) had promised that all hitherto nonprivileged people would now have the same rights along with the middle class. This promise, they argued, had been broken. Rule by business capital had replaced rule by hereditary ownership of land, and the working and other lower classes had been systematically excluded, for example, through minimization of extensions of the franchise. Instead of a society fundamentally of equals, social control essentially remained a means of rule by one class over all other classes.

The development and use of the concept of the invisible hand gradually took place in the legal-economic and social environment just described. By ignoring the remnants of and innovations in social control as well as the resulting continuation, albeit somewhat revised and newly both more subtle and with greater, hegemonic power, economists became identified with the worldview of the new hegemonic powers. Economists desired the status of scientists, the security of a safe, professional discipline, and the opportunity to make policy. They defined their subject matter narrowly so as to minimize and render unobjectionable and unnamed most manifestations of power. They changed their definition of factors of production from one set in which they were identified as social classes to another in which they were defined in terms of their assumed technical conditions as inputs.

They came to adopt a capitalist or managerial point of view in which, given some conflict of interests, the properly assumed assignment of rights always tended to be in the hands of the capital owner rather than the worker, consumer, or environmentalist. When landed interests opposed Henry George's thinking on property, which he based on property definitions and assignment promoting production and earned income rather than unearned rental income, many economists privately agreed with George's Ricardian reasoning but spoke publically against him. Economists disseminated and reinforced the doctrine of an invisible hand that augured such ontologically given harmony – among other things – that a policy of so-called laissez-faire seemed inevitable.

Hayek's much later work on both the invisible hand and the theory of economic policy in general was motivated and driven by the economic, political, and social anxiety and fear of socialism of all conceptions; the perceived military, political, and ideological threats to the western developed capitalist countries posed by the very existence and policies of the Soviet Union and the People's Republic of China; and the ensuing, often unfortunate, pathological tensions in the western democracies. The reader will recall the discussion in Essay 6 of the argument that the nature of phenomena cannot be determined by examining and arguing about definitions.

My interest in Hayek derives from my own interest in the economic role of government, in the legal-economic nexus, particularly from a positive approach. This approach has an important place for normative efforts to channel the economic role of government, to establish propaganda for economic freedom, and for selective perception. Those normative efforts constitute many of the means for working out the economic role of government. My motivation, however, is decidedly nonnormative. I seek to identify the fundamentals of the subject, whether or not they comport with my ideological, normative, subjective, and sentimental preconceptions and perspective. Overcoming my own libertarian predilections (Samuels 1974b), I have emphasized the ubiquity and importance of government in a nominally market economy (see Samuels 1992a, 1992b, 1993, 1996a, 1997, 1998; and Samuels, Schmid, and Shaffer 1994). I also sense that whatever one's normative orientation, one has a better chance of achieving it if one has solid positivist knowledge of what is actually going on than if one does not.

My objective in the remainder of this essay is to interpret and critique Hayek's three principles. I find them to be driven by one objective, namely to selectively emphasize continuity rather than change of the institutional status quo, which is to say, to limit the exercise of choice. For Hayek, as for Buchanan, among others, the emphasis on nondeliberative versus deliberative decision making, the problem of constructivism, the principle of unintended and unexpected consequences, and the principle of spontaneous order are all of a piece. That these choice-limiting principles necessarily involve choice is suggested by the fact that the Hayekian analysis was not applied to the Soviet Union.

The following conclusions are importantly based on the long and convoluted history of the treatment in economics of the idea of the invisible hand. (1) The great bulk of the literature seeking to identify the invisible hand and its functions has been a monumental waste of effort. (2) The idea of an invisible-hand process is valuable for its identification of interaction and aggregation as the basic processes. (3) Hayek's principle of unintended and unforeseen consequences is useful in conducting analyses of invisible-hand processes, but one must be wary of any analysis that results in blanket assertions of the consequences being either all benevolent or all malevolent. No empirical justification for either claim can be provided; the economic world is not that one-sided.

8.7. Lionel Robbins's Approach to the Interpretation of Smith

The problem with which I propose to continue the discussion goes something like the following. I have argued for many years that the key issue of economic policy is that of legal change, by which I mean changing the law, or legal change of law, that is, change of law by law. It seems very difficult for some people to understand one or more of these formulations is that we do not recognize as law the law we are contemplating to change. Law tends to be thought of – when it is thought of at all, and thought of favorably – as the natural order of things. It is taught that way in law schools. Such is the order by which and into which we have been simultaneously socialized and individualized. It is the larger scheme of things that, by virtue of our being raised in it, has been made a part of our own individual identity. This may be supplemented or reduced by other aspects of our own identity, such as the wealth of property rights that we sense we have and enjoy. That we may be very high on the class level of wealth and/or income also seems to be part of the natural order of things. Even absent an actual high level of income or wealth, we may identify with – to our own advantage or to that of our children and grandchildren – the mindset of those higher on the scale. Such identification is based on wishful thinking that is part of the socialization process and is all the more believable the more evident are cases that seem to support the actualization of the wish. The principal exception to personal belief in (favorable) law as the natural order of things consists of those who lobby and those who are lobbied.

Another important reason for the general difficulty in comprehending the formulations of legal change is that politics is an exceedingly subtle and vast game. Since the beginning of the nineteenth century in England, and elsewhere in Europe and North America at about the same time, the background to all politics has been the attack on, and the defense of, the received structure of power, ultimately the received structure of those who seek to control government. Earlier, the government was controlled by the landed interests. Politics then involved conflict between king and lords, between groups of lords, and between lines of succession; religion was part of the array of conflicting parties. Later, first the middle class and later the masses, notably working-class men and women, as well as children, became part of the array. Increasingly, the spread of policy consciousness tended to introduce candor into political discourse. Nonetheless, all sides seemed to feel that their side was the right side, and a variety of political absolutes were either continued or newly created.

Another reason is that politics, especially the fundraising aspects of it, is in such a state of moral squalor that reasonably decent scholars seek to avoid getting their hands dirty. Yet we cannot do away with law; by any name, law is social control.

Yet another reason is the tendency of people already at the upper hierarchical levels and of many people who imagine that they are already well on the way there and/or identify with and/or work for those elites to make no mention of the struggle for power. Numerous reasons could be given for their silence. It might be unseemly to mention it and thereby devalue their political absolutes. It might incite greater efforts by the have-nots. It might elicit punishment by those in a position to visit it.

If the preceding analysis is substantially accurate, and one does not, for whatever reason, take up such topics as the market for votes, the importance of power, outright corruption, and what Charles E. Lindblom has called the "privileged position of business" (Lindblom 1977: chapter 13 and passim), then professors, students, and the general public will not have much chance to acquire substantial knowledge of an important sphere – likely the most important sphere – of social life. Even greater ignorance will be manufactured (Samuels, Johnson, and Johnson 2007), and the worsening situation will be in part due to those who opted out of the game. Adam Smith pulled very few, if any, of his punches when it came to interpreting and criticizing the several social classes and especially those in control of government policy and of organized religion.

Compared to most of the authors of present-day works on economics, Smith was the model of political candor. It surprised late-twentieth-century readers of the *Wealth of Nations* to find in it statements that, it seemed to them, only a radical like Karl Marx would make:

Avarice and ambition in the rich, in the poor the hatred of labour and the love of present ease and enjoyment.... Wherever there is great property there is great inequality. For one very rich man there must be at least five hundred poor, and the affluence of the few supposes the indigence of the many.... It is only under the shelter of the civil magistrate that the owner of that valuable property, which is acquired by the labour of many years, or perhaps of many successive generations, can sleep a single night in security.

Civil government supposes a certain subordination. But as the necessity of civil government gradually grows up with the acquisition of valuable property, so the principal causes which naturally introduce subordination gradually grow up with the growth of that valuable property. (Smith 1976b, V.i.b.2–3, 709–10)

The rich, in particular, are necessarily interested to support that order of things which can alone secure them in the possession of their own advantages.... Civil government, so far as it is instituted for the security of property, is in reality instituted for the defence of the rich against the poor, or of those who have some property against those who have none at all. (Smith 1976b, V.I.B.12, 715)

The arguably correct interpretation of the economic role of government in Adam Smith's writings, anticipated by several people, was, for all practical purposes, first given by Lionel Robbins. Alas, Robbins's approach, elaborated and expanded by others, has had little impact on nonhistorians of economic thought and on some historians of economic thought. Successfully combating the dominant belief system of western civilization is no easy matter – and, too, it may not have been gotten altogether right.

A number of authors, beginning with Robbins, have found it useful if not imperative to work with some form of the market-plus-framework model. These same writers have found that for Smith, it is especially important to locate the market-plus-framework model, or what amounts to it, in the context of Smith's tripartite model of society. The former model envisions business strategies, legal rules, and moral rules as forming the basis of the working out of markets, law, and morality. The latter model enriches this working-out process in part by indicating the interrelations and tensions among the three spheres or domains of life. It is especially the case that neither moral rules nor legal rules (law) nor markets have a given, transcendent existence; instead, people in the three spheres interact over time such that the aggregate of their actions helps form and reform markets, moral rules, and law. Very few of those whom I will call the most sophisticated interpreters have found it necessary to exaggerate and enlarge the importance of the invisible hand. Several of them, however, have been associated with particular identifications of the invisible hand and of its functions to Smith. Robbins settled on the statesman or lawmaker. Jacob Viner and some others have concluded that the invisible hand to Smith was God. George Stigler and I, disagreeing on numerous counts, seem to have agreed, at least to some extent, that the idea and identity of the invisible hand was not as important to Smith and the history of economic thought as has been maintained by others. I may be the only historian of economic thought who has explicitly emphasized the functions of the *concept* of the invisible hand as distinguished from the functions of the particular identities assigned to the invisible hand. In any event, considering the authors of the three dozen or more books on Smith published during the last quarter-century as a group, there are both important differences of interpretation and of emphasis on perhaps every relevant topic.

Finally, if I am not mistaken, the standpoints taken by the interpreters of Smith and of the invisible hand have grown in number during the last half-century, albeit with important and suggestive precursors. Those standpoints have enriched our knowledge and insights through the introduction of philosophers and political scientists into the ranks of Smith interpreters; by the work of specialists in linguistic, ontological, and epistemological studies; and by the seeming widespread willingness of historians of economic thought and others to avoid preemptive differences and hiatuses within and between emphases on ideology, belief system, science, mythic system, and so on, both contributing to and reflecting a desire to avoid speaking past each other and to join in meaningful conversation.

The view of Smith that brings together ideas of harmony, invisible hand, laissez-faire, noninterventionism, and the like to which I refer earlier can still be usefully summarized in Robbins's language, notwithstanding the developments that have taken place in the fifty-five-plus years since the publication of *The Theory of Economic Policy in English Classical Economy*. Robbins, like most of the specialists, was not interested in whether Smith in some sense was "ultimately right," only in what was the correct interpretation of what they wrote and stood for, concluding that "they are immune from the imputation of mysticism; they are no mere Harmonielehre" (Robbins 1953: 24). Claims for harmony were relatively narrow, "very strictly limited," "no claim [was made] for any harmony at all, if the state did not behave in a certain manner and if certain conditions of the market did not prevail," that at best only "a very limited kind of harmony" would be established, "and that the long-run tendencies of society were not necessarily good at all" (idem: 25, 26). Robbins added that "it is really very hard to maintain that it gives any strong support to cosmic optimism, still less to belief in a comprehensive pre-established inevitable harmony of interests" (idem: 28; cf. 192). Indeed, the Classical economists recognized considerable conflict in society in the form of clashes of interests (idem: 25ff). The Classicists may have seemed revolutionary from a then-conventional mercantilist approach to government, but several of them were revolutionary too from the views of present-day monetarist and macroeconomic thinkers (idem: 29ff; apropos of the Classical economists as reformers, see 169ff and passim). This paragraph was written on September 21, 2008, in the midst of the first ten days or so of the seeming U.S. financial collapse. The ideological background was the earlier victory of deregulation over regulation (e.g., the repeal of the Glass-Steagall Act that had prevented the marketing of new security issues to dominate other areas of corporate policy; repeal substantially reduced investor and borrower protection; and the erosion through lapses of enforcement of arrangements requiring mortgage-granting entities to judge borrower qualifications leaving the lenders with no motive to do so, inasmuch as the lenders intended to sell blocks of mortgages to repurchasers).

Robbins summarized Ricardo as favoring "strict regulation of the note issue, holding that, in the possibility of over-issue, there lay a major danger of over-trading and financial crisis; no presumption of a universal applicability of the maxim laissez-faire seems to have crossed Ricardo's mind as he advocated the nationalization of this function" (idem: 31–32; for a strong statement by Smith in favor of necessary banking regulation, see Smith 1976a, II.ii.94; 324). No small degree of controversy surrounding various "bailouts" was conducted in terms of the invisible hand and laissez-faire. Robbins quotes John Ramsey McCulloch's "striking, though not untypical, repudiation of the principle of *laissez-faire*. 'The principle of laissez-faire may be safely trusted to in some things but in many more it is wholly inapplicable; and to appeal to it on all occasions savours more of the policy of a parrot than of a statesman or a philosopher'" (Robbins 1953, 43). Robbins quotes Nassau Senior, that "the only rational foundation of government ... is expediency – the general benefit of the community. It is the duty of a government to do whatever is conducive to the welfare of the governed. The only limit to this duty is power" (idem: 45). One interesting aspect of all this was the exceedingly rare use of invisible-hand arguments in the nineteenth century; another is the rarity of explicit elaborate discussion of whose interest is to count in the formulation of community benefit.

Robbins's statements of his interpretation of the views of the Classical economists deny the late-twentieth-century Chicago view that markets are by their nature competitive: The combination of self-interest and the market was not enough, the situation had to be competitive (idem: 58). Further, he felt that there were "strong grounds for more or less settled codes of law and morals, ... provisional only in the sense that they were all liable to the ultimate test of their ability to promote human happiness" (idem: 179, acknowledging the "fundamental difficulty ... [of] the comparability and summation of the satisfactions of different individuals."). Individualism was both an end and a means (idem: 181–94), comprising, in part, "a system of freedom of choice ... within an appropriate framework of law ..." (idem: 187), so much so that "they regarded the appropriate legal framework and the system of economic freedom as two aspects of one and the same social process" (idem: 191). Robbins did not stumble on any tautology in which an invisible hand "explained" only beneficent outcomes; for him, the Classical economists called for "the provision of a set of rules which so limited and guided individual initiative, that the residue of free action undirected from the centre could be conceived to harmonize with the general objects of public interest" (idem: 190).

The crux of Robbins's interpretation negates the conventional view that the invisible hand substantially replaces law and government; laissez-faire does not derive from the usual doctrine of an invisible hand:

> Thus, so far from the system of economic freedom being something which will certainly come into being if things are just left to take their course, it can only come into being if they are *not* left to take their course, if a conscious effort is made to create the highly artificial environment which is necessary if it is to function properly. The invisible hand which guides men to promote ends which were no part of their intention, is not the hand of some god or natural agency independent of human effort; it is the hand of the law-giver, the hand which withdraws from the sphere of the pursuit of self-interest those possibilities which do not harmonize with the public good. (idem: 56)

Robbins's account of the invisible hand seems consciously devised to counter Hayek's approach to the problem of the economic role of government. That role is within the market-plus-framework model. Robbins resuscitated the role of the lawmaker. But no specification of the identity and function of an 'invisible hand" as such adds anything to the explanation of the legal-economic nexus rendered as the market-plus-framework approach. If we constructed a model in which $X = f(a, b, c)$, nothing in explanatory power is gained by substituting d for b; so, too, calling the role of the maker of law an invisible hand adds nothing.

American conservatives and European liberals, each of varying types, tend to react to my arguments with disdain, animosity, and quizzical wonder as to how I came up with my conclusions. James Buchanan, otherwise a close friend, is serious when he says that I am subversive, as am I when I say that he has adopted the high-priest role. These folks and I tend to disagree on numerous points; for example, about whether the individual is given and independent (so-called methodological individualism, which I perceive to become normative individualism) *or* whether the individual is a product of an interactive and socializing (societizing) process. Many strongly believe in possessive individualism and would welcome the expurgation and extirpation of the system of government and its replacement with nothing or nothing much. My response is that in principle, government in particular and social control in general are inevitable, whether or not that view seems incompatible with individualism (Samuels 2007a: passim).

8.8. Institutions of Human Origin but Not of Human Design: Constructivism and Anticonstructivism, the Principle of Unintended and Unexpected Consequences, and Nondeliberative versus Deliberative Decision Making

Hayek's position in the stream of thought is typically associated with Adam Ferguson, Adam Smith, and Carl Menger, along with their argument that human institutions are of human origin but not of human design. Put aside complicating situations like that of Ferguson, for example, who also argued, against what we now call methodological individualism, that mankind has to be studied in groups – an implication latent, it seems to me, in any focus on institutions. The argument is correct: Institutions are organic and arise "spontaneously," not writ large by design.

This is as far as it goes, however. First, as Menger maintained, each generation in every society has as its calling the evaluation and revision of received institutions. These institutions may have grown up organically, spontaneously, and nondeliberatively. Each institution arguably comprises elements of both wisdom and folly, and the task is to identify them, retain the former, and correct or extirpate the latter. Thus, although the institutions have grown up organically, spontaneously, and nondeliberatively, they are to be made subject to deliberative critique and revision/reform.

Second, given that argument, it is misleading and inaccurate to say that institutions have grown up organically, spontaneously and nondeliberatively. Assume that in period one, through certain processes (see further), an institution develops. At the end of that period, or in period two, depending on one's modeling strategy, deliberative critique is undertaken that leads to institutional change. This continues through all subsequent periods; not all deliberative critique leads to institutional reform, and not all reforms are necessarily of the same type or driven by the same critique. At any point after period one, the institution is a hybrid, the result of nondeliberative and deliberative processes; at no point thereafter, that is to say, has the institution arisen in a solely organic and spontaneous manner. Institutions considered in the Ferguson-Smith-Menger-Hayek manner therefore have deliberative elements and are, in part, the result of deliberative processes.

Third, given the foregoing, it is clear that choice has to be exercised: choice as to which received institutions (each already likely a combination of nondeliberative and deliberative formation) are to be subject to critique; choice as to what that critique should be; choice as to what is folly and what is wisdom, and why; choices as to the objectives and means of institutional change; and, inter alia, choice of the mode of changing institutions, including changing the institutions constituting the mode of change.

Accordingly, one may prefer institutions that arise spontaneously and one may prefer received institutions, but institutions, following Menger, do not evolve solely organically, spontaneously, and nondeliberatively, and, because of the problem of wisdom versus folly, received institutions cannot be blindly accepted – no one likes everything in the status quo.

The principle of unintended and unexpected consequences both stands on its own and is arguably an important part of the argument that institutions are of human origin but not of human design. Human action has consequences that are neither intended nor expected by the actors. Institutions arise, although such was no purpose of the individuals whose actions inadvertently but willy-nilly led or contributed to their formation.

What is to be made of this principle? First, the principle is, of course, descriptively correct. Second, the fact of unintended and unexpected consequences does not lead people, individually or in groups/organizations, to refrain from acting. Third, whether or not one is a cynic, it is likely the case that at least in some instances, there is a difference between the ostensible intended/expected consequence and the actual objective. Fourth, some unintended and/or unexpected consequences may be desirable and others undesirable, in each case depending on who decides and the putative basis of their decision. Fifth, if spontaneously originating institutions are subject to deliberative revision, so that substantially all institutions at any point of time are hybrids, it is also the case that deliberative revision has its own unintended and unexpected consequences, such that the institution in question is a further hybrid of both deliberative and nondeliberative elements.

The question arises as to how, or through what process, unintended and unexpected consequences come about so that, for example, there are initial and continuing, seemingly spontaneous, nondeliberative elements in institutions? Alas, too little serious and sustained analysis has been made of this subject in the relevant Hayek and Hayekian literature. Yet, in a way, all the social sciences contribute to answering the question. Consider two factors: interaction and aggregation. Individuals, however motivated, interact; the result of their interaction is likely different – unintended and unexpected from their operative motivations. Aside from interaction, the aggregation of individual actions likewise produces results likely different – unintended and unexpected – from their operative motivations.

However, interaction and aggregation do not take place in a vacuum. They occur within and are structured and channeled by social system and structure – in short, institutions. So we have a fundamental dualism: Institutions are the evolving result of deliberative and nondeliberative (spontaneous) elements, and the operation of the deliberative and nondeliberative (spontaneous) elements is a result of institutions.

Another name for institutions is social control. And the problem when articulated in terms of social control not surprisingly manifests a comparable dualism: Individuals act within their respective domains of discretion (opportunity sets) being structured and channeled by social control, and social control is a function of individuals acting within their respective domains of discretion (opportunity sets).

This raises another problem. If we start with acting individuals, do all individuals enjoy the same opportunity set? Do all individuals have the same opportunity to act so as to generate unintended and unexpected consequences? Does social control (do institutions) treat all individuals alike? Do all individuals have the same opportunity to determine what the critique of received institutions should be, what is folly and what is wisdom, the objectives and means of institutional change, and, *inter alia*, the mode of changing institutions, including changing the institutions constituting the mode of change? This is the problem of equality versus hierarchy posed by Joseph Spengler.

Given that social control (institutions) exists, and given that social control can take the form of law and morals, the problem becomes one of the deliberative change of law and of morals. It is my view – and a view, I think, implicit in Hayek's analysis – that the fundamental issue is derivative of Menger's argument: The operative problem for both the analyst and policy maker is not whether there is to be institutions-social-control-law, but the critique and possible change thereof. In a nutshell, the problem is change by law of law. One can consider that law per se is coercive or that legal change (change of law) is coercive; be that as it may, such is the operative problem in the Ferguson-Smith-Menger-Hayek tradition. Inasmuch as no one wants to retain everything found in the status quo – Menger's folly – one is willy-nilly engaged in change.

However, the immediate preceding analysis assumes something that is questionable: that there is a definitive "status quo." The status quo is subject to interpretation; it is a matter of social construction in that different people define it differently. Every society, every institution, every value system, and so on is a product continuously in the making. The meaning of "the economy," "American society," "family values," "the constitution," and so on is a work of art. It is contested terrain. It is continuously under construction. "The status quo" may be a term in various syllogisms, but it is itself not an unequivocal given. It is analytically and pragmatically a primitive, undefined/unspecified term – or, rather, a term given different, selective specification by different people. The process of Mengerian critique of received institutions, the so-called status quo, is no simple matter.

Which brings me to the matter of Hayek's anticonstructivism. Just as Hayek's critique of scientism and of Enlightenment rationalism must be understood in light of his position in the Ferguson-Smith-Menger tradition and his affirmation of his own deliberative critique, so too must his critique of constructivism be understood in light of his position in that tradition: to affirm that (1) reason and science do not have the unequivocal answers to all questions, (2) the principle of unintended and unforeseen consequences, and (3) the dispersion of information throughout society both can severely limit and channel humankind's ability to design the future. However, none of the above negate or reject reason or deliberative critique or constructivism. The distribution of information and the exercise of reason in deliberative critique in the service of reconstruction of economy, polity, and society are not only called for but are part and parcel of the Mengerian argument. Selective constructivism is inherent in the body of social theory developed by Hayek. Also inherent is the influence of the structure of distribution and (especially) the structure of social control.

Especially important is the constructivism practiced by Hayek himself. It is practiced by him through his own critique of received institutions and his own proposals and suggestions for institutional change. It would be fallacious to argue that because Hayek has in mind a certain conceptual model of the free economy and so forth, that his proposals for institutional change so as to bring the existing system closer to his conceptual model does not constitute constructivism. It is constructivism no more and no less than any other agenda to restructure or otherwise change society toward some-one's notion, among others, of a free society. That they may have a different conception of freedom in mind, or a different means-ends continuum, is beside the point. To allege differently is to privilege and/or to reify Hayek's conceptual model.

Hayek, through his emphasis on the three principles, seemingly would severely limit mankind's ability to design the future through the process of working things out. But Hayek rejects neither reason nor deliberative critique nor constructivism. The exercise of reason in deliberative critique in the service of reconstruction of economy, polity, and society is not only called for but is part and parcel of the Mengerian argument. Constructivism is inherent in the body of social theory developed by Hayek. Constructivism is practiced by Hayek. It is the fundamental logic of his life's work. In a sense, his own practice constitutes the negation of his own argument.

8.9. The Invisible Hand and Intellectual History: A Glimpse

Economists do not typically view their discipline as a kaleidoscopic set of *ideas*. Almost everything – perhaps actually everything – that an econo-mist does *qua* economist has a history that turns on successive formulations of ideas and is laden with conflicts over their interpretation. The working economist *ipso facto* may be taking a position or positions on issues about ideas of which he has, no pun intended, no idea. The invisible hand, for example, is partly a matter of human interest in and response to the idea of *invisibility* – a theme of much literature.

The principal question that emerged from my studies of the use of the concept of the invisible hand has had to do with the *existence* of the invisi-ble hand. Work on that question, in turn, generated further questions – for example, can there be a difference in function between individual exam-ples or cases (of an invisible hand) and the category as a whole? And can something that, putatively, does not exist nonetheless serve a function, or functions, with material consequences? Many ancient Greeks apparently believed that whatever is thought of must exist in order to be thought of. In the twentieth century, Ludwig Wittgenstein rejected his early theory of language and meaning congruent with that belief and replaced it with a the-ory of signs, which did not assume material or other existence and which allowed for words to have the meanings ascribed to them out of, as it were, thin air. From Aristotle to numerous contemporary practitioners of phi-losophy and other specialisms, such as Anselm, Thomas Aquinas, Pierre Gassendi, René Descartes, Gottfried Wilhelm Leibniz, Thomas Reid, David

Hume, Immanuel Kant, Franz Brentano, Bertrand Russell, Frank P. Ramsey, W. V. Quine, and the early Existentialists, all have given more or less different answers to the problem of existence.

Ideas pertinent to the conduct of inquiry include *abstraction* and *fiction*. Both ideas relate to existence, at least in the sense that denial of the existence of God is internally contradictory because God exists in the mind of the denying person. Inasmuch as it seems in economics to be impossible to include every relevant variable or cause in a description or explanation, the economics of all schools has a smaller or larger degree of unrealism. Another way of making the point is to say that the conventional juxtaposition between a conceptual and an actual economy is necessarily misleading: Both are abstractions. Moreover, the pure theorist, if such a person exists (back to the question of existence!), must have some element of realism associated with an actual economy (or economies) so that his or her conceptual model can be comprehended as an economy. In other words, we always work with abstractions. Such work, however, can be – but need not be – ideologically and/or analytically presumptuous. For example, to assume, *inter alia*, that an economy has "private" property need assume thereby neither that the economist's conceptual model of property is that of a particular actual economy, nor that property is given once and for all time, that is, no change of the law of property, nor that the "public" aspect(s) of property – the *law* of property – are irrelevant. So the concept of the invisible hand, by its very nature, is an abstraction, and it exists in the minds of those who give it credibility or who do not give it credibility. The question here is whether calling "the market," or "private property," or any other identity the invisible hand – thereby defining one abstraction by another (similar to defining one metaphor by another) – adds anything to our knowledge that goes beyond saying that the Bay Front Park monkeys are the invisible hand. I have taken up the subject of economics as political language in Essay 6. Using such abstractions as primitive terms enables the surreptitious introduction of antecedent normative premises as the "economics" – in the sense of a transcendent determinate and determining absolute – and the capture and use of economics in order to control the economic role of government.

I come to the other term mentioned earlier – *fiction*. Economics is a science in the sense that it attempts to describe and/or explain the economy. That is a positive, that is, nonnormative matter, even though the decision to do so is normative. Economics is not in and of itself social control, but the introduction of normative elements enables it to be used as social control, to wit: the capture and use of economics in order to control the economic role of government. However, there are abstractions and then there are abstractions; there are fictions and then there are fictions. Moreover, the result of using abstraction is, accurately and not pejoratively, *science fiction*.

The field of law is different from the field of economics. Economics can be used as social control but arguably is not in and of itself social control. Law *is* social control. *Black's Law Dictionary* (1968, 751) defines "Fiction" as "an assumption or supposition of law that something which is or may be false is true, or that a state of facts exists which has never really taken place.... An assumption, for purposes of justice, of a fact that does not or may not exist." It also says, "A rule of law which assumes as true, and will not allow to be disproved, something which is false, but not impossible."

Just prior to the entry for "Fiction" is one for the Latin phrase, *Fictio Leges Neminem Lædit*, which is translated as "A fiction of law injures no one." This is in itself a fiction: Insofar as Law$_1$ protects Alpha's interests and leaves Beta, whose interests are not so protected, exposed to Alpha's exercise of rights given to Alpha by that law, and vice versa with Law$_2$, then any law, or any legal fiction, that effectuates a choice between parties in the same field of interest does in fact injure one of them, the one whose interests government is being used to protect. (To complete the matter somewhat, "Injure" is defined thusly: "To violate the legal right of another or inflict an actionable wrong.... To do harm to; to hurt; damage; impair," and it is followed by the Latin phrase, *Injuria absque damno*, translated as "Injury or wrong without damage ... which, therefore, will not sustain an action" [Black 1968, 924].)

8.10. Adam Ferguson

Adam Ferguson (1723–1816) was a contemporary of Adam Smith (1723–90). They were participants in overlapping circles, which included the greatest intellects in Scotland, centering in Glasgow and also in Edinburgh – a remarkable group that brought them in close contact with David Hume, Henry Home (Lord Kames), Thomas Reid, William Robertson, and others. Very few cities could claim intellectual parity with this group of citizens. London and, much later, Vienna had similar groups. Ferguson had an enormous intellect and was interested in many of the same topics and problems as Smith and, much later, Friedrich Hayek.

Of interest here are the differences between Ferguson and Hayek on matters of social theory. It is not too much to say that both Smith and Ferguson had the same, or very similar, theories, but they had some that differed materially. We focus with many other scholars on "Ferguson's most frequently quoted sentence" (Raynor 2009: 66): "Nations stumble upon establishments, which indeed are the result of human action, but not the execution of any design" (idem: 66). This may be the first articulation of the idea with which Hayek was so enamored.

Both men presumed "the positive impact of unintended consequences, a fairly common doctrine of optimism in the eighteenth century" (Weinstein 2009: 95). Both men also rejected the idea of a social contract. Ferguson, however, went further than Smith in arguing, writes Weinstein, "that since society is natural, the state of nature is society itself" (idem: 94). Both Smith and Ferguson, according to Weinstein, "[accept] that there are multiple motivations for an agent's acts and that the more negative sentiments work in concert with the more positive ones" (idem: 101).

Adam Ferguson and Adam Smith agreed that government was important and that it originated, writes Lisa Hill, in efforts to protect citizens and their property from "our equally natural tendency towards depredation" (Hill 2009: 112). Hill also writes that (quoting Ferguson), "The whole of human history testifies to the fact that social life is impossible without 'the institution of government, and the application of the penal law" (idem: 112).

Christopher J. Berry points to Ferguson's interpretive strategy of initially endorsing both commercial society and the "commercial arts." This, Berry finds, enables Ferguson to produce "a more subtle critique of commercial society" than, say, Rousseau because he recognizes "it as an important, ineradicable component of human life." Therefore, because "he does not privilege the commercial he is able to address the 'corruptions' that attend wealth (the product of commerce) ..." (Berry 2009: 151).

Berry goes on to note "the equally exigent demands of human collective life that the political arts are developed to meet. The real danger in commerce is its "privatization," "diverting humans away from, and thus undermining, the public sphere" (idem: 151). The subtlety continues, in Berry's reading of Ferguson, when he does not endorse the limitation or forbidding of commerce, on the grounds that "[s]uch a proscription not only runs against the human ambition for betterment, it also aims necessarily to impose equality" (idem: 151–2). Whereas Smith may be ultimately ambiguous (I personally find him extraordinarily clear about the fact and importance of the socialization [societization] of the individual), Hayek is not. Ferguson, Berry finds, does not privilege the political just because he "criticize[s] commercial societies for emasculating the individual." Nor does Ferguson find that "commerce per se is corrupting." Ferguson puts "the political and the commercial on the same footing, both are arts that are natural to man" (idem: 153). Moreover, the essays in Heath and Merolle make it quite clear that Hayek's methodological individualism and rejection of society as having ends fundamentally conflict with Ferguson's construction. It is surely ironic that Berry finds Ferguson declaiming against the danger of a commercial society "diverting humans away from, and thus undermining, the public sphere." Whatever the reader's views of John Kenneth Galbraith's argument in *The Affluent Society* (Galbraith 1958), Ferguson seems to be a precursor, and one with predictive power.

Whereas Heath and Merolle (2009) deal with Adam Ferguson on philosophy, politics, and society, their earlier collection (Heath and Merolle 2008) deals with Ferguson on history, progress, and human nature. David Allan takes up several very important historiographic problems (Allan 2008: 23). One concerns the different interpretations of Ferguson each based on the interpreter's own approach: a pioneering theorist of civil society, a founder of academic social science, a member of classical political economy, a representative of the tradition of classical republican or civic humanism; and his *Essays* is seen as an early exposition of historical materialism; someone on the road to free-market liberalism. This array is important for our invisible-hand purposes. At every turn, we have met different questions, each with different answers. Hayek is a principal architect of Ferguson and Smith as contributors to free-market liberalism. So too are Friedman and Stigler. If each interpreter presents Ferguson and/or Smith as a member of their group, the interpreter's own views serve to frame how Ferguson or Smith is understood. The framing is a form of presentism: Either each contemporary person's ideas are projected back to Ferguson or Smith, or some reading of Ferguson or Smith is projected forward to legitimize a contemporary identity.

Ferguson and Smith are historical personages. What they represent or how they comport with or fit into the flow of intellectual history are matters of interpretation. In the case of the invisible hand, there is nothing to interpret, but interpreters project their imagined identities into the air.

Yasuo Amoh takes up Ferguson's views on the American and French revolutions in part as to the suffrage. Ferguson did not approve of the *Ancien Régime*, but he also held that "surely the indiscriminate right of every one, whether capable and worthy, or incapable and unworthy, cannot by any means be admitted." He did approve of "distinctions of rank based on birth or property" (Amoh 2008: 83; the first is Amoh's quotation from Ferguson). If there is a difference among the English-speaking peoples between the political perspective of the late eighteenth century and that of the early twenty-first century, it is over the scope of the franchise and the correlative meaning assigned to "democracy" and the question of whose interests are to count. The matter lies just beneath the surface of many issues. In Essay 9, I take up the survival requirement in relation to Pareto Optimality, which links the invisible hand to the question of whose interests (in life!) are to count. The linkage is correlative to the linkage that Fania Oz-Salzberger (2008: 155–6 and passim) finds between the Ferguson's concept of unintended consequences and his politics of participation. The linkage relates as well to Ferguson's elevation of the unintended consequences of social interaction over the influence of great individual legislators, developed by Craig Smith (2008: 157–70), and which juxtaposes the "active genius of mankind" via social interaction to ordinary competitive politics, that is, two conflicting notions of democracy.

Possibly the most difficult problem has to do with the role played by the sources of inequality and class status. The transactional provenance of land rights can trace to grants by a monarch in reward for services and favors rendered as well as conquest. The structure of costs and prices is influenced by statutes and court decisions altering the structure of rights. Considerable economic analysis gives effect to assumptions as to which party has the rights in question (or that might be in question if more was widely known).

8.11. Ignorance and Dispersed Knowledge

We come to Hayek's emphasis on ignorance and on dispersed, localized knowledge. Hayek emphasizes "the market" as one means of organizing this knowledge. Notice, however, that the following renders his argument inconclusive: First, it is not only knowledge but interests that the operation of markets may be said to organize. Secondly, as used by economists, "the market" is a conceptual tool and this is only a form of modeling a range of activity. Thirdly, actual markets are a function of the institutions that help form and operate through them (for example, in Coase's theory of the firm, markets are a function of decisions by firms whether to self-produce or outsource; firms themselves are legal entities, and so on). Fourthly, differently structured markets organize knowledge and determine which/ whose knowledge and which/whose interests will count and in what ways. Accordingly, there is no unique Pareto-optimal solution.

Insistence on the dispersal of information throughout society is another, and important, part of Hayek's analysis though only negligibly treated here. Dispersal of information severely limits mankind's ability to design the future. To say that is to reject neither reason nor deliberative critique or constructivism. Indeed, it is closely tied to them. The exercise of reason in deliberative critique in the service of reconstruction of economy, polity, and society is not only called for and emphasized by Menger but is part and parcel of the Mengerian argument. Constructivism is inherent in the body of social theory developed by Hayek. Moreover, constructivism is practiced by Hayek. It is practiced by him through his own critique of received institutions and his own proposals/suggestions for institutional change. It would be fallacious to argue that because Hayek has in mind a certain conceptual model of the free economy, among other things, that his proposals for institutional change to bring the existing system closer to his conceptual model, in part by rearranging the marshalling of dispersed knowledge, do not constitute constructivism. It is constructivism no more and no less than any other agenda to restructure society (among other things) toward someone's notion of a free society. That they may have a different conception of freedom in mind, or a different means-ends continuum, is beside the point. To allege differently is to privilege and/or to reify Hayek's conceptual model.

8.12. Hayekian Spontaneous Order

Hayek's second principle is that of the achievement of spontaneous order through nondeliberative choice. The common examples are language, money, and the common law. Hayek's "spontaneous order" has the features indicating that (1) it is the result of both deliberative and nondeliberative factors and forces, and is therefore not solely "spontaneous"; (2) it has elements putatively both of wisdom and folly; and (3) it remains open to deliberative critique and reform. So far from negating the importance of choice, Hayek's total system provides a wide-ranging analysis of the role, nature, and limits of deliberative choice; and (4) it also has a place for tension between formulations of the optimality and spontaneous orderliness of the status quo and various critiques of the status quo – with, perhaps ironically, important places within his total system for both critique and deliberate modification of the status quo, any status quo. This is evidenced by the arrays of Hayek's own critiques and of his own proposals and suggestions for deliberative change.

Hayek has a place, in both his normative and positive analysis, for the rule of law; indeed the common law is typically given as an example of the spontaneous order system. Like the other concepts that form parts of his total system, the "rule of law" is complex and subtle. It emphasizes adherence to precedent and incremental decision making. But "adherence to precedent" should not obfuscate (1) the inexorable role of judicial choice between alternative streams of precedent. Nor should it obscure (2) the combination of deliberative and nondeliberative decision making within common, constitutional, and statute law; (3) the role of concentrated power in the lawmaking process; and, *inter alia*, (4) the fact of choice as to whose interests, which customs, and which/whose definitions – for example, of property, coercion, and so on – should count. This is part of Hayek's total system, even if some or much of it is obscured in his ideological polemics. As for the evolution of the common law, including the idea that an active invisible hand produces an optimal body of law, judges do not think of themselves – or more importantly, act – as a potted plant. Inasmuch as the concept of the rule of law became the final of Hayek's three principles and not merely an example on behalf of the other two, it is examined separately and in detail later in this essay.

Much the same thing can be said of language as an example of a Hayekian spontaneous-order process. The formation or evolution of language has organic, spontaneous-order aspects to it, but the total story is not so simple. The conflicts between prescriptive and permissive approaches to language and between different prescriptive agendas indicate the evolution of language to be a contested terrain, with both deliberative and nondeliberative elements and with critical roles for strategically situated power players. The same can be said for money and culture.

I have already credited Hayek and others for the positive – in contrast to his normative – arguments. The point here, since we have already considered the political nature of language in Essay 6, is this: In no field is nondeliberative decision making so overwhelming that it can warrant a turn away from the importance of deliberative decision making.

Two problems in writing about this topic are: (1) there is no way, certainly no independent test, by which to reach a meaningful judgment as to the relative importance of deliberative and nondeliberative decision making; (2) individual actions and developments are almost always a mixture of deliberative and nondeliberative decision making. But if one had expected Hayek to focus strongly on changing mixes of both types of decision making on the individual level, one would be disappointed.

There is ample evidence of deliberative decision making in all fields. Yes, nondeliberative decision making "strongly" contributes to the development of all fields. But in all fields, deliberative decision making is also "strong." Language change can be thought to be nondeliberative yet also be the result of deliberative efforts by parties interested in capturing the linguistic high ground and manipulating meanings in order to influence electoral and other outcomes (see White 1984; Rotunda 1986; Rodgers 1987). The monetary system of the United States evolved in a helter-skelter manner, particularly in the nineteenth century, but even during that period, the evolution was one or another mix of both types.

Terms that have entered the discussion in this book manifest not only the tension between deliberative and nondeliberative decision but a multiplicity of possibilities of meaning and of paths of development. Among these terms are capitalism, laissez-faire, Enlightenment, order, freedom, coercion, cost, rationality, self-interest, and a host of others. The linguistics of capitalism influences the paths of development taken by various economies *and* the path of development influences the linguistics of capitalism. Whether or not such a dualism of development is more, or less, important than the opportunities, ambitions, and exigencies of the business class is neither easily nor conclusively determined. This, too, confronts the two problems noted two paragraphs earlier.

George Lakoff is distinguished professor of cognitive science and linguistics at the University of California, Berkeley. He was the coauthor of one of the most influential books of the last quarter of the twentieth century (Lakoff and Johnson 1980). He has also been active in the development and use of frame analysis, an approach to meaning founded by Erving Goffman (Goffman 1974), in which framing terms help organize experience. Lakoff's 2008 book, *The Political Mind*, in chapter 14, takes up "The Problem of Self-Interest," and in chapter 15, "The Metaphors Defining Rational Action." Near the end of chapter 14, Lakoff takes up the concepts of self-interest, rationality, the invisible hand, and utility.

Lakoff begins by noting the dominance of the concept of self-interest in economic and political theorizing. "Rationality, defined in terms of the eighteenth-century-view of mind," he writes, "saw reason as primarily serving to achieve personal goals; hence it was seen as irrational to be against your self-interest. The rational actor model is a tool to maximize self-interest, called 'utility.'" Lakoff finds the concept of utility to be "strange" in two ways. First, it assumes utility is always linear; he maintains that it is far from true that a preference hierarchy is always linear because an individual can always form a nonlinear preference hierarchy. Second, it assumes that utility, if it is not economic profit (the default case), "is something that benefits you in some other way that can be meaningfully compared with profit and perhaps placed on the same scale" (Lakoff 2008: 205–6). Lakoff moves on to our major topic, saying that:

Adam Smith's "invisible hand" metaphor made seeking profit into a moral act, since it supposedly maximized the profit of all. Utility replaces economic profit with well-being. The rational actor model then is seen as maximizing overall well-being for you – that is, utility: in other words, self-interest, whatever that self-interest might be. The failure of the old view of reason calls into question the old view of self-interest with it. It's not that self-interest disappears altogether. It still exists. But it does not simply define natural behavior. It is far from the whole story. (idem: 206)

8.12.1. Digression

For my own rejection (and its implications) of conservatism versus liberalism as an opposition useful in meaningful framing (but not of framing per se or any other equivalent term), see Buchanan and Samuels, in Samuels (2007a) and in Peart and Levy (2008). Peart and Levy, and presumably Buchanan, envision our two different views of government as being between politics as exchange and politics as power. I envision politics as exchange on the basis of power, with power itself influenced by exchange. The two positions, politics as exchange and as exchange and power, as framing devices and otherwise, are obviously different. The difference extends to our different views of Adam Smith and how those views may best be utilized. The argument seems sophisticated and is accurate as to ostensible intent.

Hayek's "spontaneous order" has three features: (1) it is the result of both deliberative and nondeliberative factors and forces, and is therefore not solely "spontaneous"; (2) it has elements putatively both of wisdom and folly; and (3) it remains open to deliberative critique and reform. So far from negating the importance of choice, Hayek's total system provides a wide-ranging analysis of the role, nature, and limits of deliberative choice. It also has a place for tension between formulations of the optimality and spontaneous orderliness of the status quo and various critiques of it.

Hayek's argument selectively reinforces the status quo structure of hierarchical power and its complex relations to government. The argument ostensibly and actually – albeit superficially and selectively – limits the power of government; more importantly, it serves as an instrument of power and rule. It is ironic that a proposition that asserts minimal government and is a presumption against governmental activism is itself an instrument of governmental activism. It is a matter of misrepresentation, a fundamental defect of any body of ideas that proposes and markets the laissez-faire, noninterventionist, minimum-government approach to policy and the economic role of government.

8.13. Hayek's Normative Position in Positivist Context

Hayek was influenced by ideologies that purported to totally reconstruct economy and society and to centrally plan entire economies in detail. He was also influenced by efforts of communist parties, notably that of the Soviet Union, to pursue such paths. His normative and positive arguments against these ideologies and practices were devastating. But his arguments do not necessarily apply to partial reconstructions and to the planning inherent both therein and in government budgets writ large. His argument is not against such constructivism.

Hayek's normative arguments regarding the principle of unintended and unforeseen consequences, nondeliberative over deliberative decision making, and spontaneous order (see further in this essay) have sometimes been taken as subtle defenses of capitalism in general and of capitalist hierarchical structures in particular, as well as an exercise in antirationalism (say, of the Joseph de Maistre type). Be that as it may, his normative arguments do tend to presume a capitalist/market status quo and would give effect to sentiments supporting limited government and limited legal change of law, and ostensibly to limited government and limited change of law – though I have argued differently earlier with regard to his total system, as per Menger. But what of the problem of the more or less complete reconstruction of formerly centrally planned economies along market lines? Here, one either takes the Hayekian sentiments literally and argues "go slow," or more or less rejects them at what James Buchanan calls the constitutional level, or treats the arguments as only instrumental and pragmatic.

This subsection concludes with two vignettes. The first is from a quotation from an essay in personal history by Reeve Lindbergh, the second daughter of Charles and Anne Lindbergh. Among other things, her father was logical and factual; he was also methodical. When living on an isolated Connecticut shore, he awaited predicted strong weather conditions: "In preparation, he checked the thermometers, scanned the skies, roamed the property in his parka, and kept the household informed. He had on hand emergency food and water, flashlights, extra blankets, medical equipment, rubber rafts, snake-bite kits, and even a vial of morphine, which was probably illegal." Personal instinct and meticulous preparation had been, in his mind, critical to his survival as a pilot. But he was always wary: "'It's the unforeseen,' he would warn us. 'It's always the unforeseen'" (Lindbergh, 1998: 124; see also 129).

So far from being an injunction to do nothing, the principle of unforeseen and unintended consequences becomes, in Hayek's system – if I interpret him correctly – something like a combination of an understanding of human activism and the motto of the Boy Scouts: Be prepared. To which he would add: Don't expect too much.

The second is Frank Knight's notion that the economy is a game with economic actors/agents as players. With that in mind, consider again the American football game. The outcome of any particular play is a function of several variables, including the offensive formation, the defensive formation, the quality of the respective players, and the executions of their individual assignments in their respective formations. The same offensive formation run against different defensive formations, given the other variables, will likely generate different results – a long gain or touchdown in one case, and a loss or short gain in the other.

The result is a good example of the interaction that (among other sources) produces Adam Ferguson's principle involving results of human action but not of human design and of the principle of (potentially) unintended and/or unforeseen consequences (Ferguson 1995: 122).

The football example is a purely positive, or descriptive, one. Contrary to the frequent "conservative" conversion of the principles from a descriptive to a prescriptive, or normative, principle of policy, namely of doing little or going slow, the football example indicates that deliberative constructivism is part of the process leading to results of human action but not of human design, and is not in and of itself something that necessarily should or could be avoided (which does not necessarily negate either doing little or going slow, but does limit the reach of the critique of rational constructivism). Indeed, the use of the principles as principles of policy, which are always selective, would have the (more or less intended) effect of producing two groups: law takers and law makers. Not unlike the difference between manifest and latent function, the law takers, induced to follow the principle, would desist from active participation, leaving the field for lawmaking to those with a lawmaking rationalist social construction of reality. The language of Hayekian economics would thus preclude recognition of the foundational social-control and psychic-balm roles of the invisible hand. After all, the rationale for deploying either or both principles is precisely to influence the economic role of government along the lines of social control and psychic balm.

8.14. The Rule of Law and the Capture and Use of Government in a World of Inequality

Hayek was engaged in a quest for a principle of policy that would constrain both government activism and the political jockeying for position that largely produced what government undertook. Inasmuch as the principles of unintended and unexpected consequences and of spontaneous order underscored the elements of pure choice that inevitably had to be made in the legal-economic nexus, they could not serve as absolutist formulation. The final bastion of constraint then became the principle of the rule of law. It, too, did not succeed in accomplishing Hayek's objective. The inescapable fact on which the rule of law came to naught continued to be the inevitable necessity of choice. As much as Hayek desired to constrain legal choice, the existential reality was precisely legal choice. Moreover, the reliance on the rule of law was ironic. The intended constraint on law was to be achieved by making law supreme, in a sense at least that law was to be treated as both transcendent and beyond choice. It failed, however, because, unlike Smith, Hayek could not abide a process in which humankind had to work out the solutions to its problems.

The rule of law – or, more accurately, the idea of the rule of law – was prominent in the impeachment trial of William Jefferson Clinton. The president's prosecutors both accused him of violating the rule of law through perjury and obstruction of justice in his Paula Jones deposition, and argued that the rule of law required his removal from office. The president's defenders claimed that the rule of law was jeopardized by the use of constitutional provisions for purely political purposes. In the aftermath of the initial vote in the presidential election of 2000, the supporters of Al Gore defended his legal contest of the Florida certification of electoral delegates as based on the rule of law, and the supporters of George W. Bush likewise invoked the rule of law in claiming the conclusiveness of certification. Paul W. Kahn, a professor of law at Yale Law School and author of *The Reign of Law* (Kahn 1997), characterized the latter situation as one in which "[e]ach campaign ... ritualistically claims that it wants nothing more than 'the rule of law,' and each side accuses the other of subverting law for the sake of politics" (Kahn 2000: 13A). That description is empirically accurate.

Kahn, however, took the matter several steps further. First, he took notice that the "rule of law" is a national myth, whereas in fact law is politics. Second, he lamented the unveiling or unmasking of the rule of law as myth, and called for a return of belief.

Kahn began his argument by noting that "[t]he grand civics lesson of the past two weeks has introduced the whole nation to the deepest secret of our constitutional life. There is no line between law and politics." Hitherto, only law professors influenced by Legal Realism had "been teaching ... that the line between law and politics is illusory. Now, that knowledge has escaped the academy and threatens to subvert our faith in the rule of law" (idem: 13A).

Kahn did not claim that the rule of law is a matter of truth. Rather it is not truth; it is a myth, a myth justified by its ostensible function of generating harmony:

The rule of law is our national myth. We must believe the myth if we are to overcome our political disagreements. We need a point of reconciliation beyond our political disputes. That point is our faith in law, and the institutional locus of that faith is the U.S. Supreme Court. To be sure, we can always find the politician behind the robes of the justice, just as we can always find the man behind the robes of the priest. But faith prevents us from lifting the robe. It limits our vision to a set of symbols.

It is the Supreme Court's role to preserve this national myth. When the court speaks, it speaks in the name of the sovereign people. When it presents to us the Constitution, it purports only to hold up a mirror to the people. Its legitimacy comes neither from its knowledge of legal science nor from the justices' political appointments, but from the capacity to persuade us that the rule of law is the rule of the people. At that moment, we overcome the divide between law and politics. (idem: 13A)

Kahn's claim that the myth of the rule of law is necessary to generate order may have some truth to it but it is principally an assumption that can be carried too far. The burden must be on advocates of the claim to prove it. Much of life and of public order does not depend on myth.

At least two problems immediately arise: first, whether the defense is of the idea of the rule of law or of the privileged status of lawyers and courts; and second, whether the rule of law is to be understood to be transcendent to man or an expression of the rule of the people (popular sovereignty).

Kahn did not deny that his view is one of jurisprudential metaphysics, even jurisprudential theology. What once was the equation of the rule of law with a sovereign God is now the equation of the rule of law with the rule of the sovereign people; faith in the rule of law replaces faith in God, but to the same end, namely social control:

This is not fact, but faith – our civic religion. Neither law nor politics defines us as a nation; rather this faith in a popular sovereign who appears only in and through the rule of law. We know that political beliefs are inseparable from legal views.... No one really believes that law can end our disagreements over these issues [of policy]. Nevertheless, our faith in the rule of law unites us in a common enterprise through all these disputes. (idem: 13A)

For Kahn, the terminology of the rule of law is a mode of language, not a description of reality; in this respect at least, the concept of rule of law resembles those of natural law and natural rights as well as public interest:

This faith sets the structure of our grand national debates: Each side must claim the support of law, because in and through law it claims the right to speak for the people. Each side must accuse the other of subverting the law and thus subverting the people. Politics in its local and ordinary form is set off from law; ordinary politics can have an air of illegitimacy about it, even in our democracy. Thus, the bizarre accusation by each side that the other side was 'politicizing' an election. This claim makes sense only when we see that the call to law is a call to a faith in a higher politics. (idem: 13A)

This is itself a form of social control. Kahn takes the conventional high-priest role, notably an affirmation of rejection of wide knowledge of latent function – and their own role:

Like every faith, our national myth of law's rule can stand only so much public scrutiny. It is vulnerable just because it is a faith. There are no facts by which we can prove it. The popular sovereign is not a subject we can locate, but only a mythical figure through which we understand our history and our identity. Vulnerable as it is, however, we need it; we have no other faith standing in the wings.... So our national civics lesson may be teaching us too much about ourselves. The relentless attack of politics on law may leave us without an institution that can settle our disputes by calling us back to our civic faith.... This is the greatest danger of the present moment. The rule of law will lose its foundation as a national faith of the people. Law's rule will be seen as nothing more than another face of ordinary politics. (idem: 13A)

This brings to mind Emile Durkheim's theory of manifest and latent function in religion. When a person enters a church, Durkheim argued, he or she feels a sense of awe in the presence of the transcendent; this is the manifest function of religion. The latent function of religion, on the other hand, resides in the reenforcement of received social structure and social relations – latent, that is, in relation to the laity but not the officials of religion who appreciate the actuality of latent function. Such that one can imagine a situation in which the laity came to know about the latent function, leading the officials to wish for the reestablishment of naïve belief and manifest function in order to restore the latent function. The parallel with the rule of law is not forced.

What are we to make of this predicament, this diagnosis, and this prescription? I take a position quite opposite to that of Kahn. I do so somewhat reluctantly, because the *idea* of the rule of law encompasses worthy *ideals*; and it teaches people something of what the protection of civil rights is all about. It can provide protection against inhumane treatment under color of law. The rule of law signifies the desideratum that there is one law for all people, not only law for one group and another law for another group, say, one law for the rich and another for the poor, or one law for Protestants and another for Catholics, and so on. The rule of law signifies the desideratum of rational means-end and reasoned decision making. The rule of law signifies the desideratum of independence of legislature from executive and of judiciary from both; it especially signifies the negation of authoritarian caprice by an absolute monarch. It may also signify the desideratum of a tone of civility in political affairs, however laden with controversy. It may also signify democracy, although democracy has often been criticized for its ostensible violation of the rule of law. Allan Schmid suggests an important, if minimalist, definition of rule of law: that the judge cannot be directly bought, that decisions are not auctionable; appointment of like-minded judges is only indirect purchase. If minimalist, this definition is nonetheless important: In many countries the judiciary is in fact corrupt. But purchase and sale is one thing; pretense of the possibility and fact of objectivity and of a transcendent law to be found is quite another, and a corruption of its own.

The fact of the matter is, however, that the reality of law is nothing like these ideals. The rule of law is not self-enforcing. The rule of law is not itself constrained by the rule of law. Both law and the rule of law are matters of opinion (Dicey 1981). Among the problems with thinking otherwise are the following:

The Promotion of Special Interests: Much legislation is enacted on behalf of so-called special interests. Thus, provisions of the Internal Revenue Code have been passed to provide favorable tax treatment for specific constituency – clients of particular legislators. The same is true of amendments to the Patent Laws selectively extending the duration of particular patents. The same is true of such seemingly more general provisions as that enabling the deduction of mortgage interest from income for tax purposes.

Alpha-Beta Conflicts: When Alpha and Beta are in the same field of action, making conflicting claims of interest and of right, case law or statutory law that affirms Alpha's interest as a right ipso facto negates Beta's interest as a right. The law cannot equally apply to both. This applies to vast fields of law, perhaps most especially to economists, to those fields dealing with interests of economic significance, although this is true of law generally.

The Paradox of the Equal Treatment of Unequals: People are unequal in many ways, such as talents, wealth, and so on; this is a fact of life. A paradox arises because of this inequality: If we treat unequals equally, we may well be treating them unequally; and the only way to treat unequals equally may be to treat them unequally. Among other things, this situation enables the declarers of law to affirm either (1) that although all persons have formal equality of right, differences in position or circumstance properly operate to modify the rights; or (2) that differences in position or circumstance should not operate to modify, even to negate, the rights.

The Multiplicity of Available Law: In any situation, it is more than likely – almost axiomatic – that more than one straightforward law applies. Thus, each party to a case or other conflict can point to and invoke the law that favors its side. Each side claims that its view, and not that of the other side, comports with the rule of law. This applies to both substantive and procedural law but especially to the former. (A good example is the litigation over the Florida ballot and recount after the November 7, 2000 presidential election.)

New Rights: New rights are regularly being created in areas not previously contemplated, such as surrogate motherhood and use of the human genome and other technologies.

Conflicts within a Law: Often the various provisions of a law come into conflict in more or less novel fact situations – perhaps because the different provisions were adopted with certain fact situations in mind – fact situations that did not include the novel one.

The Division of Governmental Power: Governmental power in the United States is divided in two ways. Governmental power is divided between state and national governments (also between state and local governments) and among the several branches on each level. The conventional formula – that the legislature makes the law, the executive enforces the law, and the judiciary interprets the law – is severely flawed, actually a fiction. All three branches of government are governing; each rules/makes law in its own way – not least the judiciary. Moreover, there are inevitable tensions and conflicts between state and national governments – for example, between state legislatures and national supreme court – and between each branch on each level – for example, between common, constitutional, statutory, and administrative law.

Conflicting Interpretations: The history of constitutional law is replete with conflicting interpretations of particular provisions and of the relationships between provisions. The history of the common law is also replete with conflicting interpretations of what the law "is." In both domains, as well as if not especially in appellate judicial decisions interpreting statutes and/or relating them to constitutional provisions, the case law is replete with conflicting sequences of precedent, such that one can typically – almost always, in fact – find some chain of precedents on which to ground a decision and opinion. Judges disagree as to what is a legal rule, as to their interpretation, and as to the rules of interpretation. The rule of law is therefore instantiated and given substance by the specifics of social power, legal-economic theory, custom, institutional structure, rules and procedures of election and appointment, and so on – all of which is obfuscated by affirmation of a transcendent "rule of law" or the trope "law is found, not made."

The Exercise of Discretion: The legal system is laden with opportunities, indeed inevitabilities, for the exercise of discretion. These include prosecutorial discretion, choice of precedential sequence, choice of issues with which to frame a decision and opinion, discretion whether to take a case on appeal, and, *inter alia*, the exercise of discretion at the lowest levels of enforcement.

Lawyers' Practice: Lawyers specializing in certain areas of the law occasionally represent only plaintiffs or only defendants. Often they represent either side: in one case the plaintiff, in another the defendant. Their strategy, professed theory of the case, and legal argument in one case will be the opposite of those in the other case. The position of the client is one thing; the strategy, theory, and argument vary with the client's position.

This is all very pragmatic, instrumental, and utilitarian. In the late nineteenth century, railroad attorneys argued that their clients could/should not be subject to state statutes regulating their business because such was the preserve of the national government; when national regulation was being litigated the courts, the attorneys' argument was that railroad regulation was a state matter. In the early twentieth century, when price levels were rising, utility companies proposed the use of reproduction cost for the valuation of their rate base and their opponents proposed the use of original cost; when price levels were falling, the two sides switched positions. In the 2000 postelection imbroglios over hand recounts of votes in the contest between George W. Bush and Al Gore, the arguments were reversed depending on which side was seeking and which side was opposing a recount in different states. At the same time, each side deployed situation-specific arguments as to such matters as court versus electoral commission and federal versus state primacy.

Consider, for example, the related doctrine of "original intent." A relatively recent book on the subject (Lynch 1999) demonstrates convincingly that the notion of the original intent of the founding fathers – whatever one might think normatively of the matter – has little, if any, meaning. The author shows, *inter alia*, that during the first six Congresses, the Constitution was interpreted on the basis of immediate policy goals, including state, regional, and political interests, and not fidelity to some past position or original intent; that figures such as James Madison not only changed interpretive positions but adopted conflicting ones; that immediate policy goals influenced framers' recollections of the constitutional convention and the ratifying state conventions, the meaning of the *Federalist Papers*, and the interpretation of the Constitution; that elements of the structure of government ensconced within the Constitution were matters of compromise that neither expressed nor satisfied either compromised position; that regional interpretations became reversed, owing to changing circumstances and political expectations; that important clauses of the original Constitution and the first ten amendments – the Bill of Rights – comprised compromises of language that deferred to the future the determination of what they might be held to mean; and so on.

In another study (Neely 1999), the author shows how constitutionalism at the time of the U.S. Civil War was interpreted differently by Northerners, by the Southern Confederacy, and by Southern opponents of the Confederacy. Both Abraham Lincoln and Jefferson Davis are shown to have treated law and constitution as means to their ends, not embodiments of a transcendent "rule of law." In a related study on the question of states' rights during and after the Confederacy, McDonald (2000) shows with vast documentation how adherence to a position on an issue or to a cause dominated adherence to a particular constitutional interpretation, even to constitutionalism itself. In an effectively cognate study of civil-rights violence in Birmingham in the 1960s, McWhorter (2001) shows how far the rule of law in practice departed from the rule of law in theory and ideology, enmeshing the black-versus-white conflict with those between workers and employers, Roman Catholics and Protestants, Jews and gentiles, and communism and anticommunism – evoking memories of the vast U.S. history of the selective use of law and effective denigration of any pretext of an objective rule of law in favor of a reality of law as a weapon. And in a study of the rule of law in Britain, Ewing and Gearty (2001) document how civil liberties were judicially (and otherwise) selectively defined and administered in matters deemed to be subversive, starting well before the inception of the USSR, not least through judgments made by magistrates with direct financial interests in industrial disputes.

Consider, too, a work on constitutionalism, pragmatism, and judicial review (Lipkin 2000). Its author demonstrates the thinness and the unreality of such foundational concepts as neutral principles, objective constitutional interpretation, and constitutional legitimacy. He proposes a theory of constitutional revolutions to explain how certain decisions departed from past precedents and involved terms of legitimization inconsistent with prior jurisprudential interpretation. The *idea* of a theory of constitutional revolution is presently more important than the content of any particular theory (more or less similar to the argument in Essay 4, *supra*; but still more important is the factual premise of constitutional change).

Perhaps nowhere is the premise more dramatic, and the unrealism of the concept of the rule of law more stark, than in the domain of affirmative action. Whereas once the Constitution was invoked to uphold invidious and discriminatory unequal treatment, it has since been invoked both to uphold remedial affirmative action and to oppose that action as constituting reverse discrimination. It is the modern equivalent of sending a high priest to the presumed representative of the gods to determine the wisdom of a policy; both involve processes of legitimization, not objective decision making.

The key question to ask is not whether some abstract notion of the "rule of law" has been followed. The key question is: Which/whose interests are represented in and protected by the law for the legitimization of which the concept of the "rule of law" is invoked.

Yet it has been shown that the "rule of law," as a concept in constitutional discourse, has multiple meanings involving "mutually incompatible positions." These meanings lack "articulated theories" but have "discernible kernels of meaning." The idealized notion of the rule of law has "multiple strands or elements, which the various ideal types help to illuminate," but, while "Invocations of the Rule of Law are sufficiently meaningful to deserve attention," these invocations "are typically too vague and conclusional to dispel lingering puzzlement" (Fallon 1997: 55–6). This view may well be too charitable. Legal and constitutional language typically provides the linguistic framework of reference and argument, not the mechanism or process of transcendent unequivocal determination typically evoked by the concept of the "rule of law." Law involves choosing between claimants. The typical use of the concept of the "rule of law" functions to obfuscate the fact of choice. Law as a general category and the categories of common and constitutional law all constitute social control by their very existence, quite independent of the content of any particular decisions.

Reversal or dependence of argument consequent to a change of position seems like hypocrisy to anyone seeking "the law." But anyone familiar with the language theories of Charles Saunders Peirce and Ludwig Wittgenstein knows better. According to those theories, language has meaning as signification, as conveyor of meaning, and not, or not necessarily, as correspondence with reality or a/the true state of things. Such signification may function, and be intended, to steer imagination in certain directions and not others, but at least to convey persuasive meaning. Language, like terms, concepts and arguments, would thus not correspond to anything ontologically "real," representing instead only conceptual and methodological tools with which to organize and channel thought and exposition and to express and advance arguments. Lawyers believe in the power of people to believe in the constructs of their own imagination, and so practice this themselves, using the linguistic structure of the law for purposes of persuasion, that is, of rhetoric. "The law" and/or "rights" are convenient modes of expression, contest, and persuasion, when the specific content of law and/or of rights is precisely the point at issue. The language of common, statute, and constitutional law provides the linguistic formulations and framework of reference and argument, not mechanism of a transcendent and unequivocal "rule of law."

The possibility of misinterpreting the various arguments presented in these essays is substantial. It may be felt that my arguments open the door for change of law. I respond as follows: I am not advocating change of law. I am calling for recognition that even in the most conservative systems of economics and of government, there will be – indeed there must be – change of the law. Among those who are displeased with my argument are those who typically want to establish a presumption against the types of change of law that they dislike. Hence, they damn change of the law itself, except when "necessary," by which they mean change that promotes, or is consistent with, their own agendas. To establish that presumption is the objective of the creation or adoption and use of such metaphysical absolutes as the invisible hand, rule of law, fundamental juristic postulates, and so on. Much of the aforementioned may seem irrelevant to whether or not there is an invisible hand and what functions it performs. The invisible hand may seem absent from some or much of the aforementioned, but the linguistics of the invisible hand, whether we consider it to be a metaphor, simile, trope or something else, pervades our civil discourse. Nonetheless, the invisible hand is a mythical linguistic tool used by upper hierarchical levels in establishing, strengthening, and extending their rule.

Not surprisingly, Hutchinson (2000) goes beyond law as politics to law as a game of rhetorical justification. The writing of legal decisions, including the reaching of legal decisions, is not a process of legally reasoning to legal conclusions, fundamentally guided by the "rule of law." It is a rhetorical game in which the players only pretend to articulate or demonstrate "the law" (= legal "truth"). It is a game of justification of choices and values somehow made. The idea of the rule of law is a stratagem in this justificatory exercise, as is much of the use of the concept of the invisible hand.

Further as to hypocrisy, one readily suspects that knowledge of the falsity of the idea of the rule of law, coupled with understanding of its latent function, engenders in the minds of many politicians both further hypocrisy and contempt for the minds of the electorate.

One is therefore tempted if not compelled to say that there is no more such a thing as "the law" than there is "the market." Some pure a-institutional abstract conceptual market can be contemplated and analyzed, but actual markets are a function of the institutions, power structure, and power play/ business strategy that form and operate through them.

The law is embodied in and expressed through words that are selectively defined and selectively applied. The law as language is used in the process of defining and redefining, and making and remaking, the economy, polity, and society. The words are used as if they had given, independent, and transcendent meanings that we were trying to achieve or put into practice. But the legal system and the economy are artifacts, and the words used in describing and forming them are also artifacts. The legal and economic systems, and their institutions and words influence each other. To think otherwise is to commit the fallacy of misplaced concreteness and/or the naturalistic fallacy (that because something exists it has ontological meaning).

A basic characteristic of law is its futurity. Notwithstanding selective argumentation utilizing past cases and theories, the meaning of a law relates to how it governs relations in the future; the future is in part made through making law in the present. Moreover, much, if not all, common and constitutional law is ex post: One does not "know" "the law" until after the courts decide cases presented to it.

"The law" has two further dimensions of ambiguity. One has to do with the multiple *sources of law* and the conflicts between them. These sources include (using the terms of art) custom, morality, equity, public policy, statutes, force, past judicial precedents, opinions of experts, legal theory, and so on. The other has to do with the *mode in which law is expressed*. These modes include (again using the terms of art) the holding of a decision, the *ratio decidendi* of a case (the ground of a decision, the basis of the holding), the sequence of precedents somehow interpreted, the overriding principle or rule of which the former are manifestations or evidence, natural law, divine law, and so on. In every case, conflicting versions are present; for example, the court has to choose between rival claims of custom, between rival sets of custom, and conflicting sets or chains of precedents.

Kahn is correct: The rule of law is a myth. Law is made, not found, and this is done selectively, in large part as the ongoing product of a process in which competing parties struggle to control government/law thereby to use government/law to advance their interests – interests that are what they are, in part, due to the legal panorama in which the parties operate. The same can be said of the invisible hand. Hayek was particularly insightful to recognize that his various principles, the final one of which was the rule of law, pretty much would serve the same function and were, therefore, more or less perfect substitutes.

There is some irony in Hayek's choice of the rule of law to serve where his other principles are inadequate for his purposes. On the one hand, law is seemingly denigrated. Such vilification is common to most adherents to the doctrines of an invisible hand. On the other hand, however, it is the law itself that is praised, however much the argument is made conditional. Emphasis on the rule of law serves, first, to establish and legitimize the legal process as instrumental, if not hegemonic, in the ongoing reconstruction of law. The legal process is never hegemonic in isolation, however; it, too, is a function of the inputs made to it – perhaps ultimately, one may say, a function of social structure, power play, and language use. The second function of the concept of the rule of law is to obfuscate government as an object of capture and use, and thereby the operations of social conflict, social control, and choice in the social reconstruction of legal-economic reality. This includes but encompasses more than the tendency to identify law in rule-of-law contexts with status quo law. It also includes the process of the selective specification and specific reconstruction of the status quo, all of which are part of the process of lawmaking.

Law itself is a substitute for combat; or rather, law substitutes ideational for physical combat. There is much to be said for this. The case can be made, however, for not treating law as a myth and for not pretending both that it is not a myth and that it is an ontological absolute. People have outgrown other myths, such as the divine rule of monarchy, the divine nature of institutions, the innate inferiority of women and of blacks and other people of color, and so on. People have learned to live with rules as rules and with change of rules as change of rules – even when they are offended by them. They sense that law is policy; they have policy consciousness as to the nature and operation of institutions. Pretense to the contrary may be given lip service – and believed by some – but human social maturation seems to lead in the opposite direction.

Arguments supporting the concept of the rule of law are almost indistinguishable from claims that stable law is necessary for economic growth. Neither position is entirely false but neither is entirely correct. Claims for the necessary stability of law are generally deployed against particular undesired proposed changes in the law. As a whole, however, the claims are descriptively inaccurate: Entrepreneurial activity itself generates the need for new law, or for change of old law, both as an intended means and as an unintended by-product. Such is another ironic aspect of the use of the concept of the rule of law. The economic system called capitalism is characterized by more change of law than any other economic system; such change is part of what Joseph Schumpeter called creative destruction. The question is not whether there will or will not be law, as one might think from disputes over particular laws or particular identities given the invisible hand. The question is which law will be used to structure the economy through the capture and use of government.

There is an inevitable clash of mentalities between those who seek determinacy, certitude, and closure, and those who are comfortable with ambiguity and open-endedness. There is an apparently unusually high rate of growth of language in market or capitalist economies.

There seems to be a powerful association between rhetoric and substantive economic life that has become a feature of capitalistic development. This is presumably true of all modern economic systems but is especially noticeable in capitalism, an important source being the faster and more complex pace of socioeconomic change. Economic development promotes linguistic development: not just advertising rhetoric, but entire specialist ways of communicating that reflect in part the specialization produced by the division of labor and the stylized talk within particular institutions, such as central banks.

The actual situation is arguably that of the ultimate necessity of choice – choice that is obfuscated by the use of the concepts of the rule of law and the invisible hand. For the philosophical idealist, the inexorable necessity of choice arises because each idealist likely has a different notion of the ideal, between which choice somehow must be made. For the philosophical realist, even if everyone were a philosophical realist, the necessity of choice arises because of their conflicting definitions of reality, between which choice somehow must be made.

The ideas presented in the preceding paragraph underscore the almost incomprehensible range and complexity of the larger system in which the idea of rule of law and invisible hand exists. In the study of such topics, when one seeks to get to the bottom of things and not be seduced by the particulars of individual theories of various kinds or by pet formulations, one will inexorably find that the necessity and actuality of choice intrudes at almost every turn. And, as if in defiance of the claims of believers in the rule of law and/or the invisible hand, the operative problem soon becomes that of who is to control and use government for what purposes; or, more broadly, who is to control and use the legal-economic nexus for the purposes of continuity or change.

Recognition of the mythic nature of the concepts of the rule of law and the invisible hand could possibly engender less opportunity for dissimulation and manipulation. Recognition that law and morals constitute policy and that law is being made possibly can enable a change from the invocation of given transcendental absolutes to the discussion of ends and means. As Carl Menger argued, every generation has as its highest calling the deliberative consideration of the possible reform of the folly of received institutions. Such consideration is thwarted, or selectively channeled, by the absolutist formulation of principles of law and otherwise.

The operative situation is the burden of choice. The functional alternative to its recognition is the selective abdication of choice. The alternative to explicit recognition of the nonmythic nature of law is elite control of both the exercise and change of law. Those who treat law as something given and transcendent are law takers. They abdicate their participation in the process of making law. They leave the domain of law (and policy) to the lawmakers. These are the people who know that law is something made, an object of control and use, and act to enlist it in support of their or their clients' interests. They practice, even if they do not preach, a ubiquitous pragmatism, promoting those legal means that suit their ends.

To most people, law is akin to a foreign language: If you need it, it is there, available to be used, added to or changed. Normally people pursue the activities and relationships that constitute their private lives, ignoring direct or indirect participation in lawmaking, in order to attend to their interests and preferences as to how they use their time and energy. Their attention to and participation in civic or collective action is pragmatic. When they have a problem in, say, their occupational field, they very likely will resort to demonstrations, lobbying, and litigation – in other words, some form of collective action. The situation is one of opportunity cost. The opportunity cost of preoccupation with the activities and relationship constituting their private lives is akin to John Kenneth Galbraith's argument in *The Affluent Society* (Galbraith 1969) in the starvation of public life. They are law takers.

Two additional ironies arise. One is preaching absolutes while practicing pragmatism. (This is so common as to possibly preclude a judgment of irony.) The other is the use of concepts such as the rule of law and the invisible hand as weapons, wherein their *raison d'être* is to substitute civility and reason for force and fraud. That being the case, if enough force and fraud is avoided, the substitution may be a wise one. It depends on whose interests are protected and whose are left exposed in the substitution.

At bottom, law *is* politics – politics by other means. Law could be seen as such. Doing so, however, would tend to end mystification consequent to the idea of the "rule of law." It has been a modern mode of absolutist legitimization that has replaced or supplemented the "divine right of kings" in the strategic, linguistic game of justification. There it serves, having been joined by the invisible hand. Possibly, if the invisible hand antedates the divine right of kings, it is the latter that has joined the former. Perhaps their genesis was common.

One might not ascertain one of my major points from reading Hayek's writings and those of his disciples. They are worth reading. Hayek had a brilliant mind, and he was a serious historian of economic and social thought. Some of his followers have the same qualities. Those who unite in spirit with Hayek and urge, "Right on!" may well miss or attempt to finesse or distinguish the point away. Others may exclaim, "Say, what is going on here?"

What I have in mind is a characterization of what Hayek was doing in his lectures, speeches, and writings, what his ideas were all about. I have tried to make it clear that Hayek was a prescriptive theorist of the first rank with regard to questions of social order. There is more, however, to what a person says than is necessarily evident from their specific words and particular argumentation. In Hayek's case, and in the case of many economists and other scholars, the subtext is of enormous importance. I need not repeat his particular ideas and their history. The character of his ideas as policy requires attention with all possible candor and with neither accommodation nor compromise; otherwise, one is vulnerable to complicity in fomenting intrigue among those "who have an [intellectual if no other] interest to deceive and even to oppress the public, and who accordingly have, upon many occasions, both deceived and oppressed it" (Smith 1976a: I.xi, 267).

Friedrich Hayek sought to venerate institutions as of human origin but not of human design; to elevate anticonstructivism over constructivism; to have the principle of unintended and unforeseen or unexpected consequences ranked, in its normative form, as a forceful warning against having an activist agenda of social improvement, in all respects befitting an economist not to seek to improve the world (which is a principal reason why many economists chose economics as their college program and life's work). My point is that notwithstanding Hayek's own remonstrations, Hayek, along with numerous other Austrian School economists, have sought to conceive, create, and/or reform institutions of distinctly human design. In doing so he was in effect employing Menger's drill about the necessity to evaluate received institutions and reform them when and where necessary. That is precisely what both his insistent criticisms of existing government policies and his proposed reforms amount to.

In other words, Hayek is engaging in the very same activities that he condemns in others. Consequently, those whom he criticizes for their transgressions of the principles of his propaganda for economic freedom (to again employ Knight's language) can respond with *tu quoque* ("You also").

Hayek shares with his fellow Austrian School and Mont Pelerin Society members and with the lawyerly Federalist Society, where I suspect he has numerous supporters, a particular characteristic. That characteristic is a disjunction between, on the one hand, his sensitive and well-developed normative case (albeit one amenable to fundamental criticism) and, on the other hand, his sensitive and sometimes profound understanding of power as a problem in human society. The Austrian School as a whole has never come to grips with the two prongs of their work: the normative treatment of freedom and the nonnormative (positivist) treatment of power. Which is to say, that whereas the Austrian School economists are extremely quick to seize on and denigrate various activities by government as a threat to freedom, they have not done so in regard, for example, to the meaning of power for freedom, the varieties of freedom and of power and the relation among them, and the meaning of freedom and power for welfare economics. There are exceptions, of course. I have in mind, for example, Vilfredo Pareto, Joseph Schumpeter, and Frank Knight.

When an Austrian School economist and/or his or her alter ego are asked why they have not studied these latter questions, their response generally takes several different forms: Power is unimportant, freedom *is*. Markets prevent, control, and limit power. Under certain circumstances, markets may not be strictly competitive but by their very nature, markets are competitive at least insofar as power is diffused. The problem of our time is the concentrated power of government, not that of private business. I have even been told that, well, yes, concentration of business power, even if only in regard to its role in campaign financing and its influence in, if not control of, government, is a (more or less) serious problem. But power can only be checked by power, and having government power attempt to control business power would both extend government power and leave the rest of us caught between two leviathans. One set of responses includes the following: that no economics journal would be interested in such an article; the manuscript could not survive the review process; it would be difficult, if not impossible, to recruit qualified referees; the theories of power in other disciplines (anthropology, political sociology, general social theory, history, law, and so on) do not have the intellectual potency, capabilities, authority, dominance, (yes, power), and prestige of economic theory. Here we see both at work and some of the results of the combination of protocols (and their enforcement methods) and ironies discussed in Essay 1, Section 1.1.

The first and second generations of Austrian School (trained or influenced) economists did not fail to introduce into their more normative discussions their findings with regard to power. I have in mind particularly Carl Menger, Vilfredo Pareto, and Friedrich von Wieser, but not Eugen von Böhm-Bawerk.

8.15. Conclusion

I would summarize my view of Hayek thusly: His deep study in many realms of social theory enabled him to develop a system of thought much richer than his ideological position might lead one to expect. Hayek has given both his own normative solution to what Joseph Spengler called the problem of order and his own positive analysis of what is involved as humankind works out the problem of order (for a view that includes Hayekian ideas, see Samuels 1996b). That situation leads to a curious dilemma: The more one emphasizes his ideological position, the more question-begging it becomes, based on his own broader analysis; the more one emphasizes his complete system of thought, including his positive analysis, the more open-ended and inconclusive his ideological position becomes when applied to questions of policy.

Many, if not most, of the people who have been attracted to Hayek's work, I think, have done so because of his ideological position and the subtlety and depth of its construction. These people tend to fail to appreciate the nature and import of his larger system – and will probably find the interpretation given here to be repugnant. But if one thinks about my interpretation, Hayek is a major figure in both realms: that of the propaganda for economic freedom and that of general social theory. When one combines the two, as it were, as I have tried to do here, one ends up with a variable set of Hayekian forces: nondeliberative and deliberative social control – yes, ironically, social control. To say that any one set is a set of reasonable but readily rebuttable presumptions is rather further ironic, inasmuch as rebuttable presumptions seem to be from the deliberative, not the nondeliberative realm. An old expression says that a demand for rights is a demand for government. That is true here: The Hayekian demand for certain principles is a demand for a public or civic sector in which that demand for certain principles will successfully interact with comparable demands by others.

As for the problems of the practice of the rule of law, the source of the difficulties may be that the concept of rule of law is more broadly applied or used than is warranted. At the very least, the response to the difficulties may simply be the view that the law should be known in advance of action and that the law should be applied to all people equally, although the latter is difficult and thus problematic. Wealth effects clearly operate here. How the founding fathers, and others, subsequently interpreted the constitution, how they voted or took positions on issues, and so on seem to be matters very different than the application of, say, the criminal law to potential defendants. Be that as it may, however, the vast literature on official discretion, much of it relating to the concept of the rule of law, surely supports the belief that officials at all levels inexorably exercise discretion. The policeman, the prosecuting attorney, the judge, the jury, the appellate courts – each has opportunity, even the necessity, to exercise discretion. The various notions of the rule of law reflect several values. These include the desires to treat people equitably, to obfuscate the actual making of choices, to cast luster on or glorify the existing system and its personnel and operation, and so on. These words were initially written during the period in early 2010 when some lawyers who represented terrorist suspects in pretrial hearings were called un-American by certain critics. Similar treatment was accorded lawyers of accused communists, civil rights defendants, and organized crime.

The problems readily found with the concept of the rule of law in practice overwhelmingly derive from the nature of the subject. Government is essentially a choosing process; government is involved with choosing between values, interests, and so on. The adoption, the administration, and the enforcement of law involve at every level the ultimate necessity to choose between alternatives. There is no way to, in effect, square the circle and treat people equally. This is not solely the paradox of having to treat unequals equally, as discussed earlier in this essay. It is a matter of having to make choices that render people unequal. For example, if Alpha and Beta, otherwise equal, are in the same field of action, and an issue of, say, who can do what to whom arises, scarcity exists in the sense that the conflicting interests of both parties cannot be protected, that is, Alpha-Beta rights conflicts, also examined earlier. Moreover, the term "rule of law" is a primitive term insofar as the content of the law is not specified. The choice necessary to be made between two arguably "good, decent, and just" laws is one scenario. Another scenario involves the choice between one of those laws and a law that is manifestly monstrous. Still another scenario of frustration and grief arises, as it must, when a rule, rather than overt discretion, is chosen and it becomes all too evident that discretion must be exercised in determining how that rule is to be administered or applied. My observation is that the affirmation of the rule of law by U.S. officials when preaching to foreign governments must appear very differently when other U.S. officials, possibly the same personages, also trash some aspect of it.

It is ironic that government (or any agency of social control or decision making) is called on to ensure that necessary decisions are made. Antagonism toward government inexorably arises and tends to grow because the governing agency must make choices and in doing so aggravates some people. A more conventional but also ironic formulation posits that government is the site/institution/process where the most difficult problems are confronted – with the same result.

Pluralistic, democratic societies have several solutions for such animosity. (I acknowledge that "democracy," "rule of law," and comparable words are primitive [undefined] terms, and discourse using them lacks specificity. I have come to appreciate how difficult it is to complete a paper if one tries to clarify all such words.) Appellate processes and institutions must be available so as to avoid absolute authority. Another is provision of selection processes, open meetings, and so on to enable participation by an array of potentially disaffected as well as average persons. Still another is the careful construction of statutes, particularly in "prescribing within limits ... defining more or less specifically the scope of the agents' discretionary powers" (Knight 1960: 27).

Problems arise, of course, even in democratic societies. One problem is the result of reliance on an obfuscating absolutist formulation coupled with officials motivated by status emulation and belief in their own press releases, or decisions. Secondly, at some level, a final decision must be made for most, if not all, practical purposes for this case and for this complainant.

Thirdly, many of the circumstances in which government is called on to act involve having to choose between good or between bad. When government gets involved, as it must, in determining whether Alpha's power must be controlled or Beta be left exposed to Alpha's power, the question of the power of government itself often gets raised. But, as I have emphasized, power is involved willy-nilly.

I said a few paragraphs back that the source of the difficulties found with the concept and practice of the rule of law may be that it is more broadly applied or used than is warranted. It may well be, however, that the concept of the rule of law is going to be and perhaps should be more, not less, broadly applied or used. In fact, it is likely that the educational role of government moves people in that direction. I have in mind that due-process-type rules develop in nongovernmental fields, often characterized as the use of power to check power. It is precisely of this that much of the activism by government consists.

Likely more important than the aforementioned, however, are several other considerations. First, no conventional identity of an invisible hand with its presumptuous potential array of functions is likely to grab the headlines, if only because of the checkered reputation of the Smithian one. Secondly, invisible-hand processes are likely to become increasingly deeply studied. Thirdly, I want to make a point that is intractable but nonetheless important. I have criticized the practice of libertarians and others for applying to ordinary law the criticisms that Smith brought against mercantilism. My point here is that capitalism is more dependent on law and general social control than was the combination of monarchy and landed aristocracy and gentry. I infer from that point one corollary, namely that the capitalist nations of today have more law than did postfeudal nations of Smith's time (admittedly, even emphatically, impossible to prove); a second corollary, that there will be in the future more of both collective deliberative and nondeliberative decision making/social control; and a third, that with at least two recognitions, increased *private sector* "rule of law" will take place. One is increased recognition of problems of power (inequality) in the nominally private sector; the other is experience with and/or knowledge of due-process/rule-of-law institutions in the public sector. The two things together can overcome the metaphysics and ideology of the private-public dichotomy and its accompanying laissez-faire attitudes. The foregoing does not necessarily imply significantly less business control of government or of the new institutions; nor does it imply either necessarily greater or lesser economic growth. It may not even imply a reduced role for the concept of the invisible hand in the formulation of economic policy.

9

The Survival Requirement of Pareto Optimality

9.1. Introduction

The perceived need for the application of economic theory to economic policy – to improve society – is a declared motive of many people who become economists. Moreover, the same need is the principal technical purpose for using the concept of the invisible hand in technical economics. That this constitutes a negation of laissez-faire, however defined, is obviously significant. Consider the evident conflict with Hayek's principles. Of course, he contradicts them himself. Among other things, users of the invisible-hand concept seem to think that it facilitates the satisfactory fulfillment of the protocols under which contemporary economic theorizing and its applications take place (see Section 1.1). One need not be a cynic (although it might help) to grasp that advocates of Hayek's principles tend to apply them differently as between economies that they consider socialist and those they feel are capitalist; or that they can reach very different conclusions when a policy is evaluated using Hayek's principles. Consideration of the putative functions of the (imagined) invisible hand in Essay 3 reveals that almost every formulation centers on that task, the remaining functions being more or less substitutes for those that do and typically are treated as if they do. Much criticism is directed at the exclusion of recondite, intransigent, or uncomfortable variables; adopting assumptions that enable reaching ostensibly unique determinate results; making implicit antecedent premises; using skewed definitions of policy problems; finessing problems such as externalities and consideration of justice; massaging data and definitions; and applying theory based on a purely conceptual economy to the putatively actually existing economy despite the former being institutionally empty, with little or no examination of the correspondence of the conceptual and actual economies. Fields such as international trade have identified numerous analytical difficulties in pursuing free trade, however that term is defined.

It is neither my desire nor my need to invoke such criticisms as limitations on invisible-hand reasoning. Nor is it my wish to model a purely conceptual economy that will accomplish the reverse. I do want to examine several important problems. One problem arises with the use of concepts relating to income as "earned" and "unearned," and which turn on the definition of "productivity."

Western ideology postulates that income received without violation of the criminal law may be reckoned to have been earned, and that the acquisition of such income should be protected, not inhibited, by government. The vituperative criticism by Henry George of the unearned increment due to rent, for example, was predicated on a Malthus-Ricardo belief that people who receive truly productive incomes are compromised/disadvantaged insofar as people receive income not associated with productivity. Historically, the genesis of economic rent derives from past acts of monarchical and other favoritism, special treatment, and predatory behavior that resulted in very high percentages of landownership held in a small percentage of families, the effective attachment of political rights of governance to economic rights, and the like.

The existence of manifest inequalities aggravates some people and worries others. Not everyone applies productivity-based reasoning to incomes considered by some to be unearned. But certainly widespread is the evident desire that incomes be considered legitimate. These would include windfall profits, the capture of income by convincing legislatures and courts that one and only set of interests warrant remuneration, the increase in land values due to population growth, and so on.

It may be objected that the unearned-income argument is subjective and that its deployment would open the door to widespread revision of the many laws bearing on the distributions of opportunities, income, and wealth. Indeed, it may be objected that under such a regime, anything would go. But that is precisely the case with existing arrangements. A careful study of the actions of legislatures and courts on all levels will provide evidence of the ubiquity of successful (and unsuccessful) efforts by otherwise upstanding and conservative interests to redirect the distribution of income and wealth in their favor. Perhaps it is inevitable that the legal-economic nexus (read: political economy) will operate that way. It is not inevitable, however, that the existing (or *some* proposed) arrangement will be predicated on productivity and not manipulation of the law. The use of economics, such as productivity theory, and jurisprudence, such as the trope that law is found and not made, in both cases pretending to a nonexistent and contrived unique determinacy, does not prevent "anything goes" but does give effect to the accumulated partisan incremental definition, assignment, and structure of rights. The general rule is that prices and resource allocation are not simply a matter of supply and demand otherwise unadorned. The structure of rent, rights, externalities, and so on governs whose interest is to count.

Two propositions in economics tend to get advocates' juices flowing and their blood boiling. One is that much of the development of the theory of distribution (in economics) has been driven by controversies over the distributions of opportunity, income, and wealth both within and outside of economics. The other is that the structure of power governs the structure of distribution. Pareto was the author of a law that bears his name: that the distributions of income, wealth, and opportunity are much the same in all nations despite differences of name and form. He is also well known for his work on the circulation of, or among, the elite. Such activities are placed in a model of society that has several major interacting forces that usefully reduce to (1) belief, including forms of knowledge, (2) psychic states, and (3) power – or knowledge, power, and psychology in a system of mutual manipulation (see Pareto 1963, Samuels 1974a). For many conservative economists, "power" is not to be discussed in public.

Government is already, irresistibly and inevitably, being used to determine winners and losers, and/or getting off some people's backs and getting on others' backs. Indeed, such users, such use, and such results – and there are many of all three – provide ubiquitous examples of Pareto's emphases on the economy as a vast process of power and mutual manipulation (Robert Lee Hale's "mutual coercion") and a fundamentally Hayekian consideration of unintended and unexpected consequences. Another example is the seemingly incongruous combination of a harmonistic theory of optimality and a conflictual theory of interaction. Such a combination is, or can be, as Pareto insisted, quite flexible. The same piece of ideology-laden reasoning often can be deployed to both support and undermine a position, depending on the particular components comprising the targets' psychic states. Defenders of inequality tend to deploy to stress. Such criticism opens the door to changing the law, one way or another. One larger issue is control of the state itself. One immediate issue is how much of their income must the rich surrender in taxes to the state to finance all of the latter's activities, including welfare programs, with the cost of welfare and similar programs effectively constituting a bribe enabling the well-to-do to continue to enjoy their dominance. Critics of the bribe system will stress that such taxes are confiscation by the state; the defenders will counter that such is the price of change from one level of social maturation to another, in a manner likely not very different from what Smith meant in saying that changes in law and government would be the major defining characteristic of movement from one stage to another.

9.2. The Survival Requirement of Pareto Optimality

The example of earned income leads us to the principal problem examined in this essay. Here, we raise and treat seriously the question of survival, and do so in two contexts. First, in most countries, including the United States, there are insufficient institutional guarantees that poor individuals and their progeny, poor for whatever reason, will not be at great risk of premature death due to lack of access to medical care, food, and housing. Second, throughout the planet, the reigning preoccupation with making money and emulating the high status and increasing real income levels enjoyed by the politically and economically powerful elites – most people seem to feel that more goods are better than less – has led to the threatened extinction of all life, including humans, on the planet, possibly through the effects of global warming by various types of pollution and other practices of business and government.

The problem arises from a defect in the well-nigh universal but incomplete use of Paretian welfare economics for purposes of policy. Most economic theorists are scholars who take pride in (what they understand to be) the complete and correct logicality of their theoretical work (quite aside from the realism of their assumptions or the predictive power of their conclusions). The defect is the failure to satisfy the survival requirement comprised of both positive and normative elements applied to individual and mass survival. One positive point is that, to the extent that mainstream economic theory employs marginal analysis, the process to which it is applied, to be logically complete, that is, to have logicality, must be one of only marginal adjustments. *Death, however, is not a marginal adjustment.* The argument, so encapsulated, is as simple as that. Individuals may perish earlier than they otherwise would have to because government and private-sector decision and policy makers treated something as a matter only of comparative margins (see further in this essay) or were not mindful of whether mankind is capable of survival under the conditions of life generated by policy.

We have been discussing analytical and normative conflicts, on the one hand, between income as based on productivity and as due to economic

(Ricardian or Georgian) rent, and, on the other hand, the analytical and normative conflicts between the use and disregard (nonuse) of Pareto optimality as a decision rule, specification, construction block and/or concept of what is "best" in economics. Both problems cast a logical, quite aside from a moral, cloud over the conventional formulation of economic theory and its application to policy. It should be apparent that acceptance and/or obfuscation of the use of policies generating either problem have much to do with the control of government and its policies and their roles in the institutions through which the fundamental distributions of power, opportunity, wealth, and income are established and managed in every society.

Every phrase or clause that you have been reading has both its positive and its normative elements. Among the positive points are the logicality requirement, knowledge of externality relationships, and the modes of control and use of government in one's society (each capable of being selectively perceived). Among the normative points (and also capable of being selectively perceived) are, among others, the value assigned in decision making to the logicality requirement, the value o life, and the belief in having an economy of private enterprise and private property. The latter belief is held and deployed notwithstanding the fact that both private enterprise and private property are *social* institutions presumably predicated – for most, if not all, instances – on considerations of *social purpose*, including pragmatic and instrumental ones, and not solely, if at all, on the individualist perceptions and justifications displayed in arguments between individuals (and their attorneys), and lauded as if arguments predicated on *social* purpose are *socialist* in nature. Such people tend not to think of law, and even government, as social institutions, that is, as not discussable in any linguistic system other than one that treats them in individualist terms. Yet such folks participate in collective activities and institutions that establish and change the rules for various activities, though apparently typically turning against institutions that do not support their particular personal interests. They may combine lines of reasoning – for example, (1) individualism with naturalism and/or supernaturalism, (2) methodological individualism with methodological collectivism, (3) normative individualism with normative collectivism, and so on, simultaneously and/or sequentially, depending (as Pareto stressed in his theory of derivations) on the psychic states/belief systems/mindsets of those whose political and social preferences (with regard to continuity versus change, freedom [read: autonomy] versus control, and hierarchy versus equality) it is their purpose to manipulate. The perceptive reader will appreciate that such flexibility, multiplicity, and substitutability of lines of reasoning apply to the use of the concept of the invisible hand itself, involving witting or unwitting specification of identity and function, separately or in combination, as is evident in Essay 3. Indeed, the pragmatic flexibility, multiplicity, and substitutability of lines of reasoning is characteristic of all systems of belief or propaganda, including those said by adherents and others to pertain to economic freedom, and to most, if not all, students of ideology and propaganda. Also bearing on this discussion is the assumption, emphasized by James M. Buchanan and others, that one aspect of Pareto optimality is *consent*. The actual element of consent, however, is much narrower than Buchanan and others seem to suggest. Not all scholars are somehow attempting through their objective and scholarly work to create their propaganda for some version of economic freedom. Moreover, affirmation can be countered by disciplinary colleagues who are displeased with the term, with the revision(s) contemplated and/or in the manner newly available to them as an option. This may be because they too continue to think of the term as a primitive term or use the term to promote the group's point of view. Many discussions in Essays 3, 4, 5, 7, and 8 are also applicable to the present topics as well. Among the themes found therein are: that human beings cannot identify the meaning of words from their use; that language is political in nature; that definitions are often adopted to influence people's beliefs and to motivate and channel their behavior. A new development may exist relatively inconspicuously, having been absorbed, as it were, by interested persons in its field.

9.3. Some History of the Treatment and Disregard of the Survival Requirement in High Theory

Several eminent modern economic theorists, none generally seen as purveyors of an ideological position, have accepted, even emphasized, a survival requirement as a condition of resource allocation through markets, *ceteris paribus* the mode of receiving income and the structure of its distribution. The technical requirement of survival was recognized by Kenneth Arrow and Gerard Debreu in their epochal 1954 articles that helped transform price theory and welfare economics as well as invisible-hand thinking on the basis of their formulation of Pareto optimality. For example, in one article, Debreu articulated the survival requirement in the same sentence with the nonnegativity requirement regarding the quantity of commodities consumed, writing, "and, moreover, they [the quantity of commodities consumed] must enable the individual to survive" (Debreu 1954: 588). In a jointly authored article published the same year, Arrow and Debreu took up the "conditions under which the equations of competitive equilibrium have a solution" (Arrow and Debreu 1954: 265). The economics was, in ret-rospect, both driven by and obfuscated by the mathematics. For example, they recognized that "to have equilibrium, it is necessary that each individ-ual possess some asset or be capable of supplying some labor service that commands a positive price at equilibrium" (idem: 270). This is the logical equivalent of assuming the survival of market actors.

Paul A. Samuelson, in a 1977 discussion of the invisible hand and other matters, published under the title, "A Modern Theorist's Vindication of Adam Smith," stated that his "general finding ... provides a vindication of Adam Smith and serves, in my mind at least, to raise his stature as an economic theorist, both absolutely and in comparison with his predecessors and successors" (Samuelson 1977: 42). That is high praise indeed, coming from the foremost economist in history.

Samuelson brought to his readers' attention the key point that "precisely the *competitive* equilibrium conditions under Smith's postulated produc-tion conditions ... identifies a valid element in Smith's INVISIBLE HAND doctrine: *self-interest, under perfect conditions of competition, can organize a society's production efficiently.* (But, there need be nothing ethically opti-mal about the [consumption] specifications and their allocations among the rich and poor, the healthy and the halt!)" (idem: 47). A narrow reading of that language could focus on another defect of the new mainstream pol-icy apparatus, namely, the failure to stress that more than one optimal solu-tion to a problem exists and it is the determination and exercise of rights that importantly tends to generate the achieved solution and not vice versa. Rights cannot logically properly depend solely on solutions, for the achieved solution is a function of rights. (Rights do depend on solutions insofar as those included in solutions affect esteem and the ability to further influence law making.) A broader, richer, and more meaningful reading would also include consideration of the survival problem. (A. Alan Schmid had argued for years that different distributions of assets meant that no unique deter-minate equilibrium existed. The latter is the basis of the circularity problem in law and economics. The conflict over the uniqueness and normative nature of the actual Pareto-optimal solution was intense. The uniqueness and normative character issues received vastly more attention than did the issue of the survival requirement. For Koopmans treatment of rights, see idem; 14.)

Twenty years before Samuelson acknowledged the relevance and importance of an ethical requirement of Pareto optimality, Tjalling C. Koopmans, in his *Three Essays on the State of Economic Science*, surveyed and critiqued the economics of the allocation of resources and the price system, particularly the mathematical welfare economics of competitive equilibrium and Pareto optimality authored by Arrow and Debreu. Koopmans began his relevant discussion by saying that "[t]he hardest part in the specification of the model is to make sure that each consumer can both survive and participate in the market" (Koopmans 1957: 59). He had earlier noted that the foundation of the equilibrium model requires "some particular distribution of rights to the income from ownership of resources and from profitable production" (idem: 54), such that "the attainable set, that is, the intersection of the sum of all supply sets with the sum of all consumption sets[,] is not empty. Otherwise, not all consumers could survive, *a situation not contemplated in the definition of a Pareto optimum* we are using" (idem: 55 [emphasis added]). He noted that several earlier authors, such as Arrow and Debreu, had assumed, first, that the "aggregate supply set contains a point which supplies just a little more of every commodity than is necessary ... for every consumer to survive," and second, that "each consumer can, if necessary, survive on the basis of the resources he holds and the direct use of his own labor ..." (idem: 59). He strikingly concluded, however, that "most authors have ignored the analytical difficulty of formulating a model that ensures the possibility of survival, blithely admitting any nonnegative rates of consumption as sustainable." Koopmans presented four principal solutions (plus an additional two variations) to the "question of the survival of consumers in the Arrow-Debreu model of competitive equilibrium."

First, "given a stationary-state interpretation, it would be found best suited for describing a society of self-sufficient farmers who do a little trading on the side" (idem: 62).

Secondly, in modern society, "[o]ne 'hard-boiled' alternative would be to assume instantaneous elimination by starvation of those whose resources prove insufficient for survival, and to look for conditions ensuring existence of an 'equilibrium' involving survival of some consumers" (idem: 62).

Thirdly, "[a]n alternative more realistic for highly industrialized private enterprise societies would be to recognize the existence of income transfers through taxation and social insurance, and to look for conditions, including tax and benefit schedules, ensuring general survival in an equilibrium" (idem: 62).

A fourth alternative would be to specify lower limits on the productivity of the various types of labor ... [and] upper limits on ... minima for subsistence, so as to ensure the possibility of survival of all consumers through the sale of their labor whenever other resources are insufficient ..." (idem: 62).

A fifth alternative is said to be "a more subtle version" of the "hard-boiled" model. Each consumer's life plan would specify "the length of life compatible with his present resources, his ability to do remunerative work or shift for himself, and other aspects of his life plan. All that is to be assured by the postulates is survival of every consumer at least into the first period. The amount and initial distribution of resources and skills in the population determine the pace and extent, if any, of starvation" (idem: 62–3). The question thus must shift to the determination of individual life plans, notably individual longevity and quality of life. It is not clear that survival can be assured only ("at least") into the first period (idem: 63)

It is important to recognize Koopmans' understanding of what he is doing. He identifies his approach as follows: The first essay of this book is an attempt to communicate the logical content, and some of the underlying reasoning. It argues that, with the help of more fundamental mathematical tools, the common logical structure of received economic theories of quite diverse origin can be brought out. The descriptive theory of competitive equilibrium and the normative theory of the use of prices for the efficient allocation of resources appear as twin sides of one coin. It urges a clearer separation, in the construction of economic knowledge, between reasoning and recognition of facts (idem: vii–viii). He insists that: [T]he distinction between descriptive and normative applications is extraneous to the model. Whether a statement derived from the postulates of the model is used descriptively or normatively depends not on the logical content of the statement but on the extent to which the choices with which the model deals are regarded as subject to the influence of the user of the analysis (idem: 64).

I now turn to the reception given Koopmans' raising of the survival problem. There is not much of substance to report here, but what can be reported is immensely important. The survival problem, which Koopmans treated at length and in detail in *Three Essays*, was ignored by many, if not most, reviewers of the book, including Andreas G. Papandreou (1958) and Murray Brown (1958). John S. Chipman treated the survival problem but did so essentially obliquely. He specified the problem as having "to do with the characterization of the boundary of subsistence." Chipman made the remarkable, if not fascinating, claim that:

[m]ost writers in this field are[,] moreover, somewhat embarrassed by the fact that they must introduce a postulate to guarantee that productive capacity is high enough (or subsistence level low enough) to ensure equilibrium above subsistence; this appears quite close to assuming one's conclusion in advance. However, it should be recognized that if some such accident of nature had not come about, we would not be on earth to theorize about it, and that some economists *have* perished. It

would be of interest to explore the consequences of the introduction of a Malthusian dynamic mechanism of adjustment, or a postulate concerning automatic redistributive methods of avoiding starvation (taking in of relatives, featherbedding, etc.). (Chipman 1959: 448)

Robert M. Solow acknowledged the survival problem by dismissing it, saying that "the attention paid to the problem of the survival of consumers beyond the first period of a multiperiod model strikes me as a bit of misplaced concreteness" (Solow 1958: 178–9).

Examination of the reviews of Koopmans' *Three Essays* and of the subsequent literature makes it readily apparent that the reviewers and other writers have not refrained from calling attention to serious issues with the mathematization of economic theory and with the economic theory itself, so long as the body of economic theorists is interested in them. Examples include: the assumptions of finiteness and convexity, external economies affecting production and consumption, the representation of firms as coalitions of economic agents, compensated equilibrium, a weakened sense of irreducibility, the proofs of various lemmas, free disposal (interiority), the relation of coordination to economies of scale, and so on. Another group could include: variety in specification and in interpretation as to relevance; explicit recognition of a survival requirement; indication that an author is not impressed with the survival-requirement argument; it may be the most activist requirement aiming at competitive equilibrium; no clear explication of the survival requirement; to many economists, Koopmans' third solution smacks of socialism, implying that the very *idea* of a survival requirement is anticompetitive; a variety of formulations of the mode of achieving equilibrium and therefore of bringing about the required survival; and that nontechnical considerations have dominated both treatment and status. Discussion raises the question of whether and when moral and ideological considerations can/should take precedence over the technical requirements of economic theory, especially in the event – the typical event, I should say – of a core comprised of a set of more than one possible determinate solution. The reader is cautioned that the topics identified in both groups, especially the second, are largely the result of stretching credibility, through giving the benefit of the doubt to how much substantive content should be read into what may be merely mention. It is fair to say that the second list takes credulousness about as far as it can properly go, perhaps even beyond that point. The reason for bringing up what may be excessive laxity is not to unduly and unjustifiably enhance the reputation of high theorists in regard to the survival requirement, but to avoid failure to recognize their use of technical terms as shorthand. It is not my intention to retract or soften the conclusion that the makers of economic theory have neglected, even grossly neglected, the problem of logicality in the matter of the marginalism of Pareto optimality. Most follow, like lemmings, the conventional approach. No high theorist, however, seems to have taken up and advanced Koopmans's analysis of the survival requirement, even though, as we shall see, both other economists and noneconomists have, in various ways, unknowingly called attention to aspects of it.

If Koopmans was disappointed that the seeds he had planted did more widely germinated, he had to have been pleased with the receipt of the Nobel Prize. Moreover, the opportunity to draft his Nobel Memorial Lecture given on December 11, 1975, enabled him to elaborate his position along a number of lines. These included such questions as whether economics needed or could get along with but one definition of optimality. His opening paragraphs dramatically provided his answers:

According to a frequently cited definition, economics is the study of 'best use of scarce resources.' The definition is incomplete. 'Second best' use of resources, and outright wasteful uses, have equal claim to attention. They are the other side of the coin.

For our present purpose the phrase 'best use of resources' will suffice. However, each of the two nouns and two adjectives in this phrase needs further definition. These definitions in turn need to be varied and adjusted to fit the specific circumstances in which the various kinds of optimizing economic decisions are to be taken.

I will assume that the main interest of this gathering is in the range of applications of the idea of best use of resources, and in the ways in which the main categories of application differ from each other. (Koopmans 1976: 542)

Koopmans indicated in support of his position the varied nature of optimality already found in modeling technical production processes, its relevance to the problem of the scope of economics, its long history in economics, the sense incorporated in the notion of a "genuine optimization problem" (idem: 543); the wide range of brilliant minds that have already made important contributions; and the importance of institutions and the relations between institutions and market structures (idem: 546). Koopmans assigns considerable force to signals given by the present generation (548), to given objective functions (549), to the shifting from vectors space to function space (550); the impact of essential resource requirements (552); the survival period as a policy variable (553); population size as a decision variable (554), the problem of concern for present vis-à-vis future generations (555), and other important considerations. He concludes by noting that economists may create the pros and cons for criteria of optimality, but does not advocate them. "[T]he ultimate choice is made, usually only implicitly and not always consistently, by the procedure of decision making inherent in the institutions, laws and customs of society" (idem: 567).

In the fall of 2008, I wrote the following as part of a letter to Samuelson:

Recall that in Koopmans' *Three Essays on the State of Economic Science* (1957: 55–62), he argued that, at the very least, Pareto optimality requires the assumption or condition of a survival requirement. What reception was given his argument by other theorists and by the discipline as a whole? What is your view on the matter? (Warren J. Samuels to Paul A. Samuelson, October 7, 2008)

After examining the photocopied pages of Koopmans' *Three Essays*, Samuelson responded as follows:

I tend to connect "Pareto optimality" matters with both Arrow-Debreu "complete markets" as well as with Koopmans' *Three Essays*. Koopmans as a careful logician can be expected to worry explicitly about how to honor contracts between two people who might be capable of dying (or of going "bankrupt"). This is a legitimate preoccupation but not one that interests me a lot. (Samuelson to Samuels, November 20, 2008)

I found this response interesting but potentially evasive, as if there were something that Samuelson would rather not have publicly discussed. Koopmans was a careful logician and worried about honoring contracts in the eventuality of death or bankruptcy; these are neither entirely inappropriate nor totally irrelevant topics. They are, however, substantially irrelevant to what Koopmans had written. Let us allow Samuelson to speak for himself. His letter of November 20, 2008 continues:

Therefore, I submit to you a terse note that goes back to 1817 Ricardo–1848 J.S. Mill about wine and cloth comparative advantage competitive trade between England and Portugal. It is a case of interest because it might be the very first example of a general equilibrium. (See the "heresy" (?) in Paul Samuelson, *Journal of Economic Perspectives*, 2005.) Its equilibrium goes on in the stationary state forever when death rates and birth rates cancel out.

The point is this. Pareto's market price and production equations and unknowns *spell out the exact same story that would be spelled out by an engineer's maximizing solution* for how much 100 of I_{Port} and 100 of LEng can produce of (Global Cloth, Global Wine). What most conservative libertarian 35-year-olds fail to realize – and I put Friedman and Hayek in their company – is that there is nothing "ethically fair" in Arrow-Debreu Pareto-optimal equilibria. That's what market forces reach; but there is an infinity of *other* Pareto-optimal states not reached. Ask a Bentham-Rawls whether non-Pareto optimality A* is more fair than Pareto-optimal B* and here is the answer you could get: "Choose the non-Pareto optimal A* over the Arrow-Debreu Pareto-optimal B*.

It is more or less obvious, I think, that Samuelson was *sui generis*. He was at the top of several games – principally, but by no means only, economic theory, mathematics, and history of economic theory. I have no other reason to say so, other than to impress on the reader that Paul Anthony Samuelson was "the real deal," as the expression goes, by which I mean that he actually was what he was said to be and likely what he believed himself to be – that he more than measures up to what is said about him.

I have observed how individual economists are conspicuously the product of their advanced university training. They are also the products of the great issues of their times. The issues that were important to them and the positions they took on those issues were also of enormous importance. I want to make a point using some of the ideas of Friedrich Hayek, although without taking the view of them that seems contrived and ideological. The issues that influenced them were adopted by them both deliberatively and nondeliberatively. An overwhelming proportion of them were men and had professional academic careers.

In Samuelson's first paragraph in his letter of November 20, 2008, I found Samuelson's identification of several aspects of Koopmans' view of the world and of his place in it. Koopmans seems to have been attracted by the possibility of using complete contracts; he also has had some of the interests we tend to associate with lawyers, namely taking up potentially complex topics, such as death, which interfere with the joint plans formalized by contracts. In Samuelson's second paragraph in that letter, probably without conscious reasoning, he revealed his own career-long interest in international trade theory and policy. He called to my attention an episode of conflict between David Ricardo and other classical economists that, in Samuelson's view, "might be the very first example of a *general equilibrium*" (emphasis in the original).

Several things should be made clear. *Equilibrium* is a conceptual tool; it is very useful in analyzing the mutual impacts that the variables have on each other, but it is a conceptual construction. What goes on in equilibration may well represent more important characteristics of equilibrium, if only because the economy is so immense and so complex that we may only rarely be in a perceptual equilibrium. Even when we are in equilibrium, interactions and aggregations may be considered more important (the heart of invisible-hand processes (see Essay 10). I found it rather interesting that Samuelson went out of his way to provide me with his finding of what may have been the first – or at least an early – example of classical equilibrium theory. Why interesting? Well, in another letter to me (dated November 19, 2008, the day before the letter from Samuelson in which he declined to write an introduction to notes from Frank William Taussig [also Allyn Young and Thomas Nixon Carver], in Economics 11–12 at Harvard during the 1921–1922 academic year), Samuelson's reason for declining my invitation was that "I would not be a useful Foreword writer. My tastes are not antiquarian enough. It would not help book sales to say that this one dramatizes how much better contemporary ('Whig') economics is than back in 1921." This, despite the fact that his 1817 example from Ricardian trade theory is surely no less antiquarian than the 1921–1922 notes. Further, in his letter of November 20, 2008, Samuelson seems to accept Philip Mirowski's argument that nineteenth-century mathematics of energy was a common source of economists' use of mathematics.

When Samuelson wrote me about Taussig, he provided some interesting information. Having read some of the notes, he lamented that "[t]he reproduced copies are sometimes a bit hard for old eyes to read," but he went on to note "[s]urprising paucity of post-1890 Marshall influence. Much preoccupation with *definitions* of Smith-Ricardo-Mills-Cairnes-Walker-George" (Samuelson to Samuels, September 29, 2008). In his letter of November 19, 2008, he wrote that he "had hoped these items would enable post-2008 generations to overhear what prevailed in the Ivy League just after World War I. Taussig's Ec11 was a famous course from before 1913 and up to the 1935 autumn when Schumpeter for the first time took over both semesters for Ec11."

Candidly, I found Taussig's reflections on Mill, Cairnes, and Henry George light years away from standard present-day accounts of the post-1870 Jevons-Walras-Menger-Wicksteed-Wicksell transition from classicism to neoclassicism. Much of his is virtually pre-Marshall. (In personal conversation with him around 1937, Taussig confessed to me that after his 1916–1918 Washington service he felt unable to catch on to contemporary economic developments [i.e., contemporary developments of economic theory]).

What are we to make of the foregoing?

There is no doubt in my mind that no single explanation suffices to make sense of the behavior about which I have written here. As with explanations of the development of property rights, the causes and forms are numerous. If I understand correctly, the situation requires a compound explanation inclusive of the following as a major element.

In any event, I found in Samuelson's *obiter dicta* what appears to explain the treatment accorded Koopman's analysis of a survival requirement in Pareto Optimality.

We start with Alfred Marshall, the leading economic theorist of the late nineteenth and early twentieth centuries. Marshall was a very active person.

His activities were wide-ranging, important to others, and interesting. He was dedicated to the promotion of economics as a science. He also sought for economists to have the prestige of scientists. When I studied the period in detail, I felt that I could usefully specify the motivations of Marshall and of others like him in the following way. The prescriptions were not hidden under a barrel. Here are their motivations, as I interpreted their actions and statements:

1. Economists should have the status and esteem of men (which they principally were) of science.
2. Economists should have the related status of men of knowledge as experts in specialized fields.
3. Economists should have something to say about economic policy and the economic role of government, and thus be looked to for advice and recommendations.
4. Economists should engage in no activity that renders the discipline or the nation unsafe. Economics was to be rendered safe for the nation and the nation was to be rendered safe for economics.

These sources of status could be subsumed in a more comprehensive model, centering on knowledge, social control, and psychic balm. Pervading all sources was an identity crisis, comprising the name of the discipline; the identity and status of the founding fathers of the discipline; the identity and scope of the central problem of the discipline; and so on. The thread common to everything was (and continues to be) status emulation accompanied by conflict between objectivity and advocacy, and the irony that the activist advocacy of policy was to supplement an historic role advocating laissez-faire (see Samuels 1998 and 2000).

We are dealing with a cultural matter, itself ironic inasmuch as mainstream neoclassical economists would fairly commonly and quite invidiously compare economics as a science with (they claimed) the much softer study of culture. A principal clue was provided to me by Samuelson himself when he recommended that I examine his piece on Ricardo's recantation in his added chapter "On Machinery." Presently relevant to Samuelson was the argument that policy derived from Ohlin-Heckscher trade theory could permanently lower real wages. The reason was that Howard Ellis of Berkeley "persuaded the AER editor to turn down the Stolper-Samuelson submission" because "[i]t will weaken the case for free trade" (Samuelson 2005: 242). In an exchange of comments between Avinash Dixit and Samuelson, the idea of "muddling the case for free trade" is the principal doctrinal issue.

Why is that not only present but important? The Cambridge and Oxford dons who had chairs, professorships, and other positions, including appointment by or in the name of the reigning monarch, had the responsibility for the education and training of the upper classes. Their subtle interventions and the positions they took seem to me to have the rationale of "do not weaken the case for free trade or whatever." The adoption of a new and much more favorable rationale for British imperialism was intended to put a more acceptable face on national policy. The initial form of imperialism was the malevolent one. The ostensible new policy undertook pretty much the same ends, but the actions could be rationalized as being done for the benefit of the indigenous populations of the empire while simultaneously assuaging the conscience of the British people.

As a cultural matter, it was the mindset of a professional who identified with it as a serious business, not excess baggage – the personal professional interests of their discipline.

The matter is recognizably more complicated than one might understand upon learning of a high-priestly reaction to a development that is seen as being pursued in response to – or at least motivated by – a sense that public knowledge and discussion are a potential source of danger to status quo arrangements.

It was, it seems to me, Samuelson's professional mindset that in part drove his reaction to Taussig and to Koopmans. I wish that these matters had come up while Samuelson was still alive (he died on December 13, 2009). But they did not, at least not in such a way as to lead me to pause in my preparation of most of this book. *Mea culpa (Lata culpa)*.

Concern over the possibility of weakening the case for free trade had numerous parallels, one of which was concern over the possibility of weakening the case against socialism. Economists were now not following the lead of mathematics; they were emulating physicians and their injunction "Do no harm." The argument, however, was not conclusive. It turned on an understanding of what was harmful. The argument, could be turned around: *tu quoque*, you also. That is to say, if one believed that arguments for imperialism weakened the case for free trade and free markets (whatever was meant by those terms), the implication was to change the arguments for imperialism. However, if the danger was that arguments for free trade and free markets weakened the case for imperialism, the implication was quite the opposite.

The final step in my analysis of the survivor requirement was that the argument in its favor was overwhelmed by the multiplicity of concerns and arguments supporting the status quo and denigrating any solution that smacked of socialism. Samuelson was seeking to prevent economics from being injured by the imbroglio over socialism.

9.4. Adam Smith and the Survival Requirement

One aspect of Adam Smith's genius was his understanding of the subtleties of how things developed. If a modern scholar desires uniformity and consistency, this scholar likely would have to ignore the subtleties that do not conform to his or her system of thought. Smith understood that behavior has both its "natural" aspects and its constructivist aspects. In certain contexts, he emphasized the natural and in others, the constructed. The same is true of continuity and change, freedom and control, and other dualisms. Much of this interaction and aggregation is more or less random, but no small amount of the process of working things out concerns the question of who controls the institutions of social control, notably the state and the church. Selections are made regarding continuity and change. Here is where the levers of power operate and where selections are made regarding continuity and change; here is where the game actually played is worked out, skewed, and revised.

The point I want to elicit about the survival requirement is comprised of both positive and normative elements. The positive point is, as I have stressed earlier, that to the extent that economics, especially mainstream economic theory, employs marginal analysis, the process to which it is applied, to be logically consistent, that is, to have logicality, must be one of only marginal adjustments.

Adam Smith wrote on topics that bear on the problem of survival. Smith, it appears, would readily understand the failure of individuals and policy makers to adopt the survival requirement through, say, rejection of a meaningful welfare state. Part of his model, "Of the order in which Individuals are recommended by Nature to our care and attention," is that concern for the fate of others varies inversely to their social and physical distance from one another. (A modern expression stresses the degree of bonding.) One thread by which sympathy is habituated is family relationship; another is propinquity; still another, however, is that the strength of nature's recommendation of our support varies directly with the need of our beneficence (Smith 1976b: VI.ii.intro.i, 218–19): "... the greatly fortunate and the greatly unfortunate, the rich and the powerful, the poor and the wretched" (idem: VI.ii.I.20, 225). Smith finds that "[t]he distinction of ranks, the peace and order of society, are, in a great measure, founded upon the respect we naturally conceive for the former. The peace and order of society, is of more importance than even the relief of the miserable" (idem, VI.ii.I.20, 226).

It would not surprise Smith to learn that people tend to include other people within their considerations of well-being, but that intensity of feeling decreases as kinship and social class become more remote and physical distance becomes greater. Nor would he be surprised that the combination of one's desire for fortune, and therefore to better their condition and enhance their own rank and reputation, and this decrease in fellow feeling accompanying increasing physical distance, leads to a lack of support for programs, public or private, for aiding the poor and the infirm. He would not expect much recognition of and giving effect to a survival requirement. Nonetheless, numerous historians of economic thought and other scholars have understood Adam Smith as recognizing and lauding the merits and needs of the poor (see, for example, Rimlinger 1976).

Smith included in *The Theory of Moral Sentiments* several discussions that suggest that for him, the attitude of individuals toward other people cannot be reduced to a simple and uniform formula – that is, that specific discussions of his, no single one of which is sufficient, pertain to particular situations. Thus Smith wrote that:

The love of our own country seems not to be derived from the love of mankind. The former sentiment is altogether independent of the latter, and seems sometimes even to dispose us to act inconsistently with it ... We do not love our country merely as a part of the great society of mankind: we love it for its own sake, and independently of any such consideration, That wisdom which contrived the system of human affections, as well as that of every other part of nature, seems to have judged that the interest of the great society of mankind would be best promoted by directing the principal attention of each individual to that particular portion of it, which was most within the sphere both of his abilities and of his understanding. (Smith 1976b: VI.ii.4; 229)

Smith also wrote that:

The love of our country seems, in ordinary cases, to involve in it two different principles; first, a certain respect and reverence for that constitution or form of government which is actually established; and secondly, an earnest desire to render the condition of our fellow-citizens as safe, respectable, and happy as we can. He is not a citizen who is not disposed to respect the laws and to obey the civil magistrate; and he is certainly not a good citizen who does not wish to promote, by every means in his power, the welfare of the whole society of his fellow-citizens.

In peaceable and quiet times, those two principles generally coincide and lead to the same conduct. The support of the established government seems evidently the best expedient for maintaining the safe, respectable, and happy situation of our fellow-citizens; when we see that this government actually maintains them in that

situation. But in times of public discontent, faction, and disorder, those two principles may draw different ways, and even a wise man may be indisposed to think
some alteration necessary in that constitution or form of government, which, in its
actual condition, appears plainly unable to maintain the public tranquility, In such
cases, however, it often requires, perhaps, the highest effort of political wisdom to
determine when a real patriot ought to support and endeavour to re-establish the
authority of the old system, and when he ought to give way to the more daring, but
often dangerous spirit of innovation. (idem: VI.ii.2.11–12; 231–2)

In the United States circa 2010, some voters seem to have deserted their
Democratic, Republican, or independent position and have adopted the so-
called Tea Party position (named after the Boston Tea Party at the beginning
of the War of Independence) in a manner that exemplifies Smith's analysis.
It is difficult to establish whether a particular situation is one in which discontent leads to a desire for significant alteration, or is one in which a desire
for alteration, somehow generated, leads to discontent.

9.5. The Ubiquity of the Survival Problem

A substantial, albeit variegated, literature exists whose common thread is the
survival requirement, that is, the unwitting or witting threat to survival from
many quarters. No present necessity prompts an attempt at their systematic
or elegant exposition. First, the survival requirement arises in the number of
nutritionally adequate meals served and consumed each day, whether originating in private – say, family or household – circumstances or through
charitable or government programs. It arises in the provision of health services to the poor. It arises in the nature and distribution of housing to the
homeless. The chronically poor are not alone at risk. There are also the unemployed, unemployable, and those who are one paycheck away from needing
food, health services, housing, and possibly clothing. At risk is the survival
of children born to the poor, many of whom can trace their family history to
slavery or other systems of repression. At risk are the children whose parents
are the losers in legislative and judicial contests over rights and exposure to
the rights of the winners, contests in which they are often unwitting, passive
participants. It arises also in the numerous matters that self-interested yet
complacent persons seem unwilling to have seriously addressed, contending
that affirmative action punishes them and their children for the distributive
results of the actions and policies of earlier generations.

The problem of survival arises in several nominally different contexts, for
example, cases of ethnic or racial or religious differences, as well as those
between already established families and poor immigrants. The former
include those whose ancestors were looked down upon in the same manner

that the established families now treat present-day arrivals. In the twentieth century, Jews from Western Europe looked down upon Jews from Eastern Europe after both had emigrated to the United States or to Israel; and in Israel, invidious comparisons have been made by arrivals from Western Europe disparaging arrivals from Eastern Europe, and both groups have acted likewise toward the Palestinians and other Islamic peoples. The flow of causation is difficult to ascertain: Some have opposed programs to help those with survival difficulties because of animosity of one kind or another, whereas others oppose government programs because they do not want to pay for them through taxes. Both possibilities are mutually reinforcing; the effect with regard to survival seems to be much the same in both cases.

Second, one well-known economist of high position in both the discipline of economics and the U.S. government, Lawrence H. Summers, has ostensibly used marginalism in arguing that the lower marginal cost of waste disposal in a poor country compared with the higher marginal cost of waste disposal in a waste-producing rich country – solely because one country is rich and the other is poor – warrants disposal policies that take advantage of the different levels of marginal costs between the two countries (Summers 1992). The original memorandum, dated December 12, 1991, whose author was then chief economist for the World Bank, advocated that the Bank encourage the migration of "dirty" industries to less developed countries for the seemingly marginalist reason just stated. (Summers was subsequently appointed U.S. Treasury Secretary, the last during the Clinton Administration, subsequently made president of Harvard University, and in 2009 became head of the National Economic Council in the Obama Administration.)

But Summers's seeming exercise of marginalism is one type to which the survival requirement applies. Without provision for survival, the comparison of marginal costs begs the question whether one of the two groups is left unprotected against the very danger of nonsurvival that arises when Summers's proposal is followed. In the absence of provision of protection assuring likely survival, the reasoning employed by Summers in his infamous memo is at best pseudo-marginalism. It is the language of marginalism but not the marginalism required of Paretian marginalist economics. Its substance is that of the ideology and practice of imperialist domination. Its use of marginalist language is for purposes that not only lack provision of protection of survival, but are pursued precisely because the likely nonsurvival of many or all of one group is the low price society ala Summers has to pay for the interests of the rich to prevail over those of the poor. To sustain the answer given by Summers's memo to the question whose interests are to count is to substitute the language and policy of political absolutism for the language and logic of Pareto optimality.

One further lesson of the case of Summers's proposal is that the adoption of Pareto optimality, or any other concept of optimality, represents the choice of both the meaning of optimality and the requirements of the meaning chosen. I have in mind, for example, the role of basic goods in John Rawls's theory of justice and the role of capabilities in Amartya Sen's work.

Furthermore, Henry A. Giroux uses the work of Jane Anna Gordon and Lewis R. Gordon and others to designate as "Zombie politics" ideologies that spew out toxic gore that supports the market as the organizing template for all institutional and social relations, mindlessly compelled, it seems, to privatize everything and aim invective at the idea of big government but never at the notion of the bloated corporate and militarized state. Zombie culture hates big government – a euphemism for the social state – but loves big corporations and is infatuated with the ideology that, in Zombieland, unregulated banks, insurance companies, and other megacorporations should make major decisions not only about governing society, but also about who is privileged and who is disposable, who should live and who should die:

One of the cardinal policies of zombie politics is to redistribute wealth upwards to produce record high levels of inequality, just as corporate power is simultaneously consolidated at a speed that threatens to erase the most critical gains made over the last fifty years to curb the anti-democratic power of corporations.

Coupled with this rewriting of the obligations of sovereign state power and the transfer of sovereignty to the market is a widely endorsed assumption that regardless of the suffering, misery and problems done to human beings by these arrangements, they are not only responsible for their fate but reliant ultimately on themselves for survival. There is more at stake here than the vengeful return of an older colonial fantasy that regarded the natives as less than human, or the now ubiquitous figure of the disposable worker as a prototypical by-product of the casino capitalist order .... What we are currently witnessing in this form of zombie politics and predatory capitalism is the unleashing of a powerfully regressive symbolic and corporeal violence against all those individuals and groups who have been "othered" because their very presence undermines the engines of wealth and inequality that drive the neoliberal dreams of consumption, power and profitability for the very few .... While the state still has the power of the law to reduce individuals to impoverishment and to strip them of civic rights, due process and civil liberties, zombie politics increasingly wields its own form of sovereignty through the invisible hand of the market. (Giroux 2009: 4, 6, 8, 9)

The Giroux piece may seem rhetorically hyperactive, but it constitutes one perhaps unwitting reaction to much of the mainstream of invisible-hand writings. It also explicitly points to the problem of survival.

Fourth, in two recent books, Albino Barrera has taken up what is ultimately the survival requirement. In his *Economic Compulsion and Christian Ethics* (2005a), Barrera considers the principle of unintended consequences and how market actors can create or exacerbate poverty through the visitation of negative externalities on other people.

A pair of joint reviewers of Berrera's two books – former colleagues of mine at Michigan State University – insist on the cogency of distinguishing pecuniary from nonpecuniary externalities. The former only involve changes in prices in comparison with the latter's inefficiencies (Jeitschko and Pecchenino 2008: 398). Some four decades ago, I argued that both types of externality are analytically the same insofar as adverse impacts on others' opportunity sets are concerned (Samuels 1980). Jeitschko and Pecchenino do acknowledge, however, that:

Nevertheless, pecuniary externalities do have consequences, some of which may affect individual agents disproportionately. Indeed, as Barrera makes clear, pecuniary externalities often affect the most economically disadvantaged and may well push agents into situations of economic compulsion, that is, situations in which necessity (survival) governs economic decisions, due to no fault of their own. (Jeitschko and Pecchenino 2008: 398)

One of the limitations of the principle of unintended consequences is the difficulty of distinguishing unintended from intended consequences. Some unknown proportion of polluted areas have become so as a result of ignorance, but no small number are undertaken with knowledge aforethought – in other words, premeditated. The surreptitious shifting of costs to others has been one road to higher profit.

Barrera argues in this book that Christian (and presumably other systems of) ethics can be understood as calling for serious programs to repair the opportunity sets of those compelled to bear the costs generated, and benefited from, by others. When one considers the conditions of distance noted earlier and adds to them the surreptitious shifting of costs, the lack of even a moiety of concern for others, the belief (or rationalization) that the impoverished have chosen their poverty and take advantage of it to raid the treasury, it is not surprising that possessive individualism is not friendly to a survival requirement.

In his second book, Barrera (2005b) takes up a host of often intertwining economic and theological reasoning. The core of the argument has to do with scarcity and the problem of theodicy, that is, why bad things happen to good people, or the problem of evil. The chief stumbling block is the question of why a benevolent and omnipotent deity did not make mankind perfect. Barrera argues that notwithstanding the abundance of the Garden of Eden, after the Fall, it is scarcity that disciplines human beings and enables them to partake of God's goodness.

Another argument echoes McNeill (1976), Sen (1981) and others' reasoning that it is not overall scarcity that drives mass starvation; rather it is the historic inequality of rights and perverse, if not malevolent, incentive structures and policies adopted by governments that have other things in mind.

William H. McNeill, one of the world's foremost students of how ostensible "natural disasters" can result from the actions and inactions deliberately practiced by local and national governments, international agencies, and "private business" – a deplorable record to which must be added the neglect of preventive programs and measures and the decisions deliberately made by business managements of firms not just too large to let fail but sufficiently large enough to act strategically as if they were, or were situated like, governmental entities. some of them have the power to fend off governments, a situation enhanced by court decisions that assign to corporations the status of human beings in constitutional law. McNeill entitles his review of Ben Kiernan's *Blood and Soil: A World History of Genocide and Extermination from Sparta to Darfur*, appropriately – "Man Slaughters Man" (Kiernan 2008; McNeill 2008). And Brian Urquhart (2008) entitles his review of Jan Egeland's *A Billion Lives: An Eyewitness Report from the Frontlines of Humanity*, "The UN and the Race Against Death." The work of Amartya Sen, especially on famines, shows the disregard by certain leaders and groups of the dangers to the survival of others. From those accounts I can conclude that economists are not alone in their neglect and trivialization of the problem of survival. Like other people, economists concentrate on what appeals to them, which may well be that in which they were trained and have a vested interest in certain human capital, and avoid topics that, consciously or unconsciously, are perceived to threaten something important to them, such as their personal reputation and status, the place and status of economics as a professional academic discipline, as a body of advisors and administrators in matters of economic policy.

Fifth, inasmuch as one candidate (in various specifications) for the identity of the invisible hand is natural selection, it was not inappropriate for Robert M. Solow to have entitled his review essay on Gregory Clark's economic history of the world with the query, "'Survival of the Richest'?" (Clark 2007; Solow 2007). Whether Solow's title signals a change of view from his dismissive 1958 review of Koopmans's book is unclear.

Sixth, Jane O'Reilly entitled her review of Hillel Schwartz's book on several aspects of food, "Calories and the Crisis of Capitalism" (O'Reilly 1986; Schwartz 1986).

Seventh, an Australian columnist, David Marr, quotes another columnist and two prominent economists thusly. He quotes Jill Singer, who wrote in her column in *The Herald Sun* of the previous week that it "takes a certain person to rejoice in the suffering of others. In the real world they're called sociopaths – in politics, they're called conservatives." Marr quotes Joseph Stiglitz announcing "the death of capitalism" in *The Huffington Post* of September 16, 2008: "[The] fall of Wall Street is for market fundamentalism what the fall of the Berlin Wall was for communism – it tells the world that this way of economic organization turns out not to be sustainable. In the end, everyone says, that model doesn't work." *Per contra*, Marr also quotes Jagdish Bhagwati from the previous week's *World Affairs*:

[We] know that all analogies are imperfect, but this one is particularly dicey. When the Berlin Wall collapsed, we saw the bankruptcy of both authoritarian politics and an economics of extensive, almost universal, ownership of the means of production and central planning. We saw a wasteland. When Wall Street and Main Street were shaken by crisis, however, we witnessed merely a pause in prosperity, not a devastation of it. The presumption from which these critics start is that our markets rip – and rip us apart. But this is totally wrong for much of the world, and certainly for many developing countries that had been mired in quite the opposite problem, an anti-market fundamentalism that was reflexively and irrationally hostile toward markets and reliant on knee-jerk interventionism that went so far that Adam Smith's invisible hand was not only not seen but never felt. (Marr 2009)

Eighth, companies, especially – but not solely – public utility companies, have been thought to select the margins forming the basis of cost comparisons supporting differential charges proposed in rate-setting cases before the relevant rate-regulating state authority (Samuels: 1980). A number of utility companies offer a low-cost initial block of their service, coupled with favorable terms for payment of unpaid bills, including waiver of late charges, for those residential and small-business customers whose income position is very low. These pricing policies resulted from the deaths of poor elderly people whose electric power, heat, and/or telephone service was terminated for nonpayment of bills. Not all public utilities specialists approved of the internal cross-subsidization in pricing.

Ninth, it is widely believed that urban restricted-access highways are located in poor areas where the cost of land acquisition and construction is lower than in areas populated by rich or well-to-do people. One argument against legally mandated segregated schools, said by defenders of segregation to be separate but equal, was that in fact they were separate but unequal; and that the inequalities continued the differential investment of human capital that perpetuated all sorts of other inequalities. A related example was the provision in poor neighborhoods of simple basketball courts and crowded community pools with negligible supporting facilities, while providing expensive golf courses with elegant facilities open largely to rich people.

Tenth, "more than one billion people worldwide experience hunger daily. Sixty percent of the nearly 11 million children who die before their fifth birthday each year die due to malnutrition and hunger-related diseases" (Hazen 2009).

Eleventh, "the way the [budget] cuts are designed, people with cognitive and emotional disabilities will bear the brunt of them, and that means many seniors. Some of us will die when those cuts are implemented" (Ervin 2009: 28; the statement is quoted from a letter from Adrienne Lauby to the Director of the California Department of Social Services).

Twelfth, "the indifference of the West appalls him [Dr. Denis Mukwege, medical director of the Panzi hospital in Bukavu, Democratic Republic of the Congo]. 'How is it that people in the West can see five million people die and think nothing of it? Is it racism?'" (Podur 2009: 30)

Thirteenth, an IRS tax auditor, asked to sign off on an audit that had not yet begun, refused to essentially give the company an advance free pass; looking further, she found that the company changed the issue date of options granted to top executives to maximize their value, at the expense of unwitting stockholders – a practice that is "widespread, lucrative, and totally illegal." Neither her superiors nor the FBI or the Senate Finance Committee were interested in her findings. David Cay Johnston, a reporter for *The New York Times*, was receptive, and the *Times* published her account. Johnston reportedly rejects greed as the explanation for growing inequality. "[O]ften approvingly quoting Adam Smith: Ronald Reagan called for liberating business from government interference, in order to let the free market work its wonders. But in practice, Reaganite [and Thatcherite] policy have jiggered the system to redirect money, resources, and power upward. It is not the free market that creates inequality; it is the thousand little ratchets – taxes, subsidies, regulatory loopholes, failed enforcement, giveaways, and outright graft – that direct a free lunch to the top 0.1 percent (David Cay Johnston, "Free Lunch: How the Wealthiest Americans Enrich Themselves at Government Expense [and Stick You With the Bill]," quoted and paraphrased by Polly Cleveland in email dated March 1, 2008, 10:40 PM).

Fourteenth, President George W. Bush, two months after claiming that "We fight against poverty because hope is an answer to terror," nonetheless signed into law a farm bill that, according to critics, "increased the huge subsidies paid to American farmers, thereby ensuring that their unsubsidized counterparts in Ethiopia and the rest of the developing world would continue to have no hope of competing in the global food market [and that while] [d]rought was the proximate cause of the 2003 famine, ... the true culprit ... were the policies known as 'structural adjustment' that Western governments – under the auspices of the International Monetary Fund and World Bank – have forced on Africa since the 1980s," policies pressuring African governments to stop investing in local agriculture and instead "import food from the developed world. Structural adjustment is couched in the language of free trade, but it is really just the handmaiden of subsidy schemes that prop up farmers in the United States and Western Europe" – and an example of how the two financial institutions named earlier in this paragraph, in the guise of promoting the economic development of these states, actually serve as substitutes for more traditional means of colonial control, while failing to ensure "that everyone has enough food to eat" and that "food is produced in a sustainable manner" (Cunningham 2008: 19, 20).

Fifteenth, in the United States, an ongoing controversy – which becomes especially agitated around the Thanksgiving and Christmas holidays – takes place over whether and how many homeless, low-income, and poor people can be fed at any one location by religious and secular charitable organizations. Some communities do not enforce laws limiting the use of facilities, some enforce such laws, some make public buildings available, some neighborhoods seek to prevent such people from gathering within their environs, some pressure the homeless to leave, and some give them one-way tickets to other communities.

Sixteenth, hospitals and other medical facilities bill patients without personal medical insurance at rates higher than they receive from insurance companies for the same service or procedure. Such practice is considered corrupt by many critics.

Seventeenth, some or many insurance companies, as well as numerous outspoken conservatives, oppose as "socialized medicine" both existing and proposed government programs to provide adequate medical care for the uninsured or uninsurable. The designation that some existing or proposed program constitute "socialism" is widespread in the United States.

It seems to be the rare person who can sense the significance of the proposition that the establishment of *entitlements* may be understood as the functional equivalent of *property* in their protection of interests. Each enhances the lives and opportunities of its recipients. Each is a result of government action. It may be more likely that being already rich enhances the likelihood of becoming richer in the same manner as earlier. Rights provided by property law typically may be bought and sold. Not so with rights provided by entitlement law. The two also differ in their respective status in constitutional protection, for example, under the takings clause of the Fifth Amendment.

Eighteenth, the late twentieth and early twenty-first centuries have witnessed the largely successful efforts of several colossal food supply corporations to advance their version of globalization by adopting policies that put them in positions to control much of the world's food supply. Similar strategic moves, often with the support of various government entities, have been taken to establish private control of major sources of fresh water. These policies have followed much earlier efforts to narrow the ownership and control of oil and natural gas, and more recently the privatization of large areas of oceanic sea beds. These developments have not been unique: They parallel or reproduce one of the ways in which natural resources have become privatized by those in a position to use government to create private property, often with no serious governmental consideration of what hitherto had been held in common or of the implications for the sustainability of the organization and conduct of modern life. The same or similar approaches have been taken in the creation of markets (including those for the transfer of development rights) by government action at the behest of well-situated firms that then dominate those markets. In sum, many species and examples of property and of markets have not been the result of virgin births.

Nineteenth, it is not, however, the structures of industry and of resource ownership alone that imperil the availability of food to masses of people. The threat of mass starvation and to modern life in general may result from (1) the gradual exhaustion of supplies of oil and natural gas, and the consequent permanent oil shock(s), and (2) the reliance on nuclear energy and its dangers from operating accidents and failure to achieve safe disposal methods before engaging in the production of radioactive nuclear waste and the consequent availability of such materials to terrorists. Those threats likely will also derive from (3) Malthusian overpopulation and (4) ways of organizing living, consumption, and work that have become increasingly energy dependent. Other than exhibiting blind overconfidence and optimism derived from belief in markets and/or other identities attributed to an invisible hand (as in Essay 3), the communities of both business management

274 The Survival Requirement of Pareto Optimality

and political office holders have apparently contributed or allowed very little leadership and even less results with which to confront these threats to survival. Some or much of the predicament is (5) the result, it seems, of the failure of economists to educate and sensitize both elite groups and the general public in matters of survival. By taking the survival requirement for granted – that is, by largely ignoring the problem of survival – economists have contributed to the predicament. It also appears to me that, for reasons outlined earlier in this subsection, Adam Smith would not be surprised at such a predicament (see, in general, Monblot 2009). (The final version of this paragraph was written in April 2010, during the first week of the catastrophic discharge of enormous quantities of oil following an explosion, fire, and later collapse and sinking of an oil rig in the northern Gulf of Mexico. Among numerous and varied reactions were, first, that the event was a catastrophe of national proportions; second, that planned oil drilling off the shore of Florida should be postponed, if not canceled; third, that the drilling should proceed on schedule, if not sooner. The oil spill was the worst in history and threatened wildlife, human habitats, and shores in four states. The reportage on the event raised, typically only implicitly, the survival problem in various ways.

Twentieth, Michael Parenti echoed Bronislaw Malinovski in writing that:

a myth is not an idle tale but a powerful cultural force ... [which serves] to legitimate the existing distribution of wealth in society. Far from being innocent stories, myths [teach] acceptance of the prevailing property arrangements – to the benefit of the more prosperous property-holders .... The capitalist system has its own fundamental myths ... of the Lockean ideology ... the myth of individualism which reduces human community to a conglomeration of competing, atomized persons, each plotting his or her own gain, manifesting a loyalty to nothing but the cash nexus. And somehow the whole thing comes out for the better for everyone, thanks to Adam Smith's "invisible hand" – an invisible hand that has us all by the throat. (Parenti 1981: 425–6)

Capitalist myths, argues Parenti, also reverse the role of producer and parasite. Earlier it was "assumed that those who produced the property were the producers"; "[c]reation used to denote ownership; [while] now ownership signifies creation. Thus we speak of corporations as 'producer interests' when in fact they produce nothing. They are organizational devices for expropriating and controlling wealth. Consider also the myths of imperialism, which reverse the roles of victim and victimizer" (idem: 476–7).

Twenty-first, about one-quarter of all children in the United States receive food through food stamps, a federal welfare program. John J. Miller, writing in the *National Review*, is apparently more concerned about the effect such programs have on incentives. A critic of Miller quotes him as follows: "Seems like there *ought* to be a stigma attached to the use of welfare. A little bit of shame can go a long way toward encouraging people to find jobs. The federal government may think it's doing people a favor by providing them with access to food, but it's doing them a disservice if it also robs them on the motivation necessary to break free from dependency" (Holland 2009).

Compare the position of Paul Samuelson. In his obituary of Samuelson in *The New York Times*, Michael M. Weinstein pointed to the government activism recommended by John Maynard Keynes and applauded by Samuelson when the country had mass unemployment: "Many economics students would never again rest comfortably with the 19th-century view that private markets would cure unemployment without need of government intervention." Samuelson rejected Chicago School teaching on the subject as schizophrenic: Whereas "courses about the business cycle naturally talked about unemployment, … in economic-theory classes, joblessness was not mentioned" (Weinstein 2009). Survival is not an explicit issue here; the discussion stops just short of it, as usually happens.

Twenty-second, yet the twentieth-century view of nineteenth-century unemployment theory was erroneous, largely a result of wishful thinking and twisting of what had been written for ideological purposes. J. B. Say has been seen "to presume that a purpose of 'Say's Law' was to prove that involuntary unemployment was impossible." William J. Baumol, among others, has argued, however, that "on the contrary, J. B. Say considered unemployment to be a very real phenomenon and a very real cause for concern. Indeed, he explicitly advocated public employment as a suitable means to deal with the problem" (Baumol 1986). Survival was not an explicit issue as it was in Thomas Robert Malthus's writings on population theory.

Twenty-third, it is one of the ironies of both the history of economic thought and British political and economic history that the period in which the beliefs, policies, and practices of laissez-faire, free markets, and nonintervention were given voice, praised, and taken as epochal and conclusive by many, if not most, historians of economic thought was also the period in which British imperialism was at its zenith in both belief and practice, and that Britain's colonial system encompassed about one-fifth of the people on this planet. This "achievement" was praised (in various terms) by some people, denied by some, obfuscated by some, and ignored by some – a mix that is difficult to disentangle in terms of understanding and motive. It is testimony to the myopia and gullibility of human beings that British imperialism has not been accurately seen for what it was, and for the fraudulence of the belief that British rule was intended to and in fact did accomplish the elevation of the living conditions of the indigenous or native peoples. It does not require cynicism to suppose that the use of laissez-faire lines of reasoning was meant to influence domestic welfare state and other reformist policies, whereas the use of the rationalizations and lines of reasoning in support of imperialism was meant to influence foreign economic and military policies. Was the imposition of imperial power just something Britain awoke to one fine morning?

9.6. Conclusion

Returning to Smith, the *Wealth of Nations* is chock-full of affirmations of survival and the good life of mass consumption. The great illusion is not to be seen. At the very least, his moral sentiments do not permit him to defend the status quo distributions of income and wealth even if it comes with early death for some people. Consider the following statements by Smith:

> [W]hat improves the circumstances of the greater part [of political society] can never be regarded as an inconveniency to the whole. No society can surely be flourishing and happy, of which the far greater part of the members are poor and miserable. It is but equity, besides, that they who feed, cloath [sic] and lodge the whole body of the people, should have such a share of the produce of their own labour as to be themselves tolerably well fed, cloathed and lodged. (Smith 1976a: I.viii.36, 96)

In some places one half the children born die before they are four years of age; in many places before they are seven; and in almost all places before they are nine or ten (idem: I.viii.38, 97).

> [I]n civilized society it is only among the inferior ranks of people that the scantiness of subsistence can set limits to the further multiplication of the human species; and it can do so in no other way than by destroying a great part of the children which their fruitful marriages produce. (idem: I.viii.39, 97–8)

Smith's text continues with well-known discussions on the market for the demand for men, the liberal reward of labor and its beneficent effects on the lives of workingmen, moderation in putting labor to work, and worker motives when they are well fed (idem: I.viii.40, 41, 44, 94–101 and passim).

Whatever else can be said of the invisible hand, consideration of the survival requirement leads to several important consequences. One is that recognizing the *marginalist logic of economics requires survival as a condition of its adoption*. This is not a matter of fairness, justice, or equity. It is, I argue, a matter of what Pareto optimality calls for. Without adoption of a survival requirement, each of the second group of problems permits nonsurvival, toward class extinction in one case and species suicide in the other. Death is not something to factor into a marginal benefit–marginal cost analysis in such cases. Undoubtedly, some policy decisions inevitably include deaths in their calculations. For example, lowering the legal drinking age and raising highway speed limits each tends to increase the level of fatalities. However, because such is a narrow slice of Pareto optimality and because neither consent nor trade is directly involved, not all Paretians and non-Paretians accept comparison of marginal amounts (cost with cost, and cost with benefit; see further in this essay). At the very least, if the literature affirming the invisible hand is considered a vast set of construction plans, then consideration of a survival requirement introduces a rival relatively absolute absolute, to use Frank Knight's phrase.

The competitive equilibrium of Pareto optimality – the heart of the modern formulation of Smith's invisible hand – requires that decisions be limited to marginal decisions to which consent has been given. Otherwise, decisions would have to be admitted into analysis that permitted not only nonconsent, but nonsurvival, thereby conflicting with the marginal decisions to which Pareto optimality is limited. That is the argument. It is quite clear, or would be if the survival requirement had not been placed in a dark attic.

The survival requirement clearly applies to both the individual economic actor (with regard to income distribution) and the entirety of our species (with regard to environmental disaster, e.g., global warming or some other ubiquitous situation). Economic policy analysis, however, has substantially excluded the survival requirement from its Paretian models. This leaves virtually all analysis of economic policy silent on the issue. It also leaves the Paretian model incompletely formulated and lacking the logicality required by Pareto optimality. The same is true of global warming and its effects on survival.

Furthermore, the second and fifth of Koopmans's alternative solutions constitute or reflect the attitude of conservative higher-income people (and others) who generally attribute poverty and nonsurvival to the ostensibly dysfunctional deceased and about-to-be deceased themselves.

Some of the ubiquitous respects in which the survival requirement arises, implicitly or explicitly, are properly raised by people desirous of calling attention to the complacency and hypocrisy of both government and business policies.

Economists are neither necessarily intentionally nor equally complicit in either the practice or conduct of economics or in the adoption of policies that endanger the survival of individuals, groups of people, or of life on Earth, though their activities and beliefs could be more open to question and criticism. Their activities seem to result from inertial acts of omission and from the unthinking perpetuation of disciplinary positions (for example, on the protocols and ironies discussed in Essay 1 and the concept of the invisible hand itself) learned in undergraduate majors and in doctoral programs, and reinforced by the social controls administered by leading economists (also discussed in Essay 1) elsewhere rather than deliberate attempts to bring about or be cavalierly indifferent to death (*per contra*, see the allusion to activities and myopic claims resembling the actions of psychopaths and sociopaths noted in Essay 5). The principal omission lies in the failure to make clear the logical necessity of the survival requirement as part of serious and well-informed theoretical, methodological, and policy analyses.

The accuracy of ideological statements on both sides of such issues is not my concern. My general objective in this essay is in language that, to the greatest extent possible, accurately describes or explains arrangements. My immediate objective is in indicating the enormous range of issues to which the survival problem pertains. That is unsurprising, given what is necessary for survival in the modern world. Consider what has been cited in the nearly two dozen examples just given. Giroux writes of people treated as disposable. Parenti writes of legitimizing myths and clearly implies their role in trivializing and obfuscating loss and death to members of the lower hierarchical levels.

The survival requirement is not a minor, esoteric consideration relevant only to some theoretically, philosophically, or mathematically oriented scholars. The requirement that economic actors survive when opportunities for trade are exhausted is central to the concept of Pareto optimality: Death is not a marginal adjustment. The survival requirement is fundamental to both economic theory and economic policy formed under the aegis of neoclassical economics.

Neither individual nor group survival is a given in actual economic life. To my knowledge, no "invisible hand" has been said to guarantee "survival" and no author has named "survival" as a function performed (such as "equilibrium," for example, has been) by some identity attributed to the invisible hand. I have neither learned of nor acquired each and every example known to me of the use of the term "invisible hand," nor have I sought to do so, nor have I read every bit of relevant literature in my possession, nor have I gone completely through my notes and files to locate, assemble, and annotate each and every identification, aspect, and use of the invisible hand that I have found in the literature, nor each and every example or definition of a function thought to be performed by an/the invisible hand.

I have concentrated on topics such as logicality, concerning the marginal conditions of Pareto optimality. I have emphasized the inconclusiveness of ubiquitous arguments that assert the need to get government off our backs and that try to do so by substituting the language of methodological individualism for that of methodological collectivism. Many of our problems result, in whole or in part, from many causes, such as the distastefulness of so much collective action – which, after all is said and done, is what politics and social control are all about.

Two additional sources should not go unmentioned. One is the failure of the educational system. That system has not enabled the young student or adult to see and work from the fact that political and economic problems are problems precisely because they each can be formulated in several different ways, each formulation stating the situation in such a way as to elevate some interests over others, and thereby to empower certain interests over others.

Both of those problems engender a third, namely that decision making involves deep elements of pure choice and is, on that account if no other, arbitrary. Some interests are better versed in that opportunity than are others. The situation provides an open field to those who have the knowledge and motivation to take advantage of it.

Smith understood those things. Accordingly, he seems to have largely avoided taking positions on what has to be worked out – collectively. The final irony is that he may well have facilitated the misreading of his own works.

10

Conclusions and Further Insights

10.1. Conclusions

My study of the concept of the invisible hand encompasses a wide range of types of literature but especially that of economics. The most important are writings that use the term as explanation and/or judgment and/or a means of communication; attempt to sharpen or otherwise make sense of the term; and/or critique the foregoing uses. Given the enormous multiplicity of every aspect of the term's use, it is not always possible to categorize particular writings. And then there is the term's use in religion, fiction, the business press, politics, and so on. The overall conclusions from the study include the following:

1. That the use of the concept of an invisible hand is widespread, variegated, and imaginative, yet overwhelmingly amounts to pure assertion.
2. That the typical piece of writing on the invisible hand in economics, dealing with its ostensible identity and function(s), for example, the proposition that "the invisible hand of the market automatically allocates resources," adds nothing to knowledge that is not already contained in the proposition "the market allocates resources."
3. That it is neither necessarily nor altogether correct that it is the market that allocates resources. Inasmuch as the market can be seen as an institution and as both the product of institutions and the means through which those institutions operate, it is not the market per se that allocates resources – it is institutions. But to say that "the invisible hand of institutions allocates resources" also adds nothing to knowledge that is not already contained in the proposition "institutions allocate resources." Although many economists seem to be wedded to some version of the notion of competition, the topic of institutions is

richer with regard to the factors and forces that help form and operate through markets. That is not to decry the use of different modeling strategies. It is, however, to emphasize the importance of institutions in determining whose interests are to count, and to caution against the blind and unthinking application of any conceptual model to any actual economy.

4. The term "invisible hand" not only does not add anything to knowledge in the uses I am discussing; it serves the ideological and political purpose of obfuscating the power structure of society and its importance for making economic policy and for economic performance.

5. That the *concept* of the invisible hand, distinct from the functions of some specific identification of the invisible hand, is extremely important not only for obfuscating the role of power but for serving as a means through which certain interests are promoted and others inhibited in the total legal-economic process. The functions served by the *concept* of the invisible hand are psychic balm, social control, and the introduction of certain considerations, to the exclusion of others, into the decision-making process. These roles help account for several ironies, three of which are (a) seeking to actively control government while calling for laissez-faire, (b) seeking to serve as social control while preaching "freedom," and (c) practicing deliberative decision making while denigrating such by others.

6. That the use of the concept in one or another form (identity), by treating the subject matter in which it is used as transcendental, given, and beyond policy, that is, as absolutist formulation, caters to those who desire determinacy and closure, as if continuity always wins over change and as if no human discretion was possible. Not many centuries ago, the propositions that the king ruled on the basis of divine order and that received institutions were chosen by God served to manipulate the attitude, the will, and the opportunity of the masses of people.

7. That the contexts and contents of invisible-hand discussions are overwhelmingly ideological rather than serious, arm's length study.

8. That invisible-hand processes, not only like government but also including government, are of enormous importance. Such processes give effect to interaction and aggregation rather than to some asserted candidate for the identity of the invisible hand.

9. That Hayek's principles of spontaneous order, unintended consequences, and rule of law, *insofar as they are not selectively and ideologically used tools*, illustrate invisible-hand processes. Alas, Hayek's use is heavily ideological.

10. That the belief that invisible-hand processes are overwhelmingly beneficial, even benevolent, may or may not be true. What is beneficial, as opposed to malignant, is a matter of judgment and is highly relativist. Both opposing teams may pray to Deity before a game asking to win, but afterward, one team will have won and the other will have lost, and the result seems unlikely to have cosmic significance. In economic life, however, it matters much whether there is, by any reasonable reckoning, full employment, or that families are able to acquire health care, and so on.

11. That the key role of invisible-hand thinking has been to give the professional support of economists to beliefs allowing them to state what is and what is best; the invisible hand provides for – actually guarantees – the best of all possible worlds.

12. That in a world of less than full employment and problems owing to radical uncertainty, ubiquitous externalities, economic agents willing to gamble against regulatory undertakings, and so on, those who are injured or otherwise held back, those who have a different vision of the present and some possible future economic order, can be expected to react, even rebel, in one way or another.

13. That with one principal exception, discussion of the linguistic status of the term "invisible hand" has advanced neither linguistics nor economics. In fact, I am not convinced that linguistically the term is anything but a generic figure of speech and a primitive term. To say that A is a metaphor for B is open-ended. What if A is a metaphor for B in terms of one common point and also if C is a metaphor for B in terms of another common point: Are A and C, with no common point, related or not? The exception is the finding that the term "invisible hand" has a distinctive political significance. One can rationalize its use as a term of art, but that only masks the art – the art of manipulative rhetoric.

14. That the concept and term "invisible hand" has two attributes that help account for its popularity and seeming success in performing the functions identified in Essay 4 that go way beyond conventional functions such as coordination and efficiency to those of social control, psychic balm, and enabling one's agenda for government to appear to be at one with the nature of things. One attribute is the mystical nature of its frame of reference. It is out there, somewhere, even if we cannot quite discern it; indeed, it may fundamentally be inexplicable. Even such seemingly substantive identities of the invisible hand as the market and private property have been given a mystical, even magical,

character, as in the phrase "the magic of the market." A second attribute is its conduciveness to absolutist formulation. Lines of reasoning, of cause and effect, of transcendental existence, of inflexibility, of
independence from human discretion – such are the characteristics of
terms like the invisible hand. I began Essay 1 with several ironies and
have indicated others. Perhaps the overriding irony I have to report is
that the concept of an invisible hand, so widely deployed ostensibly
to counter politicization and social control, is itself above all else an
instrument of politicization and social control.

15. That the concept of the invisible hand has become foundational for
economics as a religion.

16. That the substantial evasion of the survival requirement for the logicality of the invisible hand based on Pareto optimality itself signifies
the irrelevance of much invisible-hand theorizing and policy making.

Smith has been widely used to interpret present-day issues, and present-
day issues have been used to interpret Smith, in both respects using the
concept as a vehicle of interpretation for other, ulterior purposes, especially
ironically, to influence policy, that is, to define reality for the purposes of policy and thereby to selectively channel the control and use of government.

The use of the term is typically treated as above choice yet is laden with
tensions – for example, between the invisible hand being true and being a
proposition serving to set minds at rest; between belief and disbelief in the
existence of an invisible hand; between rival notions of the identity and of
the functions of the invisible hand; between the invisible hand and other
regulatory or social control systems; between different conceptions of the
necessary assumptions, conditions, and limitations of the invisible hand;
and many others.

10.2. Discretion over Continuity and Change

One characteristic feature that many of the discussions in these essays have
in common is the considerable range of discretion that exists in the economy and polity, and therefore in what I have called the legal-economic
nexus. One hears that this country has due process of law and strongly
recommends it to other countries. That trope vastly understates the extent
of discretion exercised throughout government. I find that situation to be
inevitable (I do not feel any compulsion to normatively evaluate the situation). I find (as positive matters) that statements like those usually made
about the invisible hand, are, first, to no small extent exercises in symbolism

and mythology, while serving as social control *et cetera*; and, second, beg the question of what has to be worked out and thereby is finessed, obfuscated, and omitted from economic and legal models. The finessing, the obfuscation, and the omitting are inevitable. Adam Smith, in his *Theory of Moral Sentiments*, speaks of moral rules as a category, but not all of the specific moral rules that are worked out will be accepted by everyone. The substantive content of the category has to be worked out, and Smith is more concerned with the process than with the content. The same is true in law with respect to which one can favor the protection supposedly accorded by the due-process-of-law clauses of the Constitution of the United States in helping promote the rule of law but ignore the significance of several questions, including: "What constitutes an abuse of discretion?" "Yes, the rule of law, but which law is it to be?" And "When is abuse of discretion permitted and when is it prosecuted?"

It is one thing to assume and assert the existence of an invisible hand; it is something else to presume that that an imaginary invisible hand obviates – or, for that matter, controls – the process of working things out. I believe that most believers in such an invisible hand really do know that they are attempting to influence that process, however much they may overtly impugn it. These essays raise serious questions: Does an invisible hand exist? What, if any, knowledge is given by the idea of an invisible hand? What are the actual functions performed by the concept of the invisible hand? What meaning is to be assigned to terms like laissez-faire and noninterventionism? Is economics less or more important than law in such matters? What is the significance for a discipline that, for many of its practitioners, accepts the mythological concept of an invisible hand as its foundation, when the concept of an invisible hand has become a vehicle for importing into economics a particular approach to economic policy not all that different from other approaches to economic policy, all the while arguably misstating the legal foundations of our economic system and indeed of all economic systems?

10.3. The Argument and Its Meaning

For something that I claim, and hopefully convincingly show, not to exist, the invisible hand seems to have been remarkably prolific and productive. The number of mainly academic economics publications treating it in some fashion must be close to, or even more than, a thousand. The number in religion is probably a substantial multiple of that. I have no idea of the magnitude of its use in newspapers and opinion journals, but it seems to be huge.

Accordingly, if one believes that whatever is thought of must exist in order to be thought of, then the invisible hand exists. But, as was shown in Essays 2 and 3, and in other essays as well, such understanding is held in confusing ways, so much so that the term is laden with ambiguity and is inconclusive and nondispositive of the purposes for which its use was intended.

Further, if belief in something motivates behavior, and if (contrary to Hayek's principle of unintended and unexpected consequences) the belief is self-fulfilling, then the invisible hand exists. Indeed, even if the results are unintended and unexpected, they are the results of an existent invisible hand.

Unfortunately for the devotees of the invisible hand, however, the foregoing senses in which the invisible hand could be said to exist do not have substantive meaning. Consider, from Essay 3, any combination of the identity of the invisible hand and of the function(s) thought to be performed by the invisible hand. Substantive economic research and theory have already developed bodies of analysis, possibly – yes, likely – due to emphasis on some identity and/or function of the invisible hand. The deployment of invisible-hand reasoning may have suggested hypotheses and provided other help. But calling the market, the price mechanism, capital accumulation, and so on the hand's function does not in and of itself either confirm its existence or add anything to knowledge.

But is an invisible hand the cause of the results attributed to it, or is the behavior it motivates, or the goals it is used to advance, the cause of the results? What if one says that the invisible hand is comprised of the monkeys believed to reside in Bay Front Park in Miami, Florida? In this book, I have presented lines of reasoning to suggest that the concept of the invisible hand is used in ways that contribute to social control and psychic balm. Do those uses constitute the existence of the invisible hand? I have also implicitly utilized Ockham's Razor to claim that the introduction of the invisible hand as an explanatory factor adds nothing to an explanation.

Do the beliefs that motivate people constitute a domain in which, whatever else one can say about the invisible hand, the invisible hand is alive and well?

"It depends on what the meaning of the word 'is' is."

www.news.bbc.co.uk/onthisday/hi/dates/stories/september/21/newsid_2525000/2525339stm

"[It] depends what the meaning of 'Judicial Activism' is."

www.huffingtonpost.com/adam-blickstein/depends-,on-what-the-meaning_b_114750

"[It] depends what the meaning of 'the surge' is."

www.mydd.com/story/2008/7/24/114233/945

These are a few of the 163 million results received on September 26, 2008 from Google in the response to the Web search for "that depends on what one means by 'is'" – to which I will add, "It depends on what the meaning of 'domain' is."

For many people, the preceding essays are laden with disappointment. The argument seems to support and positively sanction certain practices and beliefs. But so too is the supposition or pretence that government is a fundamentally neutral and benevolent institution that those who desire to use government for social reform wish it to be. I use "social reform" (also called democracy, liberalism, pluralism, and socialism) in the historic sense of the meaningful establishment as rights for all individuals what hitherto have been the privileges of a few. Government is not the independent institution that they have imagined or pretended it to be. Government is, in fact, largely in the hands of those who, through the use or threat of what Vilfredo Pareto identified as force and fraud, control the policies of government.

Humankind seems trapped between the vision of an independent and absolutist transcendental controlling and optimizing force and government as a neutral decision-making process. Which is to say, between two groups of people each of which has its own agenda for government, even if they do not call it that, two groups each of whom has adopted absolutist formulations to such a degree that eventually they cannot even begin to understand each other, surely not to reach some accord with each other. Neither vision is correct.

These formulations can become formulas for tragedy. If each side becomes convinced that truly absolute and fundamental values and structures are at risk, that policy making is a zero-sum game, the result can be a clash of all-or-nothing positions. To some people, such a situation is a proper and principal reason for resorting to absolutist and mythical concepts, such as the invisible hand. However, such a policy readily becomes a tool in the contest between classes over the control and use of government to advance their respective agendas. Several interpreters have hailed Hayek's principle of unintended and unexpected consequences as the leading principle in the social sciences. I strongly question that designation of Hayek's version for reasons given in Essay 8. I would argue that the leading such principle is one of the following: that government is available for the capture and use of those who seek to control it; that the leaders of institutions of social control (read: power players) are always ready to use them to aggrandize on behalf of themselves and/or their institutions; and several propositions of Adam Smith, Vilfredo Pareto, and Max Weber.

The two groups have a common desire to use government for their own purposes, more than likely their own ideological, material, political, or other advantage. Smith understood this, for example, when he noted that the laborer's enjoyment of "the whole produce of his own labor ... could not last beyond the first introduction of the appropriation of land and the accumulation of stock [capital]" (Smith 1976a: I.viii.5, 82–3); that the laborers were subject to legal constraints not applicable to those who employed them (idem, I.viii.12–13, 66–7); how the dealers (businessmen) would use government regulation to increase their profits and thereby "to levy ... an absurd tax upon the rest of their fellow-citizens" whose proposals come "from an order of men, whose ... interest is ... generally an interest to deceive and even to oppress the public, and who accordingly have upon many occasions both deceived and oppressed it" (idem, I.xi.p.10, 267); and, as we have seen, "Civil government, so far as it is instituted for the security of property, is in reality instituted for the defence of the rich against the poor, or of those who have some property against those who have none at all" (idem, V.i.b.12, 715). No single chapter is devoted to these topics in either *The Theory of Moral Sentiments* or *The Wealth of Nations*. However, mercantilism is a – if not the – principal target of the latter (Book IV) and the immediately preceding quotes are taken from Smith's chapters on wages and labor markets (I.viii), on the improvement of social conditions leading directly and indirectly to raise the real rent of land, the real wealth of landlords as a share of production, their power to purchase labor or the goods produced by others (I.xi.a), and on government's expenditures on "justice" (V.i.b). The reader should notice that neither Smith nor I say that either (1) the existing structure of prices and wages, and the structure of rights which gives rise to them, or (2) some other structure of prices and wages and the rights' structure which gives rise to it, is the correct one.

The claim that society requires (belief in) some ostensibly absolutist but harmonistic agency, such as the invisible hand, is but a stratagem with which, wittingly or unwittingly, one group can capture and use for its own benefit the high ground of social control, all the while condemning social control. The invisible hand is not a solution to such a problem. It is grist for the further ideological manipulation of public opinion.

10.4. The Invisible Hand as Argument

A problem in the use of language in debate and in decision making of various types is the tendency to define issues and reality in such a way as to enable the construction of a solution that seems to be given by the nature of things as to foreclose controversy. The putative solution is seen as given, transcendent, determinate and close-ended, such that it may be said that there is nothing to argue about. The term I have employed to describe or identify such language is absolutist formulation. It serves the dual roles of psychic balm and social control.

In the field of economics, as in other fields, people postulate first principles, laws, and other propositions in order to attenuate discussion – along the lines which they prefer. Numerous such propositions have been formulated. By no means are all of them spurious – in the category that Pareto called "fraud." However, there is no litmus test with which to distinguish the correct from the incorrect. Some or many have been useful in the development of various economic ideas and concepts; others have been used to bamboozle rather than enlighten, to advance an interest.

Each group endeavors to use both materialist and idealist arguments in order to explicate and to argue over metaphysical conceptions – for us, notably, the invisible hand. These arguments have resulted in the development of theories of justice, value, and the like. The history of economic thought can be substantially explained, on a certain level of analysis, in terms of the introduction of a vast succession of arguments about the distributions of income, wealth, property and other rights, and opportunity.

These arguments have resulted in the development of theories of justice, value, and the like. The history of economic thought can be substantially explained, on a certain level of analysis, in terms of the introduction of a succession of arguments about the distributions of income, wealth, property, and opportunity.

One could argue that such arguments, such contests between theories, perhaps especially those about nonsubstantive, ontologically empty conceptions like the invisible hand, amount to a monumental misallocation of intellectual resources. There is some truth to the argument that arguing over metaphysical conceptions, even those arguably without substance, is preferable to warfare. Warfare, which has had numerous other causes, such as an egomaniacal lust and longing for the use of power, has been rampant in all areas of this planet and as far back in time as we know. It is, therefore, not clear that argument has won out over war. The argument elevating argument above war is itself an argument. Arguments presumably have both reinforced and added to what Friedrich Nietzsche called the will to power. The argument that capitalism – the market economy – preoccupation with bettering our material condition leads to a tempering of malevolent and militaristic urges is belied by the just-mentioned ubiquity of war and of "war parties" in national politics. Moreover, at the core of all theories of imperialism are the resources to be used to improve the winner's bettering of their material condition and in further future warfare. It is not for naught that the bellicose expression, a strong economy, is the basis of a strong national security; and one does not have to be a cynic to note that Department of Defense can be a euphemism for Department of Aggression.

The concept of the invisible hand has not, so far as I know, led directly and principally to any wars or other armed conflict, in either economic or religious disputes. Such disputes have led to war, and the imagery of an invisible hand has been a part of the ideational process of their legitimization. The same has been true of its principal domestic use, arguably to counter the movement referred to previously as extending the privileges of some to the rights of all. Not all the identities of the invisible hand, of course, would be amenable to such use.

The concept of an invisible hand has proven to be both durable and flexible. It has proliferated in economics almost beyond imagination and reckoning. The controversy over Nobel Awards noted in Essay 1 suggests that the conventional exaggerated accounts reveal not serious science but disciplinary backslapping and out-and-out self-promotion of economics. For all the critical work I have undertaken, I have yet to find anything to rival the invisible-hand part of our history that is both so interesting and so substantively barren.

10.5. Invisible-Hand Thinking

Adam Smith would be an important economist even without his having used the term "invisible hand." The ideology would have become the anthem of a systematic rhetoric with other borrowed or novel ideas.

There is nothing substantive about the invisible hand. The term adds nothing to economic theory. Economic theory of one type finds that competition governs resource allocation, among other things; expressing the idea in invisible-hand terms adds only an ideological patina to the account in terms of competition.

The idea of an invisible-hand process, whose results need not comport with individual expectations and/or desires, relates how interaction and aggregation drive the results. An athletic contest, such as the football game referred to in earlier essays, is a good example. Games are played within rules as is also the game, as it were, of adopting and applying rules. Such has a place for the game plans adopted by offensive and defensive coaches. There is nothing mystical or magical about it. The search for the "correct" identity and function of the invisible hand is a search for something that does not exist as such.

Hayek's principles of unintended and unexpected consequences and of spontaneous order comprise an invisible-hand process (as just mentioned) coupled with an imported additional normative, ideological premise. It supports passivity and condescension. It pretends that the results are unequivocally unique and beneficent when they are not. Hayek's affirmation of nondeliberative decision making over deliberative decision making fails on several counts, including the presumptuous identification of any institution as one or the other; the presumptuous assertion of (some) institutions as being spontaneous in their origin; the situation that even if (some) institutions did originate spontaneously, the application of Menger's principle that received institutions must be continuously examined with respect to their wisdom or folly, so that after the (assumed) initial period of "spontaneous" generation, in every period thereafter, such institutions are inevitably combinations of both types of decision making; and the evident paradox of deliberative decision making supporting nondeliberative decision making. Hayek's program, not excluding his adoption of the rule-of-law model, is a strategy of selectively minimizing change deemed undesirable. On the one hand, it is wishful thinking; on the other, it is the ideological basis of a quest for power. It is fundamentally a claim to control government, law, and language, a claim to do so by influencing and manipulating choice.

What could a person be understood to be saying when that person says something like, "well, it is clear that the Arrow-Debreu [or some other] conception of the invisible hand is competition and the allocation of resources that it generates"? Or "that competition and the allocation of resources that it generates is the Arrow-Debreu [or some other] conception of the invisible hand"?

Ordinary syntax suggests that there is something called the invisible hand, and the statement identifies its identity to be competition and its function to allocate resources. This is congruent with the raison d'être of developing theories of price formation, markets, equilibrium, efficiency (or optimality), and so forth. Ordinary syntax thus facilitates learning by introducing a concept lacking substantive content.

10.6. What Is Left of the Invisible Hand? Invisible-Hand Processes as Explanation

For the various reasons presented in the preceding essays, reliance on an "invisible hand" in economics lacks credibility. There is no invisible hand as that term is used in economics. Its continued use must at its base constitute an embarrassment. Almost all uses of the term add nothing to substantive knowledge. The exception is the invisible-hand process, as developed by Edna Ullman-Margalit (1978) and Robert Nozick (1974: 18–22, 118, 119 and passim), illustrated by the example of the football game, and either constituted or driven by interaction among agents and aggregation of interactions and their results – in short, interaction and aggregation. The invisible-hand process characterizes markets, governments, business and other organizations, and the economy as a whole.

The analysis presented in this book concludes (1) that there is no such thing as an invisible hand that identifies and moves the economy in a transcendental way, (2) that injecting an invisible hand into an argument adds no explanatory power, and (3) that the use of the concept of an invisible hand serves the purposes of social control and psychic balm as well as to inject the user's agenda for the control and use of government into the political process. The principle of unintended and unexpected consequences is in a category shared with a few other principles. Its characteristics include its potential for biased, partisan, normative use but unlike other candidates for the identity of the invisible hand, it can contribute to knowledge and it need not come with some absolutist formulation attached – a very different situation in comparison with other identifications.

There is a substantial literature that examines, and especially employs, the principle of unintended and unexpected consequences and other comparable principles, for example, the unintended consequences of war, peacekeeping operations, and unintended war itself (Aoi, de Conig, and Thakur 2007; Hagen and Bickerton 2007); a provision of a voting rights act (Blum 2007); isolated poverty (Banks 2004); increased steel tariffs (Committee on Small Business 2002); the impacts of certain herbicides on nontarget and unintended plant species (Ferenc 2001); affirmative action (Fubara 2001); constitutional amendment (Kyvig 2000); welfare reform (Witte 1998); work incentives (Mauer 1997); pregnancy (Dietz, Zpitz, Anda, and Williamson, et al. 1999); and the safety of genetically engineered foods (United States Institute of Medicine 2004). Several general analyses have been published (e.g., Boudon 1982; Dahrendorf 2000; Lal 1998; Uleman and Bargh 1989).

A small but growing and, needless to say, important group of books examines the growth of individuals engaged in terrorism. Some specialists consider Al Qaeda as a movement separate from the organization formed by Osama bin Laden. At least one author examines the role of reinforcement, under certain conditions, through the social interaction of individuals, in producing terrorists. Elements of the explanation include the principles of spontaneous self-organization and of unintended consequences. This use of the two principles is very suggestive of the value of their positivist, as opposed to their normative or ideological, use (Sagerman 2008; Sunstein 2008). A somewhat different but compatible story of Iraq, also utilizing the principle of unintended consequences, is to be found in Peter Galbraith (2008).

The invisible hand in the form of Hayek's "principle" of unintended and unexpected consequences is ubiquitous in society. I would prefer, however, to state the point without using the notion of an invisible hand, considering that, in my view, the term adds nothing substantive. Wherever one finds interaction and aggregation, the consequences are extremely likely not to be the ones intended or expected. I place quotation marks around "principle" to emphasize that the point I am making is different from that of Hayek.

Hayek claimed that the consequences of interaction and aggregation are extremely likely not to be the ones intended or expected, that planning in any organization is problematic, or that effective participation in decision making is not limited to the relative few people at the top. As Hayek's sometime *bête noire*, John Kenneth Galbraith (and numerous others) had insisted, participation in decision making extends deeply into the "lower levels" of organizational charts, as increasing numbers of individuals bring to bear their private or local knowledge. In another model, the principle is due to the division of power, including power in the form of knowledge.

Hayek typically intended to be understood as saying that the unintended and unexpected consequences, especially in regard to government, are likely to be negative or self-defeating. Negative results may well be frequently the case, but as an argument against government activity, it is inconclusive. For one thing, noninterventionists do not normally apply the normative conclusion to the agenda that they would have government adopt. For another, what is a desirable or undesirable consequence is a matter of judgment, and hence subjective, selective, and normative. And, too, the principle typically involves a bundle of hypotheses concerning what happened and why – even in the example of the football game. Finally, different legislative or judicial voters have different reasons for voting the way they do, and sometimes do not tell the operative reason why. The passage of the Sherman Antitrust Act is one example. Another is the Fourteenth Amendment and the designation of the corporation as a person. Still others are the respective efforts of Richard M. Nixon to have welfare decision making transferred to the states, where the welfare-rights movement was, compared to its influence in Congress, relatively weak; and of Charles DeGaulle to have voting for senator transferred away from Paris, to increase his power and that of his allies at the center. In each case, something different – more palatable – was given as justification.

10.7. Order, Power, and Nondeliberative Social Control

The meaning of the use of the concept of the invisible hand ultimately derives from the social process in which the use of the concept takes place. The central problem of the subject would appear to be that social order requires people in a society to be either kept ignorant of the extant degree of social control and/or led to believe in nontrue propositions functioning as psychic balm and social control. A further problem appears to be that of who determines who is so manipulated. Ruling or leading classes desire to retain power; the ruled classes, to replace those classes. It is position in hierarchy that determines the ideological position, though the prospect of mobility offers the ideological believers the possibility of recruitment, and with or without mobility, social control will not affect everyone identically. Adding to the complexity is conflict between elements of the ruling class over their respective shares. Accordingly, Frank Knight's aphorism that religion is the opiate of the masses, as well as the sedative of the classes, makes (pun intended) for quiet minds having been set both at rest in some regards and motivated in others. Such interaction may well be the ultimate invisible-hand process.

That process is fueled by differential willingness to persevere; those who control government rule by Paretian force and fraud. Most people, however, are not even aware that the process exists. Much public discussion has degraded into sound bites without depth.

In early May 2010, a marketing firm called and asked me to answer some questions. The structure of each question was the same. I was asked to give my position on something, indicating the strength with which I held that position. The first question concerned what I thought of the Florida legislature. I was then asked how much my response would be different assuming the truth of certain statements. Another question dealt with a proposed constitutional amendment requiring changes in land use and development plans to be approved by a public vote. It was followed by a similar series of questions – for example, if it is shown that the proposal came from a group of rich lawyers, or that a leading supporter of the proposal was in favor of involuntary sterilization, or if the opponents of the proposal were owners of large tracts of land, builders, and other real estate interests, in each instance how would my vote change?

The objective of the questions was to identify which positions on which issues would elicit the most favorable results from the perspective of those who financed the poll. The exercise could have been arranged by either side on the issue. A self-styled defender of private property could support the amendment inasmuch as it was intended to, and likely would, protect those property interests that sought higher remunerative uses through changing land use policy, but would have to convince a majority of those voting of the desirability of the proposed (future) changes in each case. Or the defender could desire to protect other current property interests against those who desired to change land use depending on market or other conditions. The owners of property tend to support the state of the law most favorable under the circumstances. They will support changes in the law that would enhance their interests (position in the market). They do not want changes that will injure them. They do not know what the future issues will be. A property owner with substantial and varied holdings would likely find their interest in both but in different circumstances. The owner will be able to use contradictory arguments depending on which position is at risk. The owner will prefer the venue that is easiest, lowest in terms of cost, and more likely to provide the desired opportunity results. Parties to conflicts will tend to think of the law as that version favoring them and that the law can be stated in absolutist terms. Adam Smith was not a barrister, counsel, or judge, but he understood what was going on in the legal-economic nexus in which both polity and economy were being continuously incrementally adjusted. Perhaps that helps explain why he did not discuss politics in terms of an invisible hand.

10.8. Conclusion

It is said that history is written by the victors. There is much to be said for that view. The reason is that all of us are educated historically in the mindset that has accumulated from and through history so developed and written, with usually a relatively simplistic and saccharine story inculcated in public schools. History is written to accomplish or reflect that purpose. This set of essays has been written from a point of view that recognizes that conventional history is, well, conventional history. This viewpoint does not claim to have discovered *true* history. There is no such thing, although one could argue that the point of view, centering on the multiple possible accounts of things past and present, is in itself a claim, albeit on a different level, to a true type of interpretation of history. The present account clearly does not conclude that the conventional view(s) of the invisible hand is (are) wrong, in whole or in part. I make no such claim for either that part of my mindset that is conventional or that part which is heterodox. Both "orthodoxy" and "heterodoxy" are relative terms, relative to each other, to each formulation of both terms, and to all of the possible aggregate of all of the pieces. I have found that, at least for myself, such a view – say, of "conservative" and "liberal" – makes more sense than any particular view of them, nonetheless recognizing that mine is a point of view, too. Let's say that the principle of unintended and unexpected consequences applies to the principle of unintended and unexpected consequences itself; or that Popper's statement (Popper 1957: 177) might well read, "something called science must begin with something called myths, and with something called the criticism of something called myths." Every aspect thereof has to be worked out.

It has not been my purpose in this book to further a particular agenda for government. My objective has been to help put an end to the false beliefs about government and the use of those beliefs in manipulating people's perceptions and attitudes. Whatever the nature of the institutions that comprise government, government is important. The attitudes that people have and that other people endeavor to influence have important roles in governance. People should understand what government does, how it does it, in what ways government is important, and the significance of that knowledge. The premise of that objective is the value of knowledge that is as nonnormative as possible for democratic decision making, as free of error and pretense as possible

One of Pareto's findings is that the belief system available to those who seek to manipulate political psychology is comprised of multiple tropes, each appealing to different mental states. For example, one president of the United States referred to the OPEC-determined price of oil as the "market price." This term is true of any price, however determined, found in a market. But it is not the meaning used by economists, which signifies that changes in demand in a competitive market will influence the allocation of resources rather than be used by suppliers as an instrument for capturing unearned income. Moreover, the notion of "the price" paralleling the term "the market" fails to encompass and bring forth the fact that different laws lead to different markets and thus to different prices and resource allocations. Another example is that of the advisor to that president who famously lauded the idea of economic freedom and "free to choose." But there are numerous axes along which freedom, even if only "economic" freedom, can be analyzed. One of them is "competition," which inevitably both increases and decreases freedom for different parties. It is largely ideological manipulation to claim that markets are inherently competitive and to do so without a meaningful analysis of competition, and to denigrate law when law is inevitably a set of determinants of markets and competition.

Some people will object on the grounds that such a view opens the door to undesirable changes, that it abrogates the opportunities open to various interests in influencing the opinions of others, that the approach taken here puts the foundations of the present economic order at risk, and so on. These objections can be countered and shown to be among the false beliefs. What is an undesirable change is not a given; it is open to debate. Adopting a belief system that pretends that government, in some form, can be minimized, if not fully extirpated, is grossly erroneous.

I also insist that the economic role of government in all of its details is not a purely technical matter. Government's role is inevitably laden with implicit normative premises, ultimately as to whose interests are to count.

Attention to technical details, however, can help put ideology and values in its place, and help clarify rather than confound decision making. A good example of this is the provision of meaningful health care in regard to the survival requirement. Economists who fail to identify and consider the survival requirement of Pareto optimality are, in their quest to make economics safe from public criticism, on a par with those who seem to lack concern with health care and/or rely on tropes claiming people should provide for themselves. Here is an opportunity for creativity that economists have disregarded.

My approach to the issues in which the concept of an invisible hand has had so important a role does not abrogate freedom of speech or introduce subversive ideas. Rather, it enables free and open discussion with a minimum of specious myth. It does not endanger the present economic order; it enriches discussion so as to enhance the policy choices we make and enables people to have a more solid basis for their evaluation of policies, their choice of candidates, their expectations, and their ability to perceive when they are being told nonsense or falsity. The foundation of our society is not the predominance of falsity and pretense. The reiteration and invocation of terms like "free market" and "rule of law" as well as "invisible hand" distract attention from the key issues of policy, empower those with selective perception and selective specification, and follow Pareto's recognition that a policy proposal can be supported, or opposed, by contradictory lines of reasoning directed at different groups of people.

References

Achino-Loeb. 2005. *Silence: The Currency of Power*. Edited by Maria-Luisa Achino-Loeb Berghahn Books. London.

Alvey, James E. 2003. *Adam Smith: Optimist or Pessimist?* Burlington, VT: Ashgate.

Allan, David. 2008. *Making British Culture: English Readers and the Scottish Enlightenment 1740–1830*. Routledge: London.

Amoh, Yasuo. 2008. Ferguson's Views on the American and French Revolutions, in *Adam Ferguson: History, Progress and Human Nature*, E. Heath and V. Merolle, eds., pp. 73–86. London: Pickering & Chatto.

Anderson, Harry, Nadine Joseph, and Kristine Mortensen. 1983. Explaining the "Invisible Hand." *Newsweek*, November 11: 59.

Anspach, Ralph. 1972. The Implications of the Theory of Moral Sentiments for Adam Smith's Economic Thought. *History of Political Economy* 4: 176–206.

Aoi, Chiyuki, Cedric de Coning, and Ramesh Thakur, eds. 2007. *Unintended Consequences of Peacekeeping Operations*. New York: United Nations University Press.

Arena, Richard, and Agnès Festré, eds. 2006. *Knowledge, Beliefs and Economics*. Northampton, MA: Edward Elgar.

Arnold, Thurman. 1937. *The Folklore of Capitalism*. New Haven, CT: Yale University Press.

Aronowitz, S. 1992. *The Politics of Identity: Class, Culture, Social Movements*. New York: Routledge.

Arrow, Kenneth J., and Frank H. Hahn. 1971. *General Competitive Analysis*. Edinburgh: Oliver and Boyd.

Arrow, Kenneth J., and Gerard Debreu. 1954. Existence of an Equilibrium for a Competitive Economy, *Econometrica* 22: 265–290.

Aydinonat, N. S. 2000. Invisible Hand Explanations, manuscript.

Aydinonat, N. E. 2006. Is the Invisible Hand UnSmithian? A Comment on Rothschild, *Economics Bulletin* 2: 1–9.

———. 2008. *The Invisible Hand in Economics, How Economists Explain Unintended Social Consequences*. New York: Routledge.

Ball, Terence, and J. G. A. Pocock. 1988. *Conceptual Change and the Constitution*. Lawrence: University Press of Kansas.

Banks, James G., and Peter S. Banks. 2004. *The Unintended Consequences: Family and Community, the Victims of Isolated Poverty*. Lanham, MD: University Press of America.

Barbour, Ian G. 1974. *Myths, Models and Paradigms*. New York: Harper & Row.

Barrera, Albino. 2005a. *Compulsion and Christian Ethics*. New York: Cambridge University Press.

    2005b. *God and the Evil of Scarcity*. Notre Dame, IN: University of Notre Dame Press.

Baumol, William J. 1952. *Welfare Economics and the Theory of the State*. Longmans, London.

    1986. Productivity Growth, Convergence, and Welfare: "What the Long-Run Data Show," *American Economic Review* 76(5): 1072–1085.

Bellamy, Liz. 1998. *Commerce, Morality and the Eighteenth-Century Novel*. New York: Cambridge University Press.

Bellow, Saul. 1987. *More Die of Heartbreak*. New York: William Morrow.

Berger, Peter L., and Thomas Luckmann. 1966. *The Social Construction of Reality*. Garden City, NY: Doubleday.

Berry, Christopher J. 2009. 'But Art Itself is Natural to Man': Ferguson and the Principle of Simultaneity, in *Adam Ferguson: Philosophy, Politics and Society*, E. Heath and V. Merolle, eds., pp. 143–154. London: Pickering & Chatto.

    1994. *The Idea of Luxury: A Conceptual and Historical Investigation*. New York: Cambridge University Press.

Binswanger, Hans Christoph. 1994. *Money and Magic: A Critique of the Modern Economy in the Light of Goethe's Faust*. Chicago: University of Chicago Press.

Black, Max, ed. 1962. *The Importance of Language*. Englewood Cliffs, NJ: Prentice-Hall.

Black, M. A., and Henry Campbell. 1968. *Black's Law Dictionary*, Revised Fourth Edition, St Paul, MN: West Publishing Co.

Blake, Casey, and Christopher Phelps. 1994. History as Social Criticism: Conversations with Christopher Lasch. *Journal of American History* 80: 1310–1332.

Blaug, Mark. 1968. *Economic Theory in Retrospect*, 2nd ed. Homewood, IL: Irwin.

    1978. *Economic Theory in Retrospect*, 3rd ed. New York: Cambridge University Press.

    1985. *Economic Theory in Retrospect*, 4th ed. New York: Cambridge University Press.

Bloom, Harold, ed. 1988. *Eighteenth-Century British Fiction*. New York: Chelsea House Publishers.

Bloor, David. 1976. *Knowledge and Social Imagery*. Boston: Routledge and K. Paul.

    1991. *Knowledge and Social Imagery*, 2nd ed. Chicago: University of Chicago Press.

Blum, Edward. 2007. *The Unintended Consequences of Section 5 of the Voting Rights Act*. AEI Press. New York.

Bondi, H. 1967. *Assumption and Myth in Physical Theory*. New York: Cambridge University Press.

Boorstin, D. J. 1958. E. 1981. Agricultural Economics in an Evolutionary Perspective, *American Journal of Agricultural Economics* 63: 788–795.

Bothamley, Jennifer. 2002. *Dictionary of Theories*. Detroit, MI: Visible Ink Press.

Boudon, Raymond. 1982. *The Unintended Consequences of Social Action*. London: Macmillan.

Boulding, Kenneth E. 1981. Agricultural Economics in an Evolutionary Perspective. *American Journal of Agricultural Economics* 63: 788–795.

1956. *The Image*. Ann Arbor: University of Michigan Press.

Bowring, John, ed. 1962. *Works of Jeremy Bentham*. Vol. 1. New York: Russell & Russell.

Boyle, R. R. 1954. The Nature of Metaphor. *Modern Schoolman* 31: 257–280.

Brenner, Y. S. 1979. *Looking into the Seeds of Time: The Price of Development*. The Hague: Gorcum.

Breton, Denise, and Christopher Largent. 1991. *The Soul of Economics: Spiritual Evolution Goes to the Marketplace*. Wilmington, DE: Idea House Publishing.

Brewer, Anthony. 2009. "On the Other (Invisible) hand …" *History of Political Economy* 41(3): 519–543.

Bromley, Daniel W. 2006. *Sufficient Reason: Volitional Pragmatism and the Meaning of Economic Institutions*. Princeton, NJ: Princeton University Press.

Brown, David S. 2006. *Richard Hofstadter: An Intellectual Biography*. Chicago, IL: University of Chicago Press.

Bryson, Gladys. 1968. *Man and Society*. New York: Kelley.

Buchanan, James M. 1986. *Liberty, Market, and State*. Brighton, Sussex: Sheaf.

Buchanan, James M., and Warren J. Samuels. 2008. "Politics as Exchange or Politics as Power: Two Views of Government," in *The Street Porter and the Philosopher*, S. Peart and D. Levy, eds., pp. 15–40. Ann Arbor: University of Michigan Press. Also in Warren J. Samuels et al., *The Legal-Economic Nexus*, New York: Routledge, 2002, pp. 139–201.

Buck, E. 2003. *Beethoven's Ninth: A Political History*. Chicago: University of Chicago Press.

Burke, P., and R. Porter, eds. 1987. *The Social History of Language*. New York: Cambridge University Press.

Bynum, W. F., E. J. Browne, and Roy Porter, eds. 1981. *Dictionary of the History of Science*. Princeton, NJ: Princeton University Press.

Calabresi, Guido. 1985. *Ideals, Beliefs, Attitudes, and the Law*. Syracuse, NY: Syracuse University Press.

Campbell, Joseph. 1972. *Myths to Live By*. New York: Bantam.

   2008. Thinkexist. http://thinkexist.com/quotation/every religion is true one way_or another-it_is/152697

Campbell, R. H., and A. S. Skinner. 1982. Introduction, eds., Adam Smith. New York: St. Martins.

Carver, Thomas Nixon. 1915. *Essays in Social Justice*. Cambridge, MA: Harvard University Press.

Cerruti, James. 1976. Stockholm, *National Geographic* 149, no. 1 (January 1976): 59.

Chamberlin, Edward Hastings. 1950. *The Theory of Monopolistic Competition*. Cambridge, MA: Harvard University Press.

Chipman, John S. 1959. Three Essays on the State of Economic Science by Tjalling C. Koopmans. *Journal of Farm Economics* 41: 447–449.

Chomsky, N. 1988. *Language and Politics*. New York: Black Rose Books.

Clark, Gregory. 2007. *A Farewell to Alms: A Brief Economic History of the World*. Princeton, NJ: Princeton University Press.

Clark, Henry C., ed. 2003. *Commerce, Culture, & Liberty*. Indianapolis, IN: Liberty Fund.

Clark, John Maurice. 1928. "Adam Smith and the Currents of History," in *Adam Smith, 1776–1926*. Chicago: University of Chicago Press.

Clower, Robert W., and Peter Howitt. 1998. "Keynes and the Classics: An End of Century View," in *Keynes and the Classics Reconsidered*, James C.W. Ahiakpor, ed., pp. 163–178. Boston: Kluwer.

Coats, A. W. 1975. Adam Smith's Conception of Self-Interest in Economic and Political Affairs. *History of Political Economy* 7: 132–136.

    1971. *The Classical Economists and Economic Policy*. London: Methuen.

    1969. Is There a "Structure of Scientific Revolutions?" *Kyklos* 22: 289–296.

Collins, Stephen L. 1989. *From Divine Cosmos to Sovereign State: An Intellectual History of Consciousness and the Idea of Order in Renaissance England*. New York: Oxford University Press.

Committee on Small Business. 2002. Serial No. 107–71 – Lost Jobs, More Imports; Unintended Consequences of Higher Steel Tariffs (Part II), September 25, 2002. http://frwebgate.access.gpo.gov/cgibin/getdoc.cgi?dbname=107_house_hearings&docid=f:82506.wais

Commons, John R. 1990 [1934]. *Institutional Economics*. New Brunswick, NJ: Transaction.

Corfield, P. J., ed. 1991. *Language, History and Class*. Cambridge: Basil Blackwell.

Cottrell, P. L., and D. E. Moggridge, eds. 1988. *Money and Power: Essays in Honour of L. S. Pressnell*. Basingstoke: Macmillan.

Cunningham, Brent. 2008. Cornucopia Blues, *The Nation* (September 21), pp. 39–44; a review of Thurow and Kilman 2008 and Gráda 2008.

Dahl, Robert A., and Charles E. Lindblom. 1976 [1953]. *Politics, Economics, and Welfare*. Chicago: Chicago University Press.

Dahrendorf, Lord, ed. 2000. *The Paradoxes of Unintended Consequences*. Budapest and New York: Central European University Press.

Davenport, Herbert J. 1916. *Outlines of Economics*. New York: Macmillan.

    1913. *The Economics of Enterprise*. New York: Augustus M. Kelley.

Davis, Ann. 2008. Endogenous Institutions and the Politics of Property: Comparing and Contrasting Douglass North and Karl Polanyi in the Case of Finance, *Journal of Economic Issues* 42: 1101–1122.

Debreu, Gerard. 1954. Valuation Equilibrium and Pareto Optimum, *Proceedings of the National Academy of Sciences* 40: 588–592.

Degré, G. 1985. *The Social Compulsion of Ideas*. New Brunswick, NJ: Transaction Books.

De Ruggiero, Guidi. 1937 [1933]. Liberalism, *Encyclopedia of the Social Sciences* 5: 435–443.

Desai, Meghnad. 1986. Men and Things, *Economica* 53: 1–10.

Dicey, Albert Venn. 1981 [1905]. *Public Opinion in England during the Nineteenth Century*. New Brunswick, NJ: Transaction Books.

Dixit, Avinash. 2005. The Limits of Free Trade. *Journal of Economic Perspectives* 19(1): 241–242.

Dorfman, Robert. 1983. A Nobel Quest for the Invisible Hand. *New York Times* (October 23): F15.

Eaton, Ralph Monroe. 1925. *Symbolism and Truth*. New York: Dover.

Edelman, Murray. 1964. *The Symbolic Uses of Power*. Champaign, IL: University of Illinois Press.

Egeland, Jan. 2008. *A Billion Lives: An Eyewitness Report from the Frontlines of Humanity*. New York: Simon & Schuster.

Ellul, J. 1984. *Money and Power*. Downers Grove, IL: Inter-Varsity Press.

Ely, Richard T. 1938. *Ground under Our Feet*. New York: Macmillan.

Emmett, Ross B. 2002. *Review of William B. Greer, Ethics and Uncertainty: The Economics of John Maynard Keynes and Frank H. Knight*. Northampton, MA: Edward Elgar, 2000, *Journal of the History of Economic Thought* 24: 374–376.

Ervin, Mike. 2009. "Budget Cuts Hit Home," *The Progressive*, 73 (November): 26–28.

Evensky, Jerry. 2005. *Adam Smith's Moral Philosophy: A Historical and Contemporary Perspective on Markets, Law, Ethics, and Culture*. Cambridge: Cambridge University Press.

Ewing, K. D., and C. A. Gearty. 2001. *The Struggle for Civil Liberties: Political Freedom and the Rule of Law in Britain, 1914-1945*. New York: Oxford University Press.

Fallon, Richard H., Jr. 1997. The "Rule of Law" as a Concept in Constitutional Discourse, *Columbia Law Review* 97: 1–56.

Farber, Daniel A., and Suzanna Sherry. 2002. *Desperately Seeking Certainty: The Misguided Quest for Constitutional Foundations*. Chicago, IL: University of Chicago Press.

Feibleman J. K. 1969. *The Reach of Politics: A New Look at Government*. New York: Horizon.

Ferenc, Susan A., ed. 2001. *Impacts of Low-Dose, High-Potency Herbicides on Nontarget and Unintended Plant Species*. Pensacola, FL: SETAC Press.

Ferguson, Adam. 1979 [1767]. *An Essay on the History of Civil Society*. New Brunswick, NJ: Transaction Books.

1955. *An Essay on the History of Civil Society*, edited by F. Oz-Salzberger, Cambridge: Cambridge University Press.

Fetter, Frank Albert. 1914. Davenport's Competitive Economics, *Journal of Political Economy* 22: 550–565.

1904. *The Principles of Economics*. New York: Century.

1923. Value and the Larger Economics Parts I – II, *Journal of Political Economy* 31 (October–December): 587–605, 790–803.

Fitzpatrick, P. 1992. *The Mythology of Modern Law*. New York: Routledge.

Fraser, L. M. 1937. *Economic Thought and Language*. London: A&C Black.

Friedman, L. M. 1973. *History of American Law*. New York: Simon & Schuster.

Friedman, Milton. 1978. "Adam Smith's Relevance for 1976," in Fred R. Glahe, ed., *Adam Smith and the Wealth of Nations: 1776-1976 Bicentennial Essays*, pp. 7–20. Boulder: Colorado Associated University Press.

1962. *Capitalism and Freedom*. Chicago, IL: University of Chicago Press.

2008. Glenn Johnson's Notes from Milton Friedman's Course in Economic Theory, Economics 300A, University of Chicago, Winter Quarter 1947, Marianne Johnson and Warren J. Samuels, eds., *Research in the History of Economic Thought and Methodology* 26C: 63–118.

2009. Incomplete Course Notes from Milton Friedman's Price Theory, Economics 300B, University of Chicago, Spring 1947, Marianne Johnson and Kirk Johnson, eds., *Research in the History of Economic Thought and Methodology* 27C: 159–200.

Friedman, Milton, and Rose D. Friedman. 1998. *Two Lucky People: Memoirs*. Chicago, IL: University of Chicago Press.

Fubura, Edward. 2001. Alleviating the unintended consequences of affirmative action: Achieving attitude change by invoking alternative ethical and justice frameworks, Dissertation. Michigan State University.

Gaffney, Nason, and Fred Harrison. 1994. *The Corruption of Economics*. London: Shepheard-Watrwyn.

Galbraith, John Kenneth. 1987. *Economics in Perspective: A Critical History*. Boston: Houghton Mifflin.

　　1958. *The Affluent Society*. Boston: Houghton Mifflin.

Galbraith, Peter W. 2008. *Unintended Consequences: How War in Iraq Strengthened America's Enemies*. New York: Simon & Schuster.

Gani, M. 2005. Why Teach the History of Error? EH.net (June 21). 8:19 A.M.

Garrison, Roger. 1985. Intertemporal Coordination and the Invisible Hand: An Austrian Perspective on the Keynesian Vision, *History of Political Economy* 17: 309–321.

Gatell, F. O. 1967. *The Jacksonians and the Money Power, 1829–1840*. Chicago: Rand McNally.

Geuss, R. 2001. *History and Illusion in Politics*. New York: Cambridge University Press.

Giesbrecht, Martin Gerhard. 1972. *The Evolution of Economic Society*. San Francisco: W. H. Freeman.

Giroux, Henry A. 2009. "Zombie Politics and Other Late Modern Monstrosities in the Age of Disposability," Truthout (November 17). http://www.truthout.org/111709Giroux

Goffman, Erving. 1974. *Frame Analysis: A Chapter on the Organization of Experience*. London: Harper and Row.

Gordon, Donald F. 1963. The Role of the History of Economic Thought in the Understanding of Modern Economic Theory, *American Economic Review Papers and Proceedings* 55: 119–127.

Gordon, H. Scott. 1980. *Welfare, Justice, and Freedom*. New York: Columbia University Press.

Gordon, H. Scott. 1991.Welfare, Property Rights and Economic Policy: Essays and Tributes, in Honor of H. Scott Gordon, edited by Thomas K. Rymes. McGill-Queen's University Press.

Gráda, Cormac O. 2008. *Famine: A Short History*. Princeton, NJ: Princeton University Press.

Gramm, Warren S. 1973. Natural Selection in Economic Thought: Ideology, Power, and the Keynesian Revolution, *Journal of Economic Issues* 7: 1–28.

　　1980. The Selective Interpretation of Adam Smith, *Journal of Economic Issues* 14: 119–142.

Grampp, William. 1968 . Wicksteed, Philip Henry. *International Encyclopedia of the Social Sciences*. Encyclopedia.com Feb. 3, 2011[1968] <http://www.encyclopedia.com>.

Hadley, Arthur Twining. 1986. *Economics*. New York: Putnam's.

Hagen, Kenneth J., and Ian J. Bickerton. 2007. *Unintended Consequences: The United States at War*. London: Reaktion.

Hahn, Frank H. 1973. *On the Notion of Equilibrium in Economics*. New York: Cambridge University Press.

Halévy, Elie. 1955. *The Growth of Philosophical Radicalism*. Boston: Beacon Press.

Hamilton, Alexander, James Madison, and John Jay. 1961 [1788]. *The Federalist*. Benjamin Fletcher Wright, ed. New York: Metro Books.

Hands, D. Wade. 2001. *Reflection without Rules: Economic Methodology and Contemporary Science Theory*. New York: Cambridge University Press.

Harris, N. 1971. *Beliefs in Society*. Baltimore: Penguin.

Harrison, Peter. 1990. *"Religion" and the Religions in the English Enlightenment*. New York: Cambridge University Press.

Hartz, Louis. 1990. *The Necessity of Choice: Nineteenth-Century Political Thought*. Paul Roazen, ed. New Brunswick, NJ: Transaction Books.

Hayek, Friedrich A. 1944. *The Road to Serfdom*. Chicago, IL: University of Chicago Press.

Hazen, Don. 2009. Letter to reader. AlterNet (November 10) 2:42 P.M.

Heath, Eugene, and Vincenzo Merolle, eds. 2008. *Adam Ferguson: History, Progress and Human Nature*. London: Pickering & Chatto.

Heath, Eugene, and Vincenzo Merolle, eds. 2009. *Adam Ferguson: Philosophy, Politics and Society*. London: Pickering & Chatto.

Hébert, Robert F., and Albert N. Link. 1982. *The Entrepreneur: Mainstream Views and Radical Critique*. New York: Praeger Publishers.

Heilbroner, Robert L. 1972. *The Worldly Philosophers*, 4th edition. New York: Simon & Schuster.

Henderson, John P., and John B. Davis. 1997. *The Life and Economics of David Ricardo*. Warren J. Samuels and Gilbert Davis, eds. Boston: Kluwer Academic.

Henry, John F. 1990. *The Making of Neoclassical Economics*. Boston: Unwin Hyman.

Hicks, J. R. 1981. *Wealth and Welfare*. Cambridge: Harvard University Press.

Hill, Lisa. 2009. "A Complicated Vision: The Good Polity in Adam Ferguson's Thought," in *Adam Ferguson: Philosophy, Politics and Society*, E. Heath and V. Merolle, eds., pp. 107–124. London: Pickering & Chatto.

Hirschleifer, Jack. 1960. *Price Theory and Application*. Chicago, IL: University of Chicago Press.

Hirschleifer, Jack. 1976. *Price Theory and Application*. Englewood Cliffs, NJ: Prentice-Hall.

Hirschman, Albert O. 1977. *The Passions and the Interests: Political Arguments for Capital before Its Triumph*. Princeton, NJ: Princeton University Press.

Hobsbawn, E. J. 1962. *The Age of Revolution, 1789–1848*. Cleveland, MO: World.

Hobsbawn, E. J., and T. Ranger, eds. 1983. *The Invention of Tradition*. New York: Cambridge University Press.

Hoeflich, M. F. 1986. "Afterword," in *The Politics of Language*, Ronald D. Rotunda, ed. Iowa City: University of Iowa Press.

Holland, Joshua. 2009. "Conservatives Can Really Be Heartless Bastards," *Alternet*: http://www.alternet.org/blogs/peek/144242/conservatives_can_really_be_heartless_bastards

Home, Henry, and Lord Kames. 2002 [1728]. *Essays on the Principles of Morality and Natural Religion*. Mary Catherine Moran, ed. Indianapolis, IN: Liberty Fund.

Hont, Istvan. 2005. *Jealousy of Trade: International Competition and the Nation-State in Historical Perspective*. Cambridge, MA: Harvard University Press.

Horkheimer, Max, and Theodore W. Adorno. 2002. *Dialectic of Enlightenment: Philosophical Fragments*. Gunzelin Schmid Noerr, ed. Stanford, CA: Stanford University Press.

Hunt, E. K. 1979. *History of Economic Thought: A Critical Perspective*. Belmont, CA: Wadsworth.

——— 2002. *History of Economic Thought: A Critical Perspective*. Updated Second Edition. Armonk, NY: M. E. Sharpe.

Hunt, Robert C., and Antonio Gilman, eds. *Property in Economic Context*. Lanham, MD: University Press of America.

Hutcheson, Francis. 2002 [1728]. *An Essay on the Nature and Conduct of the Passions and Affections, with Illustrations on the Moral Sense.* Aaron Garrett, ed. Indianapolis, IN: Liberty Fund.

Hutchinson, Allan C. 2000. *It's All in the Game: A Nonfoundationalist Account of Law and Adjudication.* Durham, NC: Duke University Press.

Janos, Andrew C. 1986. *Politics and Paradigms: Changing Theories of Change in Social Science.* Stanford, CA: Stanford University Press.

Jeitschko, Thomas D., and Rowena A. Pecchinino. 2008. Review of Albino Barrera, 2005a. *Compulsion and Christian Ethics.* New York: Cambridge University Press, and Albino Barrera. 2005b. *God and the Evil of Scarcity.* Notre Dame, IN: University of Notre Dame Press. *Review of Social Economy* 66: 397–402.

Jevons, W. Stanley. 1894. *The State in Relation to Labour.* London: MacMillan and Co. 2002 [1887]. *The State in Relation to Labour.* Piscataway, NY: Transaction.

Marianne Johnson and Kirk Johnson. 2009. Notes from Economics 300B by Milton Friedman, University of Chicago, Spring 1947, *Research in the History of Economic Thought and Methodology*, Vol. 27-C: 159–199.

Johnson, Marianne and Warren Samuels. 2008. Glenn Johnson's Notes from Milton Friedman's Course in Economic Theory, Economics 300A, Winter Quarter 1947, *Research in the History of Economic Thought and Methodology*, Vol. 26-C: 63–117.

Johnson, Samuel. 2005 [1755]. *A Dictionary of the English Language: An Anthology.* New York: Penguin.

Johnston, David Cay. 2007. *Free Lunch: How the Wealthiest Americans Enrich Themselves at Government Expense (and Stick You With the Bill).* New York: Portfolio. 2003. *Perfectly Legal: The Covert Campaign to Rig Our Tax System to Benefit the Super Rich – and Cheat Everybody Else.* New York: Portfolio.

Johnston, David. 1989. *The Rhetoric of Leviathan: Thomas Hobbes and the Politics of Cultural Transformation.* Princeton, NJ: Princeton University Press.

Jones, G. S. 1983. *Languages of Class: Studies in English Working Class History, 1832–1982.* New York: Cambridge University Press.

Jones, N. 1989. *God and the Money Lenders.* Boston: Basil Blackwell.

Kadish, Alon, and Keith Tribe, eds. 1993. *The Market for Political Economy: The Advent of Economics in British University Culture, 1850–1905.* London: Routledge.

Kahn, Paul W. 1997. *The Reign of Law.* New Haven, CT: Yale University Press. 2000. The "Rule of Law" is National Myth. Los Angeles Times-Washington Post News Service. *Lansing State Journal* (November 26): 13A.

Kellner, Hans. 1989. *Language and Historical Representation.* Madison: University of Wisconsin Press.

Kelsen, H. 1945. *General Theory of Law and State.* Cambridge, MA: Harvard University Press.

Kendall, K. E. 1995. *Presidential Campaign Discourse: Strategic Communication Problems.* Albany: State University of New York Press.

Kennedy, Gavin. 2009a. Adam Smith and the Invisible Hand: From Metaphor to Myth, *Economic Journal Watch* 6 (May): 239–263.

Kennedy, Gavin. 2009b. A Reply to Daniel Klein on Adam Smith and the Invisible Hand, *Economic Journal Watch* 6 (September): 374–388.

Khalil, Elias. 1990. Beyond Self-Interest and Altruism: A Reconstruction of Adam Smith's Theory of Human Conduct, *Economics and Philosophy*, 6: 255–273.

Khalil, Elias L. 2000a. Beyond Natural Science and Divine Intervention: The Lamarckian Implication of Adam Smith's Invisible Hand, *Journal of Evolutionary Economics* 10: 373–393.

2000b. Making Sense of Adam Smith's Invisible Hand: Beyond Pareto Optimality and Unintended Consequences, *Journal of the History of Economic Thought* 22: 49–63.

Kiernan, Ben. 2008. *Blood and Soil: A World History of Genocide and Extermination from Sparta to Darfur*. New Haven, CT: Yale University Press.

Kimmel, Michael S. 1988. *Absolutism and Its Discontents: State and Society in Seventeenth-Century France and England*. New Brunswick, NJ: Transaction Books.

Klein, Daniel. 2009. In Adam Smith's Invisible Hands: Comment on Gavin Kennedy. *Economic Journal Watch* 6 (May): 264–279.

Kloppenberg, James T. 1986. *Uncertain Victory: Social Democracy and Progressivism in European and American Thought, 1870–1920*. New York: Oxford University Press.

Knight, Frank H. 1947. *Freedom and Reform*. New York: Harper.

1960. *Intelligence and Democratic Action*. Cambridge, MA: Harvard University Press.

1956. *On the History and Method of Economics: Selected Essays*. Chicago, IL: University of Chicago Press.

1953. *Theory of Economic Policy and the History of Doctrine*. *Ethics* 63: 276–292.

1999. What Is "Truth" in Economics? In *Selected Essays by Frank H. Knight*, Vol. 1, Ross B. Emmett, ed. Chicago, IL: University of Chicago Press.

Koopmans, Tjalling C. 1976. Concepts of Optimality and Their Uses. *Scandinavian Journal of Economics* 78(4): 542–560.

1957. *Three Essays on the State of Economic Science*. New York: McGraw-Hill.

Kregel, Jan A. 1984. Is the "Invisible Hand" a Fallacy of Composition? Smith, Marx, Schumpeter and Keynes as Economic Orthodoxy, *Cahiers D'Économie Politique* 10–11: 33–49.

Kselman, T., ed. 1991. *Belief in History*. Notre Dame, IN: University of Notre Dame Press.

Kwas, Michael. 2000. *Privilege and the Politics of Taxation in Eighteenth-Century France: Liberté, Égalité, Fiscalité*. New York: Cambridge University Press.

Kwon, H. K. 2004. *Fairness and Division of Labor in Market Societies*. New York: Berghahn.

Kyvig, David, ed. 2000. *Unintended Consequences of Constitutional Amendment*. Athens: University of Georgia Press.

Lagermann, E. C. 1989. *The Politics of Knowledge: The Carnegie Corporation, Philanthropy, and Public Policy*. Chicago: University of Chicago Press.

Lakoff, G., and M. Johnson. 1980. *Metaphors We Live By*. Chicago: University of Chicago Press.

Lal, Deepak. 1998. *Unintended Consequences: The Impact of Factor Endowments, Culture, and Politics on Long Run Economic Performance*. Cambridge, MA: MIT Press.

Latsis, S. J., ed. 1976. *Method and Appraisal in Economics*. Cambridge: Cambridge University Press.

Lee, Soo Hee, and Christopher Williams. 2007. Institutional Foundations of Entrepreneurship: An Introduction and Cross-county Comparisons, *Journal of Interdisciplinary Economics* 18: 113–121.

Leonard, T. C. 2002. Reflection on Rules in Science: An Invisible-Hand Perspective, *Journal of Economic Methodology* 9 (2): 141–168.

Letwin, William. 1963. *The Origins of Scientific Economics*. New York: Doubleday.

Lindbergh, Reeve. 1998. Fortress Lindbergh. *The New Yorker* (August 24 and 31): 122–131.

Lindblom, Charles E. 1977. *Politics and Markets: The World's Political-Economic Systems*. New York: Basic Books.

Lipkin, Robert Justin. 2000. *Constitutional Revolutions: Pragmatism and the Role of Judicial Review in American Constitutionalism*. Durham, NC: Duke University Press.

Lubrano, Alfred. 2010. "In hard times, Americans blame the poor," *The Gainesville Sun* (February 28), pp. 1F, 4F.

Lynch, Joseph M. 1999. *Negotiating the Constitution: The Earliest Debates over Original Intent*. Ithaca, NY: Cornell University Press.

Macfie, A. L. 1967. *The Individual in Society*. London: George Allen & Unwin.

Mackie, Christopher D. 1998. *Canonizing Economic Theory: How Theories and Ideas are Selected in Economics*. Armonk, NY: M. E. Sharpe.

Mali, Joseph. 2003. *Mythistory: The Making of a Modern Historiography*. Chicago, IL: University of Chicago Press.

Marr, David. 2009. "Hurry up your majesty, we've got a republic to declare," *The Australian* (November 2). http://www.theaustralian.news.com.au/story/0,25197,26290742–20261,00.html

Marris, Robin, and Dennis C. Mueller. 1980. The Corporation, Competition, and the Invisible Hand, *Journal of Economic Literature* 18: 32–63.

Mauer, Marc. 1997. *Intended and Unintended Consequences: State Racial Disparities in Imprisonment*. Washington, DC: The Sentencing Project: 14.

McCloskey, D. 1983. The Rhetoric of Economics, *Journal of Economic Literature* 21: 481–517.

McCulloch, J. R., ed. 1946. *Adam Smith, An Inquiry into the Nature and Causes of the Wealth of Nations*. Edinburgh: Adam & Charles Black and William Tait..

McDonald, Forrest. 2000. *States' Rights and the Union: Imperium in Imperio, 1776–1876*. Lawrence, KS: University Press of Kansas.

McMahon, Martin. 2009. "She Stole My School Milk," *The Globe and Mail* (May 6). http://theglobeandmail.com/servlet/story/LAC.20090506.COLETTS06ART2007–12/T

McNally, David. 1988. *Political Economy and the Rise of Capitalism: A Reinterpretation*. Berkeley: University of California Press.

McNeill, William H. 2008. Man Slaughters Man, *The New York Review of Books*, April 17: 43–47.

   1976. *Plagues and Peoples*. New York: Doubleday.

McNulty, Paul J. 1968. Economic Theory and the Meaning of Competition, *Quarterly Journal of Economics* 82: 639–656.

McWhorter, Diane. 2001. *Carry Me Home: Birmingham, Alabama: The Climactic Battle of the Civil Rights Revolution*. New York: Simon & Schuster.

Means, H. B. 2001. *Money and Power: The History of Business*. New York: Wiley.

Medema, Steven G., and Warren J. Samuels. 1998. "Ronald Coase on Policy Analysis: Framework and Implications," in Steven G. Medema, ed., *Coaseian Economics: Law and Economics and the New Institutional Economics*, pp. 161–183. Boston: Kluwer.

Meek, R. L. 1977. *Smith, Marx & After*. London: Chapman & Hall.

Meek, R. L., D. D. Raphael, and P. G. Stein. 1978. "Introduction," in *Lectures on Jurisprudence by* Adam Smith. Oxford: Oxford University Press.

Mehrling, Perry. 1997. *The Money Interest and the Public Interest: American Monetary Thought, 1920–1970.* Cambridge, MA: Harvard University Press.

Meja, V., and N. Stehr, eds. 1990. *Knowledge and Politics: The Sociology of Knowledge Dispute.* New York: Routledge.

Mercuro, Nicholas. 2005. Government's Touch Pervades Technology. *FED TECH* 2: 16–17.

Meyers, Milton. 1983. *The Soul of Modern Economic Man.* Chicago: University of Chicago Press.

Minowitz, Peter. 2004. Adam Smith's Invisible Hands, *Economic Journal Watch* 1 (December): 391–412.

Mises, Ludwig von. 1951. *Socialism.* New Haven, CT: Yale University Press.

Mishan, E. J. 1986. *Economic Myths and the Mythology of Economics.* Atlantic Highlands, NJ: Humanities Press.

Mitchell, Wesley C. 1967. *Types of Economic Theory from Mercantilism to Institutionalism.* Joseph Dorfman, ed. New York: Augustus M. Kelley.

Mitchell, William C. 2001. "The Old and New Public Choice: Chicago versus Virginia," in William F. Shughart II and Laura Razzolini, eds., *The Elgar Companion to Public Choice*, pp. 3–2. Aldershot: Edward Elgar.

Moessinger, P. 2000. *The Paradox of Social Order.* New Brunswick, NJ: Transaction.

Monbiot, George. 2009. "Modern Life is Probably Screwed by Peak Oil, But It's Not Too Late to Avoid Mass Starvation." *Alternet* (November 19). http://www.alternet.org/module/printversion/144017

Montes, Leonidas. 2003. Smith and Newton: Some Methodological Issues Concerning General Equilibrium Theory, *Cambridge Journal of Economics* 27: 723–747.

Morrow, Glenn R. 1928. "Adam Smith: Moralist and Philosopher," in *Adam Smith, 1776 to 1926.* Chicago, IL: University of Chicago Press: 168–171.

Muller, Jerry Z. 2002. *The Mind and the Market: Capitalism in Modern European Thought.* New York: Knopf

Musgrave, Richard A. 1985. "A Brief History of Fiscal Doctrine," in Alan J. Auerbach and Martin Feldstein, eds., *Handbook of Public Economics*, Vol. 1, pp. 1–59. Amsterdam: North-Holland.

Myers, Milton L. 1983. *The Soul of Modern Economic Man: Ideas of Self-Interest: Thomas Hobbes to Adam Smith.* Chicago: University of Chicago Press.

Myrdal, Gunnar. 1969. *The Political Element in the Development of Economic Theory.* London: Kegan Paul.

Neely, Mark, Jr. 1999. *Southern Rights: Political Prisoners and the Myth of Confederate Constitutionalism.* Charlottesville: University Press of Virginia.

Neil, Robin. 2006. Book Review of *Marginal Man: The Dark Vision of Harold Innis* by Alexander John Watson. http://eh.net/bookreviews/library/1055

Nelson, W. E. 1975. *Americanization of the Common Law.* Cambridge, MA: Harvard University Press.

Nossiter, B. D. 1964. *The Mythmakers: An Essay on Power and Wealth.* Boston: Houghton Mifflin.

Novak, M. 1981. *Toward a Theology of the Corporation.* Washington, DC: American Enterprise Institute for Public Policy Research.

Novak, M., and J. W. Cooper, eds. 1981. *The Corporation: A Theological Inquiry.* Washington, DC: American Enterprise Institute for Public Policy Research.

Nozick, Robert. 1974. *Anarchy, State, and Utopia*. New York: Basic Books.

  1994. "Invisible-Hand Explanations," *American Economic Review, Papers and Proceedings* 84 (May): 314–318.

Nye, Russel B. 1975. The Thirties: The Framework of Belief. *Centennial Review* 19: 37–58.

O'Driscoll, Gerald P., Jr., ed. 1979. *Adam Smith and Modern Political Economy*. Ames: Iowa State University Press.

O'Flaherty, W. 1983. Origins of Myth-Making Man, *New York Times Book Review* (December 18): 24–25.

O'Reilly, Jane. 1986. Calories and the Crisis of Capitalism, *The New York Times Book Review* (December 7): 18–20.

Ortony, A., ed. 1979. *Metaphor and Thought*. New York: Cambridge University Press.

  ed. 1993. *Metaphor and Thought*, 2nd ed. New York: Cambridge University Press.

Outram, Dorinda. 2005. *The Enlightenment*, 2nd ed. New York: Cambridge University Press.

Oz-Salzberger, Fania. 2008. "Ferguson's Politics of Action," in *Adam Ferguson: History, Progress and Human Nature*, E. Heath and V. Merolle, eds., pp. 147–156. London: Pickering & Chatto.

Pack, Spencer J. 1994. "Adam Smith's Invisible Hand/Chain/Chaos," in *Joseph A. Schumpeter. Historian of Economics*, Laurence S. Moss, ed., pp. 181–195. New York: Routledge.

  1991. *Capitalism as a Moral System: Adam Smith's Critique of the Free Market Economy*. Aldershot: Edward Elgar.

Pagden, Anthony, ed. 1987. *The Languages of Political Theory in Early-Modern Europe*. New York: Cambridge University Press.

Parenti, M. 1981. We Hold These Myths to Be Self-Evident, *The Nation* (April 11): 425–429.

Pareto, Vilfredo. 1935 [1916]. *The Mind and Society: A Treatise on General Sociology*. Boston: Harcourt, Brace.

  1963 [1935]. *The Mind and Society: A Treatise on General Sociology*. New York: Dover [Boston: Harcourt, Brace].

  1984 [1921]. *The Transformation of Democracy*, Charles H. Powers, ed. New Brunswick, NJ: Transaction Books.

Parsons, T. 1949. *The Structure of Social Action*. Glencoe, IL: Free Press.

Pascal, Roy. 1936. Property and Society: The Scottish Historical School of the Eighteenth Century. *Modern Quarterly*. March 1938: 167–169.

Pasinetti, L. L. 1981. *Structural Change and Economic Growth*. New York: Cambridge University Press.

Peart, Sandra J., and David M. Levy, eds. 2008. *The Street Porter and the Philosopher: Conversations on Analytical Egalitarianism*. Ann Arbor: University of Michigan Press.

Peden, G. C. 1985. *British Economic and Social Policy: Lloyd George to Margaret Thatcher*. Oxford: Oxford University Press

Pocock, J. G. A. 1985. *Virtue, Commerce, and History: Essays on Political Thought and History, Chiefly in the Eighteenth Century*. New York: Cambridge University Press.

Podur, Justin. 2009. "Healing in the Congo," *The Progressive* 73 (November): 29–31.

Political Economy Club. 1876. *Revised Report of the Proceedings at the Dinner of 31st May, 1876, Held in Celebration of the Hundredth Year of the Publication of the "Wealth of Nations."* London: Longmans, Green, Reader & Dyer.

Popper, Karl. 1957. "Philosophy of Science: A Personal Report," in *British Philosophy in the Mid-Century.* 2nd ed., C. A. Mace, ed. London: Allen and Unwin.

Pound, R. 1937. *An Introduction to the Philosophy of Law.* New York: Oxford University Press.

Pufendorf, Samuel. 2002. *Of the Nature and Qualification of Religion in Reference to Civil Society.* Indianapolis, IN: Liberty Fund.

Puro, Edward. 1992. Uses of the Term "Natural" in Adam Smith's Wealth of Nations, *Research in the History of Economic Thought and Methodology* 9: 73–86.

Raphael, D. D., and A. S. Skinner. 1980. "General Introduction," in *Essays on Philosophical Subjects*, pp. 1–21. Oxford: Oxford University Press.

Rassekh, Farhad. 2009. In the Shadow of the Invisible Hand, *History of Economic Ideas*, 17 (3): 147–165.

   Four Central Propositions of the Market Economy: An Historical and Evolutionary Perspective, manuscript.

Raynor, David. 2009. "Why Did David Hume Dislike Adam Ferguson's *Essay on the History of Civil Society?*" In *Adam Ferguson: Philosophy, Politics and Society*, E. Heath and V. Merolle, eds., pp. 45–72. London: Pickering & Chatto.

Reddy, W. M. 1987. *Money and Liberty in Modern Europe: A Critique of Historical Understanding.* New York: Cambridge University Press.

Reder, Melvin W. 1982. Chicago Economics: Permanence and Change, *Journal of Economic Literature* 20: 1–38.

Rex, J. 1974. *Sociology and the Demystification of the Modern World.* Boston: Routledge & Kegan Paul.

Rimlinger, Gaston V. 1976. Smith and the Merits of the Poor, *Review of Social Economy* 34, (December): 333–344.

Robbins, Lionel. 1998. *A History of Economic Thought: The LSE Lectures.* Steven G. Medema and Warren J. Samuels, eds. Princeton, NJ: Princeton University Press.

   1953. *The Theory of Economic Policy in English Classical Political Economy.* London: Macmillan.

Robinson, J. H. 1921. *The Mind in the Making.* New York: Harper.

Rodgers, Daniel T. 1987. *Contested Truths: Keywords in American Politics Since Independence.* New York: Basic Books.

Rosen, Harvey S. 2002. *Public Finance*, 6th ed. New York: Irwin/McGraw-Hill.

Rosenberg, Nathan. 1968. Adam Smith, Consumer Tastes, and Economic Growth, *Journal of Political Economy* 76: 361–374.

   1974. Adam Smith on Profits – Paradox Lost and Regained, *Journal of Political Economy* 82: 1177–1190.

   1965. Adam Smith on the Division of Labour: Two Views or One? *Economica* 32: 127–139.

   1960. Some Institutional Aspects of the Wealth of Nations, *Journal of Political Economy* 68: 557–570.

Rothschild, Emma. 2001. *Economic Sentiments: Adam Smith, Condorcet, and the Enlightenment.* Cambridge, MA: Harvard University Press.

Rotunda, Ronald D. 1986. *The Politics of Language: Liberalism as Word and Symbol.* Iowa City: University of Iowa Press.

Rundblad, G., and D. B. Kronenfeld. 2003. The Inevitability of Folk Etymology: A Case of Collective Reality and Invisible Hands, *Journal of Pragmatics* 35: 119–138.

Sageman, Marc. 2008. *Leaderless Jihad: Terror Networks in the Twenty-First Century.* Philadelphia: University of Pennsylvania Press.

Sampson, George. 1970. *The Concise Cambridge History of English Literature.* Cambridge: Cambridge University Press.

Samuel, R., and P. Thompson. 1990. *The Myths We Live By.* New York: Routledge.

Samuels, Warren J. 2007a. Adam Smith's History of Astronomy Argument: How Broadly Does It Apply? And Where Do Propositions which "Sooth the Imagination" Come From? *History of Economic Ideas* 15: 53–78.

1973. Adam Smith and the Economy as a System of Power, *Indian Economic Journal* 20: 363–381.

2002. "An Essay on Government and Governance," in *Economics, Governance, and Law: Essays on Theory and Policy,* ed. W.J. Samuels, pp. 1–37. Cheltenham: Northhampton.

1974b. "Anarchism and the Theory of Power," in *Further Explorations in the Theory of Anarchy,* Gordon Tullock, ed., pp. 33–57. Blacksburg, VA: University Publications.

2010a. Correspondence Between Frank H. Knight, Walter B. Smith, and F. Taylor Ostrander 1933–1937, *Research in the History of Economic Thought and Methodology,* 28C: 1 – 10.

1992a. *Essays on the Economic Role of Government, Vol. 1, Fundamentals.* London and New York: Macmillan and New York University Press.

1992b. *Essays on the Economic Role of Government, Vol. 2, Applications.* London and New York: Macmillan and New York University Press.

1999. Hayek from the Perspective of an Institutionalist Historian of Economic Thought: An Interpretive Essay, *Journal des Economistes et des Etudes Humaines* 9: 279–290.

1996a. "History of Economic Thought and the Economic Role of Government, pp. 39–43," in Warren J. Samuels, My Work as a Historian of Economic Thought, *Journal of the History of Economic Thought* 18 (Spring): 37–75.

2006a. Interpreting the Bible, the U.S. Constitution, and the History of Economic Thought, *Research in the History of Economic Thought and Methodology* 24A: 79–98.

2000. Introduction to the Problem of the History of the Interwar Period. *Research in the History of Economic Thought and Methodology* 18A: 139–147.

1996b. Joseph J. Spengler's Concept of the "Problem of Order": A Reconsideration and Extension, in *Employment, Economic Growth and the Tyranny of the Market,* P. Arestis, ed., pp. 185–199. Brookfield, VT: Edward Elgar.

ed. 2003. Lectures by James S. Earley on the Development of Economics, University of Wisconsin, 1954–1955, *Research in the History of Economic Thought and Methodology* 21B: 89–271.

2010b. "Monetary Institutions and Monetary Theory: Reflections on the History of Monetary Economics," in *David Laidler's Contributions to Economics,* Robert Leeson, ed., pp. 157–211. New York: Palgrave Macmillan(including Discussion by Roger Sandilands, 203–205).

2006b. "Money, Monetary Institutions and Monetary Theory," in *David Laidler's Contributions to Economics*, Robert Leeson, ed., pp. 157–211. New York: Palgrave Macmillan(including Discussion by Roger Sandilands, 203–205).

1984. On the Nature and Existence of Economic Coercion: The Correspondence of Robert Lee Hale and Thomas Nixon Carver, *Journal of Economic Issues* 18: 1027–1048.

1974a. *Pareto on Policy*. Cleveland, OH: World.

1980. Problems of Marginal Cost Pricing in Public Utilities, *Public Utilities Fortnightly* 105 (January 31): 21–24.

1980. Problems of Marginal Cost Pricing in Public Utilities, *Public Utilities Fortnightly* 105 (January 31): 21–24.

2000. Review of Milton and Rose D. Friedman 1998, *Research in the History of Economic Thought and Methodology* 18A: 241–252.

1995. Society Is a Process of Mutual Coercion and Governance Selectively Perceived, *Critical Review* 9: 437–443.

2001. Some Problems in the Use of Language in Economics, *Review of Political Economy* 13: 91–100.

1966. *The Classical Theory of Economic Policy*. Cleveland, OH: World.

1997. The Concept of "Coercion" in Economics, in *The Economy as a Process of Valuation*, Warren J. Samuels, Steven G. Medema, and A. Allan Schmid, eds., pp. 129–207. Lyme, NH: Edward Elgar.

2004. "The Etiology of Adam Smith's Division of Labor: Alternative Accounts and Smith's Methodology Applied to Them," in *Essays on the History of Economics*, Warren J. Samuels, Willie Henderson, Kirk D. Johnson, and Marianne Johnson, eds., pp. 8–71. New York: Routledge.

1993. The Growth of Government, *Critical Review* 7: 445–460.

2009. "The Invisible Hand," in *Elgar Companion to Adam Smith*, Jeffrey T. Young, ed., pp. 195–210. Northampton, MA: Edward Elgar Publishing.

1989. The Legal-Economic Nexus, *George Washington Law Review* 57: 1556–1578.

2007b. *The Legal-Economic Nexus*. New York: Routledge.

1992c. The Pervasive Proposition, "What Is, Is and Ought to Be": A Critique, in *The Megacorp and Macrodynamics: Essays in Memory of Alfred Eichner*, William S. Millberg, ed., pp. 273–285. Armonk, NY: M. E. Sharpe.

1998. The Transformation of American Economics: From Interwar Pluralism to Postwar Neoclassicism: An Interpretive Review of a Conference, *Research in the History of Economic Thought and Methodology* 16:179–223.

Samuels, Warren J., and W. Henderson. 2004. "The Etiology of Adam Smith's Division of Labor: Alternative Accounts and Smith's Methodology Applied to Them," in *Essays on the History of Economics*, pp. 8–89. New York, Routledge.

Samuels, Warren J., Marianne Johnson, and Kirk Johnson. 2007. "The Duke of Argyll and Edwin L. Godkin as Precursors to Hayek on the Relation of Ignorance to Policy," in *The Legal-Economic Nexus*, W. J. Samuels, ed., pp. 291–398. New York: Routledge.

Samuels, Warren J., and Steven G. Medema. 2009. "Only Three Duties": Adam Smith on the Economic Role of Government, in *Elgar Companion to Adam Smith*, in Jeffrey T. Young, ed., pp. 300–314. Northampton, MA: Edward Elgar Publishing.

Samuels, Warren J., and Nicholas Mercuro. 1980. The Resolution of the Compensation Problem in Society, *Research in Law and Economics* 2: 103–128.

Samuels, Warren J., and A. Allan Schmid. 1997. "The Concept of Cost in Economics," in *The Economy as a Process of Valuation*, Warren J. Samuels, Steven G. Medema and A. Allan Schmid, eds., pp. 208–298. Lyme, NH: Edward Elgar.

Samuels, Warren J., Allan Schmid, and James D. Shaffer. 1994. "An Evolutionary Approach to Law and Economics," in *Evolutionary Concepts in Contemporary Economics*, Richard W. England, ed., pp. 93–110. Ann Arbor: University of Michigan Press.

Samuelson, Paul A. 1977. A Modern Theorist's Vindication of Adam Smith, *American Economic Review* 67: 42–49.

   1962. Economists and the History of Ideas, *American Economic Review* 52: 1–18.

   2005. The Limits of Free Trade: Response, *Journal of Economic Perspectives* 19(1): 242–244.

Samuelson, Paul A., Avinash Dixit, and Gene Grossman. 2005. The Limits of Free Trade, *Journal of Economic Perspectives* 19: 241–244.

Schlegel, Richard. 1973. Review of Nicholas Georgescu-Roegen's *The Entropy Law and the Economic Process*, *Journal of Economic Issues* 7: 475–481.

Schliesser, Eric. 2005. Some Principle of Adam Smith's "Newtonian" Methods in the Wealth of Nations, *Research in the History of Economic Thought and Methodology* 23A: 35–77.

Schmookler, Andrew Bard. 1993. *The Illusion of Choice: How the Market Economy Shapes Our Destiny*. Albany: State University of New York Press.

Schneider, Louis. 1967. *The Scottish Moralists on Human Nature and Society*. Chicago: University of Chicago Press.

Schumpeter, Joseph A. 1950. *Capitalism, Socialism, and Democracy*. New York: Harper.

Schwartz, Hillel. 1986. *Never Satisfied: A Cultural History of Diets, Fantasies, and Fat*. New York: Free Press.

Searle, J. R. 1995. *The Construction of Social Reality*. New York: Free Press.

Sederberg, Peter C. 1984. *The Politics of Meaning: Power and Explanation in the Construction of Social Reality*. Tucson: University of Arizona Press.

Sen, Amartya. 1981. *Poverty and Famines*. New York: Oxford University Press.

Sened, Itai. 1997. *The Political Institution of Private Property*. New York: Cambridge University Press.

Shackle, G. L. S. 1966. *The Nature of Economic Thought*. New York: Cambridge University Press.

   1967. *The Years of High Theory*. New York: Cambridge University Press.

Shane, Scott A. 2008. *The Illusions of Entrepreneurship*. New Haven, CT: Yale University Press.

Shapiro, Ian. 1990. *Political Criticism*. Berkeley: University of California Press.

Shell, M. 1992 [1982]. *Money, Language, and Thought*. Baltimore: Johns Hopkins University Press.

Simon, Henry C. 1948. *Economic Policy for a Free Society*. Chicago: University of Chicago Press.

Skillen, A. 1978. *Ruling Illusions: Philosophy and the Social Order*. Atlantic Highlands, NJ: Humanities Press.

Smith, Adam. 1937 [1776]. *An Inquiry into the Nature and Causes of the Wealth of Nations*, Edwin Cannan, ed. New York: Modern Library.

   1937 [1776]. *An Inquiry into the Nature and Causes of the Wealth of Nations*, J. R. M'Culloch, ed. London: Longman & Co.

1976a [1759]. *An Inquiry into the Nature and Causes of the Wealth of Nations*. Oxford: Oxford University Press.

1980. *Essays on Philosophical Subjects*, W. P .D. Wightman and J.C. Bryce, eds. Oxford: Oxford University Press.

1978. *Lectures on Jurisprudence*. Oxford: Oxford University Press.

1964. *Lectures on Justice, Police, Revenue and Arms*. New York: Kelley.

1966 [1959]. *The Theory of Moral Sentiments*. New York: Kelley.

1976b [1759]. *The Theory of Moral Sentiments*. Oxford: Oxford University Press.

Smith. Anthony. 1980. *The Geopolitics of Information*. New York: Oxford University Press.

Smith, Craig. 2008. "Ferguson and the Active Genius of Mankind," in *Adam Ferguson: History, Progress and Human Nature*, E. Heath and V. Merolle, eds., pp. 157–170. London: Pickering & Chatto.

Solow, Robert M. 1958. Review of Tjalling C. Koopmans, Three Essays on the State of Economic Science, *Journal of Political Economy* 66: 178–179.

2007. Survival of the Richest? *The New York Review of Books* (November 22): 38–41.

Spadafora, David. 1990. *The Idea of Progress in Eighteenth-Century Britain*. New Haven, CT: Yale University Press.

Spadaro, Louis M. 1978. *New Directions in Austrian Economics*. Kansas City, KS: Sheed Andrews and McMeel.

Spengler, Joseph J. 1968. Hierarchy vs. Equality: Persisting Conflict, *Kyklos* 21: 217–238.

1948. The Problem of Order in Economic Affairs, *Southern Economic Journal* 15: 1–29.

Spiegel, Alix. 2006. Psychology A La Buddha? Feb. 15, 2006.www.dharmasattva8. blogspot.com

Starr, June. 1992. *Law as Metaphor: From Islamic Courts to the Palace of Justice*. Albany: State University of New York Press.

Stigler, George J. 1965. The Economist and the State, *American Economic Review* 60: 1–18.

1976. The Successes and Failures of Professor Smith, *Journal of Political Economy* 84: 1199–1213.

Stiglitz, Joseph E. 1988. *Economics of the Public Sector*. 2nd ed. New York: Norton.

Straub, J. 2006. *Narration, Identity, and Historical Consciousness*. New York: Berghahn.

Sturtevant, E. H. 1947. *An Introduction to Linguistic Science*. New Haven, CT: Yale University Press.

1917. *Linguistic Change*. Chicago, IL: University of Chicago Press.

Summers, Lawrence. 1992. Why the Rich Should Pollute the Poor, *The Guardian* (February 2): 8.

Sunstein, Cass R. 2008. Misery and Company, *The New Republic* 239: 39–43.

Sutton, Francis X., Seymour Harris, Carl Kaysen, and James Tobin. 1956. *The American Business Creed*. Cambridge, MA: Harvard University Press.

Taylor, J. F. A. 1966. *The Masks of Society*. New York: Appleton-Century-Crofts.

Thanh, Pham Chi. 2009. Address to Second Astana Economic Forum, Economic Security in Eurasia in the System of Global Risks (11–13 March), Astana, Kazakhstan: Kazinform, March 30.

The Compact Edition of the Oxford English Dictionary. 1971. 2 vols. New York: Oxford University Press.

Thurow, Roger, and Scott Kilman. 2009. *Enough: Why the World's Poorest Starve in an Age of Plenty*. New York: Public Affairs.

Tinder, G. 1989. *The Political Meaning of Christianity: An Interpretation*. Baton Rouge: Louisiana State University Press.

Tribe, Keith. 1978. *Land, Labour and Economic Discourse*. London: Routledge & Kegan Paul.

Tribe, Laurance H. 1985. *Constitutional Choices*. Cambridge, MA: Harvard University Press.

Turner, J. 1979. *The Politics of Landscape*. Cambridge, MA: Harvard University Press.

Uleman, James S., and John A. Bargh, eds. 1989. *Unintended Thought*. New York: Guilford Press.

Ullmann-Margalit, Edna. 1978. Invisible-Hand Explanations, *Synthese* 39: 263–291.

United States Institute of Medicine . 2004. Safety Of Genetically Engineered Food Approaches to Assessing Unintended Health Effects. Committee on Identifying and Assessing Unintended Effects of Genetically Engineered Foods on Human Health. Institute of Medicine and National Reserch Council of the National Academies. Washington DC: National Academic Press.

Urquhart, Brian. 2008. The UN and the Race against Death, *The New York Review of Books* (June 26): 39–42.

Vaughn, Karen. 1979. Review of Louis M. Spadaro. 1978. *New Directions in Austrian Economics*. Kansas City, KS: Sheed Andrews and McMeel, in *Southern Economic Journal* 46: 676–678.

Veyne, Paul. 1983. *Did the Greeks Believe in their Myths? An Essay on the Constitutive Imagination*. Chicago, IL: University of Chicago Press.

Viner, Jacob. 1928. Adam Smith and Laissez Faire, in *Adam Smith, 1776–1926*. Chicago, IL: University of Chicago Press, pp. 116–155.

Viner, Jacob. 1927. Adam Smith and Laissez Faire. *Journal of Political Economy* 35: 198–232.

    1978. *Religious Thought and Economic Society*. Jacques Melitz and Donald Winch, eds. Durham, NC: Duke University Press.

    1976. *The Role of Providence in the Social Order: An Essay in Intellectual History*. Princeton, NJ: Princeton University Press.

Wagner, Peter, Björn Wittrock, and Richard Whitley, eds. 1991. *Discourses on Society: The Shaping of the Social Science Disciplines*. Boston: Kluwer Academic Sciences.

Wagner, Roy. 1986. *Symbols That Stand for Themselves*. Chicago: University of Chicago Press.

Wallace, M. 2005. All the World Is Green, *The Nation* (April 18): 25–32.

Warner, Roger. 1986. *Invisible Hand: The Marijuana Business*. New York: William Morrow.

Watson, Peter. 2002. *The Modern Mind: An Intellectual History of the 20th Century*. New York: HarperCollins.

Waterman, A. M. C. 2002. *Political Economy and Christian Theology since the Enlightenment: Essays in Intellectual History*. New York: Palgrave, Macmillan.

Weaver, Richard M. 1970. *Language Is Sermonic: Richard M. Weaver on the Nature of Rhetoric*. Richard L. Johannesen, Rennard Strictland and Ralph T. Eubanks, eds., Baton Rouge: Louisiana State University Press.

Webster's Biographical Dictionary: A Dictionary of Names of Noteworthy Persons. 1971. 1st ed. Springfield, MA: G. & C. Merriam Co.

Webster's New Universal Unabridged Dictionary. 1994. New York: Barnes & Noble.

Weinstein, Jack Russell. 2009. The Two Adams: Ferguson and Smith on Sympathy and Sentiment, in *Adam Ferguson: Philosophy, Politics and Society*, E. Heath and V. Merolle, eds., pp. 89–106. London: Pickering & Chatto.

Weintraub, E. Roy. 2002. *How Economics Became a Mathematical Science*. Durham, NC: Duke University Press.

Weintraub, E. Roy. 1991. *Stabilizing Economics: Constructing Economic Knowledge*. New York: Cambridge University Press.

Weldon, T. D. 1953. *The Vocabulary of Politics*. Baltimore: Penguin.

West, Edwin G. 1990. *Adam Smith and Modern Economics: From Market Behaviour to Public Choice*. Aldershot: Edward Elgar.

White, James Boyd. 1984. *When Words Lose Their Meaning*. Chicago, IL: University of Chicago Press.

Whorf, Benjamin Lee. 1956. *Language, Thought, and Reality*. Cambridge, MA: MIT Press.

Wight, Jonathan B. 2007. The Treatment of Adam Smith's Invisible Hand, *Journal of Economic Education* 38 (Summer): 341–358.

Wightman, W. P. D. 1980. *Introduction to Essays on Philosophical Subjects*. Oxford: Clarendon Press.

Wiles, Peter, and Guy Routh, eds. 1984. *Economics in Disarray*. New York: Basil Blackwell.

Will, George. 2002. It's Time Bush Showed Anger over Enron, *Jewish World Review* (January 16): 3.

Wilson, Thomas. 1976. "Sympathy and Self-Interest," in *The Market and the State*, Thomas Wilson and Andrew S. Skinner, eds., pp. 73–99. Oxford: Oxford University Press.

Winch, Donald. 1996. *Riches and Poverty: An Intellectual History of Political Economy in Britain, 1750–1834*. New York: Cambridge University Press.

Witte, Ann Dryden. 1998. *Unintended Consequences? Welfare Reform and the Working Poor*. Cambridge, MA: NBER.

Witte, Edwin E. 1957. Economics and Public Policy. *American Economic Review* 47: 1–21.

Wittgenstein, L. 1958. *Philosophical Investigations*. 3rd ed. New York: Macmillan.

Wuthnow, Robert. 1989. *Communities of Discourse: Ideology and Social Structure in the Reformation, the Enlightenment and European Socialism*. Cambridge, MA: Harvard University Press.

Yarbrough, Tinsley E. 2000. *The Rehnquist Court and the Constitution*. New York: Oxford University Press.

Yoder, Edwin M., Jr. 1983. Was Economics Nobel a Mistake? *Detroit News* (October 25).

Zelizer, V. A. 1994. *The Social Meaning of Money*. New York: Basic Books.

Index

abortion, 169
abstractions, 217–218
academic field of economics, 2
Adam (Bible), 128
Aeschylus, 21
affirmative action, 234–235
The Affluent Society (Galbraith), 220, 240
d'Alembert, Jean le Rond, 115
Allan, David, 220
alpha-beta conflicts, 231
al Qaeda, 291
Ambrose (Saint), 21
The American Political Tradition
(Hofstadter), 92
American Revolution, 220
Amoh, Yasuo, 220
analogy, 147–148
Anderson, Harry, 7
Annand, William, 22
Anselm, 216
anticonstructivism, 215, 241
apartheid, 169
argument, invisible hand as, 287–290
Aristotle, 201, 216
Arrow, Kenneth, 7–8, 10, 252–254, 290
attorney practice, 233
Augustine (Saint), 21
Austrian School, 202, 241–242
automaticity as function of invisible
hand, 78–79
Ayres, Clarence, 73–74

Bailey, Ronald, 28
Baltimore Chronicle & Sentinel, 28
Barrera, Albino, 268–269
Barreto, Humberto, 66

baseball analogy, 110
Basil (Saint), 21
Baumol, William J., 14, 275
Beard, Charles, 92
de Beaumarchais, Pierre Augustin Caron, 115
belief systems, 96–98, 121–122, 295
Bellow, Saul, 27
benevolence as function of invisible hand, 80
Bentham, Jeremy, 163
Berkeley, George, 24
Berry, Christopher J., 219–220
Bhagwati, Jagdish, 270
*A Billion Lives: An Eyewitness Report from the
Frontlines of Humanity* (Egeland), 269
Bill of Rights, 234
bin Laden, Osama, 291
Black's Law Dictionary, 218
Blaug, Mark, 15, 41
*Blood and Soil: A World History of Genocide
and Extermination from Sparta to
Darfur* (Kiernan), 269
von Böhm-Bawerk, Eugen, 243
Bohr, Niels, 45
Boisguilbert, 153*n*
Boulding, Kenneth, 96
Brady, Steve, 28
Brenner, Nancy, 156
Brenner, Y.S., 171–172
Brentano, Franz, 217
Brooke, Henry, 24
Brown, Charles Brockden, 26
Brown, David, 91–92
Brown, Murray, 255
Buchanan, James M., 199, 202–203, 206, 212,
225–226, 252
Burke, Edmund, 115

Ohlin, Bertil, 261
ontology of invisible hand, 164–170
  "psychic balm" and, 167–169
  social control and, 167–169
Opio, Azore, 27–28
order
  as function of invisible hand, 78
  nondeliberative social control and, 293–294
  spontaneous order (*See* spontaneous order)
O'Reilly, Jane, 270
Organization of Petroleum Exporting
  Countries (OPEC), 63, 295
original intent, 233
Ortony, Andrew, 156–157
Oz-Salzberger, Fania, 221

Pagden, Anthony, 156
Paine, Thomas, 115
Paley, William, 25, 115
Papandreou, Andreas G., 255
paradigms, multiple. *See* multiple paradigms
Parenti, Michael, 95–96*n*, 274, 278
Pareto, Vilfredo
  generally, 42, 112, 202, 242–243
  derivations, 178
  on distribution, 249
  on force and fraud, 286, 288, 293
  general sociology, 139
  on language, 139
  non-logico-experimental knowledge, 177–178
  on social control, 99–101
  on systems of belief, 96–97, 295–296
Pareto optimality
  generally, 124, 221
  as function of invisible hand, 80–81
  research protocols and ironies, 5
  survival requirement (*See* survival
    requirement of Pareto optimality)
Parsons, T., 97
Pascal, Roy, 95
Pasinetti, Luigi, 94–95
patent law, 231
Peart, Sandra J., 225
Pecchenino, Rowena A., 268
Peden, G.C., 93–94
Peirce, Charles Saunders, 235
perfect competition and invisible hand, 15, 64
Perry, Bill, 21
Philadelphia Experiment, 19
policy consciousness, 51–52, 55–56, 141, 151
political economy, 38–58

constructivism versus anticonstructivism, 215–216, 221–222, 241
deliberative versus nondeliberative decision
  making, 98, 127, 206, 212–216
fecundity of Smith's analysis, 35–37
ignorance and dispersed knowledge, 221–222
interpretation of Smith, 38–42
normative position in positivist context, 225–227
principle of unintended and unexpected
  consequences (*See* principle of
  unintended and unexpected
  consequences)
Rule of Law (*See* Rule of Law)
spontaneous order (*See* spontaneous order)
synoptic and synthetic system (*See* synoptic
  and synthetic system)
The Political Mind (Lakoff), 224
political nature of language, 136–139
politics, uses of invisible hand in, 27–29
Popper, Karl, 295
positive externalities as invisible hand, 74
Pound, Roscoe, 101
poverty and survival requirement, 265–276
power. *See* social control
pragmatism, 114, 151, 234
predictability of human behavior, 48
prescriptive epistemology, 170
price system
  as invisible hand, 61–63, 143–144, 154–155
  markets compared, 45–47, 61–63
price theory, 5–6
primitive terms, 135, 148
principle of unintended and unexpected
  consequence
  Ferguson and, 212–215
principle of unintended and unexpected
  consequences, 212–216
  generally, 281, 286, 290–292, 295
  Hayek and, 203, 206, 212–216
  invisible hand and, 67–68, 112–113, 174
  Menger and, 212–216
  Rule of Law and, 227–228, 241
  survival requirement and, 268
private property, 123
  as invisible hand, 64–65
  laissez-faire and, 181–182
  Smith on, 195
"Problem of Job," 75, 89, 128

problems of interpretation
  functions of invisible hand (*See* functions
    of invisible hand)
  identities of invisible hand (*See* identities
    of invisible hand)
  market-plus-framework model, 180,
    184–185, 208
  synoptic and synthetic system (*See* synoptic
    and synthetic system)
processes of invisible hand as explanation,
  290–293
productivity, 248
propaganda, 136, 201–203
"psychic balm"
  generally, 108, 131
  as function of invisible hand, 77, 145,
    281–282, 285
  ontology of invisible hand and, 167–169
  religion as, 89
  systems of belief and, 98
psychopathy, 124

Quesnay, François, 115
Quine, W.V., 217

Radcliffe, Ann Ward, 26
Ralph, James, 23
Ramsey, Frank P., 217
Raphael, D.D., 59, 83–84, 90
rationalism, 115, 151, 171–173
rationality and self-interest, 127, 224–225
Rawls, John, 267
Reagan, Ronald, 63, 183, 271
rebellion, 103*n*, 184
received institutions, 240–241, 290
reciprocal nature of externalities, 123–124
Reeve, Clara, 25
Reform Act of 1832, 186
regulation, 137, 189, 210
Reid, Thomas, 216, 218
The Reign of Law (Kahn), 228
religion
  Catholicism, 16, 120, 153*n*
  Christian ethics, 268
  economics and, 104, 117, 131, 283
  Enlightenment and, 115–117
  invisible hand, God as, 20, 75–76, 116,
    152–153, 166–167
  Knight on, 131, 293
  manifest and latent function, 230
  metaphors and, 195
  moral rules, God as source of, 153

  as "psychic balm," 89
  Smith and, 119–121
  supernaturalism (*See* supernaturalism)
Republicans, 108, 265
research protocols, 1–6
Ricardo, David, 15, 210, 248, 259–261
Road to Serfdom (Hayek), 201
Robbins, Lionel
  on economic role of government, 206–212
  on harmony and conflict, 16
  Hayek and, 211
  on invisible hand, 141, 145, 197
  Knight on, 200
  on legal rules, 208
  market-plus-framework model, 133
  on moral rules, 208
  on Smith, 206–212
  on social control, 75–76
Roberts, William Hayward, 25
Robertson, William, 115, 218
Roosevelt, Franklin, 100
Rosen, Harvey, 188
Rosenberg, Nathan, 40*n*, 45, 47–48, 51
Rousseau, Jean-Jacques, 115, 219
Rule of Law, 227–243
  generally, 243–246, 296
  Hayek on, 222–223, 237–238, 241
  invisible hand and, 68, 112
  ironies in, 240
  legal rules and, 232
  as myth, 237–240
  principle of unintended and unexpected
    consequences and, 227–228, 241
  problems of, 231–233
  self-interest and, 130
  spontaneous order and, 222–223
rules. *See* legal rules; moral rules
Russell, Bertrand, 217

de Saint-Simon, Henri, 115
Samuels, Warren J., 38*n*, 177, 225
Samuelson, Paul A., 7, 14–15, 187, 253,
  258–263, 275
Sand, George, 27
Say, Jean-Baptiste, 66, 275
scarcity, 128–129, 257
Schiller, Friedrich, 115
Schliesser, Eric, 86*n*
Schmid, A. Allan, 85*n*, 231
Schumpeter, Joseph, 16, 66, 238, 242
Schwartz, Hillel, 270
science, uses of invisible hand in, 28

CPSIA information can be obtained at www.ICGtesting.com
Printed in the USA
LVOW041445050113

314457LV00004B/7/P